Computer disk available

USING FORMAL DESCRIPTION TECHNIQUES

An Introduction to ESTELLE, LOTOS and SDL

Edited by
Kenneth J. Turner
University of Stirling, UK

JOHN WILEY & SONS
Chichester · New York · Brisbane · Toronto · Singapore

Other Wiley Editorial Offices

John Wiley & Sons, Inc., 605 Third Avenue,
New York, NY 10158-0012, USA

Jacaranda Wiley Ltd, G.P.O. Box 859, Brisbane,
Queensland 4001, Australia

John Wiley & Sons (Canada) Ltd, 22 Worcester Road,
Rexdale, Ontario M9W 1L1, Canada

John Wiley & Sons (SEA) Pte Ltd, 37 Jalan Pemimpin #05-04,
Block B, Union Industrial Building, Singapore 2057

British Library of Cataloguing in Publication Data

A catalogue record for this book is available from the British Library

ISBN 0 471 93455 0

Typeset from camera-ready copy supplied by the author.
Printed and bound in Great Britain by Biddles Ltd, Guildford, Surrey

Contents

List of Figures

List of Contributors

The following list gives the affiliation of contributors at the time the contributions were initially written.

Name	Affiliation	Chapter/Section
A. Azcorra	Polytechnic University of Madrid Madrid, Spain	3, 11
F. Belina	Telia Research AB Malmö, Sweden	1, 5.5, 12
F. Bertolotti	CSELT Turin, Italy	9.5
T. P. Blumer	Phoenix Technologies Ltd. Cambridge, USA	6.3, 7.3, 9.3
L. Cerchio	CSELT Turin, Italy	9.5
V. Chari	MARBEN[1] Paris, France	10
O. Færgemand	TFL Horshølm, Denmark	4
L. Ferreira Pires	University of Twente Enschede, Netherlands	3
F. M. Fournón y González-Barcia	European Space Technology Centre[2] Noordwijk, Netherlands	6.4, 7.4, 8.4, 9.4
D. Hogrefe	University of Hamburg[3] Hamburg, Germany	8.3
J. A. Mañas	Polytechnic University of Madrid Madrid, Spain	3, 9.4
T. de Miguel Moro	Polytechnic University of Madrid Madrid, Spain	7.4

[1]Now of CEGELEC, Clamart, France
[2]Now of Ericsson Telecomunicaciones, Madrid, Spain
[3]Now of University of Berne, Berne, Switzerland

Name	Affiliation	Chapter/Section
S. Pavón	Polytechnic University of Madrid Madrid, Spain	11
J. Quemada	Polytechnic University of Madrid Madrid, Spain	3, 11
T. Robles	Polytechnic University of Madrid Madrid, Spain	3
R. L. Tenney	University of Massachusetts Boston, USA	2, 5.3, 6.3, 7.3, 9.3
A. J. Tocher	BNR Europe Ltd. Harlow, England	8.4
S. Trigila	Ugo Bordoni Foundation Rome, Italy	6.5, 7.5, 8.5, 9.5
K. J. Turner	University of Stirling Stirling, Scotland	1, 5.1, 5.2, 5.4, 5.6, 6.1, 6.2, 6.6, 7.1, 7.2, 7.6, 8.1, 8.2, 8.6, 9.1, 9.2, 9.6

Foreword

The standardised FDTs *(Formal Description Techniques)* are ESTELLE, LOTOS and SDL. The roots for their development lie far in the past. CCITT *(International Consultative Committee on Telegraphy and Telephony)* started work on standardising FDTs around 1972, and ISO *(International Organization for Standardization)* around 1978.

The incentive for these developments was the growing awareness that only formal approaches to system specification, verification, analysis, implementation, testing, and operation could provide the means to control the ever-growing complexity of standards for telecommunications and OSI *(Open Systems Interconnection)*. And indeed, these standards have become tremendously complex. To be meaningful, FDTs had to become a common tool for all those involved in the system development life cycle. This implied that the FDTs had to be stable, which could be guaranteed only if they were standardised. CCITT and ISO provided the natural environment for the standardisation process.

Originally CCITT and ISO approached FDTs from quite different angles. CCITT was more oriented towards telecommunications, signalling and switching applications, whereas ISO was more oriented towards data processing applications. As time went by, CCITT and ISO grew more and more towards each other, and so in fact did the FDTs. Yet the different origins are still recognisable in the characteristics of the FDTs.

This explains an important aspect of design with FDTs: it is extremely hard to find an FDT that presents the single and universal solution to all problems involved. Indeed, if we had to start developing other FDTs today, given the experience we have gained, we would certainly come up with another set of FDTs. It is therefore more realistic, and profitable, to offer a set of complementary FDTs and leave it up to the informed user to make his or her own choice.

This is the reason why CCITT and ISO decided in 1985 that they should work closely together to advance the widespread introduction, appreciation and application of the standard FDTs. The chosen approach was to offer a set of specification examples, ordered from simple to more complex, with each example described in ESTELLE, LOTOS and SDL. The aim was to allow the reader to study and compare, and to choose the most suitable FDT for a specific application. One of the fruits of this cooperative work lies now in front of you — this book!

One of the major problems, reflected in this book and strongly marked in the development of the FDTs, is the vast complexity of systems in the application area involved. It meant that the FDTs had to be evaluated continually for their appropriateness and power of expression. You may easily imagine the number of meetings involved (for SDL alone there were more than 40 meetings involving 10 to 15 experts), the hot debates, confrontations, and disagreements among the experts while deciding on language features. It explains why the development of the FDTs took so long. The last versions were published in 1988/1989.

Yet, in spite of all the efforts to make the FDTs as powerful as possible, the reader should understand that a complex system is complex by its own virtue. It cannot be made simpler by using an FDT since the FDT acts only as a means to describe it.

However, an FDT can strongly assist in elucidating and controlling complexity. In this respect it acts like a mirror, showing the quality of the system design, its structural grace and functional consistency. But an FDT also shows structural poverty and functional deficiency. Indeed it is a mirror without mercy, forcing the designer to consider the system in all its aspects. At first you may find this cumbersome and tedious, but later on you will appreciate that it enables you to control every facet of the system. It allows you to structure a system strongly and to fill in all its functional features and details gradually, including those that are much too easily forgotten in informal approaches and are the primary source of incompatibility and errors. In this sense it is more important that you use an FDT than what FDT you use.

While you increase your experience with FDTs you will find that you will start using general purpose approaches to structuring systems, and general purpose building bricks to specify system functions. You will develop an intimate understanding of how to bind FDT concepts and constructs to the concepts and constructs of the application area. This will become part of the FDT heritage in the field of application — what is usually referred to as the architectural semantics of FDTs. To achieve this understanding has been the objective in the preparation of the various examples in this book. It will help you to move much more easily between specifications since they all share these general-purpose approaches. You are also strongly encouraged to use the idea behind this in your own field of application. After all, the quality of a formal description is more dependent on the competence of the user than on the syntax and semantics of the FDT. Of course the FDT itself has to be well designed, but it remains a tool in the hands of the user whose experience, creativity and skills determine the end result of its application.

Finally, in spite of the qualities of FDTs, there is a golden rule to which you can appeal: if you have to do something, look for someone else to do it for you! And, since it is getting more and more difficult to find Mr. Someone Else, the trick is to have tools. The book provides you with valuable information on existing tools and gives references to publications, workshops, conferences and symposia where you can get the latest information on the FDTs, their applications and their tools.

We congratulate our friend Ken Turner with the publication of this book. As the editor of the CCITT/ISO project 'Guidelines for the Application of Estelle, LOTOS, and SDL', his efforts were key to the production of a common CCITT and ISO report that is the basis of this book. We also congratulate the various authors who made significant efforts in contributing to the example specifications.

And last, but not least, we extend our best wishes to you — the reader of this book and hopefully a future user of FDTs. Your interest and involvement will be key to the success of FDTs!

Roberto Saracco
CSELT, Italy
FDT Rapporteur, CCITT
(1984–1988 Study Period)

Chris A. Vissers
University of Twente, The Netherlands
FDT Rapporteur, ISO

Preface

Readership

This book will be of interest to various groups of people:

- those who wish to learn how to use the standardised FDTs *(Formal Description Techniques)* ESTELLE, LOTOS and SDL
- those who wish to learn about formal methods and languages in general by studying the standardised ones
- those already familiar with another formal method or language who wish to compare the approaches taken by the standardised FDTs
- those already familiar with the standardised FDTs who wish to use them for specifying data communications systems and distributed systems.

For the complete beginner, the book has substantial introductory material on formal methods and the three FDTs. This is complemented by guidance on how to develop specifications and implementations using the FDTs. The treatment of the FDTs is deliberately non-mathematical to make the book accessible to a wide readership.

The book is copiously illustrated with examples since it is believed that a great deal can be learned from the work of experienced specifiers. The examples can be used to study one FDT or to compare the approaches taken by different FDTs. Although the examples mainly deal with data communications, they illustrate important principles that apply in many other application areas. The examples have been written for readers with little knowledge of data communications.

The book is suitable for self-study. It would also be appropriate as a textbook for a practical course on formal methods and languages. The examples in particular would be a useful source of material for laboratory exercises and projects. An instructor's disc has therefore been prepared as a companion to the book. It contains the ASCII text (less the commentary) of all the complete formal descriptions in the book. Major diagrams that would be useful for teaching are also included on the disc in LaTeX or PostScript form as appropriate.

Contents

Part I contains introductions to the general context of FDTs and to each FDT in particular. Chapter 1 explains why FDTs were developed, their origins and their use. Chapters 2, 3 and 4 give an introduction to ESTELLE, LOTOS and SDL respectively.

Part II illustrates each of the FDTs on a graded series of examples, starting with a simple communications service and working up to a large communications protocol. Chapter 5 specifies the Daemon Game, a simple game of chance for multiple players. Chapter 6 specifies an Unreliable Medium, a basic communications service that does not guarantee correct delivery of messages. Chapter 7 specifies a Sliding Window Protocol that can safely transfer messages over an unreliable medium in a flow-controlled manner. Chapter 8 specifies the Abracadabra Service, a connection-oriented service that embodies major features of more complex services. Chapter 9 specifies the Abracadabra Protocol that implements the Abracadabra Service over an unreliable medium.

Part III deals with development methods and tools for each of the FDTs. Chapters 10, 11 and 12 deal with development using ESTELLE, LOTOS and SDL respectively.

Part IV contains reference material for the rest of the book. Appendix A lists references and gives other sources of information on FDTs. Appendix B is an index to the main components of each example specification. Appendix C is the main index.

Editor's Corner

Like many good ideas, this book started from a jest. During an early meeting of the group that produced the corresponding CCITT and ISO/IEC reports, I happened to remark that we should perhaps sell the film rights. This had two happy consequences. It led to the establishment of the successful series of FORTE *(Formal Techniques)* conferences, and it led to this book based on the international standards work. This is something not normally possible since CCITT and ISO/IEC hold the copyright in such documents. I was delighted to have the cooperation of these organisations in allowing development of this book.

I firmly believe that FDTs have major advantages to offer the Information Technology community. Hundreds of man-years have been spent in developing the standardised FDTs and their supporting tools. Those involved have included standards bodies, academic institutions and industrial organisations. The time is ripe to capitalise on the opportunities offered by FDTs.

Development of the FDTs has involved many people. However, certain individuals stand out: E. Brinksma (University of Twente, Enschede, Netherlands) for LOTOS; O. Færgemand (TFL, Horshølm, Denmark) for SDL; R. Saracco (CSELT, Turin, Italy) for SDL; R. L. Tenney (University of Massachusetts, Boston, USA) for ESTELLE; and C. A. Vissers (University of Twente, Enschede, Netherlands) for ESTELLE and LOTOS. These people played a major part in directing the work of the corresponding standardisation groups. Their technical and political acumen deserves due recognition.

As editor, I faced major organisational, technical and editorial challenges in producing this book. The nature of the book required a high level of integration of material from contributors who were widely spread. Electronic mail was indispensable for keeping in contact with everyone and for transferring large numbers of files. Since the book contains many closely related examples in different FDTs, I worked hard to harmonise these without losing the essential character of each contributor's style. This is not just an edited book, it is an *edited* book! I gratefully acknowledge the tolerance of the contributors as I made wholesale alterations to their prized text.

The book was assembled from material that arrived via four different media, used three different text formatters, and contained diagrams produced using five different drawing tools. Everything was reduced to LaTeX, TeX and PostScript. In the hope that it may prove useful to other authors, I have included the style files and utilities I developed in this task on the instructor's disc. The utilities to format formal descriptions for LaTeX may be useful in their own right. Typographical design was undertaken by myself. The book was prepared using a NeXTstation and printed on a NeXTprinter — an environment for authors that I can recommend.

K. J. Turner
Stirling
June 1992

Acknowledgements

This book is based in part on a joint CCITT and ISO/IEC collaboration, leading to a report whose editor was also the editor of this book. Reproduction of material from the ITU/ISO Manual *Guidelines for the Application of Estelle, Lotos and SDL — October 1992* (on the basis of which the present book has been prepared) is made with the authorisation of the International Telecommunication Union (ITU) as copyright holder. The choice of the excerpts reproduced remains the sole responsibility of the authors and does not engage the ITU in any way. The ITU/ISO *Guidelines for the Application of Estelle, Lotos and SDL* can be obtained from:

International Telecommunication Union
General Secretariat — Sales Section
Place des Nations
CH-1211 Geneva 20
Switzerland

Telephone: +41-22-730-5111 Telegram: Burinterna Geneva
Telefax (2/m): +41-22-730-5194 Telex: 421 000 uit ch

ISO/IEC has also kindly permitted the use of copyright material from the report, which is published as ISO/IEC TR 10167 with the above title. Copies of this may be obtained from any ISO or IEC member, or from:

ISO	IEC
P.O. Box 56	P.O. Box 131
CH-1211 Geneva 20	CH-1211 Geneva 20
Switzerland	Switzerland

Enquiries about the ITU/ISO Manual regarding SDL descriptions must be forwarded to:

CCITT Secretariat (Study Group X — Question 6/X)
2, rue de Varembé
CH-1211 Geneva 20
Switzerland

while those regarding ESTELLE and LOTOS descriptions must be forwarded to:

ISO/IEC JTC1/SC21 (Project 1.21.45)
14430 Broadway
New York
NY 10018
USA

Chapter 1 is loosely based on some material in CCITT (1992g) and ISO (1991g). Chapter 3 derives from material produced for the ALICE project (COMETT 87/2/C/650), partly supported by the Commission of the European Communities. Sections 5.4, 6.4, 7.4, 8.4 and 9.4 stem from work originally undertaken on the SEDOS project (ESPRIT 410), partly supported by the Commission of the European Communities. Permission to include the material of Section 8.4 (copyright Northern Telecom) is gratefully acknowledged. Chapter 11 is based on material produced for the LOTOSPHERE project (ESPRIT 2304), partly supported by the Commission of the European Communities. Chapter 12 is based on the work of many people including O. Færgemand (TFL, Horshølm, Denmark), R. Bræk (Sintef-Delab, Trondheim, Norway), J. Ellsberger (Telia Research, Malmö, Sweden) and A. Ek (Telia Research, Malmö, Sweden).

The names UNIX, PostScript, and of the tools cited are trademarks of their respective owners.

P. A. J. Tilanus (PTT Research, Leidschendam, Netherlands) read a draft of the entire book with great care and attention. His helpful comments were extremely valuable in giving the book a final polish. H. W. Thimbleby (University of Stirling, Stirling, Scotland) read parts of the book and made many useful editorial suggestions.

R. Saracco (CSELT, Turin, Italy) and C. A. Vissers (University of Twente, Enschede, Netherlands) kindly commented on a draft of Chapter 1. S. Budkowski (Institut National des Télécommunications, Evry, France) and V. Chari (CEGELEC, Clamart, France) carefully read a draft of Chapter 2 and made many helpful comments.

Since the examples of Chapters 5 to 9 are based on some of those used in the CCITT and ISO/IEC report, the book has benefited from the comments of the many (and sometimes anonymous) experts who reviewed the report during its several stages of approval. Many of the contributors checked each other's contributions. However, the authors of all chapters and sections assume full responsibility for their contents.

A.-M. Halligan, the Publishing Editor, was very supportive throughout the production of the book. She dealt efficiently with many contractual and copyright problems, and was always a source of good advice on editorial matters.

K. J. Turner would like to thank his family (Beth, Duncan and Robin) for their patience and understanding of his unavailability during many long hours of difficult editing.

Part I

Introducing the FDTs

This part of the book contains introductions to the general context of FDTs *(Formal Description Techniques)* and to each FDT in particular. Individual chapters in this part are as follows:

Chapter 1 explains why FDTs were developed, their origins and their use.

Chapter 2 gives an introduction to ESTELLE.

Chapter 3 gives an introduction to LOTOS.

Chapter 4 gives an introduction to SDL.

1 The Context of FDTs[1]

1.1 The Origins of FDTs

1.1.1 *Reasons for Formal Approaches*

FDTs *(Formal Description Techniques)* derive from work over several decades on **formal specification languages** and **rigorous methods** for computer system development. The essence of such languages and methods is a mathematical underpinning that ensures precision and tractability. Conventional descriptions are usually given in natural language or in diagrams, but these are hard to make unambiguous and are hard to analyse. Errors and omissions in computer systems are often costly to rectify, and may endanger life or property. Formal approaches to development are particularly justified for systems that are:

complex. Many systems already fall into this category, and the trend is to produce even more complex systems.

concurrent. These systems exhibit complex patterns of potentially interfering behaviours that must be interwoven; concurrency arises in distributed systems, real-time systems, hardware design, and parallel processing.

quality-critical. These are systems whose failure is not dangerous but whose reliability and dependability are highly important; examples include financial applications, telecommunications, and operating systems.

safety-critical. Computers control vital systems in activities such as defence, medicine, the nuclear industry, railway signalling, telecommunications, and aircraft flight management.

security-critical. With the widespread use of Information Technology, preventing unauthorised use of information or computing facilities may be

[1]Chapter 1 is by K. J. Turner and F. Belina.

essential for reasons of national security, commercial confidence, or personal privacy.

standardised. Standards, in particular international standards, are widely used and must be interpreted uniformly if they are to have any value.

It is hardly surprising that the main areas where formal approaches have been actively pursued are safety-critical systems, (tele)communications, hardware, and defence. (Tele)communications is of particular interest to **ISO** (the *International Organization for Standardization*) and **CCITT** (the *International Consultative Committee on Telegraphy and Telephony*).

1.1.2 *The Standardisation of FDTs*

In the second half of the 1970s, ISO began work on a massive programme to produce standards for **OSI** *(Open Systems Interconnection)*. Standards for OSI and related topics are still being developed. A key issue in OSI is *openness* — a framework in which any manufacturer may produce implementations of OSI that interwork with others. It follows that standards for OSI must be unambiguous and free from implementation bias, in other words they must be precise statements of requirements. It was recognised early in the work on OSI that the standardisation process would benefit from the use of formal approaches. A preliminary meeting was held in 1980 to investigate the feasibility of this, and led to the establishment of a *rapporteur* group to produce standards for formal approaches.

The term 'Formal Description Technique' was coined to describe the languages and methods to be standardised. Although 'FDT' is now used loosely to mean any formally-based language or method, it still has the restricted meaning of the standardised techniques discussed in this book. The early studies of the ISO FDT group showed that there were a great many existing approaches that could be adopted. A number of these fell into two broad categories: those based on finite state automata, and those based on algebraic ideas. Both of these approaches were felt to be useful and to have complementary benefits, so it was decided to standardise one FDT in each category. After 8 years of work, the outcome was standards for ESTELLE (*Extended Finite State Machine Language*, ISO (1989e)) and LOTOS (*Language Of Temporal Ordering Specification*, ISO (1989l)). Vissers, Tenney and von Bochmann (1983) give a history of early FDT development in ISO.

CCITT is responsible for producing standards[2] in the field of telecommunications. Computing first began to make an impact on telecommunications with

[2]The correct CCITT term is 'recommendation', but for all practical purposes the recommendations of CCITT can be treated as standards.

the advent of SPC *(Stored Programme Controlled)* telephone exchanges. It was therefore natural for CCITT to take an interest in techniques for specifying computerised telecommunications systems. An early version of SDL *(Specification and Description Language)* was produced in 1976. Through successive four-year 'study periods', SDL was evolved from an informal diagrammatic design notation to a fully-fledged FDT. By coincidence, the most advanced version of SDL was finalised around the same time as ESTELLE and LOTOS were issued as standards. However, for some years prior to this there had been close cooperation between CCITT and ISO over the development of FDTs. SDL in fact shares some features with both ESTELLE and LOTOS: the finite state automaton concept of ESTELLE, and the algebraic data typing of LOTOS.

1.2 The Purpose of FDTs

FDTs were developed to ensure:

- **unambiguous**, **clear** and **concise** specifications
- **completeness** of specifications
- **consistency** of specifications, in isolation and relative to each other
- **tractability** of specifications
- **conformance** of implementations to specifications.

Those who are expected to benefit from the use of FDTs on standards include:

- **developers** of standards
- **implementers** who develop products complying with standards
- **testers** of conformance to standards
- **end-users** of products designed according to standards.

The use of FDTs is by no means confined to standards. Any computer system development that requires a high level of dependability and quality will benefit from the application of FDTs. There are encouraging signs that ESTELLE, LOTOS and SDL are already being applied outside their original area of (tele)communications standardisation.

Using an FDT requires care in specifying exactly what is required. A valuable byproduct of using an FDT is the discovery of errors, ambiguities and inconsistencies in the ideas that are being specified. Writing a formal description also imposes a good structure on the problem domain. In the early stages of development, an FDT is helpful in expressing requirements and problem structure. Even if development has already progressed to the stage of informal description, applying an FDT retrospectively can highlight deficiencies before they cause difficulties[3].

The main initial thrust of FDT standardisation was on language definition. This was subsequently followed by development of tutorial material, the preparation of guidelines for using FDTs[4], and writing formal descriptions of standards. The existence of standards for FDTs allows text-books to be written, justifies companies in training their staff to use FDTs, and encourages universities to include FDT teaching in their curricula.

1.3 The FDTs in Brief

All three FDTs share a common basis for specifying behaviour, namely **labelled transition systems**. These are systems whose transitions between states are labelled with associated actions. For data typing, ESTELLE uses PASCAL data types while LOTOS and SDL use algebraically specified **ADTs** *(Abstract Data Types)*. Specification with the three FDTs is illustrated with a graded series of examples in Chapters 5 to 9. These examples allow each FDT to be studied in depth on examples of increasing complexity. The examples also allow the characteristics of the three FDTs to be compared by example. Although the examples mainly emphasise OSI-like communications systems, the principles illustrated in the examples are generally applicable and should be helpful in other application domains.

1.3.1 *ESTELLE*

ESTELLE is a formally-defined specification language for describing distributed or concurrent processing systems, in particular those that implement OSI services and protocols. The language is based on widely used and accepted concepts of communicating non-deterministic state machines (automata). An ESTELLE specification defines a system of hierarchically-structured state machines. The state machines communicate by exchanging messages through bi-directional

[3]This was the case while the FDTs were being developed in CCITT and ISO. Formal descriptions of standards were developed after the fact, but it was still possible to identify problems that could be dealt with by the standardisation committees. The trend is now for formal descriptions to be developed side-by-side with informal ones.

[4]This book derives in part from ISO (1991g), a cooperative effort by CCITT and ISO to publish guidance on using FDTs.

channels between their communication ports. Messages are queued at either end of a channel. The actions of machines are specified in a derivative of standard PASCAL (ISO (1982)), so ESTELLE specifications will look familiar to many programmers.

ESTELLE allows modelling of synchronous and asynchronous parallelism between the state machines of a system. It also permits dynamic evolution of the system configuration. ESTELLE specifications can be written at different levels of abstraction, from abstract to implementation-oriented. The latter may be derived from the former with the aid of supporting tools. Since all ESTELLE concepts are rigorously defined, it has been possible to develop ESTELLE tools that accurately reflect the language.

The ESTELLE language is introduced in Chapter 2. Aspects of development with ESTELLE are dealt with in Chapter 10.

1.3.2 *LOTOS*

LOTOS was developed from a large, well-established body of theory based on CCS (*Calculus of Communicating Systems*, Milner (1989)), CSP (*Communicating Sequential Processes*, Hoare (1985)), and ACT ONE (Ehrig and Mahr (1985)). Having a well-defined mathematical foundation, LOTOS provides a solid basis for analysis and also development of reliable tools.

The basic behavioural constructs of LOTOS allow modelling of sequential behaviour, choice, concurrency and non-determinism in an unambiguous way. In addition, LOTOS permits modelling of both synchronous and asynchronous communication. The data typing part of LOTOS allows implementation-independent specifications to be given as ADTs.

LOTOS can be used to specify all the allowed behaviours of a system, i.e. the set of all behaviours that may be observed of a conforming implementation. LOTOS permits this without describing how an implementation might be achieved, or by describing particular mechanisms that achieve the required behaviour. LOTOS is therefore appropriate for the specification of open standards.

The LOTOS language is introduced in Chapter 3. Aspects of development with LOTOS are dealt with in Chapter 11.

1.3.3 *SDL*

SDL is based on an extended finite state machine model, supplemented by features for specifying ADTs (based on the same model as used in the ACT ONE part of LOTOS). This combination is supported by a complete formal semantics.

SDL provides constructs for representing structures, behaviours, interfaces and communication links. In addition, it provides constructs for abstraction, module encapsulation and refinement. All of these constructs were designed to assist the representation of a variety of telecommunications system specifications, including aspects of services and protocols. SDL is quite widely used in the telecommunications community and is well supported by a variety of tools, some of which are commercially available.

The SDL language is introduced in Chapter 4. Aspects of development with SDL are dealt with in Chapter 12.

1.4 Development using FDTs

1.4.1 *Modelling*

It is widely accepted that the key to a successful system is a thorough system specification and design. The result of the system specification and design activity is called a **specification** for brevity.

For a system there may be specifications at different levels of abstraction. A specification is the basis for deriving **implementations**. It should abstract from implementation details in order to give an overview of the system, to postpone implementation decisions, and to allow all valid implementations.

In contrast to a program, a formal specification is not intended to be run on a computer. In addition to serving as a basis for deriving implementations, a formal specification can be used for precise and unambiguous communication between people, particularly for contracts.

The use of a specification language makes it possible to analyse and simulate alternative system solutions, which in practice is impossible when using a traditional programming language due to the cost and the time delay. A specification language offers a well-defined set of concepts, improving the capability to produce a solution to a problem and to reason about the solution.

A complete description of a system contains many kinds of information. Each information item must be expressed in an appropriate language: natural, semi-formal or formal. A natural language is very good at expressing aims, wishes and intentions. It is poor at expressing details precisely and unambiguously. A formal language has the opposite properties. In a complete description of a system, different categories of languages should be used that complement each other, so that their advantages are exploited. How to achieve this is an important methodology issue.

The application domain of a system is understood ultimately in terms of the concepts of a natural language. The specification of an application in a natural language is descriptive by nature; phenomena are described as they are perceived by an observer.

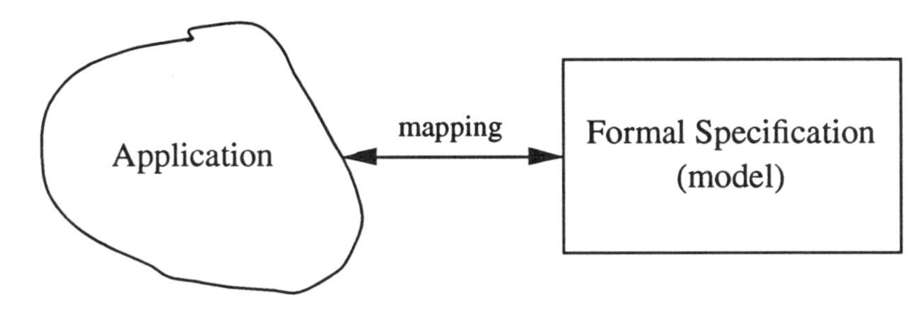

Figure 1.1: Understanding a Formal Specification

When a system is described using a specification language, the formal specification makes use of neither application nor implementation concepts; it defines rather a **model** that represents the significant properties of the system (mainly behaviour). In order to understand this model, it must be mapped to the intuitive understanding of the application in terms of natural language concepts; Figure 1.1 illustrates this point. The mapping can be done in different ways. One approach is to choose names for the concepts introduced in the formal specification that are naturally associated with application concepts. Another way is to include comments in the formal specification. This is much the same issue as the understanding of a program or algorithm that solves a problem taken from real life.

A model should have good **analytical power** to maximise the benefits of the formal approach. It should also have good **expressive power** to ease the mapping to the application. Unfortunately, analytical power and expressive power are generally in conflict: the more expressive a model is, the more difficult it is to analyse. When designing a specification language, a trade-off must be made between these two properties.

1.4.2 *Development Method*

Development using an FDT is broadly similar to conventional development, but there are distinctive features in the approach. Most development methods can be represented by a **waterfall model** in which earlier stages produce results for later stages. A typical sequence of stages in development with an FDT is:

- **requirements capture** and **analysis**
- **formal specification** of informal requirements

- **checking** the specification for consistency and for completeness with respect to the requirements
- **design steps** involving:
  - **refinement** of a specification to a more implementation-oriented form
  - **verification** (proof) that a refined specification has the essential properties of the one from which it is derived
- **implementation** of the lowest level specification
- **validation** (testing) of the implementation against the highest level specification.

The use of an FDT requires formal rather than informal specifications at all stages, thus ensuring unique interpretation. The fact that specifications are formal means that correctness-preserving transformations may be used. Alternatively, a designer may use intuition and experience to derive the next level of specification. Since there is a risk of introducing errors in this process, the lower level specification should be formally verified. This requires proof that the essential properties of the earlier specification are preserved in the new one.

The number of design steps depends on the gap between the high-level specification and the low-level implementation environment. To produce an implementation in assembler or hardware logic it would be wise to have a relatively large number of steps. To produce an implementation in a fifth generation language or a hardware design language could take rather fewer steps. It may be necessary to backtrack during design, reconsidering earlier steps that have led to an infeasible solution. Design steps progressively decide implementation details, and are central to the design process. Figure 1.2 shows the essential activities in a design step.

The specification that is input to a step can be refined by the addition of implementation detail and the removal of unwanted implementation freedoms. The refinement might be suggested by a pre-defined transformation, by general design principles, or by problem-specific heuristics. The size of the design step will be no larger than can be handled intellectually and by tools. Use of a formal method requires that an informal refinement be checked by comparing the input and output specifications of the step. Checking the validity of a refinement is a non-trivial exercise since the refinement may introduce details and features not present in the original specification, and may remove freedoms allowed in the original. A variety of relations have been developed for FDTs to handle these possibilities.

It is commonplace to design top-down and bottom-up at the same time. Top-down design is concerned with analysis and decomposition of the problem into

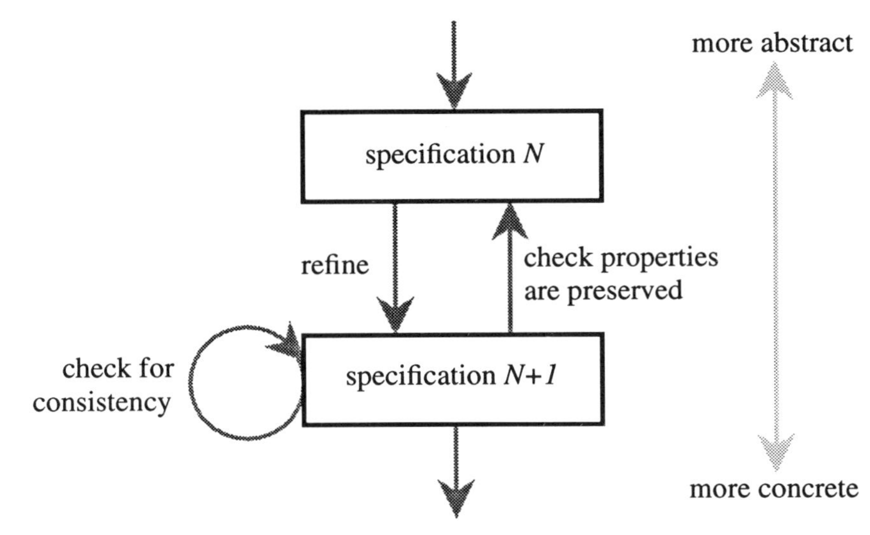

Figure 1.2: Activities in a Design Step

manageable pieces. Bottom-up design is concerned with synthesis of existing components to make new structures. A designer will often carry out some top-down analysis, and then investigate the feasibility of this by looking at whether existing components can be combined to build the required modules. FDTs help in both these aspects of design. FDTs have good features for structuring and decomposition that aid in analysis. They can also deal with systems at different levels of abstraction, allowing a high-level specification to be evolved into a low-level one. Libraries of pre-defined components can be specified and verified. By combining known components in known ways, a designer can have confidence in the results of bottom-up design. Finally, verification techniques can assess whether a proposed design meets the specified requirements.

Although a fully formal approach to development has many benefits, there may be practical reasons why it is not feasible in its entirety. The effort involved in formal specification and verification may seem to be high. However, the extra cost of formal methods is offset by the reduction in defects and the consequent avoidance of having to correct work already done. The cost of fixing a problem when a system has been distributed and installed is roughly 1000 times the cost of fixing the problem if it is identified at the specification stage. This means that formal approaches are particularly cost-effective in the early stages of development. Even if development proceeds conventionally after a formal specification has been written, benefits will still have been gained.

The possibility of verifying the correctness of a specification or design is appealing. In critical systems it may be essential to do so, regardless of the cost. Verification is unfortunately a difficult intellectual activity in which current software tools can provide only limited support. Verification may even be impossible since some properties are undecidable. There is generally a trade-off in FDT design between expressive power and verifiability. A practical alternative to verification is simulation, in which testing techniques are used to evaluate a specification or to compare two specifications. Simulation requires specifications to be capable of symbolic execution. As a deliberate decision, all three FDTs were designed to allow executable specifications to be written[5]. Of course, simulation can only ever discover the existence of errors, not prove in general that all errors have been found. However, it is a practical and valuable alternative when verification is infeasible or impossible.

1.5 Tools for FDTs

The development of tools was not an explicit objective of the FDT work in CCITT and ISO. It is not necessary to have computer tools to support FDTs since they can be used as intellectual tools. The complexity of modern computer systems and techniques is nonetheless such that software tools are extremely valuable. The existence of standards for FDTs has encouraged tool developers to develop computer support for these stable and widely accepted techniques. The rigorous nature of FDTs makes it possible to develop reliable tools to assist in the creation, analysis, and refinement of formal descriptions.

The tools that have been developed for FDTs depend to some extent on the individual character of each FDT. Some tools have been developed for research purposes, while others have been produced for entirely practical goals such as commercial development. The software tools that support FDTs can be broadly categorised as:

- **book-keeping tools** that create and maintain specifications
- **front-end tools** that operate directly on specifications
- **verification tools** that analyse properties of specifications
- **back-end tools** that are used to refine, transform, and implement specifications.

Book-keeping tools deal with the essentially 'administrative' tasks of creating and maintaining specifications. Since all three FDTs have a textual form,

[5]Non-constructive (and therefore non-executable) specifications can also be written where a high level of abstraction is required.

conventional text editors can be used. In addition, **syntax-directed editors** (also called **structure editors**) have been produced for FDTs. These editors have a knowledge of the language being edited, and can ensure that statically correct specifications are produced. **Graphical editors** have also been developed to handle formal descriptions in diagrammatic form. Other book-keeping aspects such as version control can be handled by conventional tools.

Front-end tools deal directly with specification text. The front-end tools developed for FDTs are largely ones that are available for any language. Front-end tools commonly translate the source specification into some common intermediate representation used by other tools. A **lexical analyser** turns the raw specification text into 'tokens'. A **syntax checker** verifies conformance to syntax rules. A **static semantics analyser** checks for consistent use of types, consistency of actual and formal parameters, etc. A **parser** produces the abstract syntax tree of the source specification, and is often combined with a syntax checker. An **unparser** is used to print a specification in standard forms, either in a stylised layout (**pretty-printing**) or with conversion to a new form (e.g. textual to graphical). A **cross-referencer** produces a list of identifiers, their type, and where they are defined and used. Some tools are FDT-specific, such as a **flattener** that produces a one-level specification with all nested scopes removed and identifier clashes resolved.

Verification tools are a natural accompaniment to formal languages. Some tools are independent of the choice of FDT, or could be developed for any FDT. An **algebraic simplifier** has the task of reducing expressions to a simpler or standard form. A **theorem prover** is used to help prove properties of a specification stated as theorems. Proof may be automatic, but usually requires considerable human guidance — interactive or in the form of codified proof strategies. A **proof checker** automates the verification of a supposed proof given to it, usually derived manually by a user. A **test derivation tool** generates tests from a specification to validate the corresponding implementation.

Other verification tools are used with particular kinds of FDT. The list of such tools is large, but here are some examples. A **state space analyser** is used to explore the state space of a problem, checking for unwanted deadlocks, infinite loops, unreachable states, etc. A **simulator** is used to symbolically execute a specification in order to explore its consequences. An **equivalence checker** is used to verify equivalence of two labelled transition systems according to some formally defined notion of what differences are acceptable. A **completion tool** checks for completeness of algebraically specified abstract data types. A **persistency checker** establishes that data types have been enriched without destroying their essential properties.

Back-end tools deal with refinement or implementation of specifications. An **interactive transformation tool** is used to apply correctness-preserving transformations to a specification. An **expansion tool** unfolds behaviour definitions, and so may transform a specification into a more readily implemented form. A **compiler** translates a low-level specification into code in some language. Unless a specification is already written in a very constructive way, it is necessary to refine a more abstract specification to a more concrete one before trying to compile it. Compiling a formal description does not usually produce machine code directly. Back-ends have been developed for programming languages such as C and ADA. By producing code in such languages it becomes possible to compile specifications to run on a variety of computers.

1.6 The Future of FDTs

The standardisation of FDTs has made formal approaches much more widely available to system developers. Although standardisation brings stability to a language, the language need not remain static. CCITT standards are typically revised every four years, and this has happened several times with SDL. ISO standards are reviewed every five years, so new developments in ESTELLE and LOTOS are possible in future. There has been research on new data typing formalisms for ESTELLE and for LOTOS, for example. A graphical syntax for LOTOS is currently being standardised. Features for non-determinism are being added to SDL. There is interest in object-oriented versions of all three FDTs. There are issues of real time and stochastic behaviour to be investigated. So although everyone can benefit from the existence of standards for FDTs, future enhancements can be anticipated.

Most of the tools activity to support FDTs has been to produce research prototypes, although some of this work has led to commercial products. It is very likely that more commercially available toolsets will be produced in the near future, leading to more widespread use of FDTs. These toolsets will be integrated with current development methods and languages.

Because the FDTs drew on a large body of existing research on formal languages, the development of the FDTs as languages was more a standardisation exercise than a research activity. Work on *methods* for using FDTs is comparatively recent. As experience with the FDTs has been gained, a body of knowledge has been built up on how to use the FDTs effectively throughout development. Case studies have been investigated and reported. The strengths and weaknesses of each FDT have been discovered. A future area of work will therefore be to codify methods for each FDT, and to support these methods with tools. It is quite possible that FDTs will be combined with existing practices such as structured analysis and design, object-oriented design, inspection, structured walk-throughs, etc.

The most interesting change, however, will be the increasing use of the FDTs outside the (tele)communications standards world. This has started already, and is bound to grow. There are many areas where FDTs would be of benefit such as safety-critical systems, secure systems, real-time systems, embedded systems, distributed operating systems, VLSI and hardware design. Once FDTs have permeated computer system development in general, they will have truly realised their potential.

2 Introduction to ESTELLE[1]

2.1 Introduction

ESTELLE was developed for use in describing OSI services and protocols. More generally, however, it is a technique for specifying distributed systems. It is based on the observation that communications software is often described and implemented with an underlying finite automaton model. ESTELLE builds on this by adding features to a simple finite automaton that facilitate writing complete descriptions of communication services and protocols.

A major consequence of choosing to base ESTELLE on finite automata is that descriptions are 'natural': designers may write formal descriptions based on familiar notions, and implementers are given guidance on how to implement the protocols.

ESTELLE is an outgrowth of earlier work that includes Ansart *et al.* (1982), Blumer and Tenney (1982), von Bochmann (1978), Danthine (1980), Merlin (1979) and Tenney (1980). A snapshot of the status of FDTs when the work on ESTELLE and LOTOS began is given by von Bochmann and Sunshine (1980). ESTELLE became an International Standard, ISO (1989e), in mid-1989.

The chapter begins by describing the key ideas of ESTELLE, using a very simple specification example (a simplification of the Daemon Game that is dealt with fully in Chapter 5). The language used to write ESTELLE specifications is then described.

2.2 Overview

This section gives a brief, somewhat simplified overview of the main ideas in ESTELLE: modules, channels and structuring. Subsequent sections describe ESTELLE in more detail. Modules and channels are the fundamental building

[1]Chapter 2 is by R. L. Tenney. Although he was the editor of the ESTELLE standard (ISO (1989e)) and remains its maintenance editor, the views expressed in this chapter are strictly personal and do not represent an official position of ISO or its members.

blocks of ESTELLE. Modules communicate with each other through channels, and may be structured into submodules.

2.2.1 *Modules*

The underlying model for an ESTELLE module is a finite state automaton. Finite automata are mathematical abstractions of computing devices. They are thought of as machines having a finite number of states that make transitions from state to state as they consume inputs. Finite automata come in a number of variants; the one ESTELLE uses is based on the notion of a transducer. An ESTELLE automaton accepts inputs and produces outputs as it makes transitions from state to state.

In ESTELLE modules, inputs and outputs (often called **interactions**) occur through **interaction points**. Interactions received by one module from another are queued by the receiving module.

In a typical protocol specification, the state of the automaton would correspond to the state of the connection (closed, opening, open, closing, etc.). One set of inputs would correspond to user requests (*Connect*, *Send*, etc.) and would cause the automaton to output PDUs *(Protocol Data Units)*. Another set of inputs would be accepted from the communication provider (*DataIndication*, *Reset*, etc.), and these would give rise to outputs to be sent to the user (*ReceiveResponse*, *ErrorIndication*, etc.). A transition could occur from the state named *Closed* to the state named *Opening* when a user-initiated *Connect* request was received, and a *ConnectRequest* PDU could be output as part of the transition. This is a scenario that will be familiar to most readers who have dealt with communications protocols, and they could easily complete the broad outlines of the progress of the connection.

ESTELLE modules act by making transitions from one state to another. The choice of which transition to take is determined by the current state and current input. Making a transition consists of consuming an input, changing state, and producing output. Making a transition is sometimes called **firing** the transition. ESTELLE modules allow transitions that require no input, called **spontaneous transitions**, which may have time constraints placed on them to delay their firing. In addition, ESTELLE modules may be non-deterministic, which means that the current state and current input determine a set of allowable actions, only one of which will be chosen. An implementation based on an ESTELLE specification may resolve non-determinism in any fashion desired, including always making the same choice or always making a random choice. In particular, there is no guarantee of fairness in the semantics of ESTELLE.

2.2.2 *Channels*

Modules are connected by **channels**. These form bindings from the output of one module to an (unbounded) queue associated with another module[2]. When one module initiates an interaction, the interaction is placed in a queue of another module, as determined by the binding corresponding to the channel through which the interaction is sent.

Channels do not allow arbitrary interactions to occur. Each channel has two ends, which are attached at interaction points of two modules. Each of these modules may initiate certain interactions and receive other interactions. In other words, associated with each channel are two roles that will be assumed by the modules connected to the ends of the channel. To each of these roles there corresponds a set of interactions that may be initiated (output) by the module assuming that role. These will, of course, be received by the module assuming the other role.

Modules maintain queues for receiving interactions. A module may have an individual queue for each interaction point, or it may combine the inputs from several interaction points into a common queue. A module may have at most one common queue. When a module receives an interaction, it is placed in the appropriate queue in the usual fashion (i.e. at the tail of the queue).

A module's queues are unbounded, so there is always room to accept another interaction in each queue. The module can act only on interactions that are at the head of one of its queues; it cannot tell if there are other interactions that follow it or what they are.

2.2.3 *Structuring*

From outside, an ESTELLE module is a 'black box'; nothing can be known about its inner workings except what can be observed by its outputs. From within, however, besides having states and transitions between these states, a module may be structured to contain other modules.

An ESTELLE module, sometimes called a **parent** module, may create and destroy other ESTELLE modules within itself, called **children** modules. A child module can have its own children modules. The parent module may connect the interaction points of its children modules to each other or to its own internal interaction points. It may attach its external interaction points to the external interaction points of its children, causing interactions that arrive through the attached interaction point to be received by the child. It may also share some

[2]The modules connected through a channel will be referred to as though they were distinct, but this is not always the case: a channel may loop back from a module to itself.

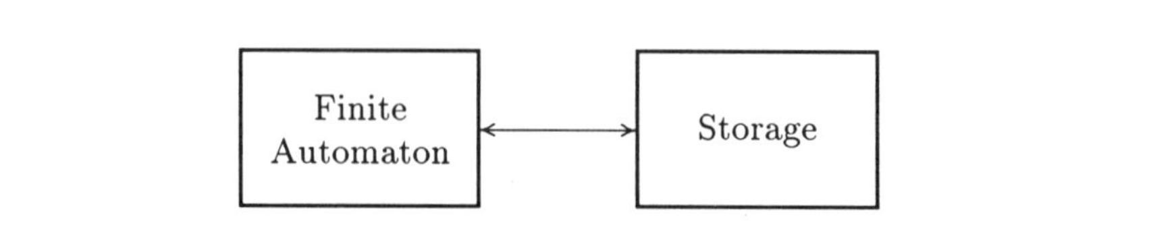

Figure 2.1: A Finite Automaton with External Storage

of its children's variables. The distinction between connecting and attaching interaction points will be dealt with in more detail in Section 2.4.

This overview has presented the major ideas of ESTELLE to give a feel for the technique. It is by no means a complete view; the next sections revisit the parts of ESTELLE that require more explanation.

2.3 Modules

This section elaborates on the simple description of ESTELLE modules given earlier. For the most part, the description will concentrate on an isolated ESTELLE module. Modules in systems are considered later.

2.3.1 *Modules as Extended Finite Automata*

The finite automaton model on which ESTELLE is based is very appealing, both for its simplicity and for its tractability to analysis. However, there is a fundamental reason that a pure finite automaton model is inadequate for complete descriptions of most communications protocols: state-space explosion. Communication protocols usually involve such things as sequence numbers. Even though the sequence numbers are finite (they are usually integers modulo some power of two), if these were to be included as part of the state of the automaton, the number of states would quickly become unmanageably large. Thus it is necessary to introduce variables, sometimes called **context variables**, and also a way of manipulating them into the usual finite automaton model.

The total state of an ESTELLE module includes the values associated with each of these variables as well as the state of the underlying automaton, which is sometimes called the **control state** or **major state** to distinguish it from the total state of the module. It is helpful to think of an automaton with external storage as pictured in Figure 2.1. Technically, the extended automaton can be thought of as functions defined on the cross product of the finite automaton and the storage.

2.3.2 *Transitions*

In ESTELLE, firing a transition is more complex than in the simple finite automaton case. The choice of action is based on the current major state, the current values of the variables, the inputs at heads of queues, and the priorities associated with transitions. The model includes non-determinism, meaning that at any given instant there may be more than one action that a module might perform. The only guarantee is that at most one of these actions will be performed. Spontaneous transitions are also supported, both with and without delay. These are discussed at length later.

The conditions that enable a transition are thought of as a guard: each must be satisfied if the transition is to be considered among those able to be fired. The conditions may include:

- the interaction at the head of a specified queue
- the current control state
- predicates based on the values of the context variables of the extended finite automaton and the values of the parameters associated with the interaction
- the status of timers
- the transition priority.

If no action is possible for any interaction at the head of any queue, and if no spontaneous transition is enabled, the module merely does nothing until the situation changes.

The selection of and changes effected by a transition form a single, indivisible, atomic action. This implies, among other things, that values assumed by variables during a transition cannot be observed from outside the module unless they remain after the transition has finished. Note, however, that no assumptions are made about the length of time required to perform the transition: this is regarded as an implementation issue.

Each transition has a priority associated with it, if not explicitly then implicitly. For a transition to be chosen, no transition of higher priority may be enabled in the module. The priority of a transition is a non-negative integer value, with lower integers corresponding to higher priorities. If no priority is explicitly given for a transition, then a priority one lower than (i.e. an integer one greater than) any explicitly given anywhere else in the module is assumed for it. If no transition has an explicit priority, all transitions may be assumed to have priority zero. The priority of a transition is fixed.

2.3.3 *Time and Delay*

As explained in Section 2.3.2, there is no time associated with the execution of a transition. However, it is possible to specify a delay that must occur before a spontaneous transition may be enabled.

Two time delays, d_1 and d_2, may be associated with a spontaneous transition, where $d_1 \leq d_2$. The transition cannot fire until the enabling conditions of its guard have remained true continuously for time d_1. Provided its enabling conditions remain continuously true, in the interval between d_1 and d_2 the transition may be considered to be enabled, but it need not be. Finally, after time d_2 has elapsed, the transition must be considered to be enabled as long as its enabling conditions continue to remain true. Firing the transition restarts its timing, so its guard must again remain continuously true for time d_1 before it can again be enabled.

If the time delays associated with a spontaneous transition are zero and infinity, then the transition may be enabled whenever the guard associated with it is satisfied, but it need never be enabled. One use of this might be to specify that when a multiplexed network connection is no longer used, it may be closed but need not be: the choice belongs to the implementer. This situation may occur in the OSI Transport Protocol (ISO (1988)).

A spontaneous transition may have a single time delay, d, specified. This has the meaning of $d_1 = d_2 = d$.

The ESTELLE semantics restrict the interpretation of time in the weakest way possible, placing only those requirements that derive from assuming that time moves forward consistently for all modules in the same subsystem (see Section 2.5). This corresponds to making no assumptions about speed of execution. It is up to the specifier or implementer to make whatever additional assumptions are necessary to guarantee timing constraints are met. The potential execution sequences of an ESTELLE specification can be regarded as forming a tree. The additional assumptions about time have the effect of pruning certain branches from the tree.

2.4 Channels

Modules communicate through channels. A parent module may connect and disconnect channels between its children. Modules cannot manage the connection of their own external interaction points.

The structuring of modules necessitates a mechanism to establish communication between a parent and its children. One way this is accomplished is through internal interaction points of the parent, which the parent itself may connect to external interaction points of a child through a channel. As with all connections through channels, either module may initiate and receive those interactions appropriate to its declared role.

To facilitate making the substructure of a module invisible to other modules, it is also desirable to be able to attach an external interaction point of a parent to an external interaction point of a child. The result of this action is to cause interactions that would have gone to the queue associated with the parent's interaction point to go directly to the queue associated with the child's interaction point. Of course, the child may itself be substructured (yielding a grandchild of the original parent), and the interaction point of the child may itself be attached to the external interaction point of the grandchild. Were this to be done, it would result in associating the parent's interaction point with the grandchild's queue.

It is important to note that connecting and attaching are quite different operations. A parent connects the external interaction points of its children so that they may communicate with each other; a module attaches one of its external interaction points to an external interaction point of a child to facilitate structuring.

As the names imply, the operations **connect** and **disconnect** are opposites, and **attach** and **detach** are opposites. An interaction point that has been connected may be disconnected, and one that has been attached may be detached. It makes no sense for a parent to detach an interaction point that it connected nor to disconnect an interaction point that it attached.

Taken together, **connect** and **attach** are said to **bind** interaction points, while **disconnect** and **detach** are said to **unbind** them. A module may output interactions through an interaction point that is not bound, but these are simply lost. Binding and unbinding may be done explicitly by the parent; unbinding is also done implicitly in a release operation.

Unbinding has different actions for its two forms. Interactions that reside in a queue remain there when the corresponding interaction point is disconnected. In contrast, interactions that reside in a queue of a child are moved to the queue of the parent when the corresponding interaction point is detached[3]. If a chain of attaches is broken in the middle, the result is that the interactions that came through the interaction point of the parent breaking the attach are returned to the end of its queue; all other interactions in the queue at the end of the attach chain are left alone.

The semantics of **attach** and **detach** are complex, but they are easily justified in the context of OSI protocols. Consider, for example, the following simple case: a protocol specification that creates a child module to manage

[3]More precisely, for a detach, those interactions that were placed in the queue of the child while it was attached are moved to the queue of the parent, but those placed in the queue while it was connected are left in the queue.

each connection. The sequence of actions begins when a user of the protocol requests that a connection be opened. This will be an interaction through an interaction point of the parent. The parent then creates a child module. Once the child is created, one of its external interaction points should be attached to the interaction point of the parent through which the original open request came, so that interactions affecting this connection can be handled by the child without intervention by the parent.

After some use, the module that initiated the connection may choose to close the connection and then quickly open another connection by issuing a second open request. Assuming asynchronous execution of these modules (as is normal), the close request and the second open request may both end up in the queue of the child, with the open request behind the close request in the queue. The close request should result in the parent releasing the child, with the result that the child's interaction point is first detached. When this happens, if the contents of the child's queue were not returned to the parent, then the open request in the child's queue would be lost. This would make the use of children modules almost impossible.

2.5 Structuring

As already indicated, an important aspect of ESTELLE is its ability to describe a module as containing submodules which may themselves contain submodules, and so forth. This is referred to as **structuring**, and may be static, dynamic, or a combination of both. The structuring of a module is invisible from outside the module. In other words, the substructure of a module cannot be inferred from the behaviour of the module.

This is very useful for OSI descriptions. If, for example, a system had to be described with two transport modules communicating through a single network module, the three modules and their channels might be statically described. However, each connection between the two transport modules could be described as being managed by a separate submodule of each of the transport modules. These submodules could be created as each connection is established and then destroyed as the connection is closed. To destroy a module, either **release** or **terminate** may be used. **Release** implicitly unbinds all interaction points, while **terminate** simply destroys them, causing any interactions in their queues to be lost. Such a transport system is shown in Figure 2.2, where the innermost modules (one for each active connection) are created each time a connection is begun and released each time a connection is ended.

Structuring leads to hierarchies of modules. There are notions of a **parent** and **child** (a module and one of its immediate submodules), of **siblings** (children of the same parent), and of **ancestors** and **descendants** (the transitive

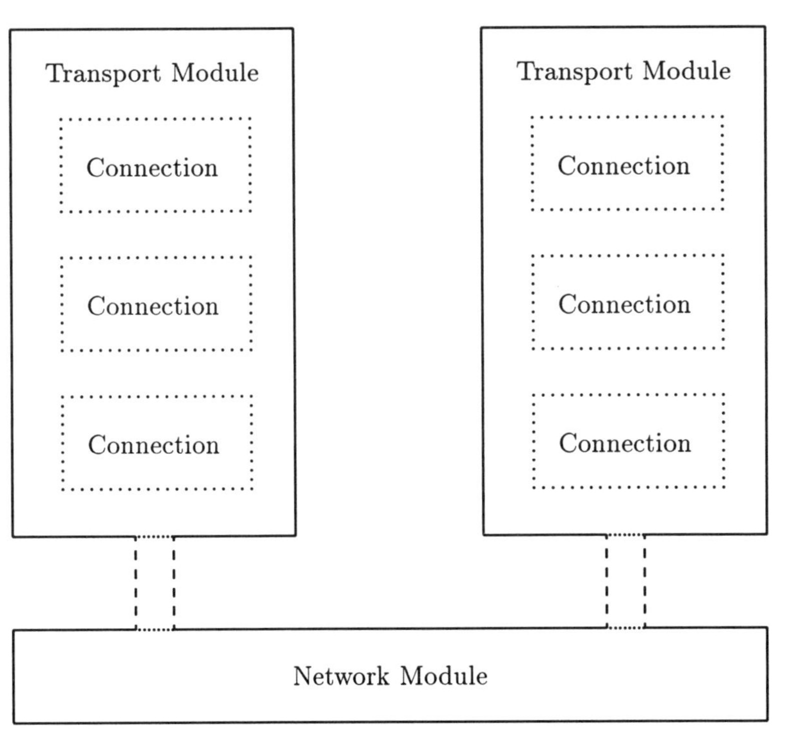

Figure 2.2: A Simple Transport Layer

closures of the parent and child relations, respectively). A parent may share those variables of a child that the child chooses to **export**. ESTELLE semantics guarantee that ancestors and descendants may never act at the same time, so there are no synchronisation problems with shared variables.

There is thus a difference between the communication and synchronisation possibilities between a module and its descendants, between siblings, or between two modules neither of which is a descendant of the other.

Synchronisation between siblings is determined by the **class** attribute of their parent: the children of a module that is declared to be a **process** run in parallel, while the children of a module that is an **activity** run sequentially in some random order, thus modelling parallelism in the usual interleaving fashion. Besides synchronisation implications, the class of a module has structural implications: an activity module may be substructured only into activity submodules, while a process module may be substructured into either processes or activities.

Each module may have an initialisation section, which is quite similar to a transition except that it does not depend on beginning in any state. The initialisation is invoked when the module is instantiated. Modules may be specified that have no transitions outside the initialisation section. In this case, the module serves simply to provide static structure and is called **inactive**.

Consider a module all of whose ancestors are inactive. It is not possible for such a module ever to be released or terminated since none of its ancestors may have a transition that could cause this. Such a module may be designated as the **root** of a subsystem. Note that other modules may also have inactive parents, but for a module to determine a subsystem, all of its ancestors must be inactive. Clearly, once they have been established during initialisation, the number of subsystems and the external connections between them are static.

A module that is the root of a subsystem must have the **systemactivity** or **systemprocess** attribute. No synchronisation is assumed between subsystems. It is sometimes convenient to think of modules within a single subsystem as being tightly coupled, while the subsystems themselves are only loosely coupled with each other.

2.5.1 *Systems of Modules*

ESTELLE modules do not generally exist in isolation, so it is necessary to understand how they interact. The actions of any subsystem are independent of the actions of any other subsystem, meaning that they run asynchronously. However, within each subsystem the actions of the modules are coordinated. It is convenient to think of subsystems as making computations step-by-step. Within the subsystem these computation steps are atomic acts.

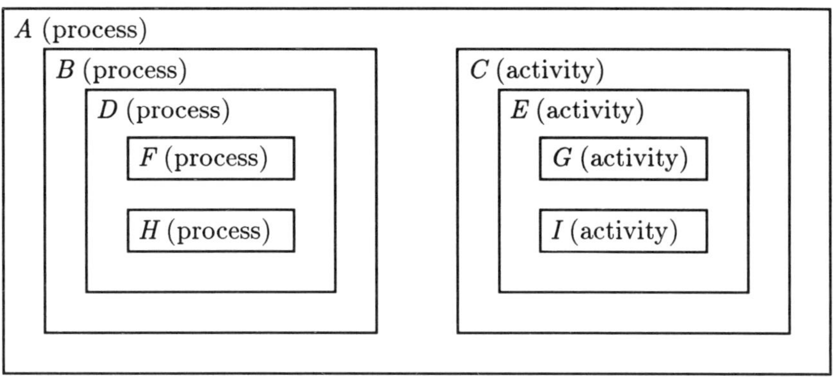

Figure 2.3: Structured Subsystem

At each computation step, each module within the subsystem selects an enabled transition to fire, if any. It does not necessarily fire this transition since its actions will be constrained by the condition of other modules in the subsystem.

Within any subsystem, ancestors always have priority over descendants. Thus if an ancestor and a descendant have enabled transitions, the descendant may not fire its transition. Starting with the root of the subsystem, modules are recursively given a chance to fire as follows. If the module under consideration has any enabled transitions, it will select one and fire it. If it does not have any enabled transitions there are two cases to consider: activities and processes. If the module is an activity, it will non-deterministically choose one of its children and give it a chance to fire. If a module is a process, it will give all of its children a chance to fire (in parallel).

A complex subsystem of modules is shown in Figure 2.3. Consider the following computation steps in this example:

- Module A has an enabled transition. In this case, only module A will fire its transition, regardless of whether other modules have enabled transitions or not. A is the ancestor of all the other modules and thus has priority over all of them.

- Modules D, F, G, H and I have enabled transitions but other modules do not. In this case, module D and one of G or I will fire their transitions.

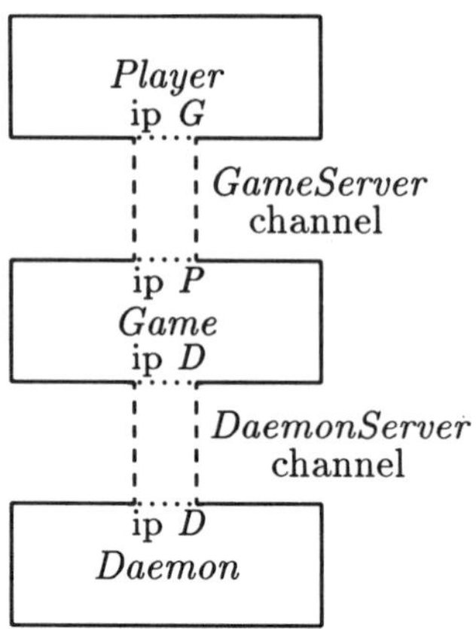

Figure 2.4: Simple Game System

D, as parent of processes F and H, has priority over them. As children of an activity, only one of G or I may fire. Since the nearest common ancestor of D and G or I is the process A, these will fire in parallel.

- Modules F, G, H and I have enabled transitions but other modules do not. In this case, both modules F and H and one of G or I will fire their transitions. This is the same as the immediately previous case, except that D has no enabled transitions so its children, F and H, fire their own transitions. As children of a process, F and H run in parallel.

Enabled process siblings are thus synchronised and run in parallel, while enabled activity siblings are interleaved.

2.6 Example

To make the ideas of ESTELLE clearer, the following sections use a simple form of the Daemon Game example elaborated in Chapter 5. Reference will be made to the Daemon Game as necessary when introducing more advanced concepts in ESTELLE.

The simple example is a game, not a communications protocol, because the aim is to concentrate on the details of ESTELLE rather than a protocol. The game is simpler than most protocols, and yet it is sufficiently complex that it provides a vehicle for explaining most of the features of ESTELLE.

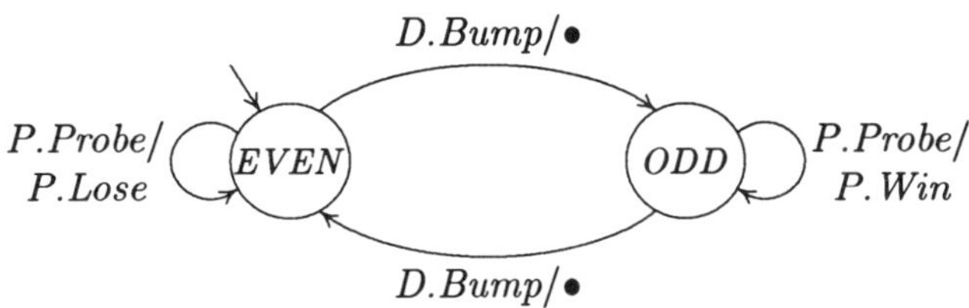

Figure 2.5: Simple Game Automaton

Imagine the following game machine: each time the player plays, the machine reports either that the player wins or loses. The choice depends on the actions of an internal 'daemon' that goes 'bump' at random times. If the daemon has made an odd number of bumps, the player wins; if the daemon has made an even number of bumps, the player loses.

As shown in Figure 2.4, this system may be modelled as three modules: the *Daemon*, the *Game* and the *Player*. These are connected through two channels, *DaemonServer* and *GameServer*.

The game machine module may be modelled as a two-state finite automaton: one state corresponds to an even number of bumps, the other to an odd number of bumps. There are four transitions as indicated in Figure 2.5. The notation for transitions is '*input/output*'. A '•' indicates an empty input or output. Two of the transitions require input from interaction point *D* associated with the *DaemonServer* channel and respond to a *Bump* by changing from *ODD* to *EVEN* or from *EVEN* to *ODD*. The other two transitions require input from interaction point *P* associated with the *GameServer* channel[4]. They respond to a *Probe* with a transition that does not change state but outputs either a *Win* or *Lose* response.

The *Daemon* and *Player* modules can be modelled as finite automata, each with a single state, as shown in Figure 2.6. The automata are trivial and can be represented easily in Estelle.

2.7 Language

This section concentrates on the language used to express specifications in Estelle. The language has three major components, each one oriented toward

[4]This channel is connected to a *Player* module, hence the choice of *P* as the identifier for the interaction point.

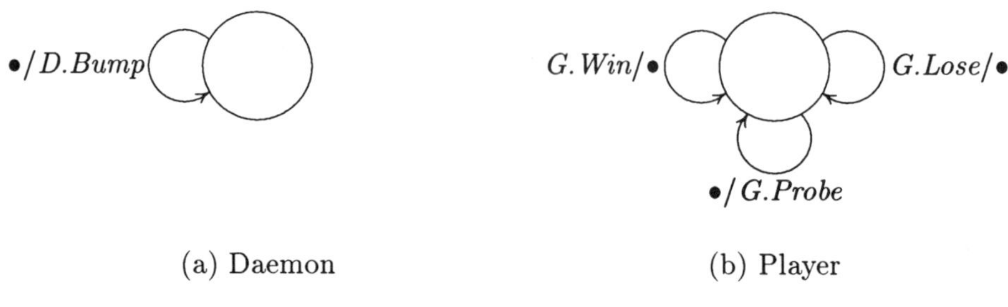

Figure 2.6: Daemon and Player Automata

expressing a different aspect of the model:

- the channels
- the actions of the finite automaton
- the structure of the system.

These components necessarily interact, but a conscious effort was made in the language design to limit the interactions between the parts as much as possible to keep the resultant language simple.

2.7.1 *Describing Channels*

A channel declaration names the two roles associated with a channel. It also determines the interactions that a module assuming a role may initiate and the parameters that accompany the interactions.

The channel descriptions for the Daemon Game system are as follows:

```
channel DaemonServer (User, Provider);
  by Provider:
    Bump;

channel GameServer (Player, Machine);
  by Player:
    Probe;                    { Player takes a turn }
  by Machine:
    Win;                      { Player wins }
    Lose;                     { Player loses }
```

Only the *Bump* interaction may pass through a *DaemonServer* channel, and it must be initiated by the module that assumes the role of the *Provider*. Three interactions may pass through a *GameServer* channel: a *Probe* initiated by a *Player* module, and *Win* and *Lose* initiated by a *Machine* module.

Note that the names of the roles are formal parameters, much like the formal parameters of a procedure in a language like PASCAL. There is nothing special about them. For example, *User* and *Provider* could be uniformly changed to *Taker* and *Giver* with no alteration in the meaning of the specification.

No temporal restrictions can be inferred from the channel description itself, e.g. a *Probe* must precede a *Win* or a *Lose*. For that it is necessary to look at how the channels are used by the modules. In many ways, a channel description behaves much like a type declaration.

Many interactions carry additional information in the form of parameters. This is indicated by including the parameters and their types with the interactions in the channel specification. One example is the *Score* interaction of the *GameServer* channel in the Daemon Game of Chapter 5.

2.7.2 *Describing Modules*

There are two aspects of an ESTELLE module that must be described: those features that can be seen externally and the actual functioning of the module itself. Thus there are two corresponding parts to the description of an ESTELLE module: the module header and the module body.

In a complete ESTELLE specification there is a (unique) outermost module. This module may have neither external interaction points nor exported variables. Furthermore, instead of being designated a module, it is designated a **specification** and its **end** is followed by a period (as is the final **end** of a PASCAL program). In addition to the usual features of a module, a specification module may declare a time scale to be used with delay clauses. It may also declare a default queueing discipline to be used in all modules for interaction points that do not declare an explicit one.

The module header lists the name of the module, its class (e.g. activity or process), and its exported variables (if any). It also describes the interaction points (**ip**) of the module. In effect, the module header establishes a module type. For the simple example, the following serves as the module header for the Game module:

```
module Game activity;
  ip
    P: GameServer (Machine) common queue;
    D: DaemonServer (User) common queue;
end; { Game }
```

The queueing discipline for each interaction point may be given in the header. Any interaction point for which the queue clause is not specified uses the default queueing discipline given for the entire specification. Of course it is an error if an interaction point has no specified queue discipline and no specification-wide default has been given.

The module body first identifies the module header to which the body applies and then describes the actions of that body. Note that several bodies may be defined for the same header; it is during instantiation that the appropriate body is selected. This can be useful when the actions of a module may change with circumstances. Consider the case of the OSI Transport Protocol (ISO (1988)) where there are five protocol classes. A single module header might be declared for a transport connection. Five bodies, one for each protocol class, might also be declared, to be chosen according to the class of the connection.

The remainder of this section is concerned with the module body. A body for the *Game* module of the simple example is as follows, corresponding to the finite automaton shown in Figure 2.5:

```
body GameBody for Game;
  state EVEN, ODD;                    { Records parity of bumps }

  initialize
    to EVEN
      begin
      end;

  trans
    { *** Player makes guess *** }
    when P.Probe
      from EVEN to EVEN
        begin
          output P.Lose
        end;
    when P.Probe
      from ODD to ODD
        begin
          output P.Win
        end;

    { *** Daemon bumped *** }
    when D.Bump
      from EVEN to ODD
        begin
        end;
```

```
        when D.Bump
          from ODD to EVEN
            begin
            end;
    end; { GameBody }
```

A module body is much like a PASCAL procedure. It may declare local types, variables, functions and procedures. As discussed later, it may even declare modules within itself. It must declare any states or sets of states used within the module. It should initialise the state of the module and any variables that must have known values. The actions of the module body are described as transitions.

Transitions

Each transition is controlled by a guard that consists of several clauses. Each clause corresponds to a keyword in ESTELLE. The transition may fire only if the guard clauses are satisfied. Beyond the usual scoping effects, the order of the clauses is immaterial. In other words, there would be no significance to writing the **when** clause before the **from** clause; the clauses could be rearranged without changing the meaning, except for changes that occur in the interpretation of variables resulting from the rearranged scopes.

The purpose of the various guard clauses is as follows:

- **when** specifies an interaction point and the interaction that must be at the head of the queue associated with that interaction point

- **from** specifies the control state (or states) that the automaton must be in

- **to** specifies the control state (or states) that the automaton may be in at the end of the transition

- **provided** specifies conditions that must hold, usually involving context variables as well as parameters from an interaction

- **priority** specifies the priority to be associated with the transition

- **any** is a macro-like schema, meaning that one copy of the transition exists for each object in the domain over which the **any** ranges, with the appropriate substitutions made

- **delay** specifies time requirements for spontaneous transitions that must be met before the transition is enabled.

The **when** clause specifies an interaction as well as the interaction point through which the interaction must have come into the module. Any parameters associated with the interaction (as specified in the channel description) are defined; their values are the ones passed with the interaction. This mechanism is much like associating values with parameters of a function, the main difference being that the names of the variables are those given in the channel definition; they may be repeated as part of the **when** clause, but they need not be.

As an example, consider how to define the *Player* module of the Daemon Game in Chapter 5. There the *GameServer* channel supports an interaction initiated by the *Machine*. It is called *Score* and has an integer parameter, *nwon*. The header of the *Player* module states that the channel is attached at interaction point *G*. Thus a transition guard could say '**when** *G.Score*' or '**when** *G.Score(nwon)*'. The meaning is the same in either case. The second form serves to remind the reader of the variables that are defined by the interaction. The first form is convenient in the case where there are many such variables and it would be cumbersome to list them each time. In the example, the integer variable *nwon* would be defined and would have the value associated with it during the transition of the *Game* module that initiated the *Score* interaction. This would be achieved with the statement '**output** *P.Score(NCorrect)*'.

If the interaction point associated with an interaction is one of an array of interaction points, the **when** clause is usually within the scope of an **any** clause, as in the following example:

```
any n : 1..3 do when ipt[n].open
  begin
    variable := n
  end
```

The **any** clause indicates a macro-like expansion of the remainder of the transition that follows it, giving in this case three transitions:

```
when ipt[1].open
  begin
    variable := 1
  end
when ipt[2].open
  begin
    variable := 2
  end
when ipt[3].open
  begin
    variable := 3
  end
```

The **from** clause specifies the state (or set of states) in which the transition is applicable. The transition may be considered only when the control state of the automaton is the specified state (or is in the set of specified states).

The **to** clause specifies the control state which the automaton will be in at the end of executing the transition. If the **to** clause specifies **same**, the control state will be the same after executing the transition as it was before executing the transition. This is particularly useful if the **from** clause contains a set of states. When considered as part of the guard of a transition, the value of the **to** clause is always *true*.

The **provided** clause is a Boolean expression that must evaluate to *true* for the transition to be enabled. As all ESTELLE functions are pure and consequently may have no side-effects, evaluation of the **provided** clause has no effect beyond returning a value of *true* or *false*. The ESTELLE keyword **otherwise** enables the specifier to give a default case, as in:

> **provided** Condition1
>
> ⋱
>
> **provided** ConditionN
> **provided otherwise**
>
> ⋱

The meaning of the **provided otherwise** clause in this case is:

> **provided not** (Condition1 or ⋱ or ConditionN)

The **priority** clause, if present, explicitly gives the priority of a transition. Otherwise, the transition has an implicit priority lower than any explicitly given. Priority is indicated by a non-negative integer value, with higher integer values representing lower priority. A transition with priority value n can be enabled only if no transition is enabled in the same module with priority value k for $k < n$.

The **any** clause is expanded like a macro, with the variable controlled by the **any** being substituted throughout its scope. The example given in discussing the **when** clause should help make this clear.

A **delay** clause may be associated only with a spontaneous transition, i.e. one that has no **when** clause. There are two forms of the clause: '*delay(d1, d2)*' and '*delay (d)*'. The second of these forms is essentially equivalent to writing '*delay(d, d)*'[5].

In the first form, *d2* may be '*', which means 'forever'. A transition may be eligible to be fired after its guard has remained true for *d1* time and must

[5]The only difference between the two forms is that '*delay(d, d)*' would evaluate *d* twice, while '*delay(d)*' would evaluate it once. Since ESTELLE expressions may have no side-effects, it is difficult to tell these two cases apart.

be eligible to be fired after *d2* time. This means that if it is the only transition available after *d2* time, it must be fired. If *d2* is forever, it may happen that the transition will never be fired.

Delay clauses may be used to establish time-dependent behaviour of protocols. For example, if a retransmission is required when a PDU is not acknowledged within a certain time, a suitable transition would be:

```
from PDUSent to same
  provided (NumRetrans < MaxRetrans)
    delay (RetransTimeout)
      begin
        ...
      end
```

If an acknowledgement of the PDU is received, the control state would be changed from *PDUSent* to another state, thus disabling the **from** part of the guard and stopping the delay timer. In a slightly more sophisticated protocol, a retransmission might be permitted after a short delay but required after a longer delay. This might be described by changing the **delay** clause above to:

```
delay (RetransPermitted, RetransRequired)
```

Transitions may have names attached to them. These have no formal meaning as far as ESTELLE semantics are concerned (they are regarded as syntactically restricted comments). They are merely for the convenience of having a way of talking informally about a specific transition. Some software tools make provision to deal with these names. The transition is named by placing the keyword **name** followed by an identifier followed by a colon before the **begin** of the transition block, as in the following example:

```
when P.Probe
  from EVEN to EVEN
    name Trans_1:
      begin
        output P.Lose
      end;
```

Nesting Transitions

To facilitate a structured programming style, transitions may be nested. Recall the transitions of *GameBody* in the simple example. Two of them require *D.Bump* interactions. With no change in meaning, they could be rewritten as follows:

```
when P.Probe
  from EVEN to EVEN
    begin
      ...
    end
  from ODD to ODD
    begin
      ...
    end

when D.Bump
  from EVEN to ODD
    begin
      ...
    end
  from ODD to EVEN
    begin
      ...
    end
```

The meaning is the same as if the '**when** *D.Bump*' clause were repeated before the second from clause. The statements between **begin** and **end** (here indicated by dots) determine the action of the transition. The two transitions that require *P.Probe* interactions have been treated similarly.

Alternatively, the transitions might be organised as follows to emphasise the actions available in each of the states[6]:

```
from EVEN
  when P.Probe
    to EVEN
      begin
        ...
      end
  when D.Bump
    to ODD
      begin
        ...
      end
```

[6]Rewriting these transitions relies on the fact that the guard clauses of a transition may be reordered without changing their meaning, so the **from** clause may be written first.

```
from ODD
  when P.Probe
    to ODD
      begin
        ...
      end
  when D.Bump
    to EVEN
      begin
        ...
      end
```

There is nothing unique about the **when** or **from** clause: any of the enabling clauses may be nested. The first keyword following **end** indicates how many of the clauses that controlled the previous transition to 'throw away'. Repeating the keyword **trans** starts a new transition structure; none of the guards of the previous transition applies after **trans**. In well-structured protocol descriptions, multiple levels of nesting are frequently used.

Freedom in nesting encourages the specification writer to organise the specification in some coherent way. A specifier who regards the specification as event-driven may choose to order the transitions by **when** clauses, and then nest the remaining clauses within the **when** clauses. Within these, the specifier may choose to order and nest the **from** clauses. Alternatively, a specifier who regards the actions of the automaton in any given state as the key idea may first choose to order and nest the **from** clauses, and then to order and nest the **when** clauses. Another specifier may choose to order by priority, using the highest priority transitions as a form of error pre-processor. This would simplify the rest of the description since transitions of ordinary priority would not have to deal with errors. In short, the nesting facility of the language helps the specifier organise ideas and convey meaning.

State Sets

As a convenience, ESTELLE allows sets of states in a **from** clause. State sets may be defined in a separate section, similar to the PASCAL **var** section (and at the same level of the language as the **var** section). A state set may be used as the **from** designator in a transition. A special designator, **same** may be used in the **to** clause (i.e. the **to** clause may be '**to same**'). This means that the control state of the automaton does not change as a result of firing the transition; it is especially useful for those transitions that apply to several states. For example, if *EITHER = [EVEN, ODD]* defines a stateset, a transition might be specified as follows (similar to those in the Daemon Game of Chapter 5):

```
from EITHER to same
  begin
    ...
  end
```

This would have the same meaning as two separate transitions:

```
from EVEN to EVEN
  begin
    ...
  end
from ODD to ODD
  begin
    ...
  end
```

PASCAL

To manipulate the variables in the storage portion of the extended finite automaton, ESTELLE uses a language based on ISO PASCAL, level 0 ISO (1982)[7]. Some changes to PASCAL have been introduced in ESTELLE, however. For example, as ESTELLE is a specification technique, integers and real numbers are considered to be integers and real numbers in the mathematical sense: implementation-dependent constraints such as maximum size or precision of real numbers are irrelevant. Similarly, those features of PASCAL that relate to file manipulation (**file**, *text*, *get*, *put*, *read*, *write*, *readln*, *writeln*, *eof*, *eoln*) were removed from ESTELLE, as was the keyword **program**. The use of **goto** was constrained as indicated below.

In keeping with the choice made for PASCAL, ESTELLE is case and font insensitive. It makes no difference if an identifier or keyword is written in bold or italic, in upper case or lower case or a combination of these.

Furthermore, to simplify the language, functions and procedures may not reference non-PASCAL objects (e.g. module variables, interaction points, interactions and states). As a consequence, the ESTELLE statements **all**, **forone**, and **exist** within a procedure or a function may use only finite ordinal types as their domain lists. As a further consequence, the ESTELLE statements **init**, **release**, **terminate**, **connect**, **disconnect**, **attach**, **detach**, and **output** cannot be used in a procedure or a function. The intention of this is to increase the visibility of the automata-based actions of a module by ensuring that they are not hidden in subroutines. An unfortunate consequence of this is to prevent simple subroutines that, for example, output error reports or output acknowledgements.

[7]Level 0 PASCAL excludes conformant arrays, which are included in level 1 PASCAL.

Procedures and Functions

Procedures and functions may, of course, be used in ESTELLE as in PASCAL. Because ESTELLE is to be used for specifications, functions may be declared as returning any defined type, not just the simple types allowed in PASCAL.

The examination of a guard for a transition will usually entail evaluating functions when evaluating the **provided** clause. As a consequence of this, and also to avoid effects of evaluation order in expressions, it is necessary that functions have no side-effects. This is ensured by requiring that all ESTELLE functions be **demonstrably pure**. The full definition of this term is given in the ESTELLE Standard, but the essential ideas are that it may alter the values of only its local variables, it may have no **var** parameters, and it may not be passed pointers or data structures containing pointers. It is also possible to express the intention that a procedure have no side-effects in ESTELLE with the keyword **pure**. If a procedure is declared pure, it must satisfy the same requirements that a demonstrably pure function does, except that a pure procedure may have **var** parameters and it may modify these.

Some functions and procedures in an ESTELLE description may be left entirely to the implementer. These are described by the keyword **primitive**. Such functions and procedures are required to be pure. They are often the access methods for data types that are declared to be '. . . '. For instance, the following declarations might be given for a stack:

StackType = . . . ;

procedure Push(value: ValueType; **var** stack: StackType);
  primitive;

procedure Pop(**var** value: ValueType; **var** stack: StackType);
  primitive;

The intent of the specification writer should be made plain with a comment to the effect that *Push* stores value into stack, while *Pop* removes the most recently pushed value from the stack provided the stack is not empty. The point is that, presumably, the system being described does not depend on how the implementer chooses to implement stacks, so details about stacks are omitted.

As ESTELLE has no abstract data typing mechanism, assumptions about primitive procedures and functions must be formalised to enable reasoning about ESTELLE descriptions that include them. Assumptions about types declared to be '. . . ' must similarly be formalised.

2.7.3 *Specifying Structure*

Some of the structure of a system is indicated by the organisation of the specification itself; nesting the description of one module inside the description of another module shows the hierarchical relationship of the modules. When instantiated, the inner module will necessarily be the child of the outer module.

Module instances are created and destroyed dynamically by the use of **init**, **release**, and **terminate** operators during transitions and initialisation. It is useful to note that an inactive module, one that has no transitions other than its initialisation, will never alter the module and connection structure it creates during its initialisation. Thus system modules (with the **systemactivity** or **systemprocess** attribute) will create a structure during initialisation that thereafter remains static.

Modules may be bound and unbound through interaction points using **connect** and **disconnect** as well as **attach** and **detach**. The following shows the initialisation of the simple game system:

```
modvar
  DaemonInstance: Daemon;
  GameInstance: Game;
  PlayerInstance: Player;

initialize
  begin
    init DaemonInstance with DaemonBody;
    init GameInstance with GameBody;
    init PlayerInstance with PlayerBody;
    connect PlayerInstance.G to GameInstance.P;
    connect DaemonInstance.D to GameInstance.D
  end;
```

First, three module variables are declared, one for each of the modules in the system. As the system initialisation is performed, these modules are initialised with their bodies. Recall that this causes an **initialize** transition of the body to be invoked. Finally, the modules are connected at their interaction points. It is not necessary to specify the type of channel that is used to connect interaction points, because this is specified as part of the module header.

2.7.4 *Additional Features*

Any

Another feature of ESTELLE that aids dealing with implementation-dependent types is the ability to declare that a constant may have any value of a given type. Thus, for example, the maximum number of retransmissions could be specified as:

```
MaxRetrans = any integer
```

Of course, it might be necessary to guarantee that *MaxRetrans* is positive. This may be done by having the initialisation of the system depend on this, as in:

```
initialize
  to StartState
    provided (MaxRetrans > 0)
      begin
        ...
      end
```

For systems with more complex tests, the tests could be collected into a Boolean-valued function that would be included as (part of) the **provided** clause of initialisation transitions.

For the example just considered, the formal semantics of ESTELLE require that some integer be chosen for *MaxRetrans* before the specification has a meaning. If the integer chosen did not exceed zero, the **provided** clause would fail to be satisfied, so initialisation could not take place and the system could not function.

Attach and Detach

As explained before, the **attach** operation associates a parent's interaction point with a child's queue. To illustrate this requires a larger specification such as that of the Daemon Game in Chapter 5. In this specification, the *Manager* module attaches its *D* interaction point to the *Distributor* module. As a consequence of this, the *Bump* interactions initiated by the *Daemon* are not placed in the queue of the *Manager*, but rather they are placed in the queue of the *Distributor*. Similarly, each time the *Manager* creates a *Game* module, it attaches its corresponding *P[GameNumber]* interaction point to the *P* interaction point of the *GameInstance*. When it releases the *GameInstance*, an implicit **detach** of the interaction point occurs, so that any interactions that remain in the *GameInstance* queue are returned to the *Manager* queue.

Output

The **output** statement is used to initiate interactions. It specifies an interaction point, an interaction, and any required values that accompany the interaction. The interaction is queued at the receiving module. The identity of the receiving module is determined by the chain of **connect** and **attach** statements that have been applied to the modules, beginning with the interaction point specified in the **output** statement. An example of an interaction without parameters is found in the simple example:

```
output P.Win
```

An example of an interaction that requires a parameter is found in the Daemon Game of Chapter 5:

output P.Score(NCorrect)

This second interaction causes the interaction *Score* with its parameter *nwon* set to *NCorrect* to be queued by the module linked to the *P* interaction point.

All, ForOne, and Exist

There are three convenient ESTELLE constructs — **all**, **forone** and **exist** — for working with finite ordinal types or with sets of modules.

The **all** statement causes a statement to be executed for each value of the ordinal type or each module of the module type specified. For example:

```
type ErrorIndication = ...;

begin
   ...
   all error : ErrorIndication do S;
   ...
end
```

This would cause the statement *S* to be executed once for each element in the type *ErrorIndication*. Note that, as with the PASCAL **for** statement, *S* may be a compound statement[8]. The **all** statement does not impose any order on the choice of elements chosen from type *ErrorIndication*, so it is not possible to predict which will be chosen first. For iteration over types, it might be imagined that the PASCAL **for** statement could be used, but as the above example shows it may not be possible to know the smallest or largest value of some types. It is thus not possible to iterate over such types without the **all** statement.

The **forone** statement is of the form:

forone x : T **suchthat** E **do** S1 **otherwise** S2

where E is a Boolean-valued expression and T is either a finite ordinal type or a module type. If T is a finite ordinal type, each x is chosen in some non-deterministic order from T until one is found for which E is satisfied. For this x, the statement *S1* is executed. If there is none, then the statement *S2* will be executed.

Similarly, if T is a module type, instantiations of module bodies of that type are examined in non-deterministic order until one is found for which E is

[8]This glosses over the possibility that S is a compound statement containing a **goto**, which might cause the statement S to be executed for only some of the elements of the domain of the **all** statement.

satisfied. Exported variables of a child may be used in such situations. For example, suppose that children are managing connections and that they maintain and export a variable named *SpareCapacity*. A statement similar to that below could be used to find a child with sufficient unused capacity to multiplex a new connection onto an existing one, or to create a new connection manager if there were no existing one with sufficient spare capacity[9]:

```
forone Connection : ConnectionManager
  suchthat
    Connection.SpareCapacity > CapacityRequired do
      begin
        ...
      end
  otherwise
    begin
      ...
    end
```

The **exist** expression is of the form:

exist x : T **suchthat** E

where again E is a Boolean-valued expression and T is either a finite ordinal type or a module type. It could be used in a situation such as the above to guarantee that the **otherwise** case would never be needed. For example, the transition could have:

```
provided exist Connection : ConnectionManager
  suchthat
    Connection.SpareCapacity > CapacityRequired
```

as part of its guard. If several *Connection* modules satisfy the **suchthat** condition, one *Connection* might be found while examining the **provided** clause and a different one may be used in executing the **forone** statement. The **exist** construct can also be used as a guard before a transition that uses an **all** statement (see the transition that cleans up after a game in Chapter 5).

Goto

ESTELLE allows a limited form of the PASCAL **goto** statement. The limitation is achieved by permitting labels to be associated only with the final **end** of a procedure or function. Consequently, any **goto** leaves the procedure or function immediately.

[9]Note that an exported variable is referenced by identifying the module body and the variable, separated by a dot.

2.8 Other Information

Real protocols and services are sufficiently complex that automatic tools are required to analyse them. There is a need for tools such as compilers, editors, path generators, verifiers and validators to support any FDT. Complete ESTELLE descriptions become quite large, so good tools are needed to make it easier to work with these descriptions. Tools for ESTELLE have been developed in a number of places around the world; some references are given in Chapter 10.

Although the tutorial in this chapter has been fairly complete, it has not been possible (nor would it have been desirable) to explain every detail of ESTELLE. The interested reader will find additional information in various places. First, there is the International Standard itself, ISO (1989e). There are tutorials on ESTELLE by Budkowski and Dembinski (1987), Dembinski and Budkowski (1989), Tenney (1992) and Linn (1987). In addition, a tutorial addendum to the International Standard is being drafted, ISO (1991t).

3 Introduction to LOTOS[1]

LOTOS was developed to define implementation-independent formal standards of OSI services and protocols. 'LOTOS' stands for Language Of Temporal Ordering Specification because it is used to model the order in which the events of a system occur. LOTOS has two very clearly separated parts. The first part provides a behavioural model derived from process algebras, principally from CCS (*Calculus of Communicating Systems*, Milner (1989)) but also from CSP (*Communicating Sequential Processes*, Hoare (1985)). The second part of the language allows specifiers to describe abstract data types and values, and is based on the abstract data type language ACT ONE (Ehrig and Mahr (1985)).

These two aspects of LOTOS guided the organisation of this chapter. Section 3.1 introduces basic concepts of the language. Section 3.2 presents the process algebra aspect of LOTOS, called **Basic LOTOS**. Section 3.4 presents the ACT ONE basis of data typing. Finally, Section 3.5 indicates how these aspects are combined as **Full LOTOS**.

The syntax and semantics of LOTOS are defined in the relevant standard (ISO (19891)). The definition has four main parts: the syntax, the static semantics, the algebraic semantics of data types, and the dynamic semantics of behaviour expressions. A description of the detailed semantics of LOTOS is beyond the scope of this introductory chapter.

3.1 Basic Concepts

Specification languages have been developed to allow modelling of systems for the purpose of analysis and design. LOTOS uses the concepts of process, event and behaviour expression as basic modelling concepts.

3.1.1 *Processes*

Systems and their components are represented in LOTOS by **processes**. A process displays an **observable behaviour** to its environment in terms of

[1]Chapter 3 is by J. Quemada, L. Ferreira Pires, J. A. Mañas, A. Azcorra and T. Robles.

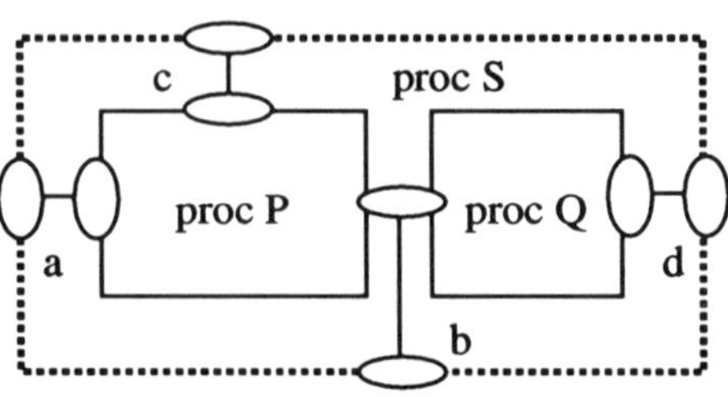

Figure 3.1: Process Structure Example

permitted sequences of observable actions. A process appears as a **black box** to its environment since the environment has no information about its internal structure and mechanisms. LOTOS processes interact with each other through **gates**.

Figure 3.1 illustrates a LOTOS process structure. In this figure, process S represents a system that interacts with its environment via gates a, b, c and d. These gates model the logical or physical attachment points between a system and its environment. Process S is the composition of processes P and Q. Process P interacts with its environment through gates a, b and c, while process Q interacts with its environment through gates b and d. Processes P and Q interact through their common gate b, and are therefore considered to belong to the environment of each other.

Figure 3.1 could correspond to the following LOTOS process definitions:

```
process S [a, b, c, d] : noexit :=

  P [a, b, c] |[b]| Q [b, d]          (* behaviour expression *)

  where

  process P [t, u, v] : noexit :=
    t; (u; stop [] v; stop)           (* behaviour expression *)
  endproc (* P *)

  process Q [x, y] : noexit :=
    x; y; stop                        (* behaviour expression *)
  endproc (* Q *)

endproc (* S *)
```

The identifiers *S*, *P* and *Q* in the example designate the corresponding processes in the LOTOS text. *P [a, b, c]* represents an instantiation of process *P*, while *Q [b, d]* represents an instantiation of process *Q*. Notice that the gate structure of these processes is explicitly described in the process instantiation through gate identifier lists (*[a, b, c]* and *[b, d]*). The operator |[*b*]| between *P* and *Q* states that these processes interact through their common gate *b*.

Process declarations are delimited by the reserved words **process** and **endproc**. Process definitions have a process identifier, a formal gate list, an optional parameter list, the process functionality, and a behaviour expression. All these language elements are discussed later. Note that process *P* in the example is declared with formal gate list *[t, u, v]* which is renamed to *[a, b, c]* when the process is instantiated (called).

In LOTOS, a **specification** is a special kind of process, namely the one that represents the whole system. The difference between a process and a specification is only syntactic, as will be explained later.

3.1.2 *Events*

LOTOS specifications describe observable behaviour of systems. The observable behaviour is the set of all possible sequences of interactions in which the system is allowed to participate. Therefore the concept of interaction is fundamental in the LOTOS model. Interactions are represented in LOTOS by **events**. Events are atomic, instantaneous and synchronous instances of interaction. Each event is associated with a gate, namely the gate at which the event takes place.

Events model real-life occurrences in an abstract way. The degree of detail required in the model determines the events to be considered. For example, data transmission through an interface could be modelled by a single event representing the whole transmission. Alternatively, the beginning and the end of the transmission could be modelled as distinct events, or events could correspond to the transmission of individual bits. All these models represent the same data transmission at different degrees of detail.

Events can only occur if *all* processes that are supposed to participate in it are ready to interact. When an event takes place, all the processes involved in the event synchronise and have a common view of the interaction. This common view is interpreted as synchronisation and communication, and guarantees that processes participating in interactions have access to the same interaction parameter values. The concept of structured event introduced in Section 3.5 clarifies these ideas.

3.1.3 *Behaviour Expressions*

The observable behaviour of a system is described in LOTOS by means of a language construct in which the sequences of allowed events are defined. This

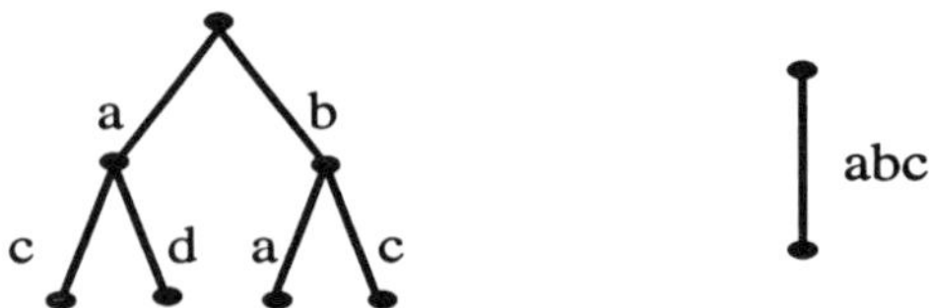

Figure 3.2: Examples of Behaviour Trees

construct is called a **behaviour expression** that defines sequences precisely in terms of the LOTOS semantic model.

Behaviour expressions can be represented graphically as **behaviour trees**. This representation is helpful in visualising the sequence of events and their dependencies, but its practical use is limited to simple cases of behaviour. Figure 3.2 depicts two examples of behaviour trees. Time in these diagrams runs down the page. Nodes represent states of a system. Arcs between nodes represent transitions between states, and are labelled with the corresponding actions.

3.2 Basic LOTOS

LOTOS without ACT ONE is called **Basic LOTOS**. Experience shows that Basic LOTOS is easier to understand than Full LOTOS; furthermore, Basic LOTOS can be generalised to Full LOTOS in a quite straightforward way.

3.2.1 *Basic Constructs*

The basic LOTOS operators are the ones which allow the representation of any finite behaviour. Other operators are introduced in order to cope with structuring, readability, and repetitive behaviour. The basic operators deal with inaction (**stop**), action prefix (';'), and choice ('[]').

Inaction

Inaction (specified with **stop**) models a situation in which a process is unable to interact with its environment. Inaction can be used to describe **deadlock**, i.e. a situation in which no more interactions are possible. Inaction is a degenerate case of behaviour. It is a kind of null behaviour expression (like an empty set) since it models the *absence* of behaviour. In behaviour trees, inaction corresponds to a node that does not lead to further branches.

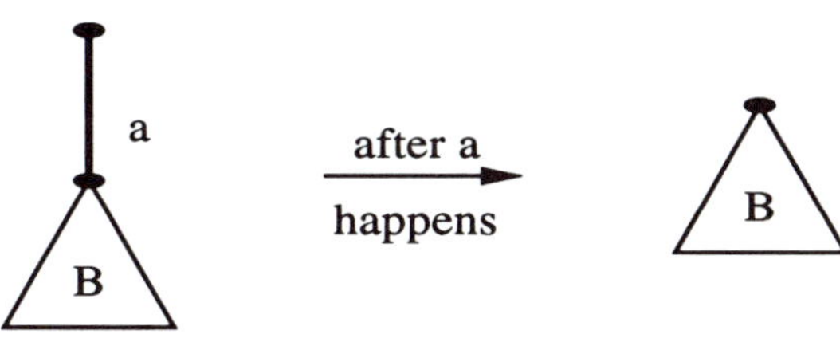

Figure 3.3: Action Prefix

Action Prefix

When representing observable behaviour, it is often necessary to indicate that an event occurs before other events. The **action prefix construct** is used when an event must occur before the following behaviour expression. The syntax element that represents an event in LOTOS is called an **action denotation**. Figure 3.3 depicts the behaviour tree associated with the generic behaviour expression *a; B* where *a* is an action denotation and *B* is a behaviour expression.

Some behaviour expressions illustrating action prefix are:

Error; (Crash; **stop**)

TelephoneFriend; Conversation; **stop**

Choice

The **choice construct** selects one of two alternative behaviours. Given behaviour expressions B_1 and B_2, B_1 *[]* B_2 behaves as B_1 or B_2 depending on whether the next event is the initial one of B_1 or B_2 respectively. Figure 3.4 shows a graphical representation of the choice operator.

Consider modelling the behaviour of a drink dispenser that accepts 10 and 20 cent coins. Introducing a 10 cent coin results in a cup of tea, while introducing a 20 cent coin results in a cup of coffee. This could be specified as:

(Coin10c; Tea; **stop**) [] (Coin20c; Coffee; **stop**)

In the behaviour expression above, B_1 is *(Coin10c; Tea;* **stop***)* and B_2 is *(Coin10c; Tea;* **stop***)*. If the environment (a user of the drink dispenser) offers *Coin10c*, behaviour B_1 can be selected; after the interaction, only the *Tea* event can occur, meaning that only tea can be delivered. Similarly, the *Coin20c* event will select behaviour B_2, and only coffee can be delivered.

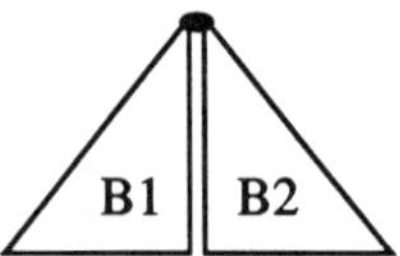

Figure 3.4: Choice Construct

3.2.2 *Internal Event*

So far, observable behaviour has been described in terms of events that represent interactions between a system and its environment. However, a system may make an internal unobservable decision that affects its future behaviour; the *effect* of the decision may be significant.

The **internal event**, represented by **i**, is a special LOTOS event that models occurrences or decisions that are internal and therefore invisible to the environment. Although invisible, the occurrence of an internal event may modify the subsequent externally observable behaviour. Examples of real-life occurrences that may be modelled as internal events are timeout, system failures, and lack of resources. The following represents a timeout situation:

(ExpectedAction; **stop**) [] (**i**; TimeOut; **stop**)

Non-determinism

From the point of view of the environment, **non-deterministic behaviour** occurs when there are multiple possibilities for behaviour that cannot be controlled by the environment. In such a case, the system may react in different ways on different occasions to the same sequence of interactions.

Non-determinism can be modelled in LOTOS in three ways, combining choice and the internal event. Suppose that P and Q are behaviour expressions and that a is an event:

(a; P) [] (**i**; Q) (* case 1 *)

(a; P) [] (a; Q) (* case 2 *)

(**i**; P) [] (**i**; Q) (* case 3 *)

Case 1 says that event a can take place initially, unless the internal event occurs and makes the system behave like Q. In this case the environment has some chance to influence the system if it acts before the internal event. Note that the concept of time is immaterial in LOTOS, so 'acting before' refers to an interpretation of the internal event as a timer or some internal activity that takes time. Case 2 says that the system decides at the occurrence of the interaction which one of the a events will take place. Case 3 says that the system will decide internally whether it should behave according to P or Q. In both cases 2 and 3, the environment cannot influence the outcome of the decision.

The following example deals with the behaviour of an airline reservation system:

```
RequestSeat;
(
   i; SeatConfirmed; stop
[]
   i; NoSeatsAvailable; stop
[]
   i; SystemNotAvailable; stop
)
```

The result of a request for reservation of seats on a flight is completely unpredictable from the point of view of a client, since a normal client does not know how the system is organised and whether there are seats available in advance. The inability of the client to influence the system is modelled with internal events.

3.2.3 *Recursion*

A behaviour is very often repetitive or even infinite. With the language constructs introduced so far this is not possible since the specification text must be finite. However, LOTOS allows repetition of behaviour to be modelled with **recursive** process instantiations.

Consider again the drink dispenser of Section 3.2.1. After one coin has been inserted, this machine can deliver tea or coffee and then stop. This is probably not the way the drink dispenser machine should operate since a dispenser that delivered only one cup of tea or coffee would be a little impractical! A more realistic dispenser could be specified as:

```
process DrinkDispenser [Coin10c, Coin20c, Tea, Coffee] : noexit :=
   Coin10c; Tea; DrinkDispenser [Coin10c, Coin20c, Tea, Coffee]
[]
   Coin20c; Coffee; DrinkDispenser [Coin10c, Coin20c, Tea, Coffee]
endproc (* DrinkDispenser *)
```

This example uses recursion to indicate that the behaviour is repetitive: after a cup of tea or coffee has been delivered then more can be dispensed.

Another example to illustrate recursion is a communications polling device. This example deals with only the polling operation, and supposes the existence of three stations:

```
process PollingOperation [StationA, StationB, StationC] : noexit :=
  StationA;
  PollingOperation [StationB, StationC, StationA]
endproc (* PollingOperation *)
```

Here the actual gate list of the recursive instantiation is cycled one place relative to the formal gate list in the process definition. This allows a cyclic repetition of events at gates *StationA*, *StationB* and *StationC*, characterising the polling.

3.2.4 *Exit*

The model of behaviour termination introduced by inaction (**stop**) is very rough since defines only abrupt termination. This kind of termination does not allow a sequence of processes, for example, which is sometimes a useful concept. LOTOS models successfully terminating processes though the **exit** construct. The interpretation of **exit** is that a special termination event[2] takes place before **stop**; this special event indicates successful termination and is distinct from any ordinary event.

Consider the following example of a login procedure:

```
process LoginProcedure [LoginReq, LoginConf, LoginAbort] : exit :=
  LoginReq;
  (
    i; LoginConf; exit
  []
    i; LoginAbort; LoginProcedure [LoginReq, LoginConf, LoginAbort]
  )
endproc (* LoginProcedure *)
```

In the example, the occurrence of *LoginAbort* is followed by a new login attempt, but the occurrence of *LoginConf* is followed by the special termination event to indicate successful termination of the login procedure. Section 3.2.7 indicates how **exit** can be used in the context of sequential composition of processes.

---

[2]The special event denoting successful termination is called δ.

3.2.5 *Parallel Composition*

Very often specifiers have to structure specifications or to represent design structures. These structures, in the case of distributed systems, are generally parallel instances of functionality. In LOTOS, behaviour expressions can be combined using the **parallel construct**.

Consider the general behaviour expression B_1 $|[g_1, \ldots, g_n]|$ B_2 in which B_1 and B_2 are behaviour expressions and $g_1, \ldots, g_n$ is a gate identifier list. In this behaviour expression, events at gates that belong to the gate identifier list can occur only with the participation of both B_1 and B_2. Events at gates that do not belong to the gate identifier list can occur with the participation of either B_1 or B_2 alone.

Return to the example of Figure 3.1. The behaviour expression:

P [a, b, c] |[b]| Q [b, d]

says that behaviour expressions *P [a, b, c]* and *Q [b, d]* synchronise at gate *b*. In this case the behaviour expressions are process instantiations, but may not be in general. As another example, consider the following behaviour expression:

(a; **stop** [] b; c; **stop**) |[a, c]| (d; a; **stop** [] c; **stop**)

Events at gates *a* and *c* in the example above can occur only with the participation of both behaviour expressions; events take place at the other gates (by inspection, *b* and *d*) with the participation of only one of the behaviour expressions.

Special Cases

Two special cases of the parallel operator can be identified by considering the extreme cases of pure interleaving and full synchronisation. These two extreme cases can be represented by language shorthands.

In the case of **pure interleaving**, interactions of the two behaviour expressions are completely interleaved, i.e. they always occur with the participation of only one of the behaviour expressions. This corresponds to the case in which the gate identifier list is empty; the shorthand notation for pure interleaving is '|||'. An example of this is the behaviour expression:

(a; b; **exit**) ||| (c; **exit**)

The equivalent[3] behaviour expression in terms of the action prefix and choice operator can be deduced by inspection:

[3]The behaviour expressions are considered to be **observationally equivalent** to each other, and so represent the same semantic model. The formalisation of the equivalence relation used falls outside the scope of this chapter.

```
    a; (b; c; exit [] c; b; exit)
[]
    c; a; b; exit
```

In the case of **full synchronisation**, interactions at any gate of the two behaviour expressions are fully synchronised, i.e. they occur with the participation of both behaviour expressions. Syntactically this is the case in which the gate identifier list contains all the gate identifiers appearing in both behaviour expressions; the shorthand notation for full synchronisation is '||'. An example of this is the behaviour expression:

```
    (a; stop [] b; c; stop)
||
    (a; stop [] i; b; c; stop [] d; stop)
```

The equivalent behaviour expression in terms of the action prefix and choice operators is:

```
a; stop [] i; b; c; stop
```

Note that behaviour expressions do not synchronise on internal events. This is due to the fact that internal events are not observable.

Multi-way Synchronisation

The concept of synchronisation occurring between two instances of activity can be generalised to more than two instances, i.e. **multi-way synchronisation**. LOTOS supports multi-way synchronisation through the combinational character of the parallel construct.

As an example, take process instances *P [a, b, c]*, *Q [a, c]* and *R [a, b]*. The following expression says that events at gate *a* can happen only with the participation of all three processes:

```
P [a, b, c] |[a]| Q [a, c] |[a]| R [a, b]
```

This example says that events at gate *a* in *Q* and in *R* can happen only with the participation of both processes. *Q [a, c]* |[*a*]| *R [a, b]* is a new behaviour expression, so events at gate *a* in *P* and in this new behaviour expression (and thus in *Q* and *R*) can happen only with the participation of both behaviour expressions. The conclusion is that interactions at gate *a* in the example above can happen only with the participation of all processes, *P*, *Q* and *R*.

3.2.6 *Hiding*

The parallel composition presented so far has a drawback: behaviour expressions cannot be 'protected' from interactions with their environment. This problem becomes clear with the example in Figure 3.1. There the environment of process *S* interacts with processes *P* and *Q*. (Notice the parallel operator |[*b*]|.) To say that events at gate *b* represent some kind of internal (unobservable) interaction, it is necessary to be able to 'hide' this gate from the environment. This can be done using the **hide construct**. The example of Figure 3.1 can be rewritten as follows:

```
process S [a, c, d] : noexit :=

   hide b in
      P [a, b, c] |[b]| Q [b, d]

   where
   ...
```

In this new specification of process *S*, events at gate *b* are not accessible to the environment. The **hide** operator contains a gate identifier list in which the specifier indicates which gates are unobservable by the environment of the behaviour expression. In the example the list has a single element, *b*. Observe that the gate list in the declaration of process *S* does not have *b*, indicating that gate *b* is no longer accessible to the environment of *S*.

3.2.7 *Sequential Composition*

Action prefix was introduced to allow the explicit representation of temporal ordering of events. Nevertheless, it is very often necessary to represent temporal ordering of behaviours. This occurs when the system presents well-determined phases. In LOTOS, temporal ordering of phases can be represented using sequential composition of behaviour expressions with the **enabling construct** '>>'.

Consider the generic behaviour expression B_1 >> B_2. The behaviour expression B_2 is **enabled** by the behaviour expression B_1 if the special δ event (**exit**) occurs in B_1. As explained earlier, **exit** indicates successful termination and allows the sequential composition of behaviour expressions. Notice that if B_1 does not terminate successfully (e.g. it deadlocks), B_2 will never be allowed.

Consider a file transfer procedure that starts with a login procedure like the one in Section 3.2.4. The behaviour expression for this system could have the following outline:

```
LoginProcedure [...] >> FileTransfer [...] >> LogoutProcedure [...]
```

3.2.8 *Disabling*

It is very often possible to identify 'normal' behaviour in systems which can be disrupted at any moment by some exceptional circumstance. Examples of exceptional circumstances are interrupts and errors. In LOTOS, disruption of behaviour is represented by the **disabling construct** '[>'.

The generic behaviour expression B_1 *[>* B_2 behaves like B_1 until an event of B_2 occurs. B_2 is said to **disable** B_1 in this case. After an event of B_2 occurs, the future behaviour is that of B_2. If B_1 terminates successfully (a δ occurs), B_2 no longer applies.

The following behaviour expression illustrates disabling:

(a; b; **exit**) [> (d; **stop**)

The equivalent behaviour expression in terms of action prefix and choice operators is:

```
   a; b; exit
[]
   d; stop
[]
   a; d; stop
[]
   a; b; d; stop
```

3.3 Basic LOTOS Examples

The Basic LOTOS operators will be illustrated with a simplified treatment of the two-key system covered in Chapter 11. This is an access control system that requires insertion of two keys before allowing access. Both keys must be inserted before one access is allowed. The keys can be extracted only after the access has occurred.

The following subsections illustrate the basic operators by providing a LOTOS behaviour expression and the corresponding semantics (behaviour tree) on the right.

The first step is the definition of the observable interface of the system. There are five abstract events for creating a model of the two-key system: *In1*, *In2*, *Access*, *Out1*, *Out2*. The first two of these represent the insertion of the keys, the third represents the access, and the last two represent the extraction of the keys.

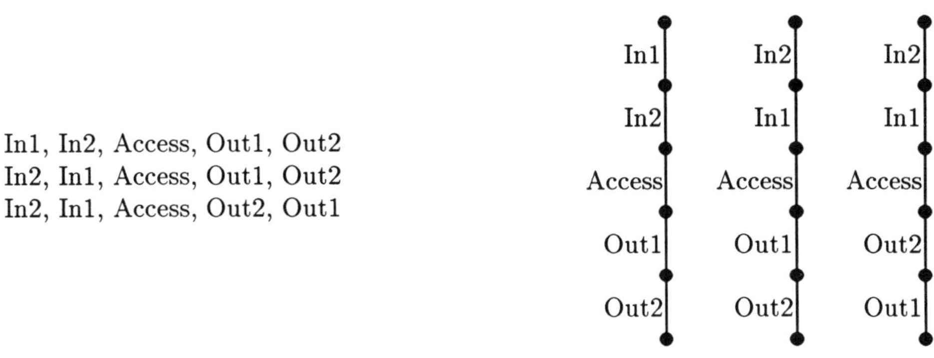

Figure 3.5: Action Prefix Operator for Two-Key System

3.3.1 *Action Prefix*

The action prefix construct allows the specification of sequences of events. This is not enough for representing the complete behaviour of the system. Sequences of events represent just possible execution traces. Some valid sequences are shown in Figure 3.5.

3.3.2 *Choice*

The action prefix and choice constructs allow the representation of trees. Now the complete behaviour of the system can be represented. The representation of the whole behaviour of the system in a tree-like form is only practicable when the number of states is small, as in the example of Figure 3.6.

3.3.3 *Processes*

Processes are used for many purposes. One important use is the creation of infinite behaviours by the use of recursion. Process *TwoKey* in Figure 3.7 allows an unlimited number of access cycles. Another important use of processes is the encapsulation of generic behaviour patterns to avoid duplication, as in process *Acc*. Gate relabelling is also used in this example.

3.3.4 *Enabling*

Enabling and **exit** allow the behaviour of a specification to be structured in phases, three in this example. Phase 1 is the introduction of both keys. Phase 2 concerns access. Phase 3 is the extraction of both keys.

```
  In1;
  In2;
  Access;
  (Out1; Out2; stop [] Out2; Out1; stop)
[]
  In2;
  In1;
  Access;
  (Out1; Out2; stop [] Out2; Out1; stop)
```

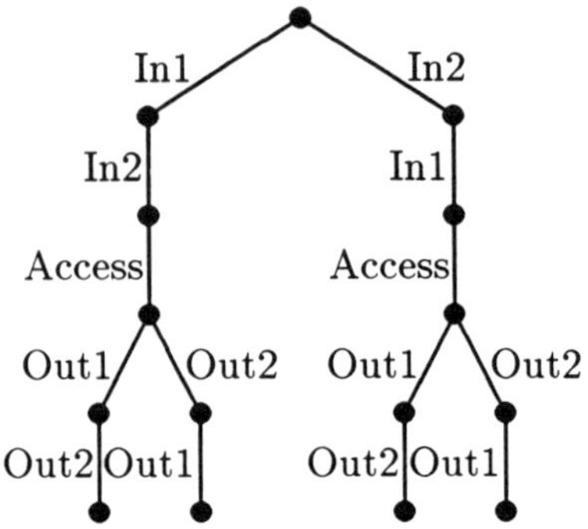

Figure 3.6: Choice Operator for Two-Key System

```
TwoKey [In1, In2, Access, Out1, Out2]

where

process TwoKey [I1, I2, Ac, O1, O2] : noexit :=
  K1; K2; Acc [I1, I2, Ac, O1, O2]
[]
  K2; K1; Acc [I1, I2, Ac, O1, O2]
endproc (* TwoKey *)

process Acc [I1, I2, Ac, O1, O2] : noexit :=
   Ac;
   (
      O1; O2; TwoKey [I1, I2, Ac, O1, O2]
   []
      O2; O1; TwoKey [I1, I2, Ac, O1, O2]
   )
endproc (* Acc *)
```

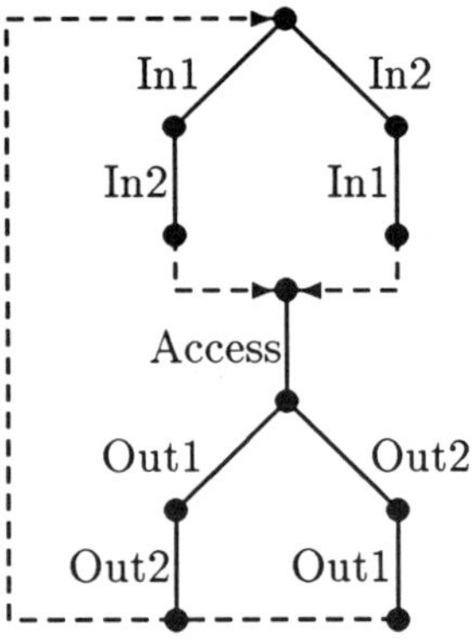

Figure 3.7: Processes for Two-Key System

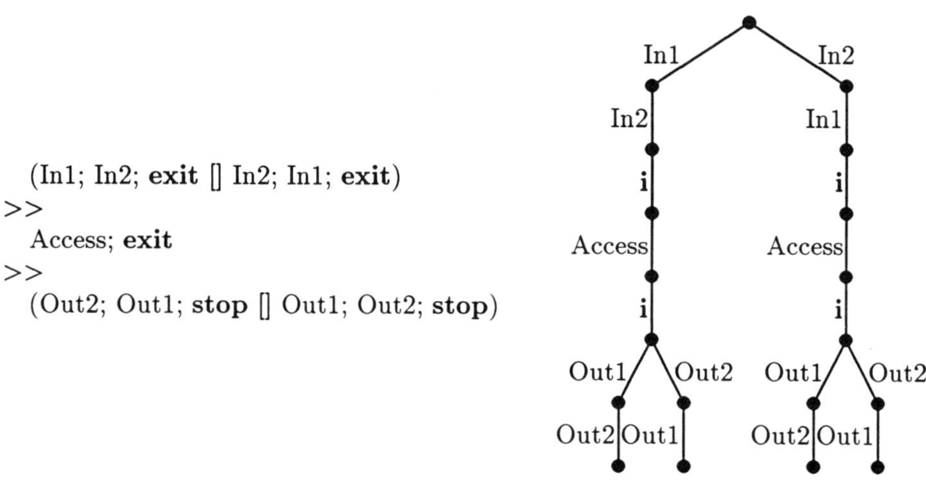

Figure 3.8: Enable Operator for Two-Key System

Notice that internal events in the behaviour tree of Figure 3.8 appear as a consequence of the way the enabling operator works. The appearance of these internal events does not modify the observable behaviour.

3.3.5 *Interleaving*

The first phase is now modelled as interleaved behaviour that deals with the insertion of keys in either order. The upper part of Figure 3.9 shows the trees of the two interleaved behaviours. The tree of the resulting interleaving composition is shown in the lower part of the figure. Both behaviours synchronise on δ despite being composed by interleaving.

3.3.6 *Synchronisation*

An alternative specification for the system uses the synchronisation operator instead of enabling. The system can be specified as a number of independent constraints on valid sequences of behaviour. The independent constraints are then composed with the parallel operator to define the system. Such a specification style is called **constraint-oriented**. A little study will show that the behaviour expression in Figure 3.10 describes the intended behaviour. The behaviour trees of the parenthesised expressions are shown on the right.

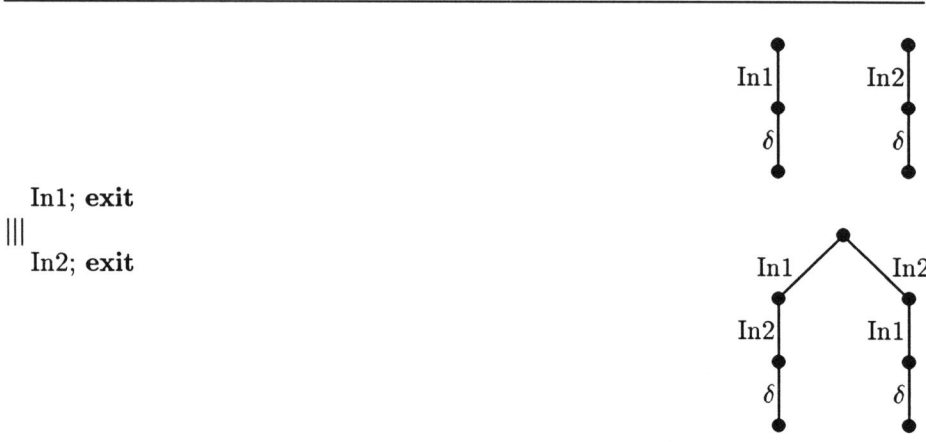

Figure 3.9: Interleaving Operator for Two-Key System

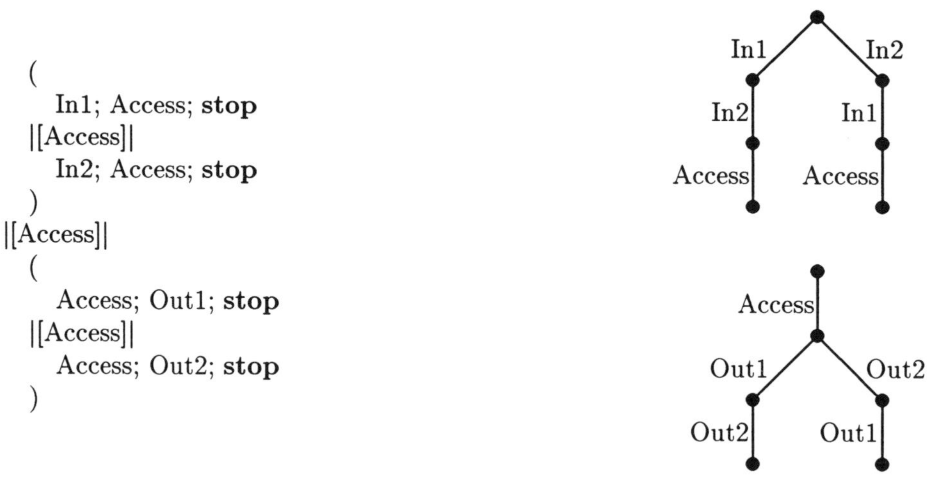

Figure 3.10: Synchronisation Operator for Two-Key System

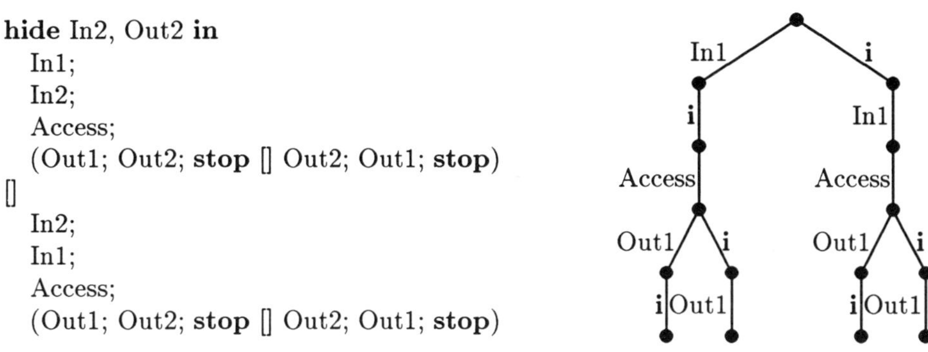
hide In2, Out2 **in**
In1;
In2;
Access;
(Out1; Out2; **stop** [] Out2; Out1; **stop**)
[]
In2;
In1;
Access;
(Out1; Out2; **stop** [] Out2; Out1; **stop**)
In1
i
i
In1
Access
Access
Out1
i
Out1
i
i
Out1
i
Out1

Figure 3.11: Hide Operator for Two-Key System

3.3.7 *Hiding*

Hiding provides a powerful abstraction mechanism. Hiding could be used with this example to obtain a one-key system out of one of the previous specifications of the two-key system. It is only necessary to hide gates *In2* and *Out2* as in Figure 3.11 to achieve this. Although there are internal events composed with the choice operator, the behaviour of the system is deterministic.

3.4 Data Types

LOTOS models data as **abstract data types** based on ACT ONE. The underlying theory is that of equational models. These have complex semantics and require complex reasoning about data terms. Since conventional methods of equational reasoning have to be applied, there are difficulties in theorem-proving.

Fortunately, most data types in real specifications may be accurately treated like conventional data structures in a programming language, with functions and procedures to manipulate them. This section presents an informal and intuitive view of data types.

3.4.1 *Basic Data Type Concepts*

There is *no* predefined data type. A LOTOS specification starts with no built-in data types. Even Booleans (truth values), explicitly required by language constructs like guards and predicates, must be defined in each LOTOS specification.

However, commonly required data types can be included from the **standard library** to save time and space. For example:

> **library**
> Boolean, Set, NaturalNumber
> **endlib**

but specifiers are completely free to use whichever data types they wish, even modifying the usual understanding of what Booleans are.

Data specifications are collected into **type** definitions. LOTOS types are not programming language types, but rather a world of things and properties. In a programming language, a Boolean type is typically a set of data values with predefined operations. In LOTOS a Boolean type is a set of data values and operations that require to be defined. Although the LOTOS view is compatible with that of a programming language, a LOTOS type also deals with properties of operations and values.

LOTOS **sorts** are distinct sets of data values. The concept of sort in LOTOS corresponds to the concept of type in many programming languages. Expressions have a definite sort. A variable can hold a value of only a specific sort.

LOTOS **operations** correspond to functions and procedures to manipulate objects. By means of operations it is possible to combine values of the same or different sorts into aggregate values, or establish relations between them.

LOTOS **equations** define which expressions are considered equal, possibly using variables that are universally quantified. For example:

$$\forall x : Nat \ . \ x + 0 = 0$$

Equations state properties that must be satisfied by (any implementation of) the objects of the type. Equational reasoning must therefore be applied to value expressions to find out whether they are equal or not. In theory this may require a complex proof, or may even be unprovable.

In actual practice, however, specifiers usually write equations that can be treated as **rewrite rules**. A rewrite rule handles transformations of expressions. The equation $LHS = RHS$ ('Left-Hand Side equals Right-Hand Side') can be treated as a rewrite rule $LHS \Rightarrow RHS$. The rewrite rule is interpreted 'an expression that matches the LHS pattern can be rewritten according to the RHS scheme'.

The intention of rewriting is to reduce an expression to its **canonical form**. If rewriting is successful, then dealing with (in)equality of two terms becomes trivial: rewrite each term to its canonical form and see whether they are identical or not.

The canonical form is unique, and is sometimes called the **normal form**. The canonical form has the following properties:

- it cannot be rewritten further
- two expressions that can be proved to be equal must yield the same canonical form after applying as many rewrites as possible.

Canonical forms are, loosely speaking, the forms used in computer programming to hold data. Data values are held in arrays, records, sets, etc. All these are (usually) directly stored in canonical form. For example, the expression *3 + 2* would normally be reduced to its canonical form of *5* rather than be preserved as an expression involving '+'.

Canonical forms are convenient, and rewriting is a simple procedure to understand. But, is it possible to avoid rewriting loops? Will the canonical form result after applying every possible rewriting? If there are several possible left-hand sides that match, is it irrelevant what order the rewriting is carried out?

For a large range of practical cases the answers to these questions are positive, so there can be confidence in the informal interpretation of the equations as rewrite rules. This chapter considers equations only as rewrite rules, and it is taken on trust that this interpretation is correct. The limitations of treating equations purely as rewrite rules are not explored here.

3.4.2 *Basic Types*

Here are some basic types to show the relevant syntax:

```
type Boolean is
  sorts Bool
  opns
    true, false :            -> Bool
    not :           Bool     -> Bool
  eqns
    ofsort Bool
      not (true) = false;
      not (false) = true;
endtype (* Boolean *)

type NaturalNumber is
  sorts Nat
  opns
    0 :                      -> Nat
    Succ :          Nat      -> Nat
endtype (* NaturalNumber *)
```

The type *Boolean* has been specified with terms of sort *Bool.* There are the usual constants *true* and *false*, and the *not* operation that complements a Boolean value. A constant in LOTOS is simply an operation with no arguments, as is the case with *true* and *false.* Since an operation always returns the same result for the same arguments, an operation with no arguments always returns the same constant value. Hopefully the equations for Booleans do not require further explanation since they are commonly used in programming.

The *NaturalNumber* type specifies whole numbers (positive or zero), which should again be familiar. The specification is based on the usual mathematical approach rather than the conventional arabic notation for numbers. The idea is to have a single constant *0*, and a *Succ* (successor) operations that yields the next value. The terms of this sort are:

0, Succ (0), Succ (Succ (0)), Succ (Succ (Succ (0))), ...

Once the above types have been specified, variables of sort *Bool* and *Nat* may be defined. Boolean expressions involving *true*, *false* and *not* may be written. There may also be natural number expressions involving *0* and *Succ.*

3.4.3 *Extension*

Types may be extended with new sorts, operations and equations. Specifying new sorts provides more sets of data values. Adding new operations expands the range of expressions that are allowed. Introducing new equations results in new properties of operations, and new ways of rewriting. Here is an extension of the natural numbers:

```
type NaturalExtended is NaturalNumber
  opns
    _ + _ : Nat, Nat -> Nat
  eqns
    forall x, y : Nat
      ofsort Nat
        x + 0 = x;
        x + Succ (y) = Succ (x + y);
endtype (* NaturalExtended *)
```

This enriches the type *NaturalNumber* with a '+' operation for addition. The operation takes two naturals and yields the natural that is their sum. The underscores before and after the operation name indicate that it is an **infix operation** (i.e. is placed between its arguments). The equations allow the new terms that may be written with '+' to be **evaluated.**

Consider now how to apply these equations to add *3* to *2*, something that would usually be written as *3 + 2 = 5* in arabic digits. The specification of '+'

works as follows, rewriting with the second equation twice and then the first equation:

```
   Succ (Succ (Succ (0))) + Succ (Succ (0))
⇒  Succ (Succ (Succ (Succ (0))) + Succ (0))
⇒  Succ (Succ (Succ (Succ (Succ (0))) + 0))
⇒  Succ (Succ (Succ (Succ (Succ (0)))))
```

3.4.4 *Combination*

Types may be combined to build more complex types. The sorts, operations and equations of each component are all included to produce the richer type. For example, a stack of natural numbers is specified with:

```
type NaturalStack is NaturalNumber, Boolean
  sorts Stack
  opns
    empty :                        -> Stack
    push :      Nat, Stack         -> Stack
    top :       Stack              -> Nat
    pop :       Stack              -> Stack
    IsEmpty :   Stack              -> Bool
  eqns
    forall n : Nat, s : Stack
      ofsort Nat
        top (push (n, s)) = n;
      ofsort Stack
        pop (push (n, s)) = s;
      ofsort Bool
        IsEmpty (empty) = true;
        IsEmpty (push (n, s)) = false;
endtype (* NaturalStack *)
```

This defines the new sort *Stack*. The empty stack is the base case for stacks. Note that this is the only operation that yields an object of sort *Stack* without using another stack as argument. The other operations (*push*, *top*, *pop* and *IsEmpty*) work on an existing value of sort *Stack*.

The equations state the expected properties: the top of a stack is the last element pushed onto it; popping a stack yields the stack prior to the last push; and finding whether a stack is empty or not requires checking whether any element has been pushed onto it.

3.4.5 Conditional Equations

The applicability of an equation may be made to depend on a Boolean condition — a **premiss**. If the premiss holds for a given set of values, the equation applies for these values; if the premiss does not hold for the values then the the equation does not apply for them. As an example, an operation to return the maximum of two naturals might be specified as[4]:

```
type NaturalMaximum is NaturalNumber
  opns max : Nat, Nat -> Nat
  eqns
    forall x, y : Nat
      ofsort Nat
        x ge y =>
          max (x, y) = x;
        y ge x =>
          max (x, y) = y;
endtype (* NaturalMaximum *)
```

Note that both equations apply when x and y are equal.

For every sort, there is an equality (denoted by the reserved symbol '=') that says whether two terms can be proved equal according to the equations. This equality may be used in conditional expressions. However, for technical reasons there is no direct way to check for inequality (in other words, there is no predefined $\neq$). The equations say which things are *equal*, but do not say which things are *unequal*. Apart from equational equality, specifiers may define their own Boolean equalities. These are operations that yield a Boolean value for two arguments of the same sort:

```
_ eq _ : Nat, Nat -> Bool
```

The specifier will provide enough equations to get a *true* or *false* result in all cases. LOTOS permits the use of these user-defined equalities in conditional expressions. In fact, *(x eq y)* is short for *(x eq y) = true*. A common reason for defining Boolean equality is so that inequality can be tested with expressions like *not (x eq y)*.

LOTOS does not support partial functions — those whose arguments are restricted. There are many cases where partial functions model reality accurately. For example, a specification of a stack would not expect to deal with expressions like *top (empty)* and *pop (empty)*. In the absence of appropriate equations, these are meaningless values in the sorts of natural numbers and stacks respectively. Some specifiers deal explicitly with errors like this, but

[4]The standard data type for natural numbers defines operations such as *ge* (greater than or equal) and *lt* (less than).

there are as many solutions as there are specifiers. Another approach is to 'protect' the use of the stack type in the behavioural part of the language, refusing to allow illegal operations.

3.4.6 *Renaming*

It is often the case that types are very similar. For instance, the example below specifies bit values and parity values. The only differences between these two types is that they normally use different names, and it is undesirable to mix these up.

```
type Bit is Boolean
  sorts Bit
  opns
    0, 1:                          -> Bit
    _ + _:        Bit, Bit         -> Bit
    _ eq _:       Bit, Bit         -> Bool
  eqns
    forall b : Bit
      ofsort Bit
        0 + 0 = 0; 0 + 1 = 1;
        1 + 0 = 1; 1 + 1 = 0;
      ofsort Bool
        b eq b = true;
        0 eq 1 = false; 1 eq 0 = false;
endtype (* Bit *)

type Parity is Bit renamedby
  sortnames
    Parity for Bit
  opnnames
    even for 0
    odd for 1
endtype (* Parity *)
```

The renaming facility of LOTOS allows a new, completely independent type to be specified by changing the names of an existing type. Both sort and operation names may be changed. If a name is not changed, the same name will be used in the new type. The Boolean operations in type *Parity* are the very same ones of *Boolean.* Type *Bit* provides *0*, *1*, '+' and *eq*. The *0* and *1* operations are explicitly renamed as *even* and *odd* respectively. They are therefore new operations, although similar to those in type *Bit.* Operations '+' and *eq* are not explicitly renamed, but since their arguments are renamed (i.e.

Bit is replaced by *Parity*), they become new operations with the same name. This a typical case of **operation overloading**, i.e. operations with the same name but different meanings according to their arguments and results.

Renaming is frequently used before extending a type. Suppose natural numbers have been specified, and that natural numbers modulo N are required. Rather than working on *NaturalNumber* and mixing everything up, it is better to create a fresh copy of *NaturalNumber* and extend it to deal with the new arithmetic. It is a way of protecting the existing type against unintentional changes.

3.4.7 *Parameterisation*

Reusability is a major goal of modern software engineering. In order to achieve this goal, it is necessary that software be decomposed into components that are made as reusable as possible; parameterisation is a technique that can greatly enhance this.

Types may be incompletely specified, leaving a gap for further information. A similar situation arises with functions or procedures in a programming language, where an algorithm may refer to formal arguments that are provided later. When the actual arguments are provided on a call, the algorithm is applied with these definite values. This can save repetitious programming, reducing the opportunities for making mistakes and simplifying maintenance.

Gaps in data types may be left for sorts and operations. These act as an interface to the generic type. Requirements may be imposed on this interface by specifying equations that must hold if actual parameters are to fill the gaps. Understanding this would require a detailed treatment of the semantics and so is omitted here.

The example below specifies a stack parameterised by some element sort:

```
type GenericStack is Boolean
  formalsorts Element
  sorts Stack
  opns
    empty :                         -> Stack
    push :     Element, Stack       -> Stack
    top :      Stack                -> Element
    pop :      Stack                -> Stack
    IsEmpty :  Stack                -> Bool
  eqns
    forall e : Element, s : Stack
      ofsort Element
        top (push (e, s)) = e;
```

```
        ofsort Stack
          pop (push (e, s)) = s;
        ofsort Bool
          IsEmpty (empty) = true;
          IsEmpty (push (e, s)) = false;
endtype (* GenericStack *)
```

3.4.8 *Actualisation*

Parameterised types may be actualised[5] — instantiated with actual parameters to fill the gaps. Two stacks are generated below by instantiating the parameterised stack with different actual arguments:

```
type NatStack is GenericStack actualizedby NaturalNumber using
  sortnames
    Nat for Element
    NatStack for Stack
endtype (* NatStack *)

type BoolStack is GenericStack actualizedby Boolean using
  sortnames
    Bool for Element
    BoolStack for Stack
endtype (* BoolStack *)
```

Actualisation involves a renaming of the components of the parameterised data type. Formal sorts and operations of the parameterised type are renamed as sorts and operations of the actual type. Actualisation differs from renaming in that new names are not invented; they must correspond to names in the actual argument. Usually, this association is explicit, but if both the parameterised type and the instantiating type have sorts or operations with identical names, the renaming may be implicit.

The definition of actualisation in LOTOS allows for additional renaming that is not strictly required for actualisation. This is not theoretically needed but is rather convenient. Sorts and operations that are not formal in the parameterised type may be renamed in the usual way. For instance, the first example above renames sort *GenericStack* as *NatStack* to avoid two definitions of a sort called *GenericStack*. For sorts and operations that are not formal, the rules for renaming apply.

[5] LOTOS syntax requires the spelling 'actualized'.

Beh. Exp. A	Beh. Exp. B	Condition	Interaction Type
$g\ !\ E_1$	$g\ !\ E_2$	$value\ (E_1) = value\ (E_2)$	value matching
$g\ !\ E_1$	$g\ ?\ x : t$	$sort\ (E_1) = t$	value passing
$g\ ?\ x : t$	$g\ ?\ y : u$	$t = u$	value generation

Figure 3.12: Interaction Types

3.5 Full LOTOS

Section 3.2 showed that Basic LOTOS allows the representation of synchronisation, but it does not allow transfer of data since the concept of data is not defined for it. Merging the pròcess algebra defined by Basic LOTOS and the abstract data type language allows both synchronisation and transfer of data, which is necessary in distributed systems.

3.5.1 *Structured Events*

In Full LOTOS, an event has a gate identifier and a list of interaction parameters called **experiment offers**. There are two kinds of experiment offer:

- a **value offer** has the form *!* v, where v is a value expression
- a **variable offer** has the form *?* $x : s$, where x is a variable of sort s.

An event can take place at a gate only the experiment offers match in sort, value and order. Interaction possibilities are summarised in Figure 3.12. As an example, the event offer:

g ! Succ (0) ? x : Bool ! false

matches:

g ? x : Nat ! true ! false

but does not match:

g ! Succ (0) ? x : Bool

nor:

g ? x : Nat ! true ! true

Value matching represents synchronisation by matching of expected values. An example of this kind of interaction is password checking, in which an interaction only occurs if the correct password value is conveyed by a user to a resource.

Value passing represents conventional **input-output** interactions. One partner supplies a value ($! \, E_1$ in Figure 3.12) and the other receives a value ($g \, ? \, x : t$ in Figure 3.12).

Value generation represents the non-deterministic selection of a value for the interaction variable from among the valid ones. It models the concept of negotiation, since both partners in the interaction must agree on a value for the interaction to take place. After the interaction occurs, the variables of both partners have the same value ($x = y$ in Figure 3.12).

3.5.2 *Conditional Behaviour*

The behaviour of a system may depend on certain conditions. The conditions may depend on past events and/or data stored by the system. These conditions are represented in LOTOS as Boolean operations involving process variables or interaction parameters. A condition may be applied before an event, or be imposed on its occurrence. The former is represented in LOTOS by guards, the latter by selection predicates.

A **guard** contains a Boolean expression, called the **premiss**, and a guarded behaviour expression. If the premiss evaluates to *true*, the guarded behaviour expression is allowed to occur. An example is a system that calculates the maximum of two natural numbers as follows:

```
process MaxCalc [input, max] : exit :=
  input ? x : Nat ? y : Nat;
  (
    [x ge y] ->                    (* x greater than or equal to y? *)
      max ! x; exit                (* output x *)
  []
    [y ge x] ->                    (* y greater than or equal to x? *)
      max ! y; exit                (* output y *)
  )
endproc (* MaxCalc *)
```

In this example, x *ge* y and x *le* y are the premisses, while *max ! x;* **exit** and *max ! y;* **exit** are their respective guarded behaviour expressions. Notice that guards need not necessarily be disjoint; they are not in this example, since when x and y are equal then both guarded behaviour expressions are allowed.

The syntax of an action denotation in Full LOTOS contains a gate identifier, an optional experiment offer list, and an optional **selection predicate**. The selection predicate contains a Boolean expression, again called the **premiss**. An interaction is allowed to occur only for interaction parameters that cause the premiss to evaluate to *true*.

The following example of a public telephone allows international calls only if the user inserts more than 50 cents:

```
process Telephone [phone] : noexit :=
  phone ? dialled : TelephoneNumber ? money : Currency
    [InternationalCall (dialled) implies (money gt Cents50)];
  (Conversation [phone] (money) >> Telephone [phone])
endproc (* Telephone *)
```

3.5.3 *Parameterised Processes*

Processes can be parameterised with data parameters. Process parameters are declared in a process definition as formal parameters. In process instantiations these parameters must be assigned corresponding values, i.e. value expressions of matching sort to be evaluated.

Consider a scheduler that deals with telephone calls, supporting a first-in-first-out queue of calls requiring attention. The data type *Queue* is assumed to be specified elsewhere with operations *Append* (add to end), *Head* (first element), *Tail* (all but first) and *IsEmpty* (at least one element). The scheduler can be specified as follows:

```
process TelephoneQueue
 [phone, transfer] (waiting : Queue) : noexit :=
  phone ? num : Client;                        (* accept a call *)
  TelephoneQueue [phone, transfer] (Append (num, waiting))
                                               (* insert call in queue *)
[]
  [not (IsEmpty (waiting))] ->                 (* check if queue empty *)
    (
      transfer ! Head (waiting);               (* transfer first call *)
      TelephoneQueue[phone, transfer] (Tail (waiting))
                                               (* remove first call *)
    )
endproc (* TelephoneQueue *)
```

The queue of calls is updated on each recursive instantiation of the process. If a call is received, it is inserted in the queue. If there is at least one call in the queue, the system is prepared to deal with the first one; it is then removed from the queue. Process *TelephoneQueue* will be instantiated beforehand in the specification with an initial queue value (probably the empty queue).

Operator	Conditions	Functionality
stop	-	**noexit**
exit	-	$<>$
exit $(v_1 \ldots v_n)$	$sort\ (v_1) = s_1, \ldots, sort\ (v_n) = s_n$	$<s_1, \ldots, s_n>$
act; B	-	*func (B)*
B_1 *[]* B_2	*func* (B_1) = *func* (B_2)	*func* (B_1)
	func (B_1) = **noexit**	*func* (B_2)
	func (B_2) = **noexit**	*func* (B_1)
	otherwise	invalid
B_1 >> B_2	-	*func* (B_2)
B_1 *[>* B_2	same as B_1 *[]* B_2	same as B_1 *[]* B_2
B_1 *parop* B_2	*func* (B_1) = *func* (B_2)	*func* (B_1)
	func (B_1) = **noexit**	**noexit**
	func (B_2) = **noexit**	**noexit**
	otherwise	invalid

act is an action denotation, *parop* is a parallel operator.

Figure 3.13: Functionality Rules

3.5.4 *Parameterised Exit*

In Full LOTOS, successful termination of behaviour expressions allows values to be conveyed with **exit**. An **exit** may therefore have a parameter list which can be filled in by value expressions. A special syntax construct **any** is introduced to indicate that any value of a sort is allowed for that parameter. Notice that the parameterless **exit** of Basic LOTOS is the special case of an empty exit parameter list. Example behaviour expressions with exit lists are:

a ? x : Nat ? y : Nat; **exit** (Add (x, y))

a ? x : Nat; **exit** (x, **any** Nat)
|||
b ? y : Nat; **exit** (**any** Nat, y)

3.5.5 *Functionality*

Each valid LOTOS behaviour expression has assigned a static characteristic called its **functionality**. The functionality of a behaviour expression is an ordered list of sorts that indicates the exit parameter list associated with this behaviour expression. The rules for the evaluation of functionality are shown in Figure 3.13. Here, **noexit** indicates that the behaviour expression does not terminate successfully at all, while < ... > indicates a list of exit parameters.

The functionality of a process is defined as the functionality of its behaviour expression and must be explicitly declared in the process definition. The functionality of a process must match that of its defining behaviour expression.

3.5.6 *Parameterised Sequential Composition*

Section 3.2.7 explained how behaviour expressions are sequentially composed in Basic LOTOS. Full LOTOS extends this concept by also allowing values to be passed between sequentially composed behaviour expressions.

The following specification defines a system that accepts a natural number and a Boolean value as inputs, and delivers the the number or its successor depending on the Boolean input:

```
   (input ? x : Nat ? s : Bool; exit (x, s))
>>
   accept y : Nat, incr : Bool in
     (
       [incr] ->
         output ! Succ (y); exit
     []
       [not (incr)] ->
         output ! y; exit
     )
```

The parameterised sequential composition differs from the parameterless sequential composition in that it contains an **accept** statement. This statement explicitly lists the parameters that are passed to the enabled behaviour expression. The functionality of the behaviour expression preceding the enable operator must match the list of variables in the **accept**.

3.5.7 *Local Value Definition*

A **local value definition** associate values with free variables in behaviour expressions. This operator allow more conciseness and better readability in specifications, since it allows (possibly large) value expressions to be replaced by a single identifier.

Consider part of the specification of a protocol entity whose behaviour depends on the contents of a protocol data unit. The protocol data unit derives from the data parameter of a service primitive. The formal specification might read:

```
g ? sp : ServPrim;
(
   [DataField (PDU (UserData (sp))) eq <>] -> ...
[]
   [DataField (PDU (UserData (sp))) ne <>] -> ...
)
```

Using a local value definition, the equivalent specification would be:

```
g ? sp : ServPrim;
(
   let data : Data = DataField (PDU (UserData (sp))) in
      (
         [data eq <>] -> ...
      []
         [data ne <>] -> ...
      )
)
```

In this case the **let** statement associates a value with the variable *data*. This makes the specification more readable and compact, particularly if *data* is used a number of times.

3.5.8 *Generalised Choice*

There are two types of **generalised choice**: choice over gates, and choice over values. These constructs are basically shorthand notations that allow more compact specifications, and can in most cases be interpreted in terms of choice and action prefix.

Choice over gates allows a choice of identical behaviour expressions with some (formal) gates to be replaced by gates from a gate identifier list. For example:

```
choice g1 in [a1, a2, a3] []
   B [g1, h1]
```

The equivalent behaviour in terms of choice is:

```
B [a1, h1] [] B [a2, h1] [] B [a3, h1]
```

Choice over values allows a choice of identical behaviour expressions with variables instantiated with different values. An example is:

```
choice x1 : s1, x2 : s2 []
   B (x1, x2)
```

where *B (x1, x2)* is a behaviour expression. The effect of the choice over values in terms of choice may depend on the behaviour expression which follows. Consider the case of a behaviour expression consisting of an action prefix expression followed by another generic behaviour expression:

```
choice x1 : s1, x2 : s2 []
  g ! x1 ! x2; B (x1, x2)
```

This is equivalent to:

```
g ? x1 : s1 ? x2 : s1; B (x1, x2)
```

Consider now a behaviour expression in which the action prefix contains an internal event:

```
choice x1 : s1, x2 : s2 []
  i; g ! x1 ! x2; B (x1, x2)
```

In this case the choice over the values is made independently from the environment. The representation of this behaviour in terms of the action prefix and choice operators would be:

```
  i; g ! v1 ! w1; B (v1, w1)
[]
  i; g ! v2 ! w1; B (v2, w1)
...
[]
  i; g ! vk ! w1; B (vk, w1)
[]
  i; g ! v1 ! w2; B (v1, w2)
...
 []
  i; g ! vk ! wl; B (vk, wl)
```

where $v_1 \ldots v_k$ is all possible values in sort s_1 and $w_1 \ldots w_l$ is all possible values in sort s_2. If s_1 or s_2 contains infinite different values, the complete representation in terms of the choice operator becomes infinite. It is therefore not possible to say that the generalised choice is always a shorthand, since it sometimes represents behaviours that cannot be interpreted in terms of choice and the action prefix operators.

3.5.9 *Generalised Parallel Construct*

The **generalised parallel construct** is another shorthand notation that allows more compact specifications. It is therefore possible to interpret the generalised parallel operator in terms of parallel compositions of behaviour expressions. For example:

> **par** g1 **in** [a1, a2, a3] *parop*
> B [g1, h1]

where *B [g1, h1]* is a behaviour expression and *parop* is a parallel operator such as '||' or '|||'. The corresponding behaviour expression in terms of the parallel operator looks like:

> B [a1, h1] *parop* B [a2, h1] *parop* B [a3, h1]

3.5.10 *Scope*

Processes may have local definitions (after the keyword **where**), in which both data types and other processes can be defined. This determines rules for access to type and process definitions by other types and processes. A **scope** is a certain piece of LOTOS text that controls the accessibility of an element: a data type, a sort, an operation, a variable, a value or a process. LOTOS has scoping rules similar to block-structured programming languages.

Global type definitions (see Section 3.5.11) can be accessed from any part of the specification, but local definitions can be accessed only by the process in which they are defined. Furthermore, some values are accessed only by behaviour expressions.

3.5.11 *Specification*

A **specification** in LOTOS is the process that represents the whole system being specified. However, there are some syntactic differences between a specification and a process, as summarised in Figure 3.14.

A **global type definition** is a type definition that is accessible to the overall behaviour expression, type definitions and processes in the specification. Global type definitions appear before the key-word **behaviour** in a specification and do not exist in process definitions.

Just for illustration, consider the system of Figure 3.1 rewritten as a specification. A global type definition might be included as follows:

Syntax Item	Specification	Process
start of definition	**specification**	**process**
global type definitions	yes	no
start of behaviour	**behaviour**	:=
end of definition	**endspec**	**endproc**

Figure 3.14: Syntactic Differences between Specification and Process

```
specification S [a, b, c, d] : noexit

  type SomeType is                    (* a global type definition *)
    sorts SomeSort
    opns SomeOpn : SomeSort -> SomeSort
  endtype (* SomeType *)

  behaviour
    P [a, b, c] |[b]| Q [b, d]

  where

  process P[a, b, c] ...

  process Q [b, d] ...

endspec (* S *)
```

3.6 Full LOTOS Examples

The capabilities of Full LOTOS will again be illustrated with the two-key system that is further developed in Chapter 11.

3.6.1 *Event Structures*

In Full LOTOS, the definition of system interfaces has to take into account the data values exchanged at gates. The combination of gates and their value parameters is usually called the **event structure**. The first thing to consider when describing a system with Full LOTOS is the definition of the event structure of the interfaces.

For the two-key system, the event structures are *KI ? x : KeyOps* and *Access*. Gate *KI* multiplexes all the lock-related interactions. The type (i.e. insertion or extraction) and instance (key 1 or 2) of lock operations are defined by the values of sort *KeyOps*. The elements of this sort are four constants — *In1*, *In2*, *Out1* and *Out2*. Gate *Access* is used for access to the system. It does not exchange data values.

The complete specification of the system with these event structures is:

```
specification TwoKeySystem [KI, Access] : noexit

  type KeyOps is
    sorts KeyOps
    opns In1, In2, Out1, Out2 : -> KeyOps
  endtype (* KeyOps *)

  behaviour
      KI ! In1; KI ! In2;
      Access;
      (
        KI ! Out1; KI ! Out2; stop
      []
        KI ! Out2; KI ! Out1; stop
      )
    []
      KI ! In2; KI ! In1;
      Access;
      (
        KI ! Out2; KI ! Out1; stop
      []
        KI ! Out1; KI ! Out2; stop
      )

endspec (* TwoKeySystem *)
```

3.6.2 *Selection Predicates*

The following changes to the specification illustrate the use of selection predicates. Predicates over *KeyOps* values have been defined to select the proper ordering of the lock operations. *IsKeyIn* checks for a key being inserted, while *IsKeyOut* checks for a key being extracted. *IsOtherIn* checks for the other key of the pair being inserted, while *IsOtherOut* similarly checks for extraction. Notice that in spite of having no parameters, the system has memory: each value identifier following a '?' is like a variable that stores a value for later use.

```
library
  Boolean
endlib

type KeyOps ...

type MoreKeyOps is KeyOps, Boolean
  opns
    IsKeyIn, IsKeyOut :         KeyOps          -> Bool
    IsOtherIn, IsOtherOut :     KeyOps, KeyOps  -> Bool
  eqns
    forall x, y : KeyOps
      ofsort Bool
        IsKeyIn (In1) = true; IsKeyIn (In2) = true;
        IsKeyIn (Out1) = false; IsKeyIn (Out2) = false;
        IsKeyOut (In1) = false; IsKeyOut (In2) = false;
        IsKeyOut (Out1) = true; IsKeyOut (Out2) = true;
        not (IsKeyIn (x) and IsKeyIn (y)) =>
          IsOtherIn (x, y) = false;
        IsOtherIn (In1, In1) = false;
        IsOtherIn (In2, In2) = false;
        IsOtherIn (In1, In2) = true;
        IsOtherIn (In2, In1) = true;
        not (IsKeyOut (x) and IsKeyOut (y)) =>
          IsOtherOut (x, y) = false;
        IsOtherOut (Out1, Out1) = false;
        IsOtherOut (Out2, Out2) = false;
        IsOtherOut (Out1, Out2) = true;
        IsOtherOut (Out2, Out1) = true;
endtype (* MoreKeyOps *)

behaviour
  KI ? op1 : KeyOps [IsKeyIn (op1)];
  KI ? op2 : KeyOps [IsOtherIn (op1, op2)];
  Access;
  KI ? op1: KeyOps [IsKeyOut (op1)];
  KI ? op2: KeyOps [IsOtherOut (op1, op2)];
  stop
```

3.6.3 *Parameters and Guards*

The following changes to the specification express the same behaviour using parameterised processes and guards. Process parameters are used as state variables, while guards place conditions on state variables for transitions to occur. The model here is of an extended finite state machine.

```
library ...

type KeyOps ...

behaviour BeforeAccess [KI, Access] (false, false)

where

process BeforeAccess
 [KI, Access] (InKey1, InKey2 : Bool) : noexit :=
  (
    [not (InKey1)] ->
      KI ! In1;
      BeforeAccess [KI, Access] (true, InKey2)
  []
    [not (InKey2)] ->
      KI ! In2;
      BeforeAccess [KI, Access] (InKey1, true)
  []
    [InKey1 and InKey2] ->
      Access;
      AfterAccess [KI] (InKey1, InKey2)
  )
endproc (* BeforeAccess *)

process AfterAccess [KI] (InKey1, InKey2 : Bool) : noexit :=
  (
    [InKey1] ->
      KI ! Out1;
      AfterAccess [KI] (false, InKey2)
  []
    [InKey2] ->
      KI ! Out2;
      AfterAccess [KI] (InKey1, false)
  )
endproc (* AfterAccess *)
```

4 Introduction to SDL[1]

4.1 Background and Notations

SDL *(Specification and Description Language)* was first the subject of a CCITT Recommendation in 1976. It was already then based on a long tradition in switching system description going back at least to the first computer-controlled telephone switches. Since the first SDL Recommendation, SDL has evolved from a small informal drawing technique to an extensive FDT. During this process, constructs for coping with large systems and an advanced concept of data types have been added. The data type concept is based on the same kernel as in LOTOS (Ehrig and Mahr (1985)). However, the language has maintained its original flavour of graphical presentation and still provides a smooth path from informality to formality in different version of the description. The recent version of SDL (SDL-88) is published as CCITT Recommendation Z.100 (CCITT (1988)) together with a User Guidelines document (CCITT (1988), Annex D) and a formal definition (CCITT (1988), Annex F).

The language is maintained by CCITT, and a new extended version is expected to be recommended in 1992. A complete definition of SDL-92 is given in CCITT (1992s).

This chapter mainly covers SDL-88, because the examples of the book are written in SDL-88. Some aspects of SDL-92 are mentioned in Section 4.8. CCITT (1991) discusses the object-oriented extensions. A few concepts have been simplified in SDL-92 compared to SDL-88; for these concepts, the SDL-92 semantics are used in this chapter.

Although the name 'SDL' indicates use for specification and description, SDL is widely used today for other purposes such as design, high-level programming and simulation.

This chapter uses the graphical representation as much as possible. However several simple language constructs have only a textual representation. The graphical representation is called GR *(Graphical Representation)*, while the textual representation is called PR *(Phrase Representation)*. Automatic translation

[1]Chapter 4 is by O. Færgemand.

between PR and GR and vice versa is always possible. The description of the PR uses the following conventions:

bold	is used for a keyword
italics	is used for a non-terminal construct
|	represents choice between different constructs
[ ]	represents an optional construct
{ }	is used to group constructs.

In most cases where some concept is described as a list, e.g. *signal identifier list*, the elements in the list are separated by commas. In the few cases where this is not so, the separator will be mentioned explicitly.

The syntax given in this chapter is not complete; optional parts of productions with no connection to the text are omitted, and so are several constructs of the language. This has been done to limit the size of the presentation. A complete presentation of the syntax is given in CCITT (1988), Annex C.

4.2 General Model of SDL

A system is described as a number of extended finite state machines communicating by exchanging messages with each other and with the environment of the system. The state machines work in parallel, and several occurrences of the same state machine may concurrently exist.

The finite state machine is extended in the sense that local variables for each machine may hold details about the history of the machine. Also branching is allowed on state transitions for splitting into several sequences of actions. The behaviour of a state machine is described by a start node, interpreted when the machine is started, and a set of transitions, interpreted when the machine receives a certain stimulus in a certain **state**. Part of a transition may be the **output** of messages. After interpreting a transition the machine enters a new state. The extended finite state machine is modelled by the **process** concept. One occurrence of a process is called a **process instance**. Interpretation of a system thus consists of interpretation of process instances. A variable is local to the process instance owning it. This locality leads to restrictions, of course: no information exchange is possible by means of access to global data. This means, for instance, that one needs to model the access to a global database by explicitly sending query messages to the database and receiving explicit response messages. However, the locality of data is an intuitive and safe model of a distributed, parallel system. All communication between a system and its environment and within a system is achieved by sending messages, rather like letters in a postal service.

A message is modelled by a **signal**. A signal may carry with it a list of values. In this case the signal must be defined with a list of data types for the values carried by the signal. The SDL term for a set of values is a **sort**. A signal is sent from one process instance to another or between the environment and process instances within the system. When sending a signal one may directly specify the process instance for which the signal is intended or leave it to the system to identify the receiving process instance. In the latter case the receiver is derived from the signal name together with the place of the sender in the system. In addition to the explicit values that may be carried by a signal, any signal carries information about the process instance which sent it, and about the process instance it is sent to. By an analogy with postal service, each letter delivered is marked with the identity of the receiver and the sender.

Address information is expressed using the sort *PId (Process Identity)*. A *PId* value identifies a process instance. All *PId* values are unique, and each time a process instance is created a new, unique *PId* value is associated with that process instance. Each process instance contains four predefined imperative *PId* expressions (see Section 4.6.2), useful for communication with other processes:

self: the instance itself

sender: the instance from which the most recently consumed signal was sent

parent: the instance that created this one (see Section 4.5.4)

offspring: the instance most recently created by this one (see Section 4.5.4).

The *PId* value *Null* is not used for an existing process. By definition, **self** will always be different from *Null*. For **sender**, *Null* indicates that no signal was consumed by the process so far. For **parent**, *Null* indicates that the **process** instance was created at system initialisation time. For **offspring**, *Null* indicates that no instance so far was dynamically created by this instance.

Communication in SDL is asynchronous, i.e. no synchronisation is required between sender and receiver. To each process instance an unlimited buffer is attached to hold all received signals not yet consumed. In the postal analogy, each process instance has its own mailbox, and it is assumed that this mailbox is always sufficiently large to hold the mail until the process instance deals with it. The mailbox is thus an unbounded buffer, which is called the input port of a process instance. No priorities are associated with the input port. However, it is possible to retain specific signals in the input port when required (see Section 4.5.3). This can be used to model priorities for signal reception. In the postal analogy, a process instance can, in certain states (e.g. 'very busy'), ask its input port to protect it from unimportant signals (e.g. 'junk mail'). Unimportant signals (the 'junk mail') are still kept in the input port. In addition to these properties of the input ports, signals may be delayed non-deterministically during transmission between major system components (channel delay, see Section 4.4.1).

The rationale behind the asynchronous communication and the channel delay is to model a distributed and loosely coupled system. A system with asynchronous communication has a looser coupling between agents than one with synchronous communication. A sender in an asynchronous system can never be stuck because another communicating agent is not ready to communicate; it is always possible to mail a letter, as opposed to establishing direct conversation with the receiver of the letter.

4.3 General Rules

4.3.1 *Nesting of Diagrams*

An SDL description consists of a number of nested structures or scopes. Most of these are shown as a diagram. A diagram is surrounded by a rectangular frame, which may be implicit if the diagram covers a whole page. A diagram which is nested in another diagram is conceptually drawn within that enclosing diagram. In order to split the complete description into separate diagrams, the actual occurrence of a nested diagram within another diagram may be replaced by a symbol referring to the inner diagram. The **reference** symbol contains the name of the inner diagram and has a shape characteristic of the diagram being referenced. Figure 4.1 shows the various reference symbols.

4.3.2 *Names*

A **name** consists of one or more **words** separated by spaces, underlines ('_') and control characters, e.g. line-feed. A word consists of alphanumeric characters and full stops ('.'), and must contain at least one alphanumeric character. Thus '3.4' is a correct word but '..' is not. A word cannot be a **keyword**. In most places, underline can be replaced by space as a separator between words. The split of a name into several words enhances the readability of a specification. An underline symbol followed by a control character is ignored. This allows a word to be split over several lines, which is very useful within the limited space of the graphical symbols.

4.3.3 *Scope of Names*

All diagrams and some constructs with no GR define a **scope**. Every name is visible in the scope in which it is defined and in all enclosed scopes. For example, a signal name defined at the system level is visible at the system level and in all scopes within the system, i.e. in the whole system.

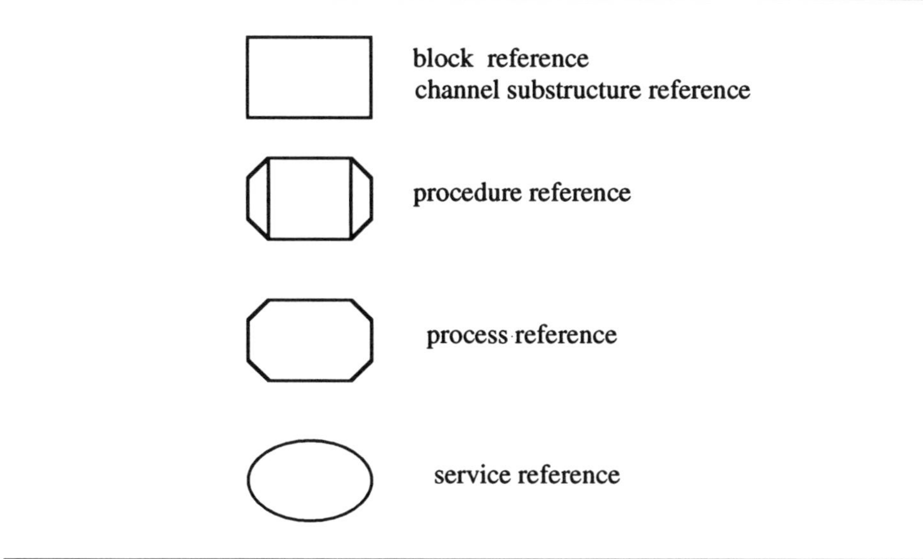

Figure 4.1: Reference Symbols

State (see Section 4.5.2) and connector (see Section 4.5.5) names have special scope rules. They are visible only within the single process or procedure[2] in which they are used. This is because states and connectors are local points-of-control within these entities.

4.3.4 *Some General Symbols*

Text Symbol

When textual definitions are needed in a diagram, a **text** symbol encloses the textual definitions in order to distinguish them from the graphical symbols. The text symbol is shown in Figure 4.2.

Comment

A comment is a piece of explanatory text insignificant for the formal interpretation of the document, rather it increases the readability. There are two kinds of comments; the distinction between them originates from the graphical representation. A special **comment** symbol (see Figure 4.3) can be attached to

[2]Similar visibility rules apply within **services**, but the service construct is not covered further in this chapter.

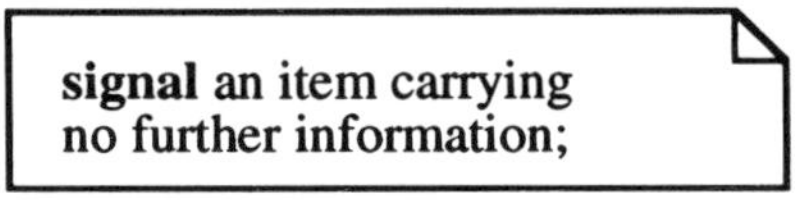

signal an item carrying
no further information;

Figure 4.2: Text Symbol

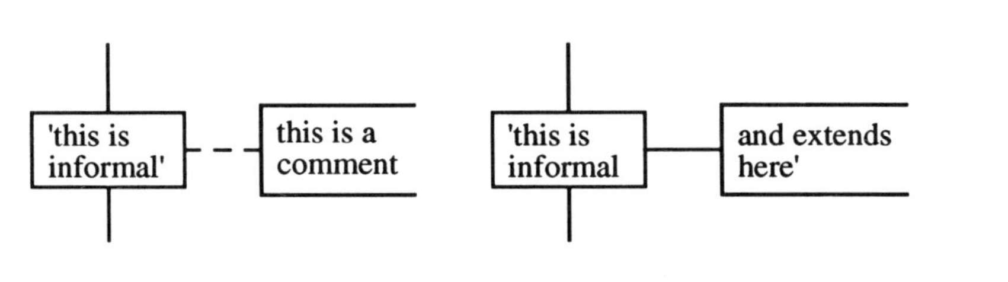

Figure 4.3: Comment and Text Extension Symbols

any symbol. It indicates that its enclosed text is a comment to the symbol it is attached to. It is also possible to define comments by enclosing any text in the characters '/*' and '*/'.

Text Extension

If text does not fit inside a symbol, it is possible to attach a **text extension** symbol (see Figure 4.3). The text extension symbol is attached by a solid line and the text in the text extension symbol is a continuation of the text in the symbol it is attached to.

4.3.5 *Informal Text*

Informal text is a piece of a specification that has no formal interpretation. It is, however, part of the specification unlike a comment. Informal text may be formalised at a later stage or be left informal, to indicate a part of the system that is not required to be formally specified. An example is shown in Figure 4.3. Informal text is written as a string of characters. Section 4.5.4 elaborates on the use of informal text.

4.4 Structure

4.4.1 *Structuring the System Level*

A system consists of a number of **blocks** connected by **channels**. A block is an enclosure for further structuring of the system, i.e. a new, nested system in its own. Channels connect the blocks with each other and with the environment of the system. A channel may be a one-way or two-way connection. It is characterised by the signals that it may carry; these constitute the **signal list(s)** of the channel. A channel has a signal list for each direction. One or two arrow heads at the middle of the channel indicate the direction(s) of the channel. Signal lists are enclosed by square brackets. Figure 4.4 shows a system diagram. The following constructs are used:

system: *s*

block references: *a, b*

channels: *c, d, e*

signals: *p, t*

signal lists: [*p*], [*p, t*], [*t*]

text symbols: used for placing textual definitions in the diagram.

Signal definitions are placed in a **text** symbol, since there is no GR for signal definitions. A *signal definition* has the format:

signal *signal name* [(*sort identifier list*)];

When several signals are conveyed on a channel or signal route (see Section 4.4.2) it is useful to define a shorthand for the list of signals. A *signal list definition* attaches a name to this:

signallist *signal list name* = *signal identifier list*;

The signal list name can then be used as a shorthand. A signal list name is distinguished from signal names by enclosing it in parentheses.

4.4.2 *Partitioning*

A block may be described by a block **substructure** diagram or a block diagram. The two diagrams give different perspectives on the internals of a block. A block substructure is used for further partitioning, whereas the block diagram defines the behaviour of a block in terms of the processes contained in the block. It is possible to give both diagrams for the same block. This is useful if one wants to state the behaviour of a block at several levels of detail. Before interpreting the system it is necessary to indicate which alternative in each block to interpret.

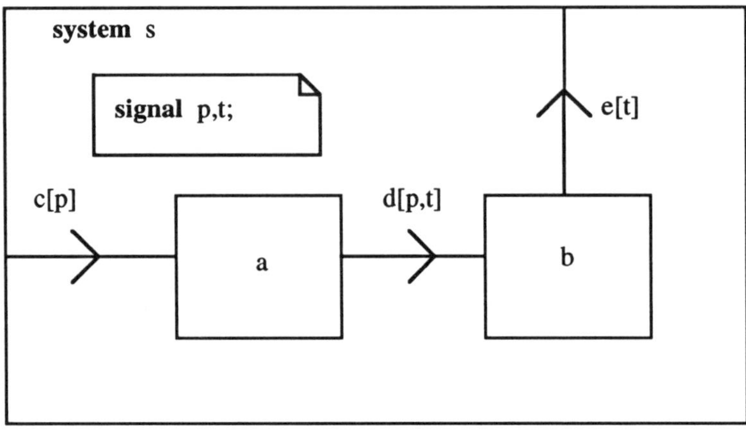

Figure 4.4: Example of a System

Block Substructure

Partitioning into block substructure implies partitioning a block into subblocks which in turn are blocks. This implies new channels within the block substructure. A block substructure looks very much like a system. In fact, a system is a substructure except that signals and sorts defined at the system level are visible outside the system because they are used in communication with the environment of the system. Names defined within a substructure scope are not visible outside that scope according to the normal visibility rules. Figure 4.5 shows a substructure for block *b* from the example in Figure 4.4. The following new construct is used here:

connection points: *d* and *e* are references to the enclosing structure, and indicate how the channels of the surroundings (*d* and *e* in Figure 4.4) are connected to channels in the substructure.

Follow the route of signal *t* from block *a*. It first enters channel *d*, then continues on channel *c1* (*t* must pass along *c1*, since *c4* can only carry signal *p*). The signal then enters block *a1*. The further processing of *t* inside *a1* is not indicated in the substructure diagram. The interfaces of a substructure must match its surroundings, i.e. signals carried by channels of the surroundings leading to or from the substructure must also be carried on channels in the substructure connected to the surroundings of the substructure.

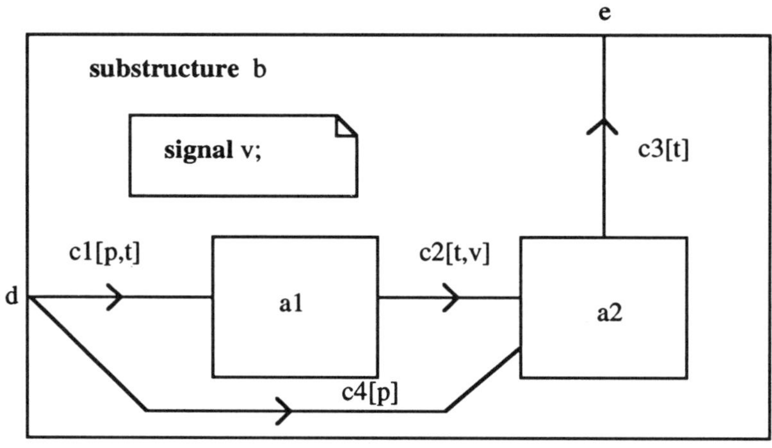

Figure 4.5: Example of a Substructure

Block Diagram

A block consists of processes connected by **signal routes**. A signal route is a communication path without delay; this makes a signal route different from a channel. The conceptual difference between a channel and a signal route is that a channel connects entities in a distributed system, whereas a signal route connects entities at the same node in the distributed system. Going back to the postal analogy, a channel is like a sorting office or main distribution route where delay is inevitable. A signal route, however, is local distribution of letters by a postman. Delivering letters locally can be done without the delay of the public mail system. The syntactic difference between signal routes and channels is that the arrow heads are put in the middle of channels and at the end of signal routes.

The buffering inherent in channels introduces an additional state component, which is not always desirable, so SDL-92 allows for channels without delay. Channels without delay have same semantics as signal routes and therefore the same notation; the arrow heads are placed at the end of the zero-delay channel instead of at the middle.

Figure 4.6 shows the block diagram for the block *a1* in Figure 4.5. The following new constructs are used here:

signal routes: *ri, r2, r3*

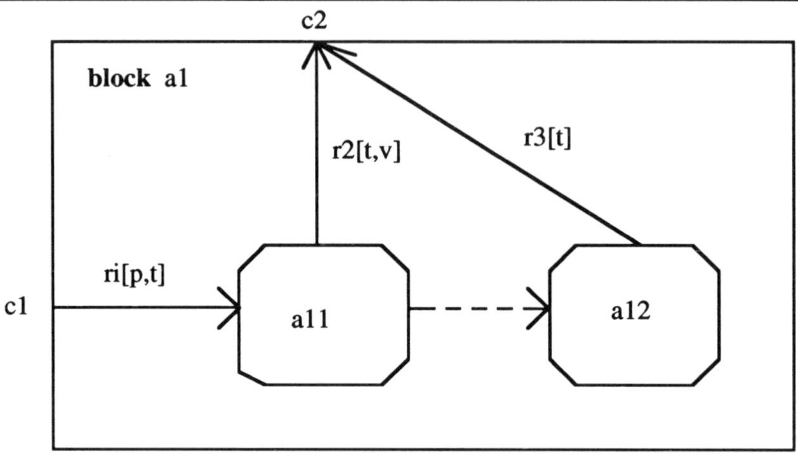

Figure 4.6: Example of a Block

process references: *a11* and *a12*, indicating that diagrams for processes *a11* and *a12* describe the actual behaviour of part of the system

dashed arrow: a dashed **create** arrow, indicating the relation 'can dynamically create' between processes, i.e. an instance of process *a11* may dynamically create an instance of process *a12* (see Section 4.5.4).

Channel Substructure

It is possible to describe a channel further as a composite entity. This is useful when describing layered protocols, or when modelling unreliable communication media. The description of the interconnection medium, which can be described as a lower layer virtual protocol or a model of a physical communication medium, is expressed by giving a substructure for the channel. When interpreting the system, the original channel will not be interpreted, rather its substructure. Figure 4.7 shows a reference to a **channel substructure** in block substructure *b*. The following new constructs are used here:

channel substructure reference: *c3*, indicating that the detailed behaviour of the channel is described in a separate diagram

dashed line: this connects the channel substructure reference symbol and the channel.

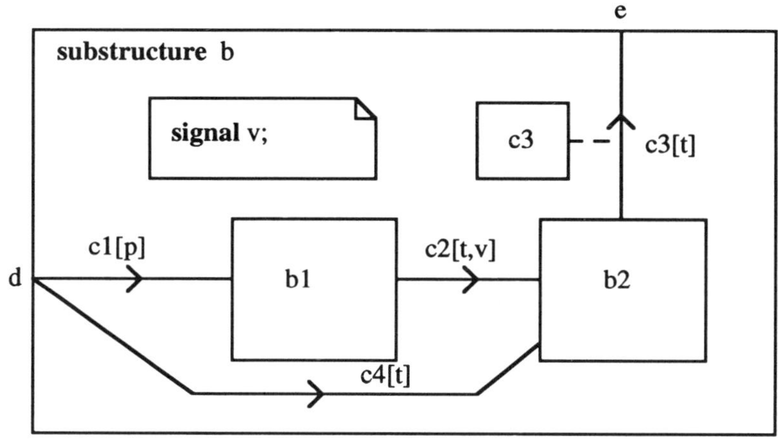

Figure 4.7: Example indicating Channel Substructure

A channel substructure has the same components as a block substructure. Figure 4.8 shows the channel substructure corresponding to channel *c3* in Figure 4.7. The names at the frame connection points of the channel substructure diagram are names of the blocks which the substructured channel connects. Environment **env** always denotes the surroundings of the substructured entity. In this example, **env** denotes the system scope.

In Figure 4.8, a one-way communication on the channel *c3* is refined into a two-way communication between the blocks *cs1* and *cs2* using the new channels *cf (channel forwards)* and *cb (channel backwards)*. This example illustrates the refinement of a file system where the signal *t* holds a whole file and the signals *r, i, n* within the channel substructure correspond to a record, the number of record in the file, and getting the next record respectively.

4.4.3 *Macros*

A **macro** is a part of a diagram or text which can be used in more than one place in a description. In the following, only macro diagrams will be described. A macro diagram can be used in any diagram. The use of a macro at a certain place in a diagram is indicated by the **macro call** symbol, shown in Figure 4.9. A macro may be called with actual macro parameters which are then substituted for the macro formal parameters in the call. Macro formal parameters are indicated by **fpar**. In the macro call, the lines connected to the macro call

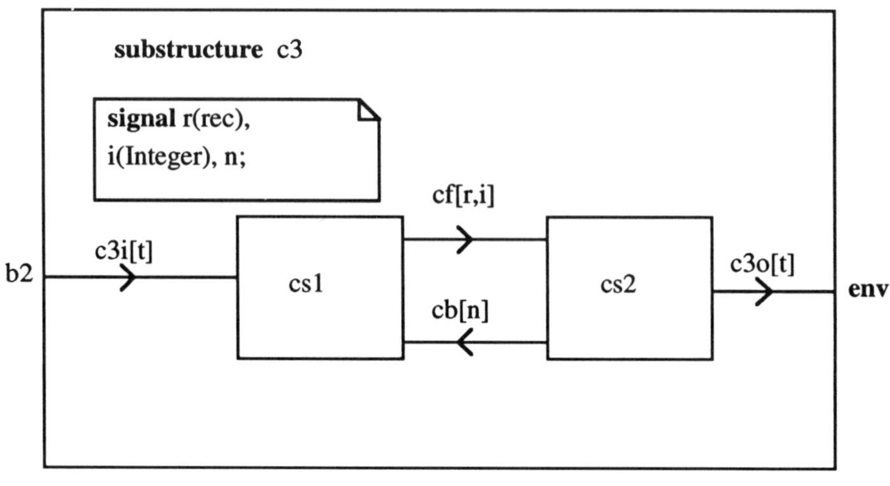

Figure 4.8: Example of a Channel Substructure

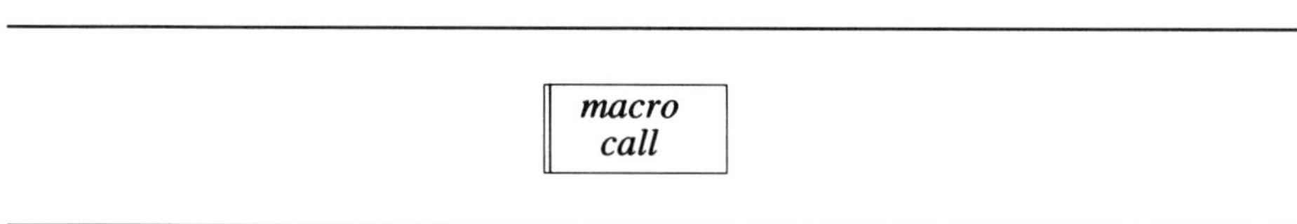

Figure 4.9: Macro Call Symbol

symbol are connected to the lines in the macro definition according to the names of the entry points in the definition. The macro concept is powerful, but there are few semantic rules associated with macros, e.g. no type checking of macro actual/formal parameters is possible. Figure 4.10 shows the macro definition *t* with entry/exit points *a*, *b* and *c* and formal parameter *x*. Figure 4.11 shows one call of this macro. Note that *k* will convey a non-negative value on both branches.

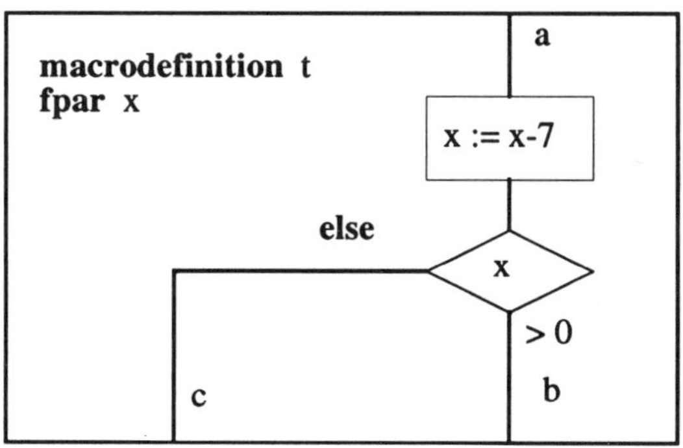

Figure 4.10: Example Macro Definition

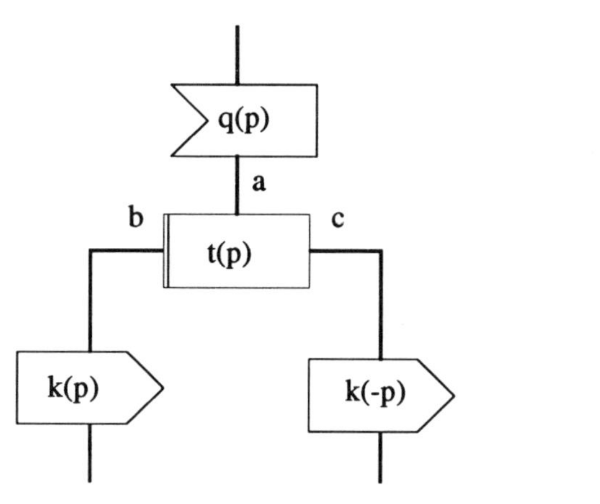

Figure 4.11: Example Macro Call

4.5 Behaviour

4.5.1 *Lifetime of a Process*

After describing the structure of the system (the blocks and process references) and the associated interfaces (channels and signal routes with signal lists), the behaviour of the system can be described. This is done by describing **processes**.

Be careful to distinguish between the definition of a process and the various instances of a process. The definition is the template for prescribing the behaviour of process instances. The instances are objects in the interpreted system. A process has the following features:

lifetime: an instance is created either at system initialisation or dynamically by another **process** instance (see Section 4.5.4); it ceases to exist when it interprets a **stop** symbol (see Section 4.5.1)

parameters: the actual values are assigned by the parent process instance during the dynamic creation of the instance

variables: these form in combination with the control state, the complete state of the instance

input port: it receives and holds signals until consumption

input-set, output-set: the sets of signals used by the process, i.e. the interface of the process; the input-set is especially important for understanding the convenient shorthands used in **inputs** and **saves**.

The format of a process diagram is shown in Figure 4.12. A *process heading* has the format:

process *process name* [*number of instances*] [**fpar** *formal parameter list*]

where the *number of instances* has the format:

([*initial numbers*] [, [*maximum numbers*]])

and a *formal parameter* has the format:

variable name list sort identifier

The *initial numbers* value denotes the number of instances for the process created at system initialisation, i.e. by static creation. It is optional and defaults to 0. The *maximum numbers* value denotes the maximum number of process instances of the process that may exist at any time. It is optional, and when omitted implies no limit. The following example shows the heading of a process:

process p (1, 5) **fpar** x Integer;

where *(1, 5)* means that one instance of the process will be created at system initialisation time, i.e. statically, and that a maximum of 5 instances can exist concurrently. Process *p* has one formal parameter of name *x* and sort *Integer.*

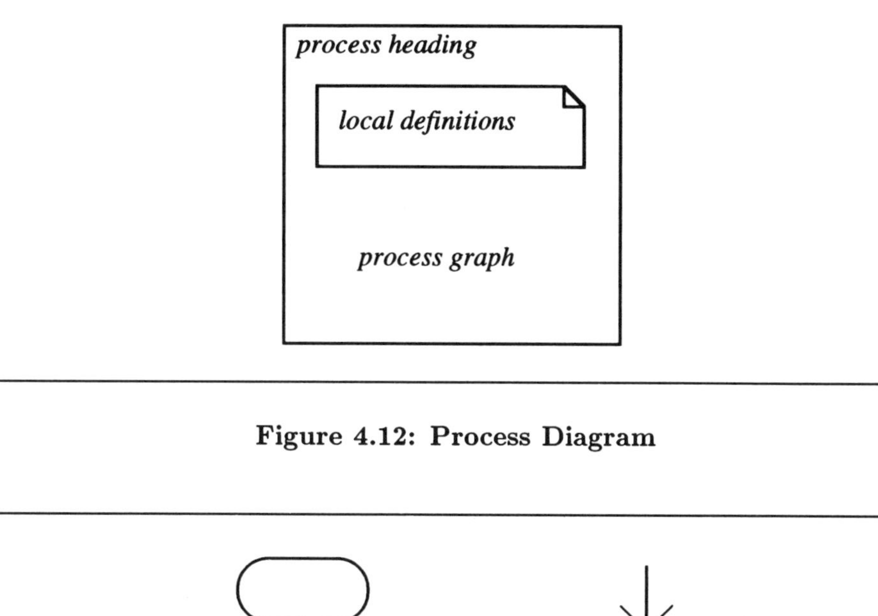

Figure 4.12: Process Diagram

Figure 4.13: Start and Stop Symbols

Initiating a Process Instance

Interpretation of a process instance starts by:

- assigning the value of the actual parameters to the formal parameters of the process
- creating and possibly initialising the variables of the process
- interpreting the start node of the **process graph**.

The start node is indicated by the **start** symbol as shown in Figure 4.13. No text is written inside this symbol. The start node is a normal transition.

Terminating a Process Instance

Interpretation of a process graph stops when the **stop** symbol is processed. This symbol is shown in Figure 4.13. It is possible for several stop symbols

Figure 4.14: State Symbol

to appear in a process. When interpretation of the graph stops, the process instance ceases to exist.

4.5.2 *State*

When a process is in a state it accepts stimuli from its input port. These stimuli can be signals received by the input port or expired timers (see Section 4.5.6). Spontaneous transitions from states is added in SDL-92 (see Section 4.8.2). The **state** symbol is shown in Figure 4.14. A *state list* has the format:

state name list | ∗ [(*state name list*)]

where '∗' indicates all states of a process. If a process reacts in the same way to the same stimulus in all states, this notation can be used. The optional *state name list* after '∗' indicates all states except those in the list.

The same state may appear at several places in a process. This is advantageous if the description is structured with respect to received signals instead of being structured with respect to states.

4.5.3 *Initiating a Transition*

The basic way of initiating a transition is through input of a signal from the input port of the instance. However, by using the syntactic shorthands **continuous signal** and **enabling condition** it is possible to initiate a transition based on a logical condition. By means of the **save** construct it is possible to change the order of signal consumption.

Consuming Signals

The **input** symbols connected to the state indicate:

- the variables that are assigned the values carried by the consumed signal
- the transition initiated by consuming the signal.

Figure 4.15: Input Symbol

Before the input symbol corresponding to the consumed signal is interpreted, the value of **sender** gets updated so that it denotes the *PId* value of the process that sent the signal. The input symbol is shown in Figure 4.15. An *input list* has the format:

stimulus list | ∗

where a *stimulus* has the format:

{*signal identifier* | *timer identifier*} [(*variable identifier list*)];

The symbol '∗' indicates reception of all valid input signals and timers that are not mentioned in a certain state. The set of valid input signals consists of signals conveyed by signal routes to the process and signals defined locally in the process. The notation is used if a process reacts in the same way to all stimuli in a certain state.

Keeping Signals in the Input Port

Every valid input signal not mentioned in a state (without the **input** ∗ shorthand attached) will implicitly be consumed by the process in the state. In such a case the input results in an empty transition leading back to the same state. Signals not explicitly mentioned in an input are thus effectively discarded. To retain signals in the input port, the **save** construct must be used.

Mentioning a signal in a **save** attached to a state means that the signal will not be retrieved from the input port and consumed in that state. Eventually it will be consumed in a successive state where it is not mentioned in a **save**. The same mechanism can be used for timers (see Section 4.5.6). The **save** symbol is shown in Figure 4.16. A *save list* has the format:

signal or timer identifier list | ∗

where a *signal or timer identifier* has the format:

signal identifier | *timer identifier*

The symbol '∗' indicates saving of all valid input signals and timers that are not mentioned in a certain state. This is useful for modelling a persistent input port where a signal is always explicitly dealt with.

Figure 4.16: Save Symbol

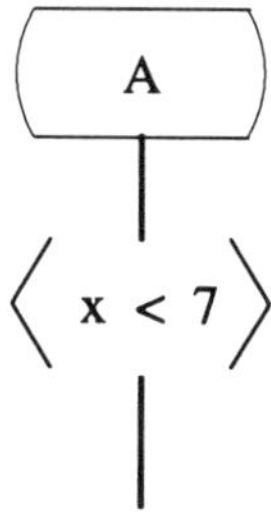

Figure 4.17: Example of Continuous Signal

Continuous Signals

A **continuous signal** allows the initiation of a transition without signal reception. The transition following the continuous signal will be taken only if its Boolean condition has the value *True*. A continuous signal is convenient for describing situations that do not lend themselves naturally to signal reception. Figure 4.17 shows such a situation, where a process can spontaneously leave state A if x is less than 7.

The priority for initiating a continuous signal is lower than that for initiating signal reception, i.e. a transition can only be initiated by a continuous signal if no signal can be consumed.

Enabling Conditions

An **enabling condition** is a continuous signal followed by an input. The input will be consumed only if the Boolean condition of the continuous signal has the value *True*. This construct is useful for modelling conditional consumption of a signal.

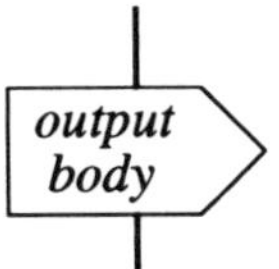

Figure 4.18: Output Symbol

4.5.4 *Transition*

A transition may contain the following actions:

output: to send signals

task: to change the value of variables

create: to create process instances

decision: to branch into alternative sequences

call: to activate procedures

set, reset: to manipulate timers (see Section 4.5.6).

Sending a Signal

Sending a signal is indicated by an **output** symbol. The symbol with its output body is shown in Figure 4.18. An *output body* has the format:

send signal address information

where a *send signal* has the format:

signal identifier [(*expression list*)]

and *address information* has the format[3]:

[**to** *receiver*] [**via** [**all**] *path*];

The *expression list* applies only if the signal is defined to convey values. The expressions must be of appropriate sorts according to the definition of the *signal identifier*.

The *receiver* is a *PId* value that denotes a uniquely identified receiving instance or the identifier of a process. If it is a *PId* value, it may utilise the information in **self**, **sender**, **offspring** or **parent** expressions. If *receiver* is

[3]The use of **all** and a process identifier as *receiver* are in SDL-92 extensions relative to SDL-88.

a process identifier, the signal is sent to an arbitrary instance of the process denoted. The *path* denotes a list of communicating paths that are the signal routes and channels on which the signal sent must be conveyed. The keyword **all** denotes a broadcast of the signal via all communication paths mentioned in *path*. By analogy with the postal service, the *receiver* is the address details normally written on an envelope, and the *path* is the optional sticker 'via Air Mail'.

If the **to** clause is omitted, the *receiver* is decided from the static structure solely. This may introduce some non-determinism into the addressing. Again by analogy with the postal service, omitting the *receiver* results in less well defined actions by the postal service to deliver the letter correctly. (Non-determinism in the case of no *receiver* is a simplification in SDL-92 compared to SDL-88.)

Changing the Value of Variables

Values of variables are manipulated in tasks that can be informal or formal. Although SDL is an FDT, informal specifications are formally *(sic)* allowed in:

- tasks
- questions and answers of decisions
- axioms in sort definitions.

These constructs deal with the formal handling of data, but they are internal to a process or sort. This ensures formality in the interfaces but allows informality within process and sort definitions. Informal text must, of course, be formalised before the description can be considered complete, but in some cases a description with some informal text left may be useful. This might apply:

- during development work, when the formal description has not yet been fully elaborated
- when parts of the specification are intentionally left open-ended.

Syntactically, informal text is written as a character string. Naturally, there are no interpretation rules for informal text. Figure 4.19 shows the format of formal and informal tasks. An *assignment statement* has the format:

variable identifier := *expression*

Figure 4.20 shows an example where the same meaning (hopefully) is expressed by formal and informal tasks.

The **set** and **reset** operations on timers (described in Section 4.5.6) and the **export** operations (described in Section 4.5.8) are also written inside the **task** symbol, but they are conceptually not tasks.

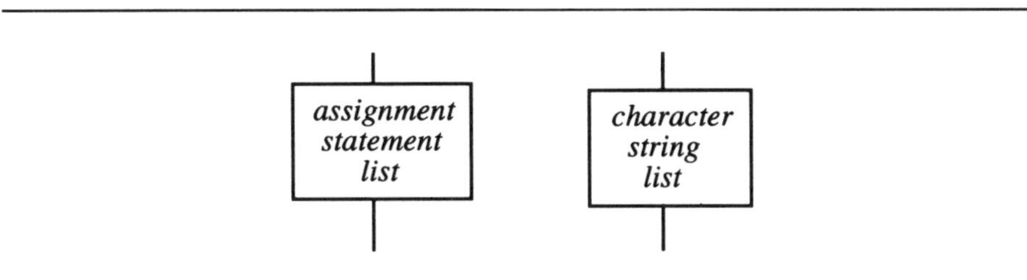

Figure 4.19: Formal and Informal Tasks

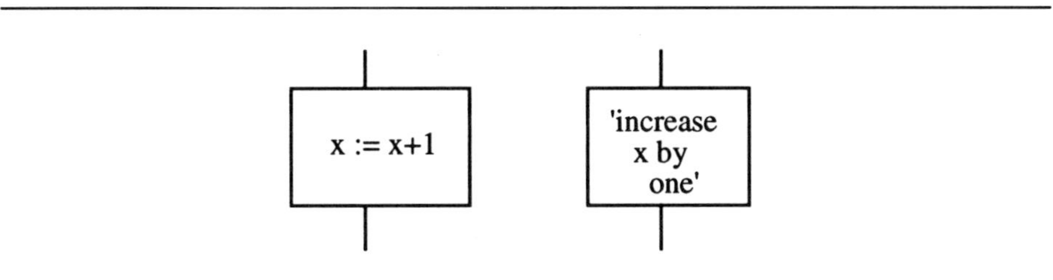

Figure 4.20: Example of 'Equivalent' Formal and Informal Tasks

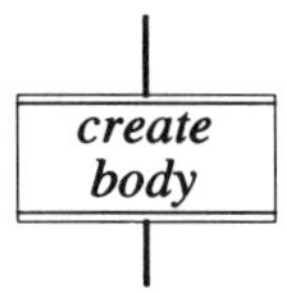

Figure 4.21: Create Symbol

Creation of Process Instances

Dynamic creation of a process instance can be requested by an existing instance in the same block. The reason for restricting creation to processes within the same block is the visibility rules: the name of the process for which a new instance is created must be visible to the creating instance. In practice, this restriction means that every block must contain at least one process with a non-zero *initial numbers*. Such a process is often referred to as a monitor process for the block.

Dynamic creation is indicated by a **create** symbol. The symbol is shown in Figure 4.21. A *create body* has the format:

process identifier [(*actual parameter expression list*)]

During creation, the values of the actual parameters are assigned to the formal parameters of the created process instance.

If an attempt is made to interpret a create symbol when the maximum number of instances of the process already exist (as indicated in *number of instances*), no instance is created and **offspring** of the process attempting the create has the value *Null*.

Branching

Branching in a transition is expressed by the **decision** symbol. A decision can be formal or informal. It consists of a question (formal or informal) followed by a number of branches, each associated with an answer (formal or informal). The format of the decision symbol with its associated *question* is shown in Figure 4.22. A *question* has the format:

informal text | *expression*

while each *answer* has the format:

(*informal text*) | (*value range list*) | *informal text* |
value range list | **else**

An example of a formal answer is : −5, 2:3, >4. This *value range list* corresponds to the values −5, 2, 3, 4, ...

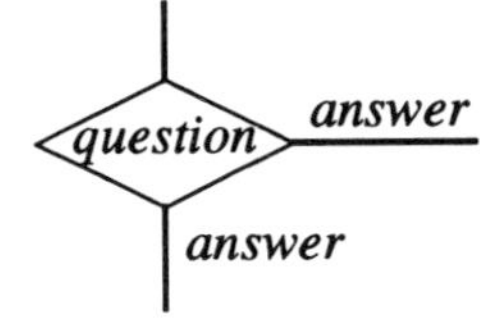

Figure 4.22: Decision Symbol

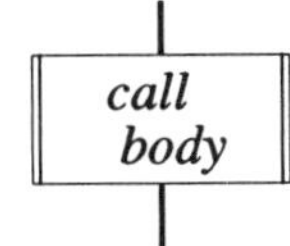

Figure 4.23: Procedure Call Symbol

If the *question* is *informal text* then there is no formal semantics for branching. How the *answer* branches are connected to the symbol is not defined in the language, since it will be likely to depend on the actual number of branches of a decision.

Calling Procedures

Part of a process can be described in a **procedure**. The definition of procedures is described in Section 4.5.7. The **procedure call** symbol with its call body is shown in Figure 4.23. A *call body* has the format:

procedure identifier [(*actual parameter expression list*)]

4.5.5 *Terminating a Transition*

Nextstate

A transition is terminated by a **nextstate** symbol containing the name of the next state. This symbol is the same as the **state** symbol, and the combined use of **state** and **nextstate** in the same symbol is often preferable. The **nextstate** symbol is shown in Figure 4.24. A *next state* has the format:

state name | -

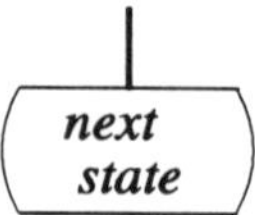

Figure 4.24: Nextstate Symbol

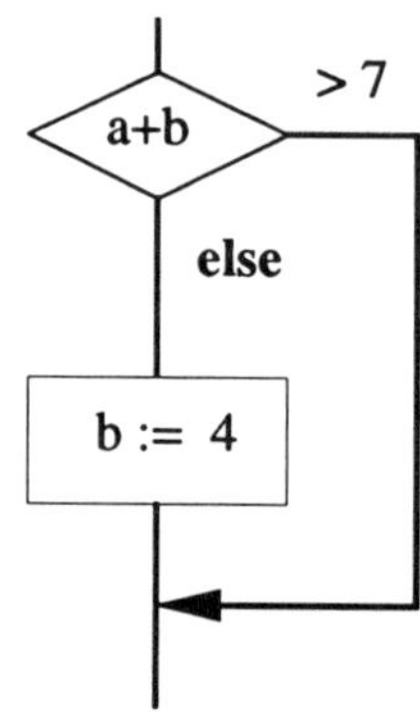

Figure 4.25: Merging Transitions

where '-' indicates that the next state is the same as the originating state of the transition, i.e. there is no change in the state name.

Connector

Branches of transitions can directly merge as illustrated in Figure 4.25. If this is not convenient for drawing, out-connectors and in-connectors can be used as shown in Figure 4.26. Several out-connectors may be used with the same in-connector.

Unrestricted use of connectors can lead to unreadable diagrams showing little useful structure. Some conventions should be imposed on the use of connectors. However, these conventions are not part of the language definition.

4.5.6 *Time*

For handling time, there are facilities:

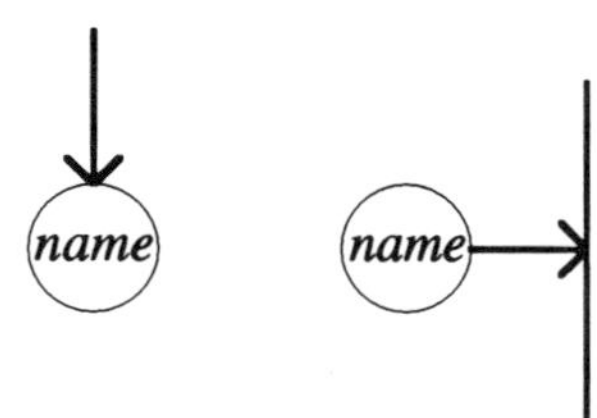

Figure 4.26: Out-Connectors and In-Connectors

- to deal with values associated with time in two predefined sorts, *Time* and *Duration*
- to read the actual time
- to do time supervision by means of **timers**
- to react to expired **timers**
- to inspect the status of **timers**.

Sorts Associated with Time

The two predefined sorts for handling time are *Time* and *Duration*. *Time* expresses moments in time, whereas *Duration* expresses time intervals. Both have similar properties as the predefined sort *Real*. This means that *Time* and *Duration* values are written as decimal floating-point numbers. It is not part of the language to relate values of *Time* and *Duration* to real-world time denotations like '5.25 pm GMT'.

Reading the Actual Time

The actual, global time is read by the imperative **now** operator (see Section 4.6.2) that returns a value of sort *Time*. It is assumed that a global time can be read by process instances. Of course, only local assumptions based on reading a global time can be made by processes in a distributed system. How time proceeds in the interpretation of a process instance is left for the particular implementation.

Time Supervision

Time supervision is handled through the use of **timers**. A timer is similar in concept to a signal. A *timer definition* has the format:

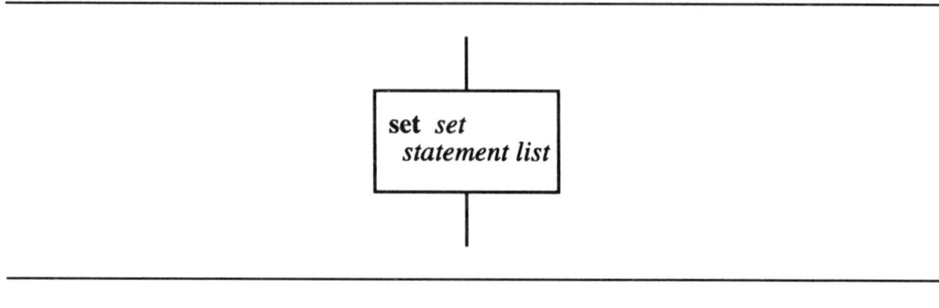

Figure 4.27: Set in Task Symbol

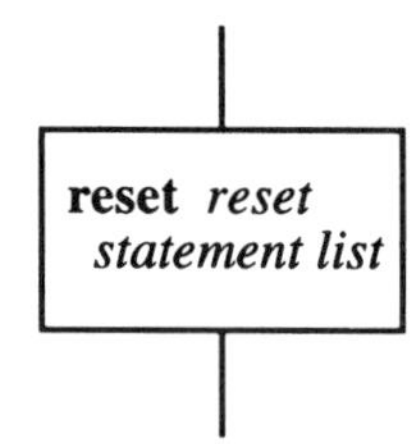

Figure 4.28: Reset in Task Symbol

timer *timer name* [(*sort identifier list*)];

The optional *sort identifier list* can be used to distinguish between several instances of the same timer by supplying different values for each instance according to the sort list.

It is possible to **set** and **reset** a timer. A timer is set with an expiry time. When the expiry time is reached, a signal with the name of the timer is inserted in the input port of the process instance. Eventually, this signal can be handled in an input, which holds the name and values of the timer.

The keywords **set** and **reset** are written inside a task symbol. Use of **set** is shown in Figure 4.27. A *set statement* has the format:

(*time expression*, *timer identifier* [(*expression list*)])

The *time expression* denotes the expiry time, i.e. the time when a signal with the name *timer identifier* and the parameters indicated by *expression list* will be inserted in the input port.

A timer is cancelled by a **reset** statement. Use of **reset** is shown in Figure 4.28. A *reset statement* has the format:

timer identifier [(*expression list*)]

Setting a timer, which is already set, implies overwriting the original expiry time. Setting a timer to an earlier expiry time than the actual time **now**, causes an immediate insertion of the timer signal in the input port. Resetting a timer that is not set has no effect.

When the timer is set and neither consumed from the input port nor reset, it is said to be active. An imperative Boolean operator **active** (see Section 4.6.2) returns the status of a timer. An *active expression* has the format:

active(*timer identifier* [(*expression list*)])

4.5.7 *Procedure*

A procedure is a parameterised part of a process with its own scope, for sorts and variables, for example. It has a local scope for states and connectors. Other kinds of names from the enclosing scope (e.g. variables, synonyms and sorts) are visible in the procedure. A procedure can have two kinds of parameters, **in** and **in/out**:

- Actual parameters corresponding to formal **in** parameters are expressions, and the values of these expressions are assigned to the formal parameters. This kind of parameter passing is 'call by value'.
- Actual parameters corresponding to formal **in/out** parameters are variable identifiers, and the formal parameters are synonyms for these variables during the interpretation of the procedure. This kind of parameter passing is 'call by reference'.

The format of a procedure diagram is shown in Figure 4.29. A *procedure heading* has the format:

procedure *procedure name* **fpar** *procedure formal parameter list*

where a *procedure formal parameter* has the format:

[**in** | **in/out**] *variable name list* *sort identifier*

A **procedure graph** contains the same symbols as a process graph except that the start symbol is replaced by the **start procedure** symbol, and the stop symbol is replaced by the **return** symbol. The specific procedure symbols are shown in Figure 4.30. When the procedure is called, the interpretation begins in the start procedure symbol, and control returns to the calling process or procedure when the return symbol is interpreted.

4.5.8 *Communication via Shared Values*

Values can be communicated between process instances only by means of signal interchange since all variables are local to process instances. In some cases

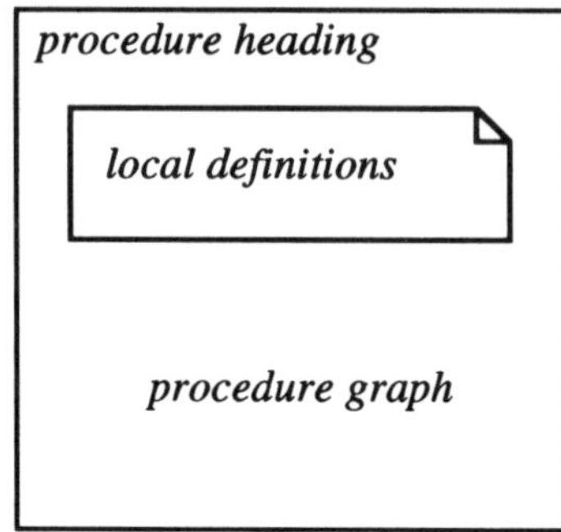

Figure 4.29: Procedure Diagram

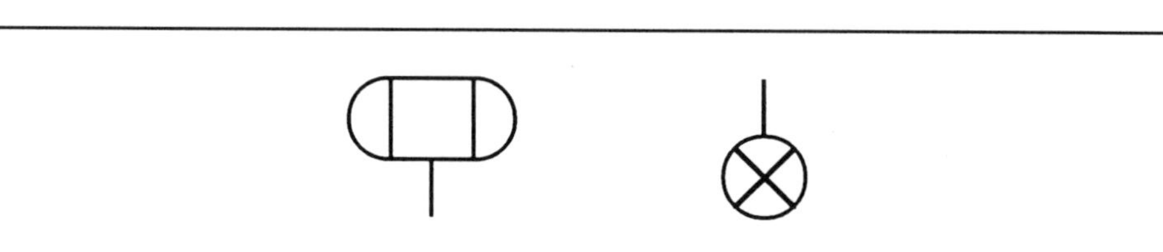

Figure 4.30: Procedure Start and Return Symbols

Figure 4.31: Export Operation in Task Symbol

this is not a very elegant approach, e.g. when the behaviour of one process depends on a value maintained by another process. The use of **view/reveal** and **import/export** allows such relations. The most important difference between **view/reveal** and **import/export** is that **import/export** includes an explicit **export** operation that restricts reading of composite variables to well-defined situations. Another difference is that **import/export** is based on signal interchange.

Reading within a Block

In the case of a **revealed** variable, the value of a variable may be read within the same block by any process instances that has introduced the name of the variable in a **view** definition. A *view definition* has the format:

viewed *viewed name* *sort identifier*

The variable in the owning process must have the attribute **revealed** in its variable declaration (see Section 4.6.2). The value of the variable can then be read through the imperative **view** operator (see Section 4.6.2) with the format:

view(*viewed name*, [*PId expression*])

The **view** construct is an exception to the rules of signal interfaces, and is not recommended in general. It is part of SDL for backwards compatibility with early versions of SDL.

Export and Import of Values

Export and import can be used for reading values from other instances all over the system. This construct is a shorthand modelled by signal interchange in the basic language model. The variable whose value is to be exported must have the attribute **exported** in its declaration. The owning instance can then make the actual value of the variable available to other processes by using the **export** construct in a task symbol. The format of the **export** operation is shown in Figure 4.31.

The importing process must introduce the name in an *import definition* of the format:

imported *imported name sort identifier*

The importing process obtains the most recently exported value of the variable through an imperative *import operation* (see Section 4.6.2) of the format:

import(*import name* [, *receiver*])

The *sort identifier* used in the variable declaration of the exporting process must be the same as the *sort identifier* used in the importing process. The use of the *receiver* value is as for *output*.

4.6 Data

4.6.1 *Introduction*

Any value belongs to a certain **sort**. A **sort** defines a set of values constructed by **literals** and **operators**. A **literal** is a name of a value, e.g. *7* and *007* are valid literals for the same *Integer* value. The operator '+' is an example of an *Integer* operator. The sort of a variable defines the set of values that can be stored in the variable.

The semantics of operators are expressed by **axioms**. An axiom is an equation that defines the expression on the left hand side to have the same value as the expression on the right hand side. The expressions are called terms. The basic model (Ehrig and Mahr (1985)) implies that two terms denote different values if they are syntactically different and not made equal by axioms, either directly or indirectly.

The semantics of a type (sort and operators) is not defined solely by the axioms given in the definition of the type, but by all visible type definitions that mention the sort operators. Data types are not represented graphically using GR syntax.

4.6.2 *Use of Data*

Variable

A variable is defined in a process and is local to a process instance. A *variable definition* has the format:

dcl [*attribute*] *variable name list sort identifier* [:= *initial value*];

where an *attribute* has the format:

revealed | **exported** | **revealed exported** | **exported revealed**

The attributes **revealed** and **exported** define a variable as being respectively **revealed** and **exported** (see Section 4.5.8).

As an example, the definition of an *Integer* variable *x* with initial value *7* looks like:

dcl x Integer := 7;

Expression

In addition to **literals** and **operators**, expressions contain synonyms, conditional expressions, imperative operators and accesses to variables.

Expressions are written in the usual style. A number of predefined operators exist, e.g. '+' and **or**. They are written using infix notation, e.g. $A + B$, *A* **or** *B*. The predefined operators have the normal binding priority, e.g. in $2 * 3 + 4$, '*' takes priority over '+'. User-defined operators are normally used in prefix form, e.g. an operator *opx* taking *a*, *b* and *c* as operands in an expression is written *opx(a,b,c)*.

As an example of an expression, the variable *x* introduced above can be used in:

(x > 0) **and** True **or** (x < 0) **and** False

The operator **and** takes priority over **or** so the expression has the same value as $x > 0$.

Overloading of operators is allowed, so the same operator may be used in different contexts, e.g. '+' can be used both in *Real* and *Integer* expressions.

A synonym is a name for the value of an expression. It is useful for attaching a symbolic name to some general value. A *synonym definition* has the format:

synonym *synonym name* [*sort identifier*] = *ground expression*;

The *sort identifier* may be omitted if the sort can be derived from the expression. An example of a synonym for an *Integer* expression is:

synonym number_of_deposits = 0;

A conditional expression denotes one of two expressions depending on a condition. A *conditional expression* has the format:

```
if Boolean expression
    then Expression1
    else Expression2
fi
```

If the *Boolean expression* evaluates to *True* the value of the *conditional expression* is *Expression1* else it is *Expression2*. As an example, *x* can be assigned according to some condition:

```
x :=
    if overdrawn
        then number_of_withdrawals
        else number_of_deposits
    fi;
```

Name	Literals	Operators
Boolean	*True*, *False*	**not**, **and**, **or**, **xor**, =>
Char	characters enclosed by ' '	<, <=, >, >=
Integer	..., -1, 0, 1, ...	−, +, −, ∗, /, <, <=, >, >=, *Float*, *Fix*
Natural	0, 1, 2, ..	as *Integer*
Real	..., -1, 0, 1, ... -9.99, ..., 5.86, ...	−, +, −, ∗, /, <, <=, >, >=
PId	*Null*	none
Duration	as *Real*	+, −, >, ∗, /
Time	as *Real*	+, −, −, <, <=, >, >=
Charstring	characters enclosed by ' '	*MkString*, *Length*, *First*, *Last*, //, *(index)*, *SubString(string, start position, length)*

Figure 4.32: Predefined Sorts with their Literals and Operators

An imperative operator is an operator whose result does not depend solely on the values of its parameters. The imperative operators are:

now: the actual time

self, parent, offspring, sender: *PId* expressions for addressing

import: imported value

view: viewed value

active: status of timer

any: any value of a sort (SDL-92 only).

Predefined Sorts

Many specifications can be written without defining new sorts because a wide selection of predefined sorts are available. The predefined sorts are listed together with their literals and operators in Figure 4.32.

Integer and *Real* both provide '−' for negation and binary subtraction. *Float* and *Fix* are used to convert between *Integer* and *Real*. *Natural* is a **syntype** (see Section 4.6.5) of non-negative *Integers*. The predefined number sorts have radix 10. *PId* is further described in Section 4.2. *Charstring* is based on the string generator described in Section 4.6.4. *MkString* accepts a *Char* and returns a

Charstring of length 1. '//' is the concatenation operator. The expression *(index)* is used for indexing in extracting or modifying one *Char* in the *Charstring*.

In addition to the operators explicitly defined for a sort, all sorts have the Boolean operators '=' and '/=' (different from) predefined.

4.6.3 *Definition of New Sorts*

A data *sort definition* consists of a **signature** and **properties** in the format:

newtype *data sort name*
signature properties
endnewtype [*data sort name*];

The *signature* defines the literals and the operators with the sorts of their operands and result. The *properties* value defines the semantics of the literals and operators.

A sort definition may also contain constructs which map the spelling of the literals onto the values of the sort, e.g. it is necessary to formally define that the literal *7* has the same value as *007*. This is not further elaborated here.

Signature

A *signature* has the format:

literals *literal list*
operators *operator signature list*

where an *operator signature* has the format:

operator name : *argument sort list* –> *result sort*

The elements in an *operator signature list* are separated by ';'.

Properties

The *properties* are given as a list of *equations*. The elements in *properties* are separated by ';'. An *equation* has the format:

unquantified equation | *quantified equation* |
conditional equation | *informal text*

where an *unquantified equation* has the format:

left hand term == *right hand term*

The symbol '==' denotes the defining equality of an equation, whereas '=' denotes a Boolean operator.

In axioms it is possible to use so-called axiomatic variables, which are names representing any value of a certain sort in the axiom. If the sort of an axiomatic variable cannot be uniquely determined from its use, it must be explicitly introduced in a *quantified equation* of the format:

for all *value name list* **in** *sort identifier* (*properties*)

Name	Parameters
String	element type, empty list literal
Array	element type, index type
Powerset	member type

Figure 4.33: Predefined Generators

A *conditional equation* holds when some restrictions, written as *unquantified equations*, are met. The elements in an *unquantified equation list* are separated by ';'. A *conditional equation* has the format:

unquantified equation list ==> *unquantified equation*

The *unquantified equation* is considered only if the equations in the *unquantified equation list* can be derived from other equations of the sort.

Finally, it is possible to stipulate properties of a sort as informal text instead of as formal equations[4].

4.6.4 *Generator*

A **generator** is a parameterised type that can be instantiated to form more complete type definition. It may have the following kinds of parameters: type, literal, operator, constant. The use of generators will be described with only the predefined sort generators shown in Figure 4.33.

Charstring is an example of an instantiation of *String* with the parameters *Char* and '' (empty *Charstring*). *Array* corresponds to an explicitly described function from index sort to item sort. There are no requirements that the index sort of an array is discrete and limited. *Powerset* means a set (not the mathematical meaning of a set of subsets).

A number of operators are available for these predefined generators, e.g. indexing an array and insertion of a member into a *Powerset*.

4.6.5 *Syntype*

A **syntype** is a sort with a restricted set of values with respect to the **newtype** it is based on. An example is the formulation of the predefined sort *Natural*:

syntype Natural = Integer **constants** >= 0;
endsyntype Natural;

[4]SDL-92 allows for alternative definitions of sorts, see Section 4.8.4.

4.6.6 *Shorthands*

Some convenient shorthands for sort definitions are available. They can be mapped onto the constructs described so far. It is possible to base a new sort definition on existing ones by using **inheritance**[5]. This is used for the definition of *Duration*, for example, which inherits features from *Real*. The inheriting sort may add operators, literals and axioms.

The ordering of values of a sort can be indicated by including the word **ordering** in the *operator signature list* of the sort. If the same sort includes a non-empty *literal list*, the literals are implicitly ordered in ascending order. For example, adding **ordering** to the sort *Colour* implies that *Red* < *Yellow*, *Yellow* < *Blue* and *Blue* < *Green*.

A **structure sort** is a composite sort whose values consist of a list of field values. This concept appears as a list, record, tree, etc. in many languages. An example of a structure definition is the definition of the sort *Car*:

```
newtype Car;
    struct
        Brand Manufacturer,
        Year Natural,
        Paint Colour,
        Licence_Number Natural,
        Owner Citizen;
    adding
    literals Herbie;
    axioms BrandExtract!(Herbie) == Volkswagen;
endnewtype Car;
```

This example defines *Car* as a structure. For use in axioms, a **struct** sort has the following operators implied:

Make!:	to build a value from the individual field values
*field name*Modify!:	to modify one field
*field name*Extract!:	to extract one field.

In the example above, *BrandExtract!* extracts the *Brand* field and thus indicates that a *Herbie* car is a *Volkswagen*.

Accessing a field of a **struct** in an expression outside the data type definition or for variable access is denoted by writing the name of the **struct** followed by '!' and the field name. For the following declarations:

```
dcl Vehicle Car, Joe Citizen;
```

the expression:

```
Vehicle!Owner := Joe;
```

[5]This is the only use of inheritance in SDL-88. The object-oriented extensions in SDL-92 allow for a more general use of inheritance in specialisation of types (see Section 4.8.1).

assigns *Joe* as the owner of *Vehicle.* A **struct** value is constructed by enclosing the field values with '(.' and '.)', as in:

```
Vehicle := (. Ford, 1970, Red, 17, Joe .);
```

4.6.7 *Example*

A sort with literals *Red, Yellow, Blue* and *Green* and no explicit operators has the definition:

```
newtype Colour;
   literals Red, Yellow, Blue, Green;
endnewtype Colour;
```

For a value of this sort, the predefined operators '=' and '/=' are available, e.g. one can ask if a *Colour* variable has the value *Red.* Now extend the definition with a *Mix* operator for mixing colours:

- mixing a colour with itself results in same colour
- the order of mixing has no importance
- mixing *Yellow* and *Blue* results in *Green.*

```
newtype Colour;
   literals Red, Yellow, Blue, Green;
   operators Mix: Colour, Colour -> Colour;
   axioms
      Mix(c, c) == c;
      Mix(c1, c2) == Mix(c2, c1);
      Mix(Yellow, Blue) == Green;
endnewtype Colour;
```

These axioms do not exclude the mixing of colours other than *Yellow* and *Blue,* but they do not indicate the result of other possible mixings. (In fact they state that other mixings do not yield *Green.*) The example also illustrates that the literals are just names for some values; a sort can contain values without literals.

4.7 Summary of Symbols

Figure 4.34 shows all symbols of SDL-88, and gives section references except for those symbols marked with '-' which have not been covered.

4.8 New Language Developments

Although it is intended to keep the language stable, SDL-92 has evolved slightly from SDL-88. Changes to SDL-88 are mainly extensions except for a few cases of simplifications. The approach protects the investment in tools, education and work based on SDL-88. This section briefly describes the major extensions.

4.8.1 *Object Orientation*

SDL-92 contains concepts for object-oriented structuring. These concepts include system, block, process and service types that can be instantiated in different contexts. These types have gates which can be connected to communication paths in specific contexts. In addition to these new types, SDL-92 also considers signals, procedures and sorts as types.

A general type (called the **supertype**) can be specialised into more specific types (called **subtypes**). In this specialisation, the subtype **inherits** the properties of the supertype. Specialisation allows a subtype:

- to add properties to those of its supertype and
- to redefine properties marked as virtual in its supertype.

Properties can, for example, be definitions enclosed in the type or state transitions for process types, service types and procedures.

Types can be parameterised. Parameterisation encourages re-use of definitions in different contexts of the same system. A **package** concept allows re-use across systems. A package consists mainly of types.

4.8.2 *Non-Determinism*

Two constructs have been added to SDL-92 for describing non-determinism: spontaneous transitions and undecided values.

A **spontaneous transition** allows non-deterministic initiation of transitions. Several spontaneous transitions may be attached to the same state. A spontaneous transition is denoted by an extension of the format for an *input list*, having value **none**.

An **undecided value** is generated by the new imperative operator **any** (see Section 4.6.2). The operator takes a sort as operand and returns any value of that sort. An *any expression* has the format:

any(*sort identifier*)

As an example, **any** *(Boolean)* returns *True* or *False* in a non-deterministic way. Based on this operator, an undefined decision is introduced. It is denoted by a decision symbol containing the keyword **any** without *answers* indicated.

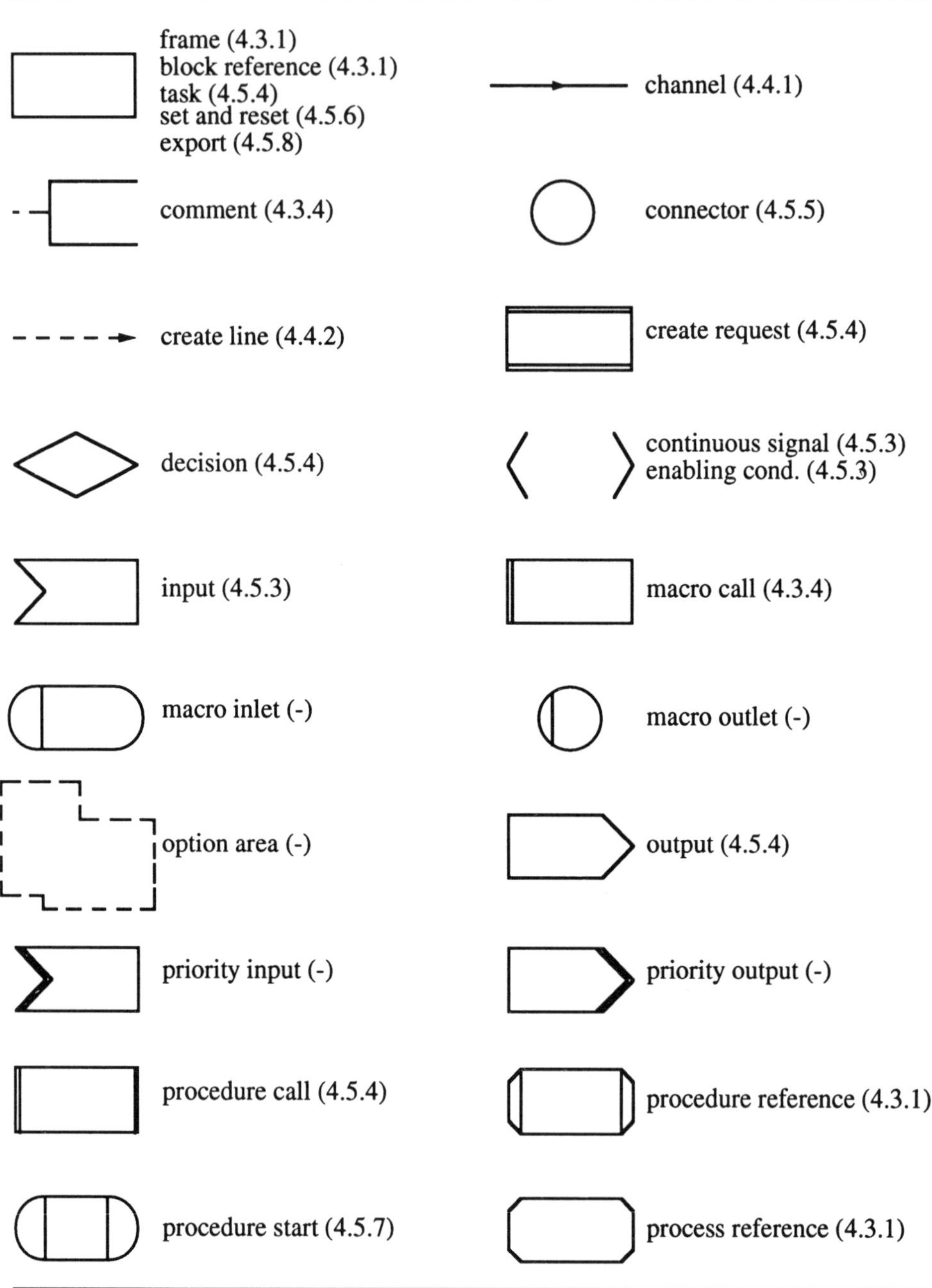

Figure 4.34: Table of Symbols

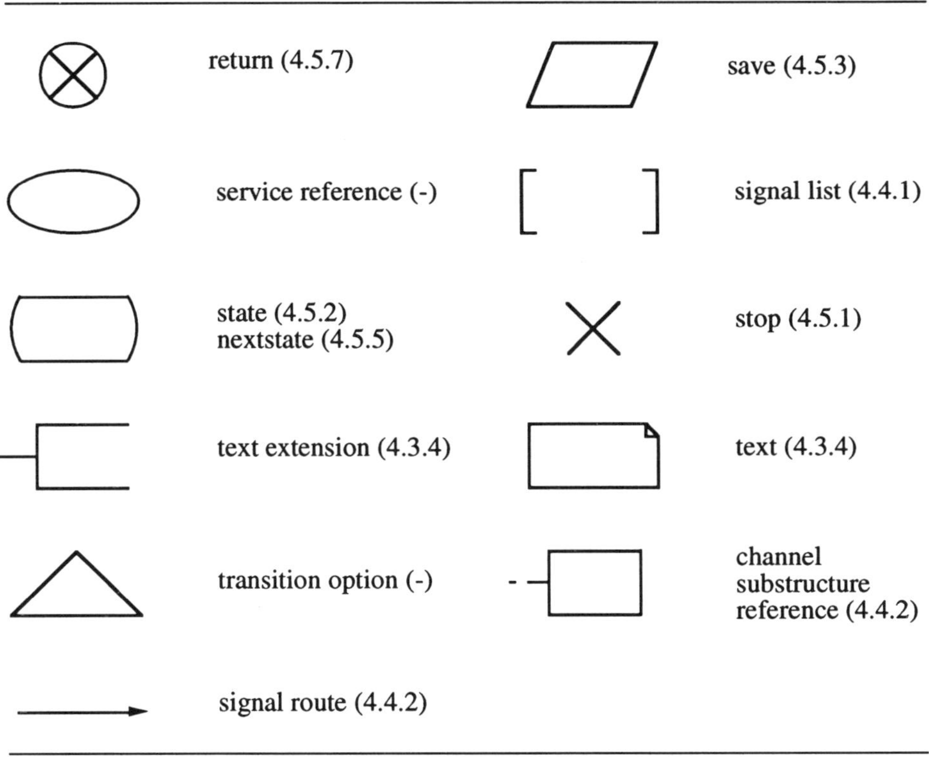

Figure 4.34 *(continued)*

4.8.3 *Extended Procedure Calls*

Procedures that return values are allowed in SDL-92. This implies that procedures can be used in expressions. Remote procedure calls have also been added. This allow a process to call a procedure in another process as if it were defined locally.

The combination of value-returning procedures and remote procedure calls results in a more elegant model than signal interchange in cases of two-way communication.

4.8.4 *Alternatives to Axioms*

SDL-92 offers two alternatives to the axiomatic definition of operators. The properties of an operator can be described by means of a value-returning procedure (without side-effects such as input or output). Instead of giving the properties of a sort in SDL, one may state the *signature* solely and refer to another data formalism (e.g. ASN.1 or C) for supplying the behaviour of the operators of the sort. This opens up the possibility of future links between SDL and other data formalisms

Part II

Specification with the FDTs

This part of the book illustrates each of the FDTs on a graded series of examples, starting with a simple communications service and working up to a large communications protocol. Although the examples have a flavour of data communications, they illustrate general aspects of the FDTs that apply to many other application areas. The examples have been written for readers with little knowledge of data communications, so they should be comprehensible to everyone. The reader should have a working knowledge of the FDTs from Part I of the book before tackling Part II. Individual chapters in this part are as follows:

Chapter 5 specifies the **Daemon Game**, a simple game of chance for multiple players.

Chapter 6 specifies an **Unreliable Medium**, a basic communications service that does not guarantee correct delivery of messages.

Chapter 7 specifies a **Sliding Window Protocol** that can safely transfer messages over an unreliable medium in a flow-controlled manner.

Chapter 8 specifies the **Abracadabra Service**, a connection-oriented service that embodies major features of more complex services.

Chapter 9 specifies the **Abracadabra Protocol** that implements the Abracadabra Service over an unreliable medium.

All the formal descriptions of one example can be read in order to compare the FDTs. Alternatively, all the formal descriptions in one FDT can be read in order to learn how to use it effectively. For some chapter *N*, each example is presented in the following format to facilitate comparison:

Section N.1 gives the informal description of the example that was used to write the formal descriptions.

Section N.2 lists and resolves the faults, omissions and ambiguities that were found in the informal description during the writing of the formal descriptions.

Section N.3 describes the example formally in ESTELLE.

Section N.4 describes the example formally in LOTOS.

Section N.5 describes the example formally in SDL.

Section N.6 summarises the lessons learned from writing the formal descriptions.

Note that the informal descriptions are given just as they were first shown to the specifiers. The errors in the informal descriptions have deliberately not been corrected. The reason for this is that one of the major benefits of using FDTs is to identify errors. By leaving the informal descriptions in their original form, it becomes clearer where the writing of formal descriptions uncovered problems.

The reader might find it educational to scrutinise the informal descriptions for deficiencies before reading what the authors of the formal descriptions found to be wrong. (The lists of errors reported in this book are not guaranteed complete!) The formal descriptions reflect the corrected informal descriptions. The lists of errors have the secondary benefit of indicating the classes of deficiencies that are found in informal descriptions. The conclusion of each chapter tries to categorise and generalise the errors that were found.

To assist reference to the formal descriptions, each major component (type, channel, procedure, process, block, module) is indexed in Appendix B at the end of the book. The formal descriptions of the examples have been harmonised wherever possible. Inevitably there are differences in approach since the characteristics of an FDT often dictate a particular architecture and style of description. At the most fundamental level the FDTs take different views of interactions. Even for one FDT the approach varies from author to author and example to example. This is only to be expected since writing a formal description is hardly a mechanical process; if it were, then it would not need human judgment and skill.

The formal descriptions have been checked with tools as thoroughly as practicable. This is not to say that they are perfect! A formal description may indeed have errors; it would be surprising if the formal description of a large or complex system could be written faultlessly. The important point, however, is that a formal description is unambiguous; it can be *proven* to be wrong in a way that an informal description cannot.

5 Daemon Game

This chapter describes the interface to a multi-player game of chance. Although not presented as a communications example, the game illustrates important features found in many communications systems. Non-determinism and concurrency also arise in this game – major issues in more complex problems. The game was originally devised by R. L. Tenney as a graded series of examples to illustrate ESTELLE.

5.1 Informal Description[1]

The **Daemon Game** is a simple game having several players. The game is the system that is to be defined in a chosen FDT. The players belong to the environment of this system.

In the system there is a daemon that generates *Bump* signals randomly. A player has to guess whether the number of generated *Bump* signals is odd or even. The guess is made by sending a *Probe* signal to the system. The system replies by sending the signal *Win* if the number of the generated *Bump* signals is odd, otherwise by the signal *Lose*.

The system keeps track of the score of each player. The score is initially 0. It is increased by 1 for each successful guess (signal *Win* is sent), and reduced by 1 for each unsuccessful guess (signal *Lose* is sent). A player can ask for the current value of the score by the signal *Result*, which is answered by the system with the signal *Score*.

Before a player can start playing, the player must log in. This is accomplished by the signal *Newgame*. A player logs out by the signal *Endgame*. The system allocates a player a unique identifier on logging in, and de-allocates it on logging out. The system cannot tell whether different identifiers are being used by the same player.

[1] Section 5.1 is by K. J. Turner, based on the original description by R. L. Tenney.

5.2 Errors in the Informal Description[2]

5.2.1 *Presence of Daemon*

Should the daemon be an integral part of the description, or is it an artefact of the informal explanation?

It was not intended that the daemon be part of the system description. However, it was decided to include formal descriptions with and without a daemon in order to show how FDTs can be used to express external behaviour and internal structure. Two versions of the daemon game have therefore been formalised: an explicit version that features the daemon, and an implicit version that does not.

5.2.2 *Login to a Current Game*

What should happen if a player who is already logged in tries to issue *Newgame* again? The informal description does not clearly cover this case.

The intention was to treat games like 'Bingo' game panels with buttons for input and indicators for output. *Newgame* should therefore be allowed to happen in a current game, but should be ignored.

5.2.3 *Attempted Play before Login*

What should happen if a player issues any signal other than *Newgame* before logging into a game? The informal description says that a player must first log in, but does not say what happens if *Newgame* is not the first signal.

The intention was to allow *Probe*, *Result*, or *Endgame* when a game is not current, but to ignore these signals.

5.2.4 *Identification of Players and Games*

The informal description precludes the case of logging into a current game, because it implies that a further login will result in a new game. This contradicts the intended behaviour as described in Section 5.2.2. Presumably some identifiers are needed, but how should they be allocated and what should they distinguish?

The intended behaviour was that each game should be distinguished from the system's point of view by some identifier. The system was not intended to be able to tell which player (or even players) were issuing signals for a game. A player should therefore be able to play multiple games simultaneously without

[2]Section 5.2 is by K. J. Turner, based on problems found by the authors of the formal descriptions.

the system knowing; the players should be an anonymous part of the environment of the system.

5.2.5 *Player Use of System Signals*

What should happen if the player issues *Win*, *Lose*, or *Score* signals?

The intention was to disallow such behaviour: it simply must not happen, as opposed to happening but be ignored.

5.2.6 *Interruption of Probe or Result*

Should it be allowable for another signal to be processed by the system between *Probe* and *Win/Lose*, or between *Result* and *Score*?

The intention was that *Probe* and *Result* should be followed by their respective responses before any other signal is processed.

5.2.7 *Counting of 'Bump' Signals*

In deciding whether a player wins or loses, is it necessary to use the count of *Bump* signals since the system started or since that game started?

The intention was to count the number of *Bump* signals since a game started.

5.3 Formal Description in ESTELLE[3]

5.3.1 *Formal Description with Explicit Daemon*

Figure 5.1 shows the architecture of the daemon game description in ESTELLE using an explicit daemon; a description without an explicit daemon is given in Section 5.3.2. Interaction points are shown as circles and labelled by their names. Those marked with a central dot are bound both by a **connect** and an **attach** and thus logically continue the path of interactions to or from a child module. The description of *ManagerBody* illustrates the dynamic structuring capabilities of ESTELLE. Declaring the *Manager* module to be a **systemprocess** is a way to guarantee fairness in the service provided to the players, because the *Game* modules will be synchronised.

Definitions of bodies for the *Player* and the *Daemon* are not described, as these are not relevant to the description: each may behave in any way consistent with the corresponding channel definition. A *Player* instance corresponds to

[3]Section 5.3 is by R. L. Tenney.

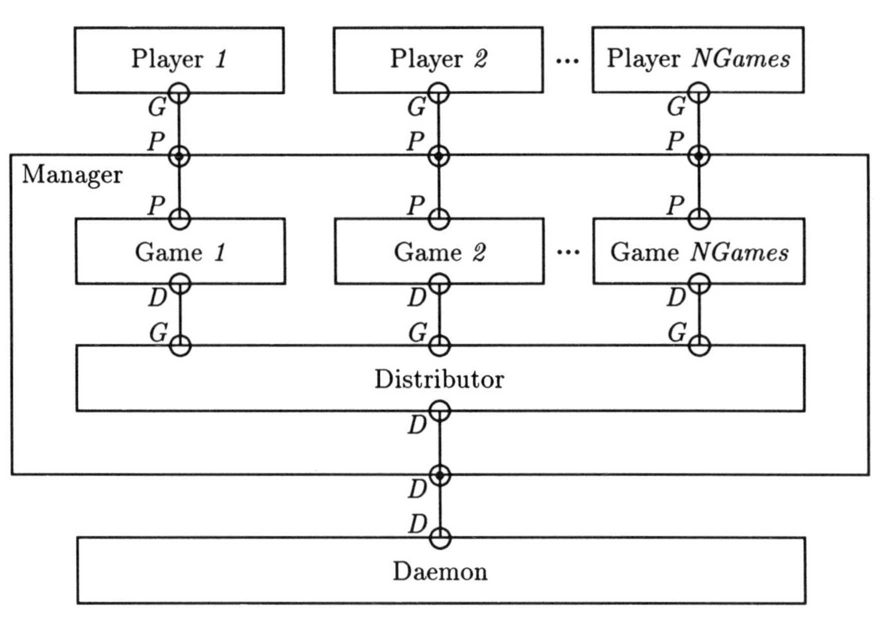

Figure 5.1: Explicit Daemon Game in ESTELLE – Architecture

one game played by a person (with each person possibly playing more than one game).

The *Manager* handles the instantiation and eventual removal of game instances, as the players initiate and terminate them. Once it has established the game, the *GameServer* channel is **attached** by the *Manager* to the newly established games, so that the remaining interactions between the player and the game require no mediation by the *Manager.* The shared variable *Done* is used by the game to indicate to its manager-parent that its user has finished play, so the game should be removed (**released**). This approach is one of several possible; it was chosen to show the use of shared variables.

The game modules simply implement the rules of the game as given in the informal description. The *Distributor* module distributes the daemon's *Bump* signal to each of the games.

The daemon game was originally invented as a graded series of examples, each more complex than the next, to explain ESTELLE. In its original, simplest version, the game had no beginning and no end: it allowed one player, and it did not report a score. In this case, it is unnecessary to have the complex structure given here since there are only empty *Daemon* and *Player* modules, and a *Game* module that has states and no variables. Each version of the game in the series forced the use of more complex ESTELLE constructs until the most complete version of the game (approximating the one given here) made use of a fairly large subset of ESTELLE. The informal description of the game given here was initially written by augmenting the old, original informal description; perhaps that affected some of the design choices.

```
specification DaemonGame;

const NGames = any integer;        { Game limit of implementation }

channel DaemonServer (User, Provider);
  by Provider:
    Bump;

channel GameServer (Player, Machine);
  by Player:
    Probe;                         { Player takes a turn }
    Result;                        { Player requests the score }
    Newgame;                       { Player initiates a game }
    Endgame;                       { Player terminates a game }
  by Machine:
    Win;                           { Tells Player of win }
    Lose;                          { Tells Player of loss }
    Score (nwon: integer);         { Tells Player of score after Result }
```

```
module Daemon systemprocess;
  ip D: DaemonServer (Provider) individual queue;
end; { Daemon }

body DaemonBody for Daemon;
external;

module Player systemprocess;
  ip G: GameServer (Player) individual queue;
end; { Player }

body PlayerBody for Player;
external;

module Manager systemprocess;
  ip
    P: array [1..NGames] of GameServer (Machine) common queue;
    D: DaemonServer (User) common queue;
end; { Manager }

body ManagerBody for Manager;

  module Distributor process;
    ip
      G: array [1..NGames] of DaemonServer (Provider)
        common queue;
      D: DaemonServer (User) common queue;
  end; { Distributor }

  body DistributorBody for Distributor;

  trans
    when D.Bump
      begin
      { Distribute the Bump to all games }
        all i: 1 .. NGames do
          output G[i].Bump
      end;
  end; { DistributorBody }
```

```
module Game process;
  ip
    P: GameServer (Machine) common queue;
    D: DaemonServer (User) common queue;
  export Done: boolean;
end; { Game }

body GameBody for Game;
  var NCorrect: integer;
  state EVEN, ODD;                { Records parity of bumps }
  stateset EITHER = [EVEN, ODD];

  initialize
    to EVEN
      begin
        NCorrect := 0;
        Done := false;
      end;

  trans
    { *** Player makes a guess *** }
    when P.Probe
      from EVEN to EVEN
        begin
          NCorrect := NCorrect - 1;
          output P.Lose
        end;
      from ODD to ODD
        begin
          NCorrect := NCorrect + 1;
          output P.Win
        end;

    { *** Player wants the score *** }
    when P.Result
      from EITHER to same
        begin
          output P.Score(NCorrect)
        end;

    { *** Player is done *** }
```

```
    when P.Endgame
      from EITHER to same
        begin
          Done := true          { Cause Manager to stop game }
        end;

    { *** Player requests a new game *** }
    when P.Newgame
      from EITHER to same
        begin
          { Ignore Player's error }
        end;

    { *** Daemon generates Bump *** }
    when D.Bump
      from EVEN to ODD
        begin
        end;
      from ODD to EVEN
        begin
        end;
end; { GameBody }

{ The actual manager description begins here }
modvar
  GameInstance: Game;
  DistributorInstance: Distributor;

state MANAGING;

initialize
  to MANAGING
    begin
      init DistributorInstance with DistributorBody;
      attach D to DistributorInstance.D;
    end;

trans
  any GameNumber: 1..NGames do

    { *** Player requests a new game *** }
```

```
        when P[GameNumber].Newgame
          begin
            init GameInstance with GameBody;
            attach P[GameNumber] to
              GameInstance.P;
            connect GameInstance.D to
              DistributorInstance.G[GameNumber];
          end;

        { *** Ignore Player's errors *** }
        when P[GameNumber].Probe
          begin
          end;
        when P[GameNumber].Result
          begin
          end;
        when P[GameNumber].Endgame
          begin
          end;

    trans
      { *** Clean up after game *** }
      provided exist GameBody: Game suchthat GameBody.Done
        begin
          all GameBody: Game do
            if GameBody.Done then release GameBody
        end;
end; { Manager }

{ Here is the body of the specification itself }
modvar
  DaemonInstance: Daemon;
  ManagerInstance: Manager;
  PlayerInstance: array [1..NGames] of Player;

initialize
  begin
    init DaemonInstance with DaemonBody;
    init ManagerInstance with ManagerBody;
    all i: 1 .. NGames do
```

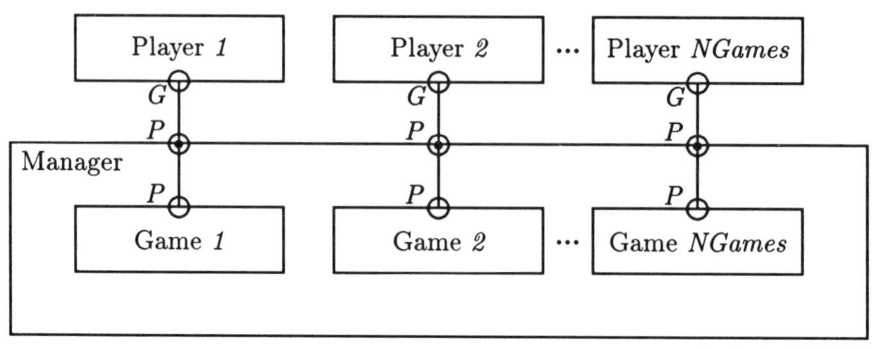

Figure 5.2: Implicit Daemon Game in ESTELLE – Architecture

```
            begin
              init PlayerInstance[i] with PlayerBody;
              connect ManagerInstance.P[i] to
                PlayerInstance[i].G
            end;
          connect DaemonInstance.D to ManagerInstance.D;
        end;
      end. { DaemonGame }
```

5.3.2 *Formal Description without Explicit Daemon*

This alternative approach to describing the Daemon Game avoids explicit representation of the daemon. The description given in Section 5.3.1 was written to reflect the informal description more naturally. However, it was recognised that there was no way a player could distinguish between a system that had a central daemon and a system where the effect of the daemon was purely non-determinism. The architecture of the alternative description without the daemon is shown in Figure 5.2. Note that no *Distributor* module is needed.

In reading the specification itself, note that there are no longer any bumps from a daemon to be stored by the *Game* module. There is therefore no longer any need for it to maintain a state, so the *GameBody* does not have a **state** declaration nor do any of its transitions have a **from** or **to** clause.

Although some parts of the specification are the same as in Section 5.3.1, they have been repeated here for completeness.

```
      specification DaemonGame;
```

```
const NGames = any integer;        { Game limit of implementation }

channel GameServer (Player, Machine);
  by Player:
    Probe;                         { Player takes a turn }
    Result;                        { Player requests score }
    Newgame;                       { Player initiates a game }
    Endgame;                       { Player terminates a game }
  by Machine:
    Win;                           { Tells Player of win }
    Lose;                          { Tells Player of loss }
    Score (nwon: integer);         { Tells Player of score after Result }

module Player systemprocess;
  ip G: GameServer (Player) individual queue;
end; { Player }

body PlayerBody for Player;
external;

module Manager systemprocess;
  ip P: array [1..NGames] of GameServer (Machine) common queue;
end; { Manager }

body ManagerBody for Manager;

  module Game process;
    ip P: GameServer (Machine) common queue;
    export Done: boolean;
  end; { Game }

  body GameBody for Game;
    var NCorrect: integer;

    initialize
        begin
          NCorrect := 0;
          Done := false;
        end;
```

```
  trans
    { *** Player makes a guess *** }
    when P.Probe
      begin
        NCorrect := NCorrect - 1;
        output P.Lose
      end;

    when P.Probe
      begin
        NCorrect := NCorrect + 1;
        output P.Win
      end;

    { *** Player wants the score *** }
    when P.Result
      begin
        output P.Score(NCorrect)
      end;

    { *** Player is done *** }
    when P.Endgame
      begin
        Done := true                { Cause Manager to stop game }
      end;

    { *** Player requests a new game *** }
    when P.Newgame
      begin
        { Ignore Player's error }
      end;

end; { GameBody }

{ The actual manager description begins here }
modvar GameInstance: Game;

state MANAGING;

initialize
  to MANAGING
```

```
      begin
      end;

  trans
    any GameNumber: 1..NGames do

      { *** Player requests a new game *** }
      when P[GameNumber].Newgame
        begin
          init GameInstance with GameBody;
          attach P[GameNumber] to
            GameInstance.P;
        end;

      { *** Ignore Player's errors *** }
      when P[GameNumber].Probe
        begin
        end;
      when P[GameNumber].Result
        begin
        end;
      when P[GameNumber].Endgame
        begin
        end;

  trans
    { *** Clean up after game *** }
    provided exist GameBody: Game suchthat GameBody.Done
      begin
        all GameBody: Game do
          if GameBody.Done then release GameBody
      end;
end; { Manager }

{ Here is the body of the specification itself }
modvar
  ManagerInstance: Manager;
  PlayerInstance: array [1..NGames] of Player;

initialize
```

```
    begin
      init ManagerInstance with ManagerBody;
      all i: 1 .. NGames do
        begin
          init PlayerInstance[i] with PlayerBody;
          connect ManagerInstance.P[i] to
            PlayerInstance[i].G
        end;
    end;
  end. { DaemonGame }
```

5.4 Formal Description in LOTOS[4]

5.4.1 *Formal Description with Explicit Daemon*

The top-level structure of the LOTOS description is as follows. The gates are:

P: for all communication between players and the system; interactions are tagged with the identifier of a game in order to distinguish them

D: an internal gate for communication between the daemon and the games; a *Bump* signal is represented purely by synchronisation at *D*, i.e. there is no value in the event.

The data types are:

Identifier: for distinguishing games

IdentifierSet: for indicating the identifiers that may be used to distinguish games

Integer: for scoring

Signal: for interactions between players and the system.

The processes are:

System: for explaining the top-level specification behaviour; this is decomposed into the independent constraints on permitted games

[4]Section 5.4 is by K. J. Turner, with early input from W. F. Chan (University of Stirling, Stirling, UK).

NoGame: for describing the behaviour of a game which is not current (i.e. not logged into)

Game: for describing the behaviour of a game that is current (i.e. logged into)

Daemon: for describing the behaviour of the daemon.

The major decision taken in writing the description was whether to represent the daemon explicitly. In the following description, the daemon is explicitly represented as a process that interacts with game processes. The daemon process is responsible for generating *Bump* signals. The description was written this way in order to reflect the informal description more naturally. However, the philosophy of LOTOS is to describe only *observable* behaviour, so this style of description is unnatural in LOTOS. An alternative description without an explicit daemon is therefore given in Section 5.4.2.

The LOTOS description shows a clear separation between static aspects (the data typing) and dynamic aspects (the behaviour). The data typing draws on already established data types, which are defined in an Annex to the LOTOS standard. The description of the data types concerns itself with implementation-independent aspects; for example, scores are described as mathematical integers, not as bit patterns.

The behaviour description illustrates the 'constraint-oriented' style in which LOTOS can be used. In this style, behaviour is decomposed into largely separate constraints which are then combined using the appropriate LOTOS operators (mainly parallel composition). In the description, the overall system behaviour is expressed in terms of game behaviours. These in turn are expressed in terms of the login/logout behaviour and game-playing behaviour. The data typing also shows a similar modularity, whereby more complex data types (e.g. *IdentifierSet*) are built out of simpler ones.

The whole description of the system is parameterised by the gate at which external communication occurs with players (*P*), and by the set of game identifiers which may be used (*Ids*). The system never terminates (**noexit**).

```
specification DaemonGame [P] (Ids : IdSet) : noexit

   library
     Boolean, Set                       (* From standard library *)
   endlib
```

The following type defines game identifiers. The only formal property that identifiers have is that they are distinct. This is explained by giving a base value (*BaseId*) and an operation for reaching all other identifier values (*NextId*). Equality (*eq*) and inequality (*ne*) are defined for game identifiers.

```
type Identifier is Boolean
  sorts Id
  opns
    BaseId              : -> Id
    NextId              : Id -> Id
    _eq_, _ne_          : Id, Id -> Bool
  eqns
    forall Id, Id1, Id2 : Id
      ofsort Bool
        BaseId        eq BaseId         = true;
        BaseId        eq NextId (Id)    = false;
        NextId (Id)   eq BaseId         = false;
        NextId (Id1)  eq NextId (Id2)   = Id1 eq Id2;
        Id1 ne Id2                      = not (Id1 eq Id2)
endtype (* Identifier *)
```

The following type actualises the standard library data type *Set* to define a set of game identifiers. A set of game identifiers is a parameter to the overall description.

```
type IdentifierSet is Set actualizedby Identifier, Boolean using
  sortnames
    Id        for Element
    Bool      for FBool
    IdSet     for Set
endtype (* IdentifierSet *)
```

The following type defines the integers (..., -1, 0, 1, ...) in terms of a 0 value, an 'add one' operation (*Inc*), and a 'subtract one' operation (*Dec*). The *Inc* and *Dec* operations are inverses.

```
type Integer is
  sorts Int
  opns
    0           : -> Int
    Inc, Dec    : Int -> Int
  eqns
    forall n : Int
      ofsort Int
        Inc (Dec (n)) = n;
        Dec (Inc (n)) = n
endtype (* Integer *)
```

The following type defines the signals between the players and the system. With the exception of *Score*, these signals are constants.

```
type Signal is Integer
  sorts Sig
  opns
    Newgame, Endgame, Probe,  Win, Lose, Result : -> Sig
    Score : Int -> Sig
endtype (* Signal *)
```

The following behaviour expression describes the entire game. It is parameterised by the given gate and set of identifiers. The internal gate *D* is used for communication between the daemon and system processes.

```
behaviour
  hide D in System [P, D] (Ids) |[D]| Daemon [D]

where
```

The following process describes the overall behaviour of the system. It sets up games independently in parallel one by one, assigning each of them a unique identifier from the given set. The effect is that all possible games are immediately available and are not created on demand. However, the games must all synchronise on signals from the daemon at gate *D*. The process is non-terminating, since all the games are.

```
process System [P, D] (Ids : IdSet) : noexit :=
  choice Id : Id []
    [(Card (Ids) eq Succ (0)) and (Id IsIn Ids)] -> (* One Id *)
      NoGame [P, D] (Id)
  []
    [(Card (Ids) gt Succ (0)) and (Id IsIn Ids)] -> (* Several Ids *)
      (
        NoGame [P, D] (Id)
      |[D]|
        System [P, D] (Remove (Id, Ids))
      )

  where
```

The following process describes the behaviour of a game when it is not current (i.e. logged into). The process is non-terminating, since on completion of a game it offers to start a new game. Unwanted signals from the player or the daemon are discarded while a game is not in progress.

```
process NoGame [P, D] (Id : Id) : noexit :=
  P ! Id ! Newgame;                                   (* Start game *)
  (
    (* start with score 0 and even Bumps *)
    Game [P, D] (Id, 0 of Int, false) >> NoGame [P, D] (Id)
  )
[]
  P ! Id ! Probe; NoGame [P, D] (Id)                  (* Ignored *)
[]
  P ! Id ! Result; NoGame [P, D] (Id)                 (* Ignored *)
[]
  P ! Id ! Endgame; NoGame [P, D] (Id)                (* Ignored *)
[]
  D; NoGame [P, D] (Id)                               (* Bump *)

  where
```

The following process describes the behaviour of a current game. Only the parity of the number of *Bump* signals is relevant, so the actual number of the signals is not stored. The process is entered after *Newgame*, and terminates once *Endgame* is received.

```
process Game [P, D] (Id : Id, Total : Int, Odd : Bool) : exit :=
  P ! Id ! Newgame;             (* Ignored *)
  Game [P, D] (Id, Total, Odd)
[]
  P ! Id ! Probe;               (* Check count of Bumps *)
  (
    [Odd] ->                    (* Count is odd? *)
      P ! Id ! Win; Game [P, D] (Id, Inc (Total), Odd)
  []
    [not (Odd)] ->              (* Count is even? *)
      P ! Id ! Lose; Game [P, D] (Id, Dec (Total), Odd)
  )
[]
  P ! Id ! Result;              (* Return score *)
  P ! Id ! Score (Total); Game [P, D] (Id, Total, Odd)
[]
  P ! Id ! Endgame;             (* Finish game *)
  exit
[]
  D;                            (* Change parity on Bump *)
  Game [P, D] (Id, Total, not (Odd))
endproc (* Game *)
```

```
        endproc (* NoGame *)

    endproc (* System *)
```

The following process describes the behaviour of the daemon. It simply generates an endless series of event offers at the *D* gate, corresponding to *Bump* signals.

```
    process Daemon [D] : noexit :=
      D; Daemon [D]
    endproc (* Daemon *)

  endspec (* DaemonGame *)
```

5.4.2 *Formal Description without Explicit Daemon*

It was recognised that there was no way a player could distinguish between a system that had a central daemon and a system that had one independent daemon per game process. Descriptions of these two systems in LOTOS would be observationally equivalent. If two players sent *Probe* at almost the same time and one received *Win* while the other received *Lose*, they would conclude that the system had internally generated *Bump* in between the two signals. This would be true no matter how close in time the two *Probe* signals were. Since the two *Probe* signals could never be simultaneous in LOTOS and could not be determined to be simultaneous in the real world, the players could not observe whether there were one or many daemons in the system. This illustrates a deep difference found between some FDTs. FDTs such as LOTOS model concurrency by interleaving of events, whereas others model simultaneity using the concept of 'true concurrency'.

Having no central daemon process, or for that matter any daemon processes at all, reflects the emphasis in LOTOS on observational behaviour. A well-written LOTOS description will focus on the sequences of interactions that can be externally observed, and will avoid unnecessary and implementation-dependent detail. To this extent, the informal description is weak because it describes a particular mechanism for implementing the system, not the externally required behaviour. The informal description is an example of over-specification, which must be carefully avoided in standards.

The formal description in Section 5.4.1 has one daemon for the whole system. However, since the daemon is simply a source of non-determinism, it can be dispensed with altogether. The manifestation of the daemon is that a player receives a *Win* or *Lose* signal after a *Probe*. It is therefore not necessary to model the *Bump* signals (which are, after all, invisible from the outside), nor to count whether an odd or even number has occurred. Such non-determinism is simply hidden as an internal event in the LOTOS description. The following description dispenses with the internal gate *D* and the *Daemon* process. The formal description is substantially the same as the one in Section 5.4.1, so informal commentary is provided only where there are significant differences. The data types are identical and so are not repeated here.

```
specification DaemonGame [P] (Ids : IdSet) : noexit

    library ...

    type Identifier is ...

    type IdentifierSet is ...

    type Integer is ...

    type Signal is ...
```

The top-level behaviour expression does not have to introduce a hidden gate for communication with the daemon. There is therefore no *D* gate for a daemon in this or the following processes.

```
behaviour
  System [P] (Ids)

where
```

Since the game processes do not have to synchronise jointly with a daemon, they are completely independent. This leads to a simpler definition of the system as a set of parallel game processes. The base case for recursion (an empty identifier set) has behaviour **stop**. Since the game processes never synchronise and do not terminate, it is not necessary to describe the base case specially.

```
process System [P] (Ids : IdSet) : noexit :=
  choice Id : Id []
    [Id IsIn Ids] ->
      (NoGame [P] (Id) ||| System [P] (Remove (Id, Ids)))
  where
```

It is not necessary for a game to check for *Bump* signals, nor to record the parity of the current number of *Bumps*. Instead, when a player probes the system, a non-deterministic *Win/Lose* decision is made.

```
  process NoGame [P] (Id : Id) : noexit :=
    P ! Id ! Newgame;                    (* Start game *)
```

```
        (
          (* start with score 0 *)
          Game [P] (Id, 0 of Int) >> NoGame [P] (Id)
        )
      []
        P ! Id ! Probe; NoGame [P] (Id)        (* Ignored *)
      []
        P ! Id ! Result; NoGame [P] (Id)       (* Ignored *)
      []
        P ! Id ! Endgame; NoGame [P] (Id)      (* Ignored *)

        where

        process Game [P] (Id : Id, Total : Int) : exit :=
          P ! Id ! Newgame;             (* Ignored *)
          Game [P] (Id, Total)
        []
          P ! Id ! Probe;               (* Check count of Bumps *)
          (
            i ;                         (* Count assumed odd *)
            P ! Id ! Win; Game [P] (Id, Inc (Total))
          []
            i ;                         (* Count assumed even *)
            P ! Id ! Lose; Game [P] (Id, Dec (Total))
          )
        []
          P ! Id ! Result;              (* Return score *)
          P ! Id ! Score (Total); Game [P] (Id, Total)
        []
          P ! Id ! Endgame;             (* Finish game *)
          exit
        endproc (* Game *)

      endproc (* NoGame *)

    endproc (* System *)

  endspec (* DaemonGame *)
```

5.5 Formal Description in SDL[5]

5.5.1 *Formal Description with Explicit Daemon*

The formal description with an explicit daemon is shown in Figure 5.3. The following commentary refers to the parts of this figure.

DaemonGame System Diagram

The *DaemonGame* system contains only block, *Game*, that is referenced in the system diagram. The system diagram thus gives only an overview of the system, indicating the constituent blocks and channels that connect the blocks with each other and with the boundary of the system. Detailed descriptions are given in other diagrams.

Note that an SDL system may ignore some possible sequences of signals coming from the environment. For example, a *Probe* signal coming from a player who has not logged in is ignored by *DaemonGame*. In other words, the allowed behaviour of the environment is specified indirectly in the SDL system description.

Game Block Diagram

The *Game* block has two process types, *Monitor* and *Game*. There is a single *Monitor* process that is created at the same time as the system is created. There may be many *Game* processes that are created dynamically, one for each player.

A player is regarded as a process in the environment of the system. Each process in SDL is given a unique address of sort *PId*, and each signal carries the address of the sending process. Thus when a player logs in by the signal *Newgame*, the address is known to the system and a *Game* process is created for the player. The process presents itself by sending the signal *Gameid* to the player and takes care of the rest of the game session.

The *Monitor* process has the task of creating *Game* processes and distributing *Bump* signals to all the *Game* processes. There is a need to introduce some new signals (*Gameover* and *Gameoverack*) between *Monitor* and *Game* to terminate a game session in a safe way.

This approach to the architecture is rather natural. A unique *Monitor* process is necessary to receive signals from the environment (*Newgame* and *Bump*) that cannot be addressed to a specific process since these signals are sent without an address.

The relation between the *Monitor* and *Game* processes could be simplified by addressing the *Endgame* signal to *Monitor*. This would then update its record of players and *Game* processes, passing the signal to the *Game* process

[5]Section 5.5 is by F. Belina.

in question. However, this would require a coupling between a player and the corresponding *Game* process in the *Monitor* process.

Monitor Process Diagram

The *Monitor* process registers new players, creates a *Game* process for each of them, and distributes *Bump* signals to all the *Game* processes. If a registered player tries to log in, then no action is taken.

Registered players and created *Game* processes are recorded in variables of sort *Pidset*, a set of process addresses. Note that no record is kept for the coupling between a player and the corresponding *Game* process.

The description of *Pidset* is based on the pre-defined generator *Powerset* and is included in the process diagram. Note that operator names ending with '!' are used only within axioms. The *unique!* operator is part of the description of the pre-defined sort *PId*. It creates a unique *PId* value (process address) based on the given *PId* value. The *take!* operator returns a *PId* value from a *Pidset* by trying all possible *PId* values starting with *null*. The *take* operator returns an element of a *Pidset*. Variables of sort *Pidset* will have the default initial value *empty*.

Game Process Diagram

A *Game* process is created for a new player to take care of the rest of the game session. The address of the player is given in the formal parameter *player*. When a player logs out, the *Monitor* process must be informed by signal *Gameover* in order to stop sending *Bump* signals to the *Game* process. The *Game* process can then terminate.

Textual Representation

SDL/PR is a textual representation that is mainly used as a standard interchange format. To give a flavour of it, this chapter includes the SDL/PR corresponding to the SDL/GR diagrams; only the diagrams are given for the other examples in this book. A software tool was used to convert the graphical representation into the textual representations. The textual representations make use of remote descriptions to separate the description into different levels of abstraction. The textual representation of Figure 5.3 is as follows.

```
system DaemonGame;

  signal
    Newgame, Probe, Result, Endgame, Gameid, Win, Lose,
    Score (Integer), Bump;
```

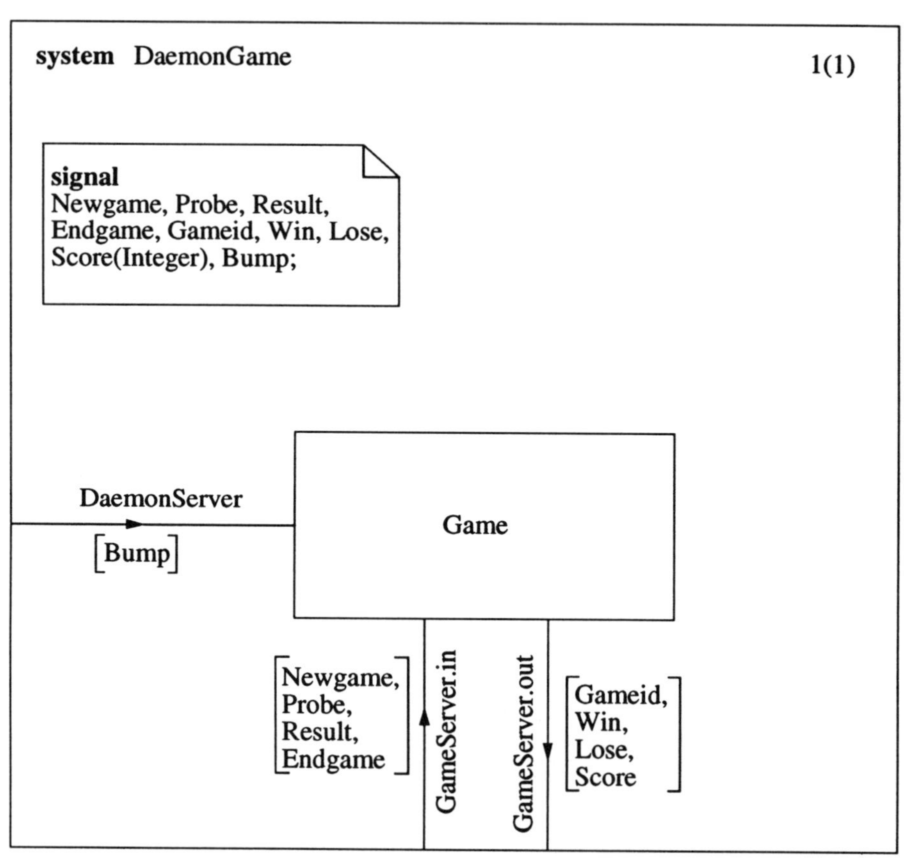

Figure 5.3: Explicit Daemon Game in SDL – Graphical Description

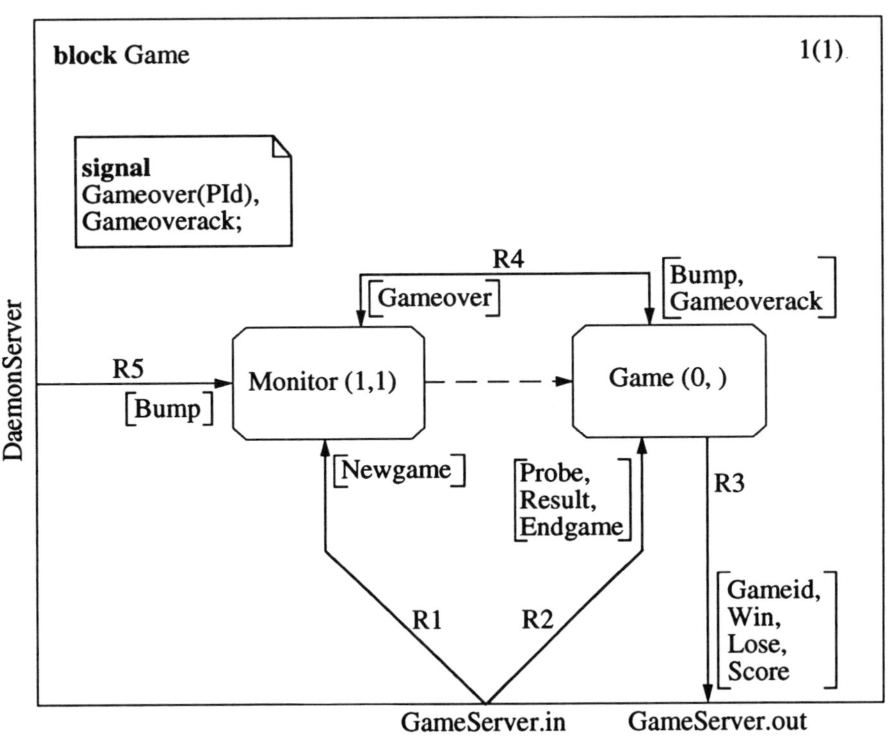

Figure 5.3 *(continued)*

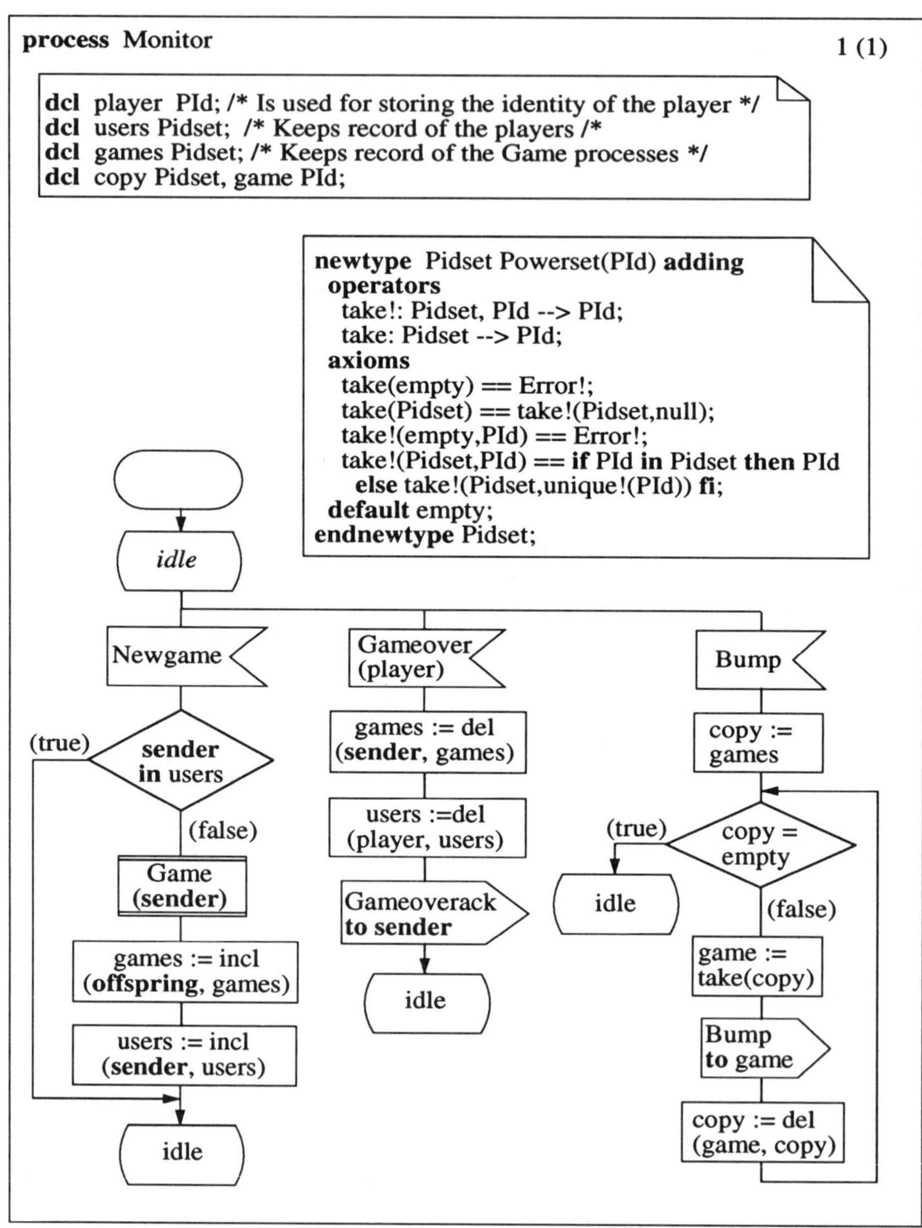
process Monitor
1 (1)
dcl player PId; /* Is used for storing the identity of the player */
dcl users Pidset; /* Keeps record of the players /*
dcl games Pidset; /* Keeps record of the Game processes */
dcl copy Pidset, game PId;
newtype Pidset Powerset(PId) adding
operators
take!: Pidset, PId --> PId;
take: Pidset --> PId;
axioms
take(empty) == Error!;
take(Pidset) == take!(Pidset,null);
take!(empty,PId) == Error!;
take!(Pidset,PId) == if PId in Pidset then PId
else take!(Pidset,unique!(PId)) fi;
default empty;
endnewtype Pidset;
idle
Newgame
Gameover
(player)
Bump
(true)
sender
in users
(false)
Game
(sender)
games := incl
(offspring, games)
users := incl
(sender, users)
idle
games := del
(sender, games)
users :=del
(player, users)
Gameoverack
to sender
idle
copy :=
games
(true)
copy =
empty
idle
(false)
game :=
take(copy)
Bump
to game
copy := del
(game, copy)

Figure 5.3 *(continued)*

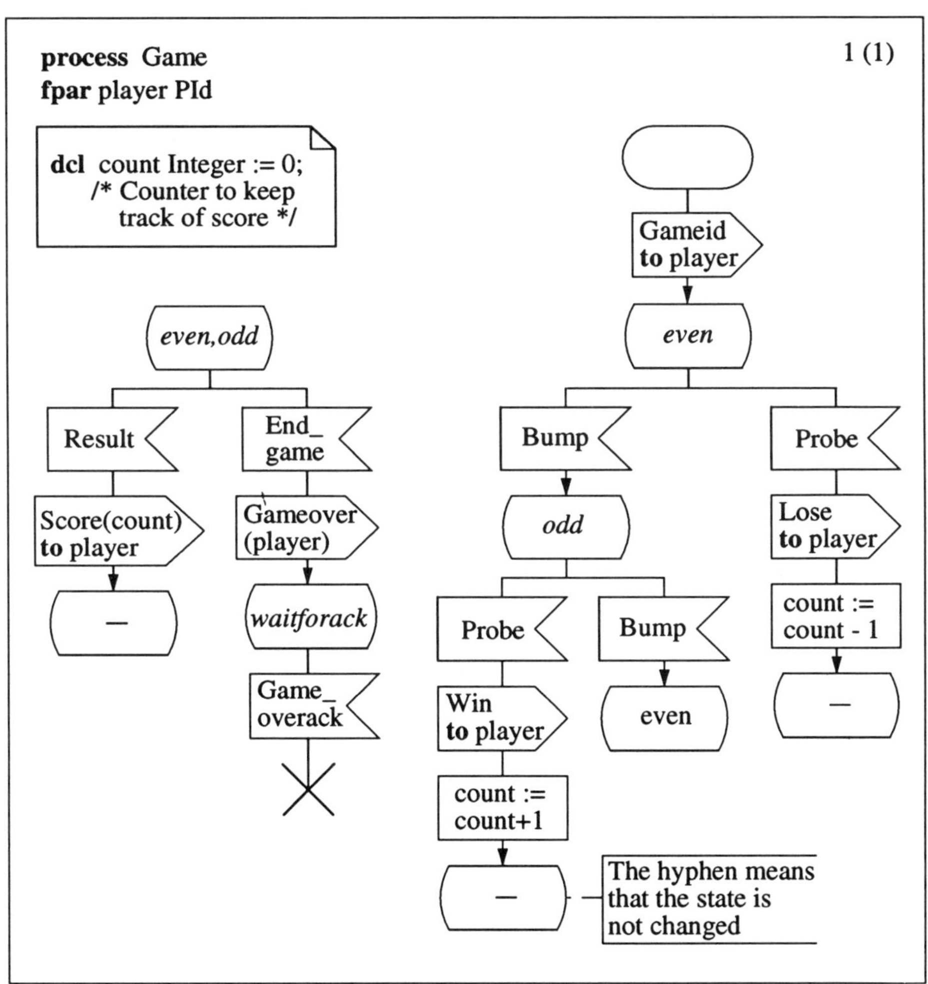

Figure 5.3 *(continued)*

```
  channel GameServer.in
    from env to Game
      with Newgame, Probe, Result, Endgame;
  endchannel GameServer.in;

  channel GameServer.out
    from Game to env
      with Gameid, Win, Lose, Score;
  endchannel GameServer.out;

  channel DaemonServer
    from env to Game
      with Bump;
  endchannel DaemonServer;

  block Game referenced;

endsystem DaemonGame;

block Game;

  connect GameServer.in and R1, R2;
  connect GameServer.out and R3;
  connect DaemonServer and R5;

  signal
    Gameover (PId), Gameoverack;

  signalroute R1
    from env to Monitor
      with Newgame;
  signalroute R2
    from env to Game
      with Probe, Result, Endgame;
  signalroute R3
    from Game to env
      with Gameid, Win, Lose, Score;
  signalroute R4
    from Game to Monitor
      with Gameover;
    from Monitor to Game
      with Bump, Gameoverack;
```

```
    signalroute R5
      from env to Monitor
        with Bump;

    process Monitor (1, 1) referenced;

    process Game (0, ) referenced;

  endblock Game;

  process Monitor;

    dcl player PId;                  /* Is used for storing the identity
                                     of the player */
    dcl users Pidset;                /* Keeps record of the players */
    dcl games Pidset;                /* Keeps record of the Game processes */
    dcl copy Pidset, game PId;

    newtype Pidset Powerset (PId) adding
      operators
        take! : Pidset, PId -> PId;
        take : Pidset -> PId;
      axioms
        take (empty) == Error!;
        take (Pidset) == take! (Pidset, null);
        take! (empty, PId) == Error!;
        take! (Pidset, PId) ==
          if PId in Pidset
            then PId
            else take! (Pidset, unique! (PId))
          fi;
      default empty;
    endnewtype Pidset;

    start;
      nextstate idle;

    state idle;
      input Newgame;
        decision sender in users;
          (true) :
          (false) :
```

```
            create Game (sender);
            task games := incl (offspring, games);
            task users := incl (sender, users);
        enddecision;
        nextstate idle;
    input Gameover (player);
        task games := del (sender, games);
        task users := del (player, users);
        output Gameoverack to sender;
        nextstate idle;
    input Bump;
        task copy := games;
        grs1 :
        decision copy = empty;
          (true) :
            nextstate idle;
          (false) :
            task game := take (copy);
            output Bump to game;
            task copy := del (game, copy);
            join grs1;
        enddecision;

endprocess Monitor;

process Game;

  fpar player PId;

  dcl count Integer := 0;             /* Counter to keep track of score */

  start;
    output Gameid to player;
    nextstate even;

  state waitforack;
    input Gameoverack;
    stop;

  state even, odd;
    input Result;
      output Score (count) to player;
```

```
        nextstate -;
      input Endgame;
        output Gameover (player);
        nextstate waitforack;

    state odd;
      input Probe;
        output Win to player;
        task count := count + 1;
        nextstate -;                /* The hyphen means that the state
                                       is not changed */
      input Bump;
        nextstate even;

    state even;
      input Bump;
        nextstate odd;
      input Probe;
        output Lose to player;
        task count := count - 1;
        nextstate -;

  endprocess Game;
```

5.5.2 *Formal Description without Explicit Daemon*

The formal description without an explicit daemon is shown in Figure 5.4. The following commentary refers to the parts of this figure. As the version without a daemon is based closely on the version with a daemon, only the differences are noted below.

DaemonGame System Diagram

A construct for non-determinism has been introduced in place of the daemon so as to represent the non-deterministic behaviour of the game. As a consequence, the *Bump* signal has been removed and all the diagrams have been simplified.

Game Block Diagram

In the *Game* block, the interaction between *Monitor* and *Game* processes has been simplified. Since a game session can be terminated in an easier way, the *Bump* and *Gameoverack* signals have been removed.

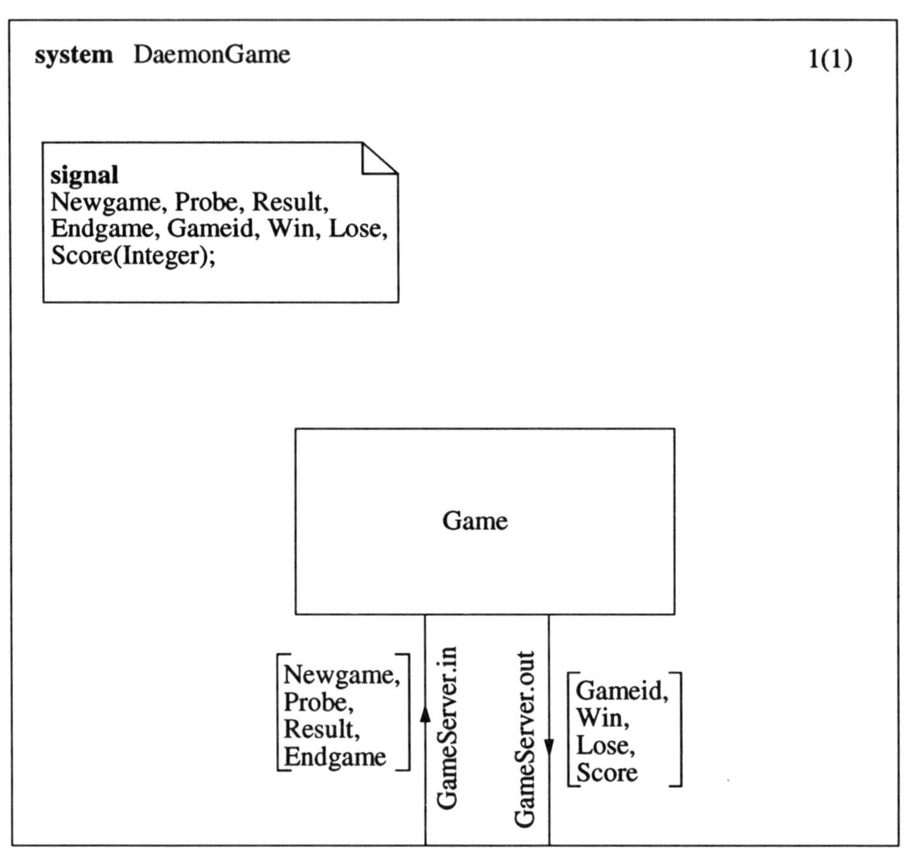

Figure 5.4: Implicit Daemon Game in SDL – Graphical Description

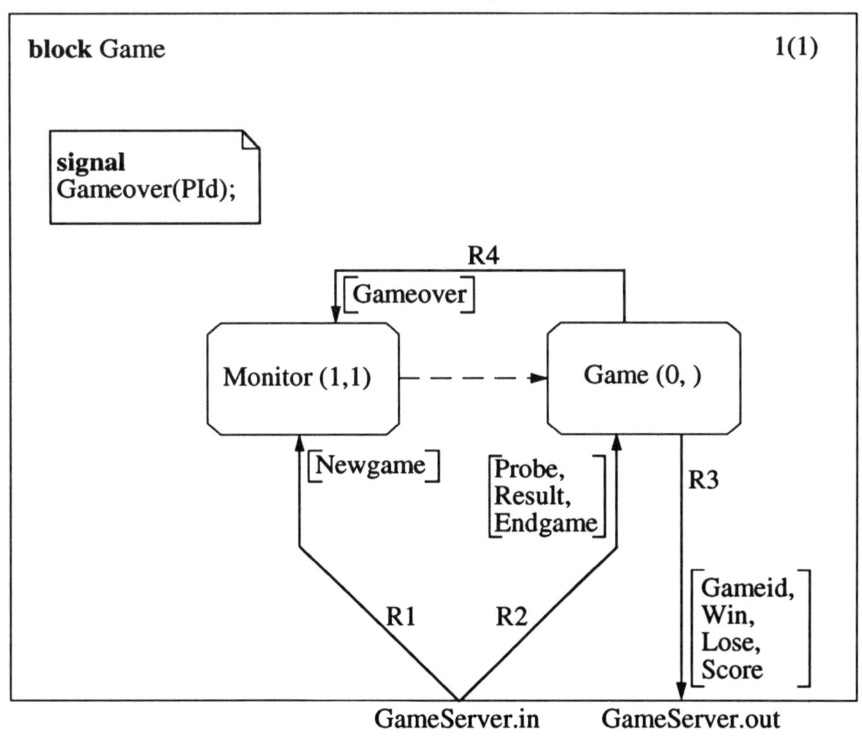

Figure 5.4 *(continued)*

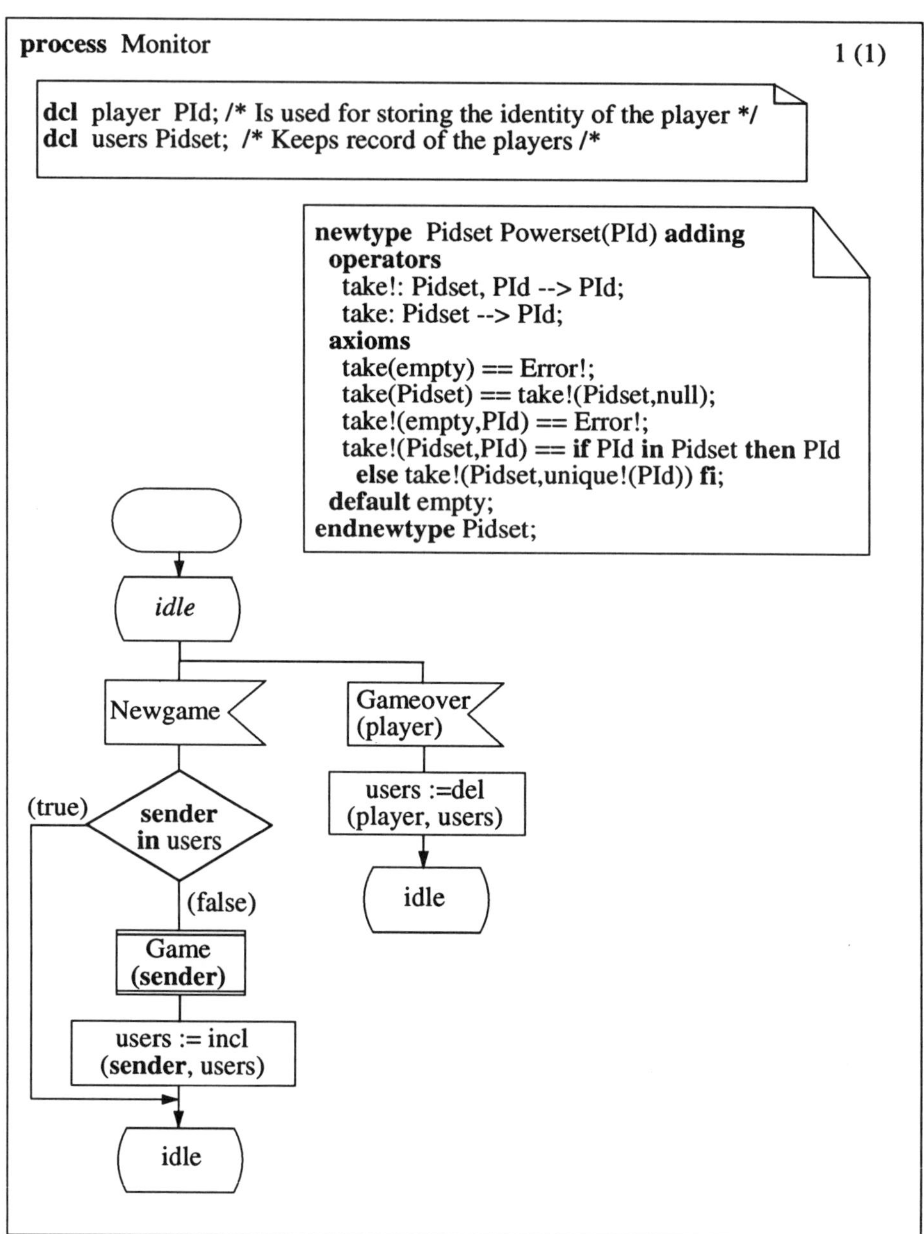
process Monitor
1 (1)
dcl player PId; /* Is used for storing the identity of the player */
dcl users Pidset; /* Keeps record of the players /*
newtype Pidset Powerset(PId) **adding**
operators
take!: Pidset, PId --> PId;
take: Pidset --> PId;
axioms
take(empty) == Error!;
take(Pidset) == take!(Pidset,null);
take!(empty,PId) == Error!;
take!(Pidset,PId) == **if** PId **in** Pidset **then** PId
else take!(Pidset,unique!(PId)) **fi**;
default empty;
endnewtype Pidset;
idle
Newgame
Gameover (player)
(true)
sender in users
(false)
Game (sender)
users := incl (sender, users)
idle
users :=del (player, users)
idle

Figure 5.4 *(continued)*

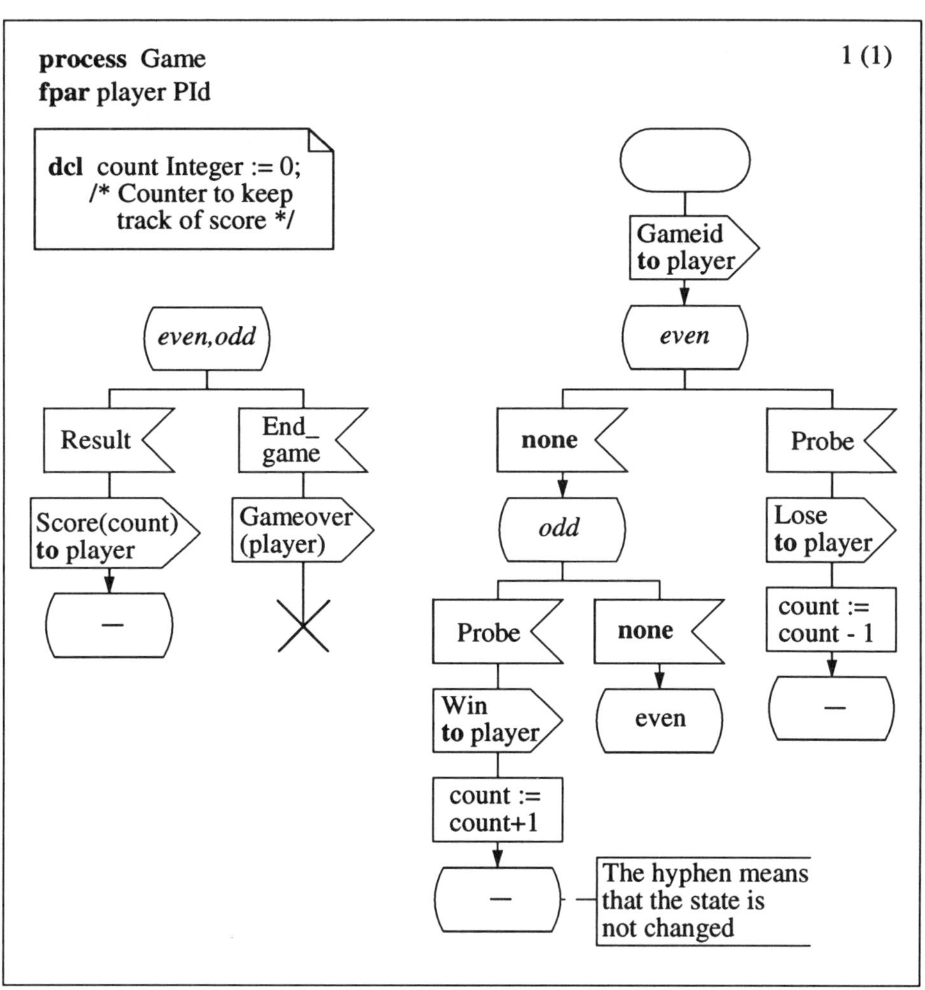

Figure 5.4 *(continued)*

Monitor Process Diagram

In the *Monitor* process, the transitions for the signals *Bump* and *Gameoverack* have been removed.

Game Process Diagram

In the *Game* process, the reception of *Bump* signals has been replaced by spontaneous transitions, using the keyword **none** in place of the signal name *Bump.* The effect is the same, namely a spontaneous state transition between *even* and *odd.* The process can now terminate directly without waiting in the state *waitforack* for the signal *Gameoverack.*

Textual Representation

The textual representation of Figure 5.4 is as follows. Since substantial parts of this are the same as in Section 5.5.1 they have been omitted.

```
system DaemonGame;

  signal
    Newgame, Probe, Result, Endgame, Gameid, Win, Lose,
    Score (Integer);

  channel GameServer.in ...

  channel GameServer.out ...

  block Game referenced;

endsystem DaemonGame;

block Game;

  connect GameServer.in and R1, R2;
  connect GameServer.out and R3;

  signal Gameover (PId);

  signalroute R1 ...
  signalroute R2 ...
  signalroute R3 ...
  signalroute R4
    from Game to Monitor
      with Gameover;
```

```
   process Monitor (1, 1) referenced;

   process Game (0, ) referenced;

endblock Game;

process Monitor;

   dcl player PId;               /* Is used for storing the identity
                                 of the player */
   dcl users Pidset;             /* Keeps record of the players */

   newtype Pidset ...

   start;
      nextstate idle;

   state idle;
      input Newgame;
         decision sender in users;
            (true) :
            (false) :
               create Game (sender);
               task users := incl (sender, users);
         enddecision;
         nextstate idle;
      input Gameover (player);
         task users := del (player, users);
         nextstate idle;

endprocess Monitor;

 process Game;

   fpar player PId;

   dcl count Integer := 0;       /* Counter to keep track of score */

   start;
      output Gameid to player;
      nextstate even;
```

```
state even, odd;
  input Result;
    output Score (count) to player;
    nextstate -;
  input Endgame;
    output Gameover (player);
    stop;

state odd;
  input Probe;
    output Win to player;
    task count := count + 1;
    nextstate -;             /* The hyphen means that the state
                             is not changed */
  input none;
    nextstate even;

state even;
  input none;
    nextstate odd;
  input Probe;
    output Lose to player;
    task count := count - 1;
    nextstate -;

endprocess Game;
```

5.6 Conclusion[6]

It is remarkable that such an apparently simple example should result in so many different interpretations. It took several iterations among the authors of the descriptions to determine exactly what the original intentions were. The conclusions from this example are as follows:

- It is difficult to be precise about even simple things.

- It is commonly forgotten to describe all error cases. Failure to do so often results in problems of incompatibility between implementations of a complex description.

[6]Section 5.6 is by K. J. Turner.

- It is easy to be unclear about the responsibilities of different parts of a system, and how these parts should view each other.

- The description of a system may be unintentionally biased towards an implementation by giving irrelevant detail. This may exclude other, valid implementations.

6 Unreliable Medium

The Daemon Game of Chapter 5 provides a service to its users, the players. A communications medium also provides a service – it attempts to transfer messages on behalf of the protocol entities that use it. An absolute guarantee of delivery can never be given by a medium; errors such as message loss or corruption may occur. This chapter illustrates how an unreliable medium may be formally described. In communications terms, the medium supports a point-to-point, bidirectional connection-less service.

6.1 Informal Description[1]

The **Unreliable Medium** operates between two points, and supports full duplex (two-way, simultaneous) transfer of messages. No acknowledgement is given of whether a message is delivered successfully or not. The medium is unreliable in that it may lose, corrupt, duplicate or re-order messages.

The medium service 'M' is intended to support a one-way transfer protocol such as the sliding window protocol (Chapter 7). It therefore allows a transmitter at one end to send data messages and a receiver at the other end to confirm their arrival with acknowledgement messages.

6.2 Errors in the Informal Description[2]

6.2.1 *Delivery of Corrupted Messages*

Does the medium deliver corrupted messages, or are they discarded within the medium?

The medium was intended to deliver corrupted messages, and the protocol to detect this by some unspecified means.

[1] Section 6.1 is by K. J. Turner.

[2] Section 6.2 is by K. J. Turner, based on problems found by the authors of the formal descriptions.

6.2.2 *Transfer of Data and Acknowledgements*

Does the medium support data and acknowledgement service primitives, or does the protocol have to encode this information in protocol data units?

The intention was that data messages and acknowledgement messages be dealt with separately by the medium.

6.2.3 *Corruption of Messages*

Can acknowledgement messages as well as data messages be mishandled in the medium?

The intention was that loss, duplication or re-ordering of acknowledgements could occur. However, an acknowledgement message could never be corrupted into a data message nor vice versa since they are handled separately (see Section 6.2.2).

6.3 Formal Description in ESTELLE[3]

Figure 6.1 shows the architecture of the unreliable medium description in ESTELLE. The medium is described quite simply as a single module with interaction points *MT* (for use by a protocol transmitter) and *MR* (for use by a protocol receiver). Its unreliable behaviour is hidden by the procedure *mung*[4], which is defined only in outline. The medium description has been written to avoid irrelevant details such as how to re-order or lose messages in the medium; this is implementation-dependent detail inside *mung*. In general, an ESTELLE description is parameterised by its **primitive** procedures and functions and depends on their operation. For example, if there were no guarantee that *mung* would eventually allow messages to be delivered in unaltered form, a protocol could not use the medium effectively. The medium is expected to perform an operation within some maximum delay.

The transitions in the following are numbered only for convenient reference.

```
specification UnreliableMedium;

default individual queue;

type
  SeqType = integer;                  { Sequence number type, >= 0 }
  UserDataType = ...;                 { Some suitable type, e.g. a string }
```

[3]Section 6.3 is by R. L. Tenney and T. P. Blumer.

[4]It is reputed that the slang word 'mung' is short for 'modify until no good'.

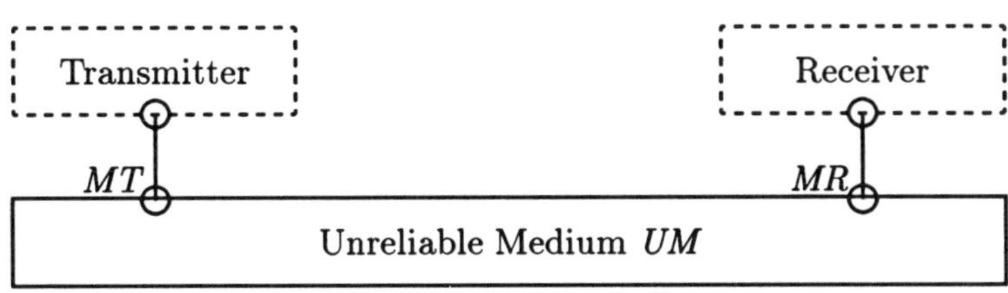

Figure 6.1: Unreliable Medium in ESTELLE – Architecture

```
  DTPDUType =                      { Data message }
    record
      Seq: SeqType;
      Msg: UserDataType;
    end;
  AKPDUType =                      { Acknowledgement message}
    record
      Seq: SeqType;
    end;
  QueueData =                      { Queue data item }
    record
      Seq: SeqType;
      Msg: UserDataType
    end;
  QueueType = ...;                 { Some suitable queue structure,
                                   e.g. a linked list }

channel Tx(Transmitter, Medium);
  by Transmitter:
    MDTreq(PDU : DTPDUType);
  by Medium:
    MAKind(PDU : AKPDUType);

channel Rx(Receiver, Medium);
  by Receiver:
    MAKreq(PDU : AKPDUType);
  by Medium:
    MDTind(PDU : DTPDUType);
```

```
module UM systemprocess;
  ip
    MT : Tx(Medium);
    MR : Rx(Medium);
end;

body UMBody for UM;
  const MaxDelay = any integer;  { implementation maximum delay }

  { The following procedures and functions manipulate queues in
    the usual fashion }

  procedure initqueue(var q: QueueType);
  primitive;

  procedure enqueue(Data: QueueData; var q: QueueType);
  primitive;

  procedure dequeue(var Data: QueueData; var q: QueueType);
  primitive;

  function isempty(q: QueueType): boolean;
  primitive;

  { The following procedure models the unreliability of the medium.
    It may lose, corrupt, duplicate or re-order some of the entries of
    the queue, q, and may also leave it unaltered. }

  procedure mung(var q: QueueType);
  primitive;

  var
    TtoR: QueueType;              { Transmitter to receiver queue }
    RtoT: QueueType;              { Receiver to transmitter queue }

  initialize
    provided ( MaxDelay > 0 )
      begin { 1 }
        initqueue(TtoR);
```

```
      initqueue(RtoT);
    end;

trans
  when MT.MDTreq
    var QueueElement: QueueData;
    begin { 2 }
      QueueElement.Seq := PDU.Seq;
      QueueElement.Msg := PDU.Msg;
      enqueue(QueueElement, TtoR);
    end;
  when MR.MAKreq
    var QueueElement: QueueData;
    begin { 3 }
      QueueElement.Seq := PDU.Seq;
      enqueue(QueueElement, RtoT);
    end;

trans
  provided not isempty(TtoR)
    delay(0, MaxDelay)
      var
        PDUtoSend: DTPDUType;
        QueueElement: QueueData;
      begin { 4 }
        mung(TtoR);
        if not isempty(TtoR) then
          begin
            dequeue(QueueElement, TtoR);
            PDUtoSend.Seq := QueueElement.Seq;
            PDUtoSend.Msg := QueueElement.Msg;
            output MR.MDTind(PDUtoSend);
          end
      end;

  provided not isempty(RtoT)
    delay(0, MaxDelay)
      var
        AKtoSend: AKPDUType;
        QueueElement: QueueData;
```

```
        begin { 5 }
          mung(RtoT);
          if not isempty(RtoT) then
            begin
              dequeue(QueueElement, RtoT);
              AKtoSend.Seq := QueueElement.Seq;
              output MT.MAKind(AKtoSend)
            end
        end;
  end; { UMBody }

{ Here is the body of the specification itself }

modvar
  UMInstance : UM;

initialize
  begin
    init UMInstance with UMBody;
  end;
end. { UnreliableMedium }
```

6.4 Formal Description in LOTOS[5]

The medium could be represented as a process with two gates, or with a single gate and two service access points. The representation with one gate *m* has been chosen since it is more general and just as abstract as the one with two gates.

An outline representation of a protocol supporting a service at gate *s* over the medium would be:

```
specification Protocol [s] (...) : noexit

  behaviour
    hide m in
      ProtocolEntities [s, m] (...) || UnreliableMedium [m] (...)

  where
```

[5]Section 6.4 is by F. M. Fournón y González-Barcia.

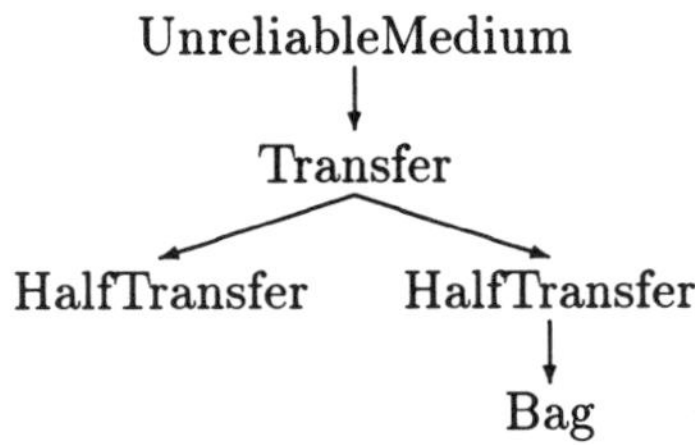

Figure 6.2: Unreliable Medium in LOTOS – Process Decomposition

process ProtocolEntities [s, m] (...) : **noexit** ...

process UnreliableMedium [m] (...) : **noexit** ...

endspec (* Protocol *)

However, the description of the medium service in this chapter is self-contained. Figure 6.2 shows the decomposition of the processes in the description.

The medium service is a very simple one. In most services, the constraints at the top level are concerned with acceptance of primitives and transfer of data. For the unreliable medium, however, the acceptance constraints are missing because there are no restrictions: indications or requests are accepted at all times.

The full duplex transfer of data from one end to the other is decomposed into two identical simplex (one-way) links. Each of these links is described using a process that behaves like a bag (a set with duplicates).

The basic elements of the medium service are the MSAPs *(Service Access Points)* it supports, the SPs *(Service Primitives)* exchanged at these points, and the SDUs *(Service Data Units)* carried by those primitives.

The service is accessed via the *m* (medium) gate.

specification UnreliableMedium [m] : **noexit**

Only the Boolean data type from the standard library is required.

library
Boolean
endlib

The specification of MSAPs provides two distinct values (*mt* and *mr*) for the transmitting and receiving ends.

```
type MSAPs is
  sorts MSAP
  opns mt, mr : -> MSAP
endtype (* MSAPs *)
```

Nothing definite is said in the informal description about the service data units of the medium except that there are data messages and acknowledgement messages. A protocol would embed protocol messages in medium service data units, encoded in some way. Nothing is also known about the detection of corrupted messages in the protocols, but it can be assumed that this would be part of the protocol encoding/decoding functions. Thus, the most abstract and general view of the informal description is as a set of distinct messages[6] (just *data* and *ack* here) with an undefined *Corrupts* operation that checks if one service data unit is a corruption of another. Several SDU values may be a corruption of a given SDU.

```
type SDUs is Boolean
  sorts SDU
  opns
    data, ack :                        -> SDU
    Corrupts :          SDU, SDU       -> Bool
endtype (* SDUs *)
```

The medium service primitives have three kinds of operations: constructors for requests and indications (*MDTreq, MDTind, MAKreq, MAKind*), a selector to extract a service data unit (*SDUOf*), and recognisers for request and indication primitives (*IsMreq, IsMind*)[7].

```
type MSPs is SDUs, Boolean
  sorts MSP
  opns
    MDTreq, MDTind : SDU    -> MSP
    MAKreq, MAKind : SDU    -> MSP
    SDUOf :          MSP    -> SDU
    IsMreq, IsMind : MSP    -> Bool
```

[6]In the description of the sliding window protocol in Section 7.4, this type is replaced by the more specific one of protocol data units. It would be convenient to have separate specification modules, but LOTOS does not support these.

[7]In more complex descriptions, each type of service primitive would be identified with a natural number to simplify the definition of recognisers.

```
    eqns
      forall sp : MSP, sdu : SDU
        ofsort SDU
          SDUOf (MDTreq (sdu)) = sdu;
          SDUOf (MDTind (sdu)) = sdu;
          SDUOf (MAKreq (sdu)) = sdu;
          SDUOf (MAKind (sdu)) = sdu;
        ofsort Bool
          IsMreq (MDTreq (sdu)) = true;
          IsMreq (MDTind (sdu)) = false;
          IsMreq (MAKreq (sdu)) = true;
          IsMreq (MAKind (sdu)) = false;
          IsMind (sp)           = not (IsMreq (sp));
  endtype (* MSPs *)
```

As noted earlier, the medium service has only transfer constraints.

```
  behaviour
    Transfer [m]

  where
```

Process *Transfer* is composed of two identical halves, each representing a simplex link from one MSAP to the other. It is a matter for the protocol to decide how to use these links (e.g. for only the transmitter to originate data messages).

```
  process Transfer [m] : noexit :=
    HalfTransfer [m] (mt, mr) ||| HalfTransfer [m] (mr, mt)

    where
```

Process *HalfTransfer* accepts a request primitive and passes it as a **medium object** to a *Bag* process forked from itself.

```
    process HalfTransfer [m] (transmitter, receiver : MSAP) : noexit :=
      m ! transmitter ? sp : MSP [IsMreq (sp)];
      (
        HalfTransfer [m] (transmitter, receiver)
      |||
        Bag [m] (receiver, Object (sp))
      )

      where
```

The simplex link represented by *HalfTransfer* handles medium objects. An object is created from a request primitive, can be corrupted, and can give rise to indication primitives. The medium carries an object presented as a service request, and delivers it transformed into an service indication. Corruption of objects affects only their data, not their kind. Several object values may be a corruption of a given object.

```
type Objects is MSPs, SDUs, Boolean
  sorts Obj
  opns
    Object :        MSP            -> Obj
    Indication:     Obj            -> MSP
    Corrupts :      Obj, Obj       -> Bool
  eqns
    forall sdu, sdu1, sdu2 : SDU
      ofsort MSP
        Indication (Object (MDTreq (sdu))) = MDTind (sdu);
        Indication (Object (MAKreq (sdu))) = MAKind (sdu);
      ofsort Bool
        Corrupts (Object (MDTreq (sdu1)),
         Object (MDTreq (sdu2))) =
          Corrupts (sdu1, sdu2);
        Corrupts (Object (MDTreq (sdu1)),
         Object (MAKreq (sdu2))) =
          false;
        Corrupts (Object (MAKreq (sdu1)),
         Object (MDTreq (sdu2))) =
          false;
        Corrupts (Object (MAKreq (sdu1)),
         Object (MAKreq (sdu2))) =
          Corrupts (sdu1, sdu2);
endtype (* Objects *)
```

Process *Bag* delivers the objects it receives in any order. It also deals with loss, corruption and duplication of objects. All these actions happen in a non-deterministic way, represented by choices preceded by an internal event. Corruption of objects is represented as a choice of corrupted value.

```
process Bag [m] (sap : MSAP, obj : Obj) : noexit :=
  i;                          (* Object discarded *)
  stop
[]
```

```
      i;                         (* Object duplicated *)
      (Bag [m] (sap, obj) ||| Bag [m] (sap, obj))
    []

      i;                         (* Object corrupted *)
      (
        choice newobj : Obj []   (* Choose corruptions of object *)
          [Corrupts (newobj, obj)] ->
            Bag [m] (sap, newobj)
      )
    []
      i;                         (* Object delivered *)
      m ! sap ! Indication (obj); stop
    endproc (* Bag *)

  endproc (* HalfTransfer *)

endproc (* Transfer *)

endspec (* UnreliableMedium *)
```

6.5 Formal Description in SDL[8]

The formal description is shown in Figure 6.3. The description demonstrates that the conceptual view of a service provider as an abstract queue manager can be supported by SDL. The transmitter and receiver are assumed to be located in the environment and to use a proper transfer protocol (e.g. a sliding window protocol) to cope with the unreliability of the medium. The description therefore consists only of a system *UnreliableMedium* containing a block *Medium*.

The block *Medium* communicates with the environment via two bidirectional channels: *mt* (to the medium from the environment – the transmitter), and *mr* (from the medium to the environment – the receiver). Within the block, each channel splits into two (unidirectional) signalroutes: channel *mt* splits into signalroutes *mtd* for data and *mta* for acknowledgements, and channel *mr* splits into signalroutes *mrd* for data and *mra* for acknowledgements.

Treatment of data within the medium is handled by process *MsgManager* whose behaviour is described by a sequence of operations on a queue of data items, asynchronously triggered by a 'guard' process *MsgHazard*. Similarly,

[8]Section 6.5 is by S. Trigila.

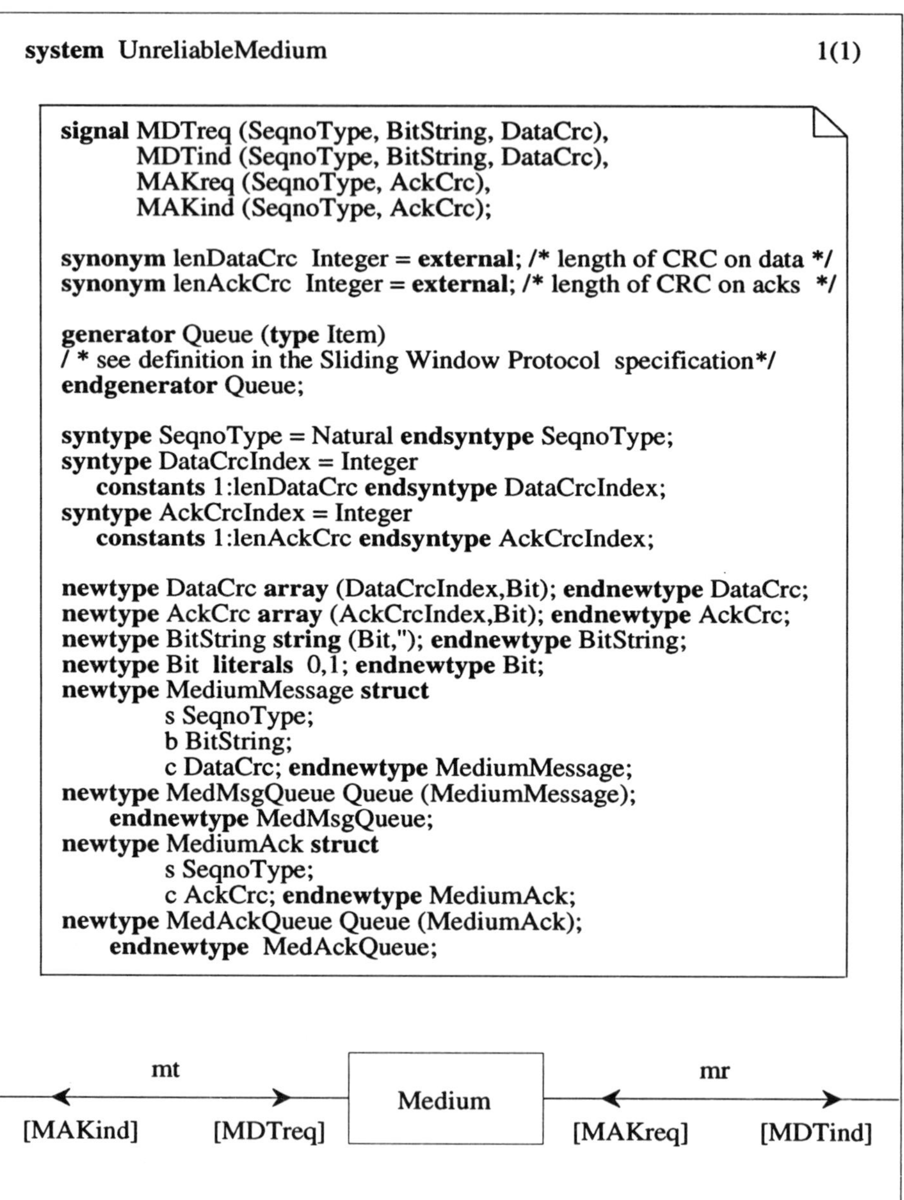

system UnreliableMedium
1(1)
signal MDTreq (SeqnoType, BitString, DataCrc),
MDTind (SeqnoType, BitString, DataCrc),
MAKreq (SeqnoType, AckCrc),
MAKind (SeqnoType, AckCrc);
synonym lenDataCrc Integer = external; /* length of CRC on data */
synonym lenAckCrc Integer = external; /* length of CRC on acks */
generator Queue (type Item)
/ * see definition in the Sliding Window Protocol specification*/
endgenerator Queue;
syntype SeqnoType = Natural endsyntype SeqnoType;
syntype DataCrcIndex = Integer
constants 1:lenDataCrc endsyntype DataCrcIndex;
syntype AckCrcIndex = Integer
constants 1:lenAckCrc endsyntype AckCrcIndex;
newtype DataCrc array (DataCrcIndex,Bit); endnewtype DataCrc;
newtype AckCrc array (AckCrcIndex,Bit); endnewtype AckCrc;
newtype BitString string (Bit,''); endnewtype BitString;
newtype Bit literals 0,1; endnewtype Bit;
newtype MediumMessage struct
s SeqnoType;
b BitString;
c DataCrc; endnewtype MediumMessage;
newtype MedMsgQueue Queue (MediumMessage);
endnewtype MedMsgQueue;
newtype MediumAck struct
s SeqnoType;
c AckCrc; endnewtype MediumAck;
newtype MedAckQueue Queue (MediumAck);
endnewtype MedAckQueue;
mt
Medium
mr
[MAKind]
[MDTreq]
[MAKreq]
[MDTind]

Figure 6.3: Unreliable Medium in SDL – Graphical Description

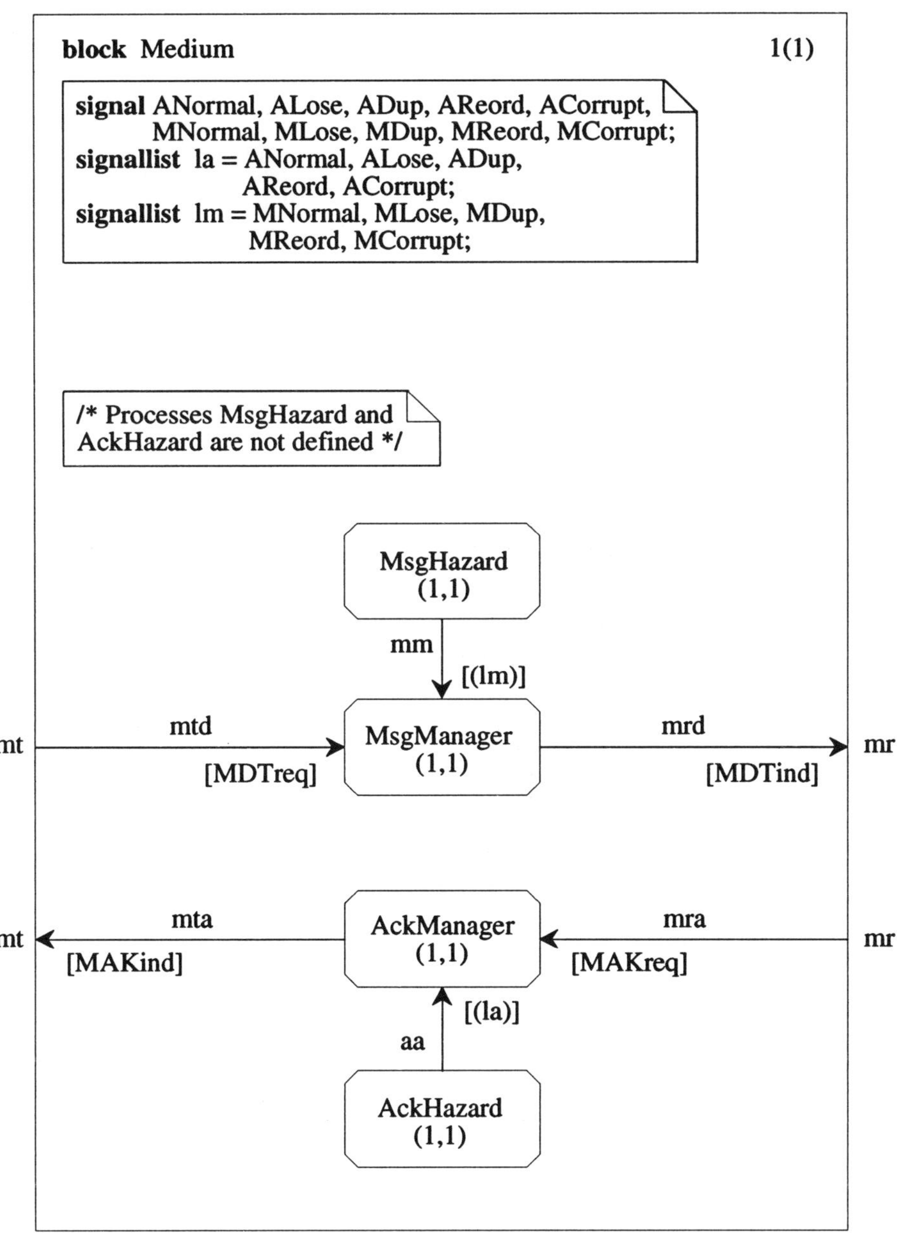

Figure 6.3 *(continued)*

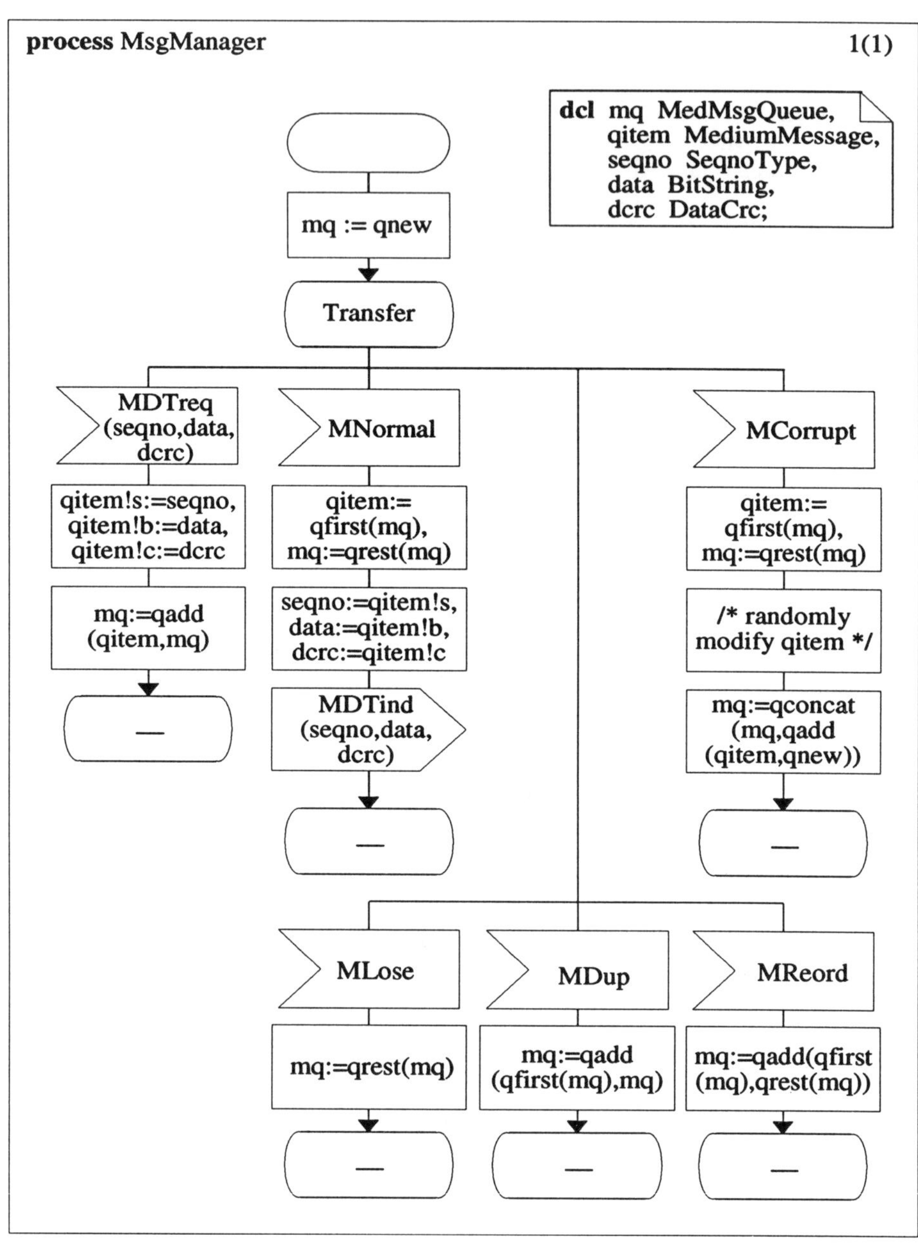

Figure 6.3 *(continued)*

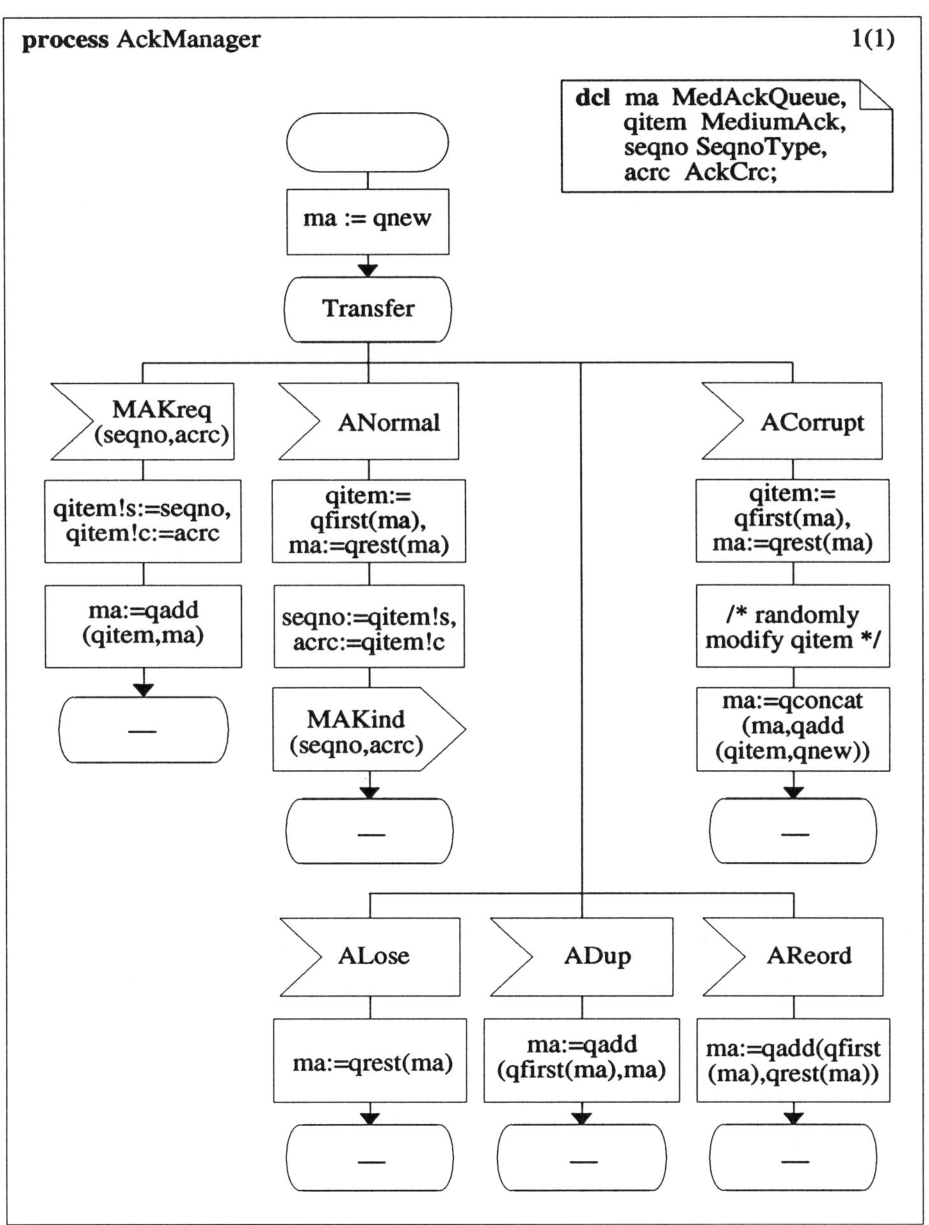

Figure 6.3 *(continued)*

treatment of acknowledgements within the medium is handled by process *Ack-Manager* whose behaviour is described by a sequence of operations on a queue of data items, asynchronously triggered by a 'guard' process *AckHazard*. For realism, it has been assumed that messages and acknowledgements carry a CRC *(Cyclic Redundancy Check)* that is used to detect corruption.

A medium can be considered as a transfer service provider between two points. The idea of describing a service provider as an abstract queue manager is well-known in OSI *(Open Systems Interconnection)*. The specific queue management policy determines the kind of service. In the formal description of the unreliable medium the queue management is specialised to reflect its characteristics. Whenever signal *MDTreq* is received, a new item is added to the queue. From time to time the first item is removed from the queue and the corresponding signal *MDTind* issued, or 'unfair' operations are performed on the queue. The overall set of non-deterministic factors causing all this is summarised in process *MsgHazard* which 'suggests' to *MsgManager*, via suitable signals, the operation to be carried out on the queue: normal delivery, loss, duplication, reordering or corruption. The same possibilities apply for acknowledgements, dealt with by *MAKreq*, *MAKind*, *AckHazard* and *AckManager*.

The signals *MNormal* and *ANormal* trigger fair operations on the queues of data and acknowledgements, whereas *MLose*, *MDup*, *MReord*, *MCorrupt*, *ALose*, *ADup*, *AReord* and *ACorrupt* trigger unfair operations. In the process bodies of *MsgManager* and *AckManager*, unfair operations are described by means of standard functions on the abstract data type *queue*. Process bodies for *MsgHazard* and *AckHazard* are left undefined[9]. In fact they summarise something that is beyond control of the specifier and as such cannot be described. An SDL specifier would best avoid their appearance by simply locating them in the environment. They have been shown explicitly here for the sake of greater clarity.

When describing a system with SDL, it is completely up to the specifier where to position its boundary with the environment. In the formal description, the medium was considered as a system on its own because the protocol was not of interest. If the protocol were relevant, it would be possible to move the system boundary and include the description of the protocol entities. The block *Medium* itself could be reused entirely in this larger description, except that signal and data definitions at system level would have to be enriched to reflect the protocol.

[9]This section uses strict SDL-88. An alternative approach is shown in Section 5.5.2, where the spontaneous transition feature of SDL-92 has been used to model non-determinism

6.6 Conclusion[10]

Even with this small example there were still useful lessons to be learned in writing the formal descriptions. It is tempting to assume that a commonly used concept (an unreliable medium in this case) will be understood in the same way by everyone. The conclusions from this example are as follows:

- It is important to define the boundary of a system clearly. In this case, the boundary between the medium and the protocol using it were not clearly drawn in the informal description. Clarification was needed of where to locate functions such as detection of corruption and identification of message types.

- The range of errors a system may cause needs to be carefully stated. For example, it is vital for a protocol to know exactly what kinds of error may occur in the medium (e.g. corruption of message data content but not message type).

- Before writing a formal description of a system, it is worth formally describing its infrastructure first. The unreliable medium supports the sliding window protocol of Chapter 7. Problems resolved in formalising the medium saved effort in writing the much larger description of the protocol.

[10]Section 6.6 is by K. J. Turner.

7 Sliding Window Protocol

A sliding window protocol is one of the simplest protocols, yet it illustrates important flow control and error recovery mechanisms found in many communications systems. Sequence numbering and windows are used for flow control. The protocol is designed to operate over an unreliable medium and so employs sequence numbering and acknowledgements. The protocol described in this chapter could be supported by the unreliable medium described in Chapter 6. The seminal paper on the sliding window protocol, Stenning (1976), described the protocol in a PASCAL-like language and investigated its correctness.

7.1 Informal Description[1]

The **Sliding Window Protocol** supports a unidirectional flow of data with a positive handshake on each transfer. An acknowledgement window is used for flow control. The protocol supports the sliding window service 'S' over an unreliable medium service 'M' that may lose, corrupt, duplicate or re-order messages. It is assumed that the corruption of messages can be reliably detected by the protocol by some unspecified means such as a checksum. The protocol has no connection or disconnection procedures.

7.1.1 *Sequence Numbering*

The transmitter sends a sequence number with each message. A sequence number is unbounded and is incremented for each new message. The first message transmitted has sequence number 1.

The receiver sends an acknowledgement when it receives a message. The acknowledgement carries a sequence number that refers to the last message successfully transferred to the receiving user. If an acknowledgement has to be sent before a successful reception (e.g. the first message was corrupted), it is given sequence number 0.

[1] Section 7.1 is by K. J. Turner, derived from the narrative and programs in Stenning (1976).

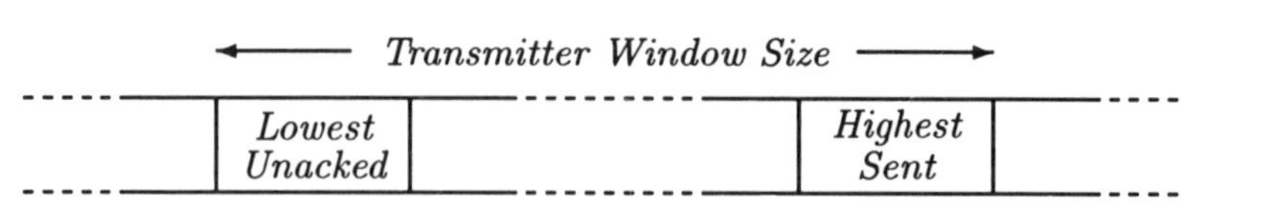

Figure 7.1: Sliding Window Protocol – Transmitter Window

7.1.2 *Transmitter Behaviour*

The transmitter maintains a window of sequence numbers as shown in Figure 7.1. This gives the lowest sequence number for which an acknowledgement is awaited, and the highest sequence number so far used. The window size is limited to the value *TWS (Transmitter Window Size)*.

The transmitter behaves initially as (1) below, and then loops doing (2), (3) and (4) where possible:

(1) *LowestUnacked* is set to 1, *HighestSent* to 0 and *TWS* to a positive value dependent on the implementation.

(2) If the current window size (*HighestSent* – *LowestUnacked*) is less than *TWS*, then a message with the next sequence number (*HighestSent* + 1) may be transmitted. In this case, *HighestSent* is incremented and a timer for that message is started.

(3) If an acknowledgement is received that is not corrupted and has a sequence number not less than *LowestUnacked*, then all timers for messages up to and including that sequence number are cancelled. In this case, *LowestUnacked* is set to the sequence number following the acknowledged one.

(4) If a timeout occurs, then the timers for all messages transmitted after the timed out one are cancelled. All these timed out messages are retransmitted (in sequence, starting with the earliest) and have timers started for them.

7.1.3 *Receiver Behaviour*

The receiver maintains a window of sequence numbers as shown in Figure 7.2. This gives the lowest sequence number that is awaited and the highest sequence number that has been received. The window size is limited to the value *RWS (Receiver Window Size)*.

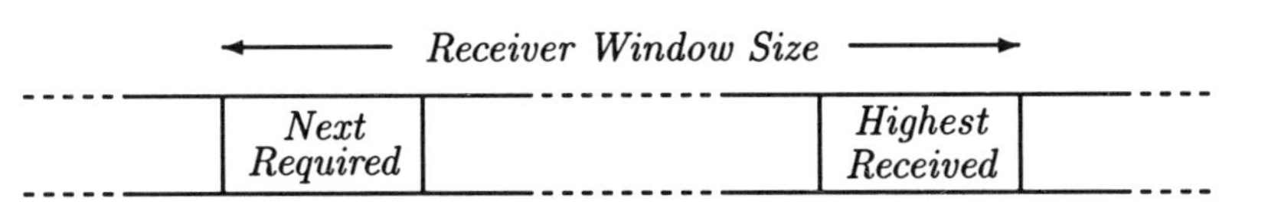

Figure 7.2: Sliding Window Protocol – Receiver Window

The receiver behaves initially as (1) below, and then loops doing (2) and (3) where possible.

(1) *NextRequired* is initialised to 1, and *TWS* to to a positive value dependent on the implementation.

(2) If a message is received that is not corrupted, has not already been received, and is within the maximum receive window (defined by *NextRequired* and *RWS*), then all messages from *NextRequired* up to but not including the first unreceived message are delivered to the receiving user[2]. In this case, *NextRequired* is set to the sequence number of the next message to be delivered to the receiving user.

(3) If a message is received under any circumstances, an acknowledgement giving the sequence number of the last delivered message (*NextRequired* − 1) is returned.

7.2 Errors in the Informal Description[3]

7.2.1 *Window Size*

In Sections 7.1.2 and 7.1.3, do *TWS* and *RWS* need to have the same value? What should happen if these parameters are not positive?

The window sizes are intentionally allowed to be different. If a window size is not positive, the protocol should simply fail to transmit messages ($TWS \leq 0$) or receive them ($RWS \leq 0$).

[2]There may be no such messages if there is a gap due to misordering.

[3]Section 7.2 is by K. J. Turner, based on problems found by the authors of the formal descriptions.

7.2.2 *Flow Control*

Section 7.1.3 is unclear as to what 'delivery' of a message means. Does it mean dispatch by the receiver to its user or receipt by its user? These may not be the same if there is buffering or delay between the receiver and its user.

Since the interface between the receiver and its user depends on the implementation, it is not reasonable to restrict the meaning of 'delivery' in the informal description. Similarly, the concept of 'delivery' in a formal description depends on the particular FDT used.

7.2.3 *Value of Time-Out Period*

Is the timeout period mentioned in Section 7.1.2 fixed for all implementations, fixed for one implementation, or dynamically variable?

The timeout period was meant to be left open, i.e. to be specified at a lower level of description.

7.2.4 *Receiver Window Size*

In Section 7.1.3, should the receiver initialise *RWS*? The informal description refers to *TWS*.

It was intended that *RWS* be initialised. The mention of *TWS* was a typographical error.

7.2.5 *Sequence of Operations*

In Sections 7.1.2 and 7.1.3, do the phrases '(2), (3) and (4)' and '(2) and (3)' mean a sequence in time, or a set of operations that may be carried out in parallel?

A sequence in time was intended.

7.2.6 *Transmit Window Size*

Figure 7.1 and the definition of 'current window size' of Section 7.1.2 are inconsistent.

The value '$HighestSent - LowestUnacked + 1$' should have been defined as the current window size.

7.2.7 *Receive Window Size*

Section 7.1.3 says that a message may be processed if its sequence number lies 'within the maximum receive window'. Is the upper bound of this included in this range (i.e. $NextRequired + RWS$)?

The upper bound is not included. The text should have read 'within the current receive window (*NextRequired* + *RWS* − 1)'.

7.2.8 *Retransmission on Timeout*

What are 'all these timed out messages' mentioned in Section 7.1.2? Only one message has in fact timed out. The phrase might also mean all the messages following, but not including, the timed out one.

The intention was that the timed out message and all messages sent later be retransmitted.

7.3 Formal Description in ESTELLE[4]

The architecture of the formal description is shown in Figure 7.3. All the modules of the description are **systemprocesses**, and so run asynchronously. As these modules are not refined into submodules, the global behaviour would not change if they were designated **systemactivities**. The crucial point is that they are distinct systems. An explicit *Timer* module was chosen for two reasons:

- it shows a way to manage timeouts without using **delay** clauses directly, although an ESTELLE description of a timer module would obviously use these; **delay** clauses are used for timeouts in the example of section 9.3
- it seemed to model the informal requirements more closely.

The *Timer* module is not described because it was felt that it would make the text longer without really adding much information to the example. Unless cancelled, the *Timer* module generates an interaction for each data interaction that arises, in order to ensure retransmission.

The sliding window protocol is unusual in several ways. For example, its data flow is unidirectional, leading to a few peculiarities in the architecture of the formal description such as having distinct and different modules acting as peers.

The transmitter uses primitive procedures and functions to buffer messages until they are acknowledged. *BuffSave* stores a PDU (*Protocol Data Unit* – a message) by its sequence number and data. *BuffFree* discards the buffered message with a given sequence number. *BuffRetrieve* extracts the buffered data with a given sequence number. The transmitter also uses *Corrupted* (to check if a PDU has been corrupted in transit) and *PDUDT* (to construct a data PDU).

The receiver has corresponding primitive procedures and functions to buffer messages until they need to be delivered. *PDUSave* stores a PDU. *PDURetrieve*

[4]Section 7.3 is by R. L. Tenney and T. P. Blumer.

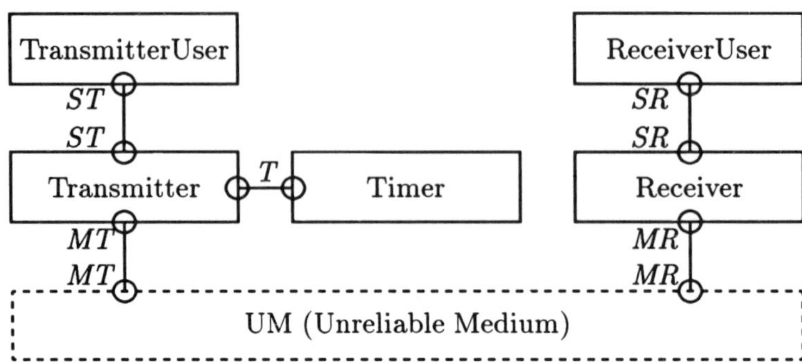

Figure 7.3: Sliding Window Protocol in ESTELLE – Architecture

extracts the buffered PDU for a given sequence number. The receiver also uses *Corrupted* (to check if a PDU has been corrupted in transit), *PDUAK* (to construct an acknowldegement PDU) and *UserData* (to extract the data part of a PDU).

```
specification SlidingWindowProtocol;

default individual queue;

type
  SeqType = integer;                 { Sequence number type, >= 0 }
  UserDataType = ...;                { Some suitable type, e.g. a string }
  DTPDUType =                        { Data message }
    record
      Seq: SeqType;
      Msg: UserDataType;
    end;
  AKPDUType =                        { Acknowledgement message}
    record
      Seq: SeqType;
    end;

channel TxUser(User, Transmitter);
  by User:
    SDTreq(Data : UserDataType);
```

```
channel RxUser(User, Receiver);
  by Receiver:
    SDTind(Data : UserDataType);

channel Tx(Transmitter, Medium);
  by Transmitter:
    MDTreq(PDU : DTPDUType);
  by Medium:
    MAKind(PDU : AKPDUType);

channel Rx(Receiver, Medium);
  by Receiver:
    MAKreq(PDU : AKPDUType);
  by Medium:
    MDTind(PDU : DTPDUType);

channel Time(Transmitter, Timer);
  by Transmitter:
    TimeReq(Seq : SeqType);
    TimeCanc(Seq : SeqType);
  by Timer:
    TimeResp(Seq : SeqType);

module TransmitterUser systemprocess;
  ip ST : TxUser(User);
end;

body TransmitterUserBody for TransmitterUser;
external;

module ReceiverUser systemprocess;
  ip SR : RxUser(User);
end;

body ReceiverUserBody for ReceiverUser;
external;

module UM systemprocess;
  ip
    MT : Tx(Medium);
    MR : Rx(Medium);
end;
```

```
{ The body for the UM module is given in Section 6.3 }

body UMBody for UM;
external;

module Timer systemprocess;
  ip T : Time(Timer);
end;

body TimerBody for Timer;
external;

module Transmitter systemprocess;
  ip
    ST : TxUser(Transmitter);
    MT : Tx(Transmitter);
    T  : Time(Transmitter);
end;

{ Transmitter module body }

body TransmitterBody for Transmitter;

  const TWSMax = any integer;   { Maximum window size }

  state SENDING;

  { Save user data in buffer until acknowledgement }

  procedure BuffSave(s : SeqType; d : UserDataType);
  primitive;

  { Free user data buffer entry after acknowledgement }

  procedure BuffFree(s : SeqType);
  primitive;

  { Retrieve user data entry from buffer }

  function BuffRetrieve(s : SeqType) : UserDataType;
  primitive;
```

```
{ Returns true if the PDU is corrupted }

function Corrupted(PDU : AKPDUType) : boolean;
primitive;

{ Construct a DT PDU from the user data and sequence number }

function PDUDT(s : SeqType; d : UserDataType) : DTPDUType;
primitive;

var
  LowestUnacked : SeqType;
  HighestSent : SeqType;
  TWS : integer;

initialize
  to SENDING
    provided (TWSMax > 0)
    begin
      LowestUnacked := 1;
      HighestSent := 0;
      TWS := TWSMax;
    end;

trans

  { Transmit while window not full }
  from SENDING to same
    when ST.SDTreq
      provided HighestSent - LowestUnacked + 1 < TWS
        begin
          HighestSent := HighestSent + 1;
          output T.TimeReq(HighestSent);
          output MT.MDTreq(PDUDT(HighestSent, Data));
          BuffSave(HighestSent, Data);
        end;

  { Receive acknowledgement }
  from SENDING to same
    when MT.MAKind
```

```
        provided (PDU.Seq >= LowestUnacked) and
         (PDU.Seq <= HighestSent) and not Corrupted(PDU)
          var S : SeqType;
          begin
            for S := LowestUnacked to PDU.Seq do
              begin
               output T.TimeCanc(S);
               BuffFree(S);
              end;
            LowestUnacked := PDU.Seq + 1;
          end;

        { Receive acknowledgement not in window }
        provided otherwise
          begin
            { Ignore this acknowledgement }
          end;

    { Timer response }
    from SENDING to same
      when T.TimeResp
        provided (Seq >= LowestUnacked) and
         (Seq <= HighestSent)
          var S : SeqType;
          begin
            for S := Seq to HighestSent do
              begin
               output T.TimeCanc(S);
               output MT.MDTreq(PDUDT(S, BuffRetrieve(S)));
               output T.TimeReq(S);
              end;
           end;

        provided otherwise
          begin
            { Ignore timer response for sequence number outside
            window, e.g. when an acknowledgement arrives just as
            the timer responds }
          end;

end; { TransmitterBody }
```

```
module Receiver systemprocess;
  ip
    SR : RxUser(Receiver);
    MR : Rx(Receiver);
end;

{ Receiver module body }

body ReceiverBody for Receiver;

  const RWSMax = any integer; { Maximum window size }

  state RECEIVING;

  { Construct an AK PDU, given the sequence number }

  function PDUAK(S : SeqType) : AKPDUType;
  primitive;

  { Retrieve PDU with sequence number S from buffer, returning a
  PDU with sequence number 0 if not in buffer }

  function PDURetrieve(S : SeqType) : DTPDUType;
  primitive;

  { Save the PDU in the buffer }

  procedure PDUSave(PDU : DTPDUType);
  primitive;

  { Returns true if the PDU is corrupted }

  function Corrupted(PDU : DTPDUType) : boolean;
  primitive;

  { Return the user data from the given PDU }

  function UserData(p : DTPDUType) : UserDataType;
  primitive;

  var
    NextRequired : SeqType;
```

```
    HighestReceived : SeqType;
    RWS : integer;

initialize
    to RECEIVING
      provided RWSMax > 0
        begin
          NextRequired := 1;
          HighestReceived := 0;
          RWS := RWSMax;
        end;

trans

    { Receive message in window }
    from RECEIVING to same
      when MR.MDTind
        provided (PDU.Seq >= NextRequired) and
         (PDU.Seq < NextRequired + RWS) and
          not Corrupted(PDU)
          var
            S   : SeqType;
            TPDU : DTPDUType;
            Done : boolean;
          begin
           PDUSave(PDU);
           S := NextRequired;
           Done := false;

           { Retrieve each PDU from buffer and send to user.
           Stop at first gap in buffer, i.e. the first PDU not
           received (sequence number 0 returned). }
           repeat
            TPDU := PDURetrieve(S);
            if TPDU.Seq = S then
             begin
              { Extract user data from PDU and send to user }
              output SR.SDTind(UserData(TPDU));
              S := S + 1;
             end
            else
             { Reached gap in buffer }
```

```
            Done := true;
          until Done;
          NextRequired := S;
          output MR.MAKreq(PDUAK(NextRequired - 1));
        end;

      { Receive message that is not in window or corrupted }
      provided otherwise
        begin
          output MR.MAKreq(PDUAK(NextRequired - 1));
        end;

  end; { ReceiverBody }

{ Main body for SlidingWindowProtocol }

modvar
  TransmitterInstance : Transmitter;
  ReceiverInstance : Receiver;
  TransmitterUserInstance : TransmitterUser;
  ReceiverUserInstance : ReceiverUser;
  UMInstance : UM;
  TimerInstance : Timer;

  initialize
    begin
      init TransmitterUserInstance with TransmitterUserBody;
      init ReceiverUserInstance with ReceiverUserBody;
      init TransmitterInstance with TransmitterBody;
      init ReceiverInstance with ReceiverBody;
      init UMInstance with UMBody;
      init TimerInstance with TimerBody;

      connect TransmitterUserInstance.ST to TransmitterInstance.ST;
      connect ReceiverUserInstance.SR to ReceiverInstance.SR;
      connect TransmitterInstance.MT to UMInstance.MT;
      connect ReceiverInstance.MR to UMInstance.MR;
      connect TransmitterInstance.T to TimerInstance.T;
    end;
  end. { SlidingWindowProtocol }
```

7.4 Formal Description in LOTOS[5]

7.4.1 *Architecture of the Formal Description*

The sliding window protocol is an asymmetrical protocol in the sense that it is composed of two different entities: the *Transmitter* at the sending side, and the *Receiver* at the receiving side. Since the service provided by this protocol has not been explicitly defined, different approaches could be taken when representing the communicating entities and the architecture of the protocol.

One approach would be to consider each entity as a whole. In this way, the transmitter user would access the service via a gate *ut*, and the transmitter would access the medium via the gate *mt*. Similarly, the receiver user would access the service via a gate *ur*, and the receiver would access the medium via the gate *mr*.

An alternative approach would be to consider both entities together. In this way, the service provided by the sliding window protocol would be accessed via a single gate *s*, and the protocol would access the medium via a single gate *m*. Service access points would be used to distinguish the different entities involved. This approach is in line with the way OSI services and protocols are defined, and does not reduces the generality or abstractness of the specification. It is the approach chosen here.

An outline representation of the protocol and its supporting medium would be:

```
specification SlidingWindowProtocol [s, m] (...) : noexit

  behaviour
    (TransmitterEntity [s, m] (...) ||| ReceiverEntity [s, m] (...))
  ||
    UnreliableMedium [m] (...)

  where

  process TransmitterEntity [s, m] (...) : noexit ...

  process ReceiverEntity [s, m] (...) : noexit ...

  process UnreliableMedium [m] (...) : noexit ...

endspec (* SlidingWindowProtocol *)
```

[5]Section 7.4 is by F. M. Fournón y González-Barcia and T. de Miguel Moro.

This chapter contains only the specification of the protocol. The specification of the unreliable medium in Chapter 6 is used in part for the protocol. The style of the specification is constraint-oriented. At the top level, the behaviour of the protocol is divided into two constraints, *TransmitterEntity* and *ReceiverEntity*. Each of these entities is further divided into the constraints related to one gate (local constraints) and the constraints involving both gates. The local constraints comprise those for gate *s* and those for gate *m*. The constraints involving both gates are further decomposed into simpler processes.

The basic elements of the protocol are the SAPs *(Service Access Points)* it supports, the SPs *(Service Primitives)* exchanged at these points, the SDUs *(Service Data Units)* carried by those primitives, and the PDUs *(Protocol Data Units)* in which they are embedded.

The overall structure of the specification in terms of the nesting of definitions is:

```
specification SlidingWindowProtocol

  library

  type SSAPs
  type SSDUs
  type SSPs
  type PDUs
  type EnrichedNat
  type MSAPs
  type MSPs

  behaviour

  process TransmitterEntity
    process LocalConstraints
      process SGate
      process MGate
        process MGate1
  process TransmitterConstraints
      type TimerSignal
      process AllTimers
        process Timer
          process AnyTimer
          process Identification
            type NaturalMod
      type PDUQueue
      process Transmitter
```

```
            process Sender
            process AckRec
              process ReleaseQueue
            process TimeOut
              process Retransmission
            process IgnoreAckedAck
        process PDUCorrectness
        process IgnoreCorruptedPDU
      process ReceiverEntity
        type PDUSet1
        type PDUSet
        type PDUSetIndexed
        process LocalConstraints
          process SGate
          process MGate
        process Receiver
          process Receiver1
            process DeliverMessages
          process IgnoredPDU
          process SendAck
              type NatMinus
```

7.4.2 *Top-Level Specification*

The sliding window protocol provides its service through the *s* gate, and accesses the medium via the *m* gate. The overall specification is parameterised by the maximum window sizes (*tws*, *rws*).

```
specification SlidingWindowProtocol [s, m] (tws, rws : Nat ) : noexit
```

Natural numbers, Booleans and sets are required from the standard library.

```
library
  NaturalNumber, Boolean, Set
endlib
```

7.4.3 *Top-Level Data Types*

The specification of SAPs provides two distinct values (*ut* and *ur*) for the transmitting and receiving ends.

```
type SSAPs is
  sorts SSAP
  opns ut, ur : -> SSAP
endtype (* SSAPs *)
```

Nothing definite is said in the informal description about the data units carried by the protocol except that there are data messages and acknowledgement messages. Thus, a sort with distinct values would be enough. For testing purposes, however, and in order to use a set of PDUs later, equality (*eq*) has been defined so that (in)equality of PDUs can be defined. Just two data messages (*data1*, *data2*) are specified.

```
type SSDUs is Boolean
  sorts SSDU
  opns
    data1, data2 :                        -> SSDU
    _eq_ :              SSDU, SSDU        -> Bool
  eqns
    forall data : SSDU
      ofsort Bool
        data1 eq data2          = false;
        data2 eq data1          = false;
        data eq data            = true;
endtype (* SSDUs *)
```

Service primitives have three kinds of operations: constructors for requests and indications (*UDTreq*, *UDTind*), a selector to extract a service data unit (*DataOf*), and recognisers for request and indication primitives (*IsUDTreq*, *IsUDTind*)[6].

```
type SSPs is SSDUs
  sorts SSP
  opns
    UDTreq, UDTind :            SSDU    -> SSP
    IsUDTreq, IsUDTind :        SSP     -> Bool
    DataOf :                    SSP     -> SSDU
  eqns
    forall sp : SSP, sdu : SSDU
      ofsort SSDU
        DataOf (UDTreq (sdu)) = sdu;
        DataOf (UDTind (sdu)) = sdu;
```

[6]In more complex descriptions, each type of service primitive would be identified with a natural number to simplify the definition of recognisers.

```
            ofsort bool
              IsUDTreq (UDTreq (sdu))          = true;
              IsUDTreq (UDTind (sdu))          = false;
              IsUDTind (sp)                    = not (IsUDTreq (sp));
      endtype (* SSPs *)
```

Protocol Data Units

With respect to the protocol data units, only the structure but not actual encoding is given in the informal description. In general, medium service data units would carry the encoded representation of the PDUs. Another data type would therefore be required for mapping between that encoded format and the logical structure. Since no encoding is defined for the sliding window protocol, no intermediate mapping is required.

There is another implication of the absence of this encoding. The corruption of PDUs has to be 'reliably detected'. Without an encoded format, it cannot be guessed how corruption arises or how it can be detected. The only way of representing this is with an extra operation *Corrupt* and an *IsCorrupted* predicate.

(In)equality of PDUs is also defined. This is necessary when defining *PDUSet* later, based on the *Set* type from the standard library. There, *eq* and *ne* are formal operations that require to be actualised.

```
      type PDUs is SSDUs, NaturalNumber, Boolean
        sorts PDU
        opns
          MakeDTPDU :      SSDU, Nat        -> PDU
          MakeAKPDU :      Nat              -> PDU
          DataOf :         PDU              -> SSDU
          SeqNo :          PDU              -> Nat
          IsCorrupted :    PDU              -> Bool
          IsDTPDU  :       PDU              -> Bool
          IsAKPDU :        PDU              -> Bool
          Corrupt :        PDU              -> PDU
          _eq_, _ne_ :     PDU, PDU         -> Bool
        eqns
          forall sn, sn1, sn2 : Nat, data, data1, data2 : SSDU,
           pdu, pdu1, pdu2   : PDU
            ofsort SSDU
              DataOf (MakeDTPDU (data, sn))            = data;
            ofsort Nat
              SeqNo (MakeDTPDU (data, sn))             = sn;
              SeqNo (MakeAKPDU (sn))                   = sn;
```

```
            ofsort Bool
              IsCorrupted (MakeDTPDU (data, sn))      = false;
              IsCorrupted (MakeAKPDU (sn))            = false;
              IsCorrupted (Corrupt (pdu))             = true;
              IsDTPDU (MakeDTPDU (data, sn))          = true;
              IsDTPDU (MakeAKPDU (sn))                = false;
              IsAKPDU (MakeDTPDU (data, sn))          = false;
              IsAKPDU (MakeAKPDU (sn))                = true;
              IsCorrupted (pdu) =>
                IsDTPDU (pdu)                         = false;
              IsCorrupted (pdu) =>
                IsAKPDU (pdu)                         = false;
              Corrupt (pdu1) eq Corrupt (pdu2)        = pdu1 eq pdu2;
              not (IsCorrupted (pdu1)) =>
                pdu1 eq Corrupt (pdu2)                = false;
              not (IsCorrupted (pdu2)) =>
                Corrupt (pdu1) eq pdu2                = false;
              IsDTPDU (pdu1), IsAKPDU (pdu2) =>
                pdu1 eq pdu2                          = false;
              IsDTPDU (pdu2), IsAKPDU (pdu1) =>
                pdu1 eq pdu2                          = false;
              MakeDTPDU (data1, sn1) eq MakeDTPDU (data2, sn2) =
                (data1 eq data2) and (sn1 eq sn2);
              MakeAKPDU (sn1) eq MakeAKPDU (sn2)= sn1 eq sn2;
              pdu1 ne pdu2                            =
                not (pdu1 eq pdu2);
      endtype (* PDUs *)
```

Finally, the number *1* is defined for convenience as a short way of saying '*Succ (0)*'.

```
      type EnrichedNat is NaturalNumber
        opns 1 : -> Nat
        eqns
          ofsort Nat
            Succ (0) = 1;
      endtype (* EnrichedNat *)
```

Medium Service Data Types

The medium service has data types for service access points and service primitives, but in place of the service data units of Section 6.4 there are protocol data units.

```
type MSAPs is
  sorts MSAP
  opns mt, mr: -> MSAP
endtype (* MSAPs *)

type MSPs is PDUs, Boolean
  sorts MSP
  opns
    MDTreq, MDTind : PDU      -> MSP
    MAKreq, MAKind : PDU      -> MSP
    PDUOf :          MSP      -> PDU
    IsMreq, IsMind : MSP      -> Bool
  eqns
    forall sp : MSP, pdu : PDU
      ofsort PDU
        PDUOf (MDTreq (pdu))= pdu;
        PDUOf (MDTind (pdu))= pdu;
        PDUOf (MAKreq (pdu))= pdu;
        PDUOf (MAKind (pdu))= pdu;
      ofsort Bool
        IsMreq (MDTreq (pdu)) = true;
        IsMreq (MDTind (pdu)) = false;
        IsMreq (MAKreq (pdu)) = true;
        IsMreq (MAKind (pdu)) = false;
        IsMind (sp)           = not (IsMreq (sp));
endtype (* MSPs *)
```

7.4.4 *Top-Level Behaviour*

The sliding window protocol provides its service through the *s* gate, and accesses the medium via the *m* gate. At the top level, the protocol is split into two asymmetrical entities, *TransmitterEntity* and *ReceiverEntity.* Each one has as parameters the service access points and the maximum window size.

```
behaviour
  [tws gt 0] ->
    TransmitterEntity [s, m] (ut, mt, tws)
|||
  [rws gt 0] ->
    ReceiverEntity [s, m] (ur, mr, rws)

where
```

7.4.5 *Transmitter Entity*

The *TransmitterEntity* process is divided into the constraints local to each gate, and the constraints related to both gates. The latter ones accept only correct PDUs from the medium, ignoring the incorrect ones.

```
process TransmitterEntity [s, m]
 (ssap : SSAP, msap : MSAP, tws : Nat) : noexit :=
  LocalConstraints [s, m] (ssap, msap)
||
  (
    (
      TransmitterConstraints [s, m] (tws)
    |[m]|
      PDUCorrectness [m]
    )
  |||
    IgnoreCorruptedPDU [m]
  )

  where
```

Transmitter Local Constraints

The *LocalConstraints* process is divided into the constraints at gate *s* and at *m*.

```
process LocalConstraints [s, m]
  (ssap : SSAP, msap : MSAP) : noexit :=
  SGate [s] (ssap)
|||
  MGate [m] (msap)

  where
```

The constraint at gate *s* always allows service requests at the *ssap* service access point.

```
process SGate [s] (ssap : SSAP) : noexit :=
  s ! ssap ? sp : SSP [IsUDTreq (sp)];
  SGate [s] (ssap)
endproc (* SGate *)
```

The constraints at gate *m* are also simple: once the first service request has been dealt with, any indication is allowed or any request with a data PDU.

```
process MGate [m] (msap : MSAP) : noexit :=
  m ! msap ? msp : MSP
    [IsMreq (msp) and IsDTPDU (PDUOf (msp))];
  MGate1 [m] (msap)

  where

  process MGate1 [m] (msap : MSAP) : noexit :=
    m ! msap ? msp : MSP
      [IsMreq (msp) and IsDTPDU (PDUOf (msp))];
    MGate1 [m] (msap)
  []
    m ! msap ? msp : MSP [IsMind (msp)];
    MGate1 [m] (msap)
  endproc (* MGate1 *)

endproc (*MGate *)

endproc (* LocalConstraints *)
```

Transmitter Constraints

The constraints involving both gates are divided into those dealing with timers and those dealing with the transmitter itself. The *Transmitter* process is initialised with the maximum window size, a highest sequence number sent of 0, a lowest unacknowledged sequence number of 1, and an empty retransmission queue.

```
process TransmitterConstraints [s, m] (tws : Nat) : noexit :=
  hide t in
    AllTimers [t] (tws + 1, 0)
  |[t]|
    Transmitter [s, m, t] (tws, 0, 1, empty)

  where
```

Timers

Although the actual passage of time cannot be represented in LOTOS, the events of timer expiry as well as timer set-up or release can be modelled. The informal description does not specify the actual period before a time-out occurs. This can be easily represented in LOTOS because the time elapsed between any two consecutive events is always undefined. Timer events are signalled through the *t* gate. A timer can be set or reset and can expire.

```
type TimerSignal is
  sorts TimerSignal
  opns set, reset, expired : -> TimerSignal
endtype (* TimerSignal *)
```

A maximum of *tws + 1* timers are required, so there is one timer for each transmitted PDU awaiting acknowledgement by the receiver. Each timer is identified by the sequence number of the transmitted PDU, calculated modulo *tws + 1*.

```
process AllTimers [t] (MaxId, TimerId : Nat) : noexit :=
  [TimerId lt MaxId] ->
    (
      AllTimers [t] (MaxId, TimerId + 1)
    |||
      Timer [t] (MaxId, TimerId)
    )

  where

  process Timer [t] (MaxTimer, TimerId : Nat) : noexit :=
    AnyTimer [t]
  ||
    Identification [t] (MaxTimer, TimerId)

    where
```

Process *AnyTimer* behaves as an entity waiting to be set up, and then expires if it is not disrupted by a reset. Process *Identification* ensures that *AnyTimer* deals with events for the appropriate timer.

```
    process AnyTimer [t] : noexit :=
      t ? AnyId : Nat ! set;
      (
        (* The amount of elapsed time is undefined *)
        t ? AnyId : Nat ! expired;
        exit
      [>
        t ? AnyId : Nat ! reset;
        exit
      )
    >>
      AnyTimer [t]
    endproc (* AnyTimer *)
```

```
        process Identification [t] (MaxTimer, TimerId : Nat) :
         noexit :=
          t ? Identifier : Nat ? AnySignal : TimerSignal
            [TimerId = (Identifier Mod MaxTimer)];
          Identification [t] (MaxTimer, TimerId)

          where

          type NaturalMod is NaturalNumber
            opns _Mod_ : Nat, Nat        -> Nat
            eqns
              forall x, y : Nat
                ofsort Nat
                  x Mod 0                = x;
                  x lt y =>
                    x Mod y              = x;
                  x Mod y                = (x + y) Mod y;
          endtype (* NaturalMod *)

        endproc (* Identification *)

      endproc (* Timer *)

    endproc (* AllTimers *)
```

PDU Queues

A queue[7] of PDUs has a constructor (*Put*) and two selectors (*First* and *Remove*). No recognisers are required in the body of the specification. Note that the description of the queue is incomplete; for example, equations such as:

```
First (empty) = ...;
Remove (empty) = ...;
```

have not been included. With equations like these the data types become more complicated and less clear, distracting the reader from the real meaning of the specification[8]. The alternative of avoiding selectors and replacing them with constructors and the **choice** operator can be unsatisfactory because ADT operations are 'simulated' with behavioural constructs and dispersed throughout the specification. For an implementor, this use of **choice** may be difficult or even impossible to translate to executable code.

[7]The library type *String* could have been used here, but it was felt to be less intuitive.

[8]LOTOS strictly speaking requires data types to be specified completely, although this may not be required in normal mathematical practice. For example, the usual definition of division of numbers is quite acceptable even though division by zero is undefined.

```
type PDUQueue is PDUs, Boolean
  sorts PDUQueue
  opns
    empty :                                -> PDUQueue
    Put :          PDU, PDUQueue           -> PDUQueue
    First :        PDUQueue                -> PDU
    Remove :       PDUQueue                -> PDUQueue
  eqns
    forall pdu, pdu1, pdu2 : PDU, pq : PDUQueue
      ofsort PDU
        First (Put (pdu, empty)) = pdu;
        First (Put (pdu1, Put (pdu2, pq))) =
          First (Put (pdu2, pq));
      ofsort PDUQueue
        Remove (Put (pdu, empty)) = empty;
        Remove (Put (pdu1, Put (pdu2, pq))) =
          Put (pdu1, Remove (Put (pdu2, pq)));
endtype (* PDUQueue *)
```

Transmitter Behaviour

The transmitter can either send messages (process *Sender*), receive acknowledgements and empty the retransmission queue (process *AckRec*), ignore acknowledgements for already acknowledged messages (process *IgnoreAckedAck*) or deal with a time-out (process *TimeOut*). Unacknowledged PDUs are kept in a queue for retransmission.

```
process Transmitter [s, m, t]
 (tws, hs, lu : Nat, rq : PDUQueue) : noexit :=
  (
    Sender [s, m, t] (tws, hs, lu, rq)
  []
    AckRec [m, t] (hs, lu, rq)
  []
    TimeOut [m, t] (hs, lu, rq)
  []
    IgnoreAckedAck [m] (hs, lu, rq)
  )
>>
  accept hs, lu : Nat, rq : PDUQueue in
    Transmitter [s, m, t] (tws, hs, lu, rq)

  where
```

Sending a Message

The *Sender* process accepts a message from the user if the window is not full. Then a data PDU is constructed and sent to the receiver, a timer is started, the highest sequence number sent is incremented, and the PDU is put in the queue for possible retransmission.

```
process Sender [s, m, t] (tws, hs, lu : Nat, rq : PDUQueue) :
 exit (Nat, Nat, PDUQueue) :=
   s ? ssap : SSAP ? sp : SSP [hs lt (lu + tws)];
   (
      let pdu : PDU = MakeDTPDU (DataOf (sp), hs + 1) in
         m ? msap : MSAP ! MDTreq (pdu);
         t ! hs + 1 ! set;
         exit (hs + 1, lu, Put (pdu, rq))
   )
endproc (* Sender *)
```

Reception of an Acknowledgement

If an acknowledgement is received whose sequence number is greater than or equal to the last unacknowledged one and less or equal to the highest one sent, the corresponding queued messages are released.

```
process AckRec [m, t] (hs, lu : Nat, rq : PDUQueue) :
 exit (Nat, Nat, PDUQueue) :=
   m ? msap : MSAP ? msp : MSP
      [(SeqNo (PDUOf (msp)) ge lu) and
         (SeqNo (PDUOf (msp)) le hs)];
   ReleaseQueue [t] (hs, SeqNo (PDUOf (msp)), rq)

   where
```

In the *ReleaseQueue* process, the timers are also reset and *LowestUnacked* is set to the sequence number of the received acknowledgement plus 1.

```
process ReleaseQueue [t] (hs, sn : Nat, rq : PDUQueue) :
 exit (Nat, Nat, PDUQueue) :=
  let pdu : PDU = First (rq) in
     t ! SeqNo (pdu) ! reset;
     (
        [SeqNo (pdu) lt sn] ->
           ReleaseQueue [t] (hs, sn, Remove(rq))
     []
```

```
        [SeqNo (pdu) eq sn] ->
          exit (hs, sn + 1, Remove(rq))
      )
    endproc (* ReleaseQueue *)

  endproc (* AckRec *)
```

Error Conditions

The last event that can affect the *Transmitter* process is the expiry of a timer. If this happens, all the messages queued after the timed out one are retransmitted.

```
process TimeOut [m, t] (hs, lu : Nat, rq : PDUQueue) :
 exit (Nat, Nat, PDUQueue) :=
   t ? sn : Nat ! expired [(sn le hs) and (sn ge lu)];
   Retransmission [m, t] (sn, rq)
>>
   exit (hs, lu, rq)

   where
```

Before the actual retransmission of each message takes place, its corresponding timer is reset.

```
    process Retransmission [m, t] (sn : Nat, rq : PDUQueue) :
     exit :=
      let pdu : PDU = First (rq) in
        m ? msap : MSAP ! MDTreq (pdu);
        t ! SeqNo (pdu) ! reset;
        t ! SeqNo (pdu) ! set;
        (
          [SeqNo (pdu) lt sn] ->
            Retransmission [m, t] (sn, Remove(rq))
        []
          [SeqNo (pdu) eq sn] ->
            exit
        )
    endproc (* Retransmission *)

  endproc (* TimeOut *)
```

Acknowledgements whose sequence number corresponds to released PDUs or to unsent ones are ignored.

```
process IgnoreAckedAck [m] (hs, lu : Nat, rq : PDUQueue) :
 exit (Nat, Nat, PDUQueue) :=
   m ? msap : MSAP ? msp : MSP
     [(SeqNo (PDUOf (msp)) lt lu) or
       (SeqNo (PDUOf (msp)) gt hs)];
   exit (hs, lu, rq)
endproc (* IgnoreAckedAck *)

endproc (* Transmitter *)

endproc (* TransmitterConstraints *)
```

Finally, process *PDUCorrectness* ensures that *TransmitterConstraints* sees only uncorrupted PDUs. *IgnoreCorruptedPDU* absorbs those that are corrupted.

```
process PDUCorrectness [m] : noexit :=
  m ? msap : MSAP ? msp : MSP
    [not (IsCorrupted (PDUOf (msp)))];
  PDUCorrectness [m]
endproc (* PDUCorrectness *)

process IgnoreCorruptedPDU [m] : noexit :=
  m ? msap : MSAP ? msp : MSP [IsCorrupted (PDUOf (msp))];
  IgnoreCorruptedPDU [m]
endproc (* IgnoreCorruptedPDU *)

endproc (* TransmitterEntity *)
```

7.4.6 *Receiver Entity*

The *ReceiverEntity* process comprises the constraints local to each gate, and the constraints pertaining to both gates. The *Receiver* process is initialised with the maximum window size, a next required sequence number of 1, and an empty set of received PDUs.

```
process ReceiverEntity [s, m]
 (ssap : SSAP, msap : MSAP, rws : Nat) : noexit :=
  LocalConstraints [s, m] (ssap, msap)
||
  Receiver [s, m] (rws, 1, {} of PDUSet)

  where
```

Sets of PDUs

A set of PDUs is used almost everywhere in the receiver. This is made from the *Set* type in the standard library, enriching it with operations for handling indexes. Firstly, *Set* is instantiated using *PDU* for elements.

```
type PDUSet1 is Set actualizedby PDUs using
  sortnames
    PDU      for Element
    Bool     for FBool
endtype (* PDUSet1 *)
```

Now, a *PDUSet* instance of the type is created with elements *PDUs*. This would allow sets of other sorts of elements without destroying *Set*. Although both actualisation and renaming could have been done in the same type definition, it is perhaps clearer this way.

```
type PDUSet is PDUSet1 renamedby
  sortnames PDUSet for Set
endtype (* PDUSet *)
```

Finally, the type is enriched with operations to access PDUs in the set using their sequence numbers as an index. This avoids defining and handling sets of sequence numbers as well. Calls to *GetPDU* are guarded so that is used only when the given sequence number is known to be present.

```
type PDUSetIndexed is PDUSet
  opns
    _IsSeqNoIn_ :      Nat, PDUSet      -> Bool
    GetPDU :           Nat, PDUSet      -> PDU
  eqns
    forall sn : Nat, pdu : PDU, pduset : PDUSet
      ofsort Bool
        SeqNo (pdu) eq sn =>
          sn IsSeqNoIn Insert (pdu, pduset) = true;
        SeqNo (pdu) ne sn =>
          sn IsSeqNoIn Insert (pdu, pduset) =
            sn IsSeqNoIn pduset;
        sn IsSeqNoIn {} = false;
      ofsort PDU
        SeqNo (pdu) eq sn =>
          GetPDU (sn, Insert (pdu, pduset)) = pdu;
        SeqNo (pdu) ne sn =>
          GetPDU (sn, Insert (pdu, pduset)) =
            GetPDU (sn, pduset);
endtype (* PDUSetIndexed *)
```

Receiver Local Constraints

The local constraints are very simple, allowing certain primitives at only the receiver service access points. Indications only are allowed at the *s* gate.

```
process LocalConstraints [s, m] (ssap : SSAP, msap : MSAP) :
 noexit :=
  SGate [s] (ssap)
|||
  MGate [m] (msap)

  where

  process SGate [s] (ssap : SSAP) : noexit :=
    s ! ssap ? sp : SSP [IsUDTind (sp)];
    SGate [s] (ssap)
  endproc (* SGate *)
```

At the *m* gate, an indication is allowed and then a request carrying an AK PDU.

```
  process MGate [m] (msap : MSAP) : noexit :=
    m ! msap ? msp : MSP [IsMind (msp)];
    m ! msap ? msp : MSP
      [IsMreq (msp) and IsAKPDU (PDUOf (msp))];
    MGate [m] (msap)
  endproc (* MGate *)

endproc (* LocalConstraints *)
```

Receiver Behaviour

The receiver keeps every message received in a *PDUSet* and sends an acknowledgement. All received PDUs whose sequence numbers are consecutive are delivered to the user. An acknowledgement is sent in reply to an ignored PDU.

```
process Receiver [s, m] (rws, nr : Nat, ps : PDUSet) : noexit :=
  (
    Receiver1 [s, m] (rws, nr, ps)
  []
    IgnoredPDU [m] (rws, nr, ps)
  )
>>
  accept nr : Nat, ps : PDUSet in
    Receiver [s, m] (rws, nr, ps)
```

```
        where
```

The messages stored in the *PDUSet* must not be corrupted, must have a sequence number that falls in the receiver's maximum window size *rws*, and must not already have been received.

```
        process Receiver1 [s, m] (rws, nr : Nat, ps : PDUSet) :
          exit (Nat, PDUSet) :=
          m ? msap : MSAP ? msp : MSP
            [not (IsCorrupted (PDUOf (msp))) and
              (SeqNo (PDUOf (msp)) lt (nr + rws)) and
                (SeqNo (PDUOf (msp)) ge nr) and
                  (PDUOf (msp) NotIn ps)];
          DeliverMessages [s, m] (nr, Insert (PDUOf (msp), ps))

          where
```

Consecutive messages are delivered to the user and removed from the queue by process *DeliverMessages* The process is finished when a gap is found in the set of stored messages.

```
          process DeliverMessages [s, m] (nr : Nat, ps : PDUSet) :
           exit (Nat, PDUSet) :=
            [nr IsSeqNoIn ps] ->
              (
                let pdu : PDU = GetPDU(nr, ps) in
                  s ? ssap : SSAP ! UDTind (DataOf (pdu));
                  DeliverMessages [s, m] (nr + 1, Remove (pdu, ps))
              )
          []
            [not (nr IsSeqNoIn ps)] ->
              (
                SendAck [m] (nr)
              >>
                exit (nr, ps)
              )
          endproc (* DeliverMessages *)

        endproc (* Receiver1 *)
```

PDUs not handled by the receiver are ignored, but an acknowledgement is sent anyway. The *Pred* operation is defined for the sequence numbers (naturals) in order to be able subtract 1.

```
process IgnoredPDU [m] (rws, nr : Nat, ps : PDUSet) :
 exit (Nat, PDUSet) :=
  m ? msap : MSAP ? msp : MSP
    [IsCorrupted (PDUOf (msp)) or
      (SeqNo (PDUOf (msp)) ge (nr + rws)) or
        (SeqNo (PDUOf (msp)) lt nr) or (PDUOf (msp) IsIn ps)];
  SendAck [m] (nr)
>>
  exit (nr, ps)
endproc (* IgnoredPDU *)
```

Finally, an acknowledgement is sent to the transmitter for sequence number '*NextRequired* – 1'.

```
process SendAck [m] (sn : Nat) : exit :=
  m ? msap : MSAP ! MAKreq (MakeAKPDU (Pred (sn)));
  exit

  where

    type NatMinus is NaturalNumber
      opns Pred : Nat -> Nat
      eqns
        forall n : Nat
          ofsort Nat
            Pred (Succ (n)) = n;
    endtype (* NatMinus *)

endproc (* SendAck *)

  endproc (* Receiver *)

endproc (* ReceiverEntity *)

endspec (* SlidingWindowProtocol *)
```

7.5 Formal Description in SDL[9]

The architecture of the formal description is a natural mapping between the structuring features of SDL and the layering concepts of OSI. The *SlidingWindowProtocol* system is modelled as the composition of three blocks, *TransmitterEntity*, *ReceiverEntity* and *Medium*. The transmitter and receiver users are

[9]Section 7.5 is by S. Trigila.

located in the environment: they interact with the system via two service access points modelled by means of two unidirectional channels, *st* (from the environment to *TransmitterEntity*) and *sr* (from *ReceiverEntity* to the environment). The channels *st* and *sr* carry the signals *SDTreq* and *SDTind* respectively. These model interactions between the user and the provider of a unidirectional data transfer service.

The *TransmitterEntity* sends data over the medium (*MDTreq* signal) and gets acknowledgements from it (*MAKind* signal) by using bidirectional channel *mt*. Conversely, the *ReceiverEntity* gets data from the medium (*MDTind* signal) and sends acknowledgements over it (*MAKreq* signal) by using bidirectional channel *mr*. The *TransmitterEntity* block consists of a process type *Transmitter*, instantiated just once at system start-up time. The *ReceiverEntity* block consists of a process type *Receiver* that is also instantiated once at system start-up time.

The *Medium* block is given in Section 6.5 rather than here because it is not an integral part of the protocol specification. Although the SDL description of the sliding window protocol is not meant to include a formal description of the medium, many of the protocol features arise from the nature of the medium. Of course, a formal description of the block *Medium* would be essential in order to simulate the protocol or to validate it against the required service.

The informal description does not suggest any names for protocol data units, so *DT* is used for data and *AK* for acknowledgements. According to the principles of OSI, the *TransmitterEntity* and *ReceiverEntity* should interact with the *Medium* via service primitives such as *Mreq* and *Mind* in order to convey protocol data units. In order to avoid mapping between service data units and protocol data units, the informal description made the simplification that the medium distinguishes between data and acknowledgements. The formal description therefore uses '*MDTreq*' instead of '*Mreq (DT)*', '*MDTind*' for '*Mind (DT)*', '*MAKreq*' for '*Mreq (AK)*', and '*MAKind*' for '*Mind (AK)*'. Four corresponding signals have been defined. From this point of view, *Medium* can be thought of as just a block performing transfer and renaming of signals (requests becoming indications in both directions).

The informal description requires an individual timer to be set for each message sent. This is dealt with in SDL by using a timer *tim* with multiple instances referred to by a value in the range *[0..tws]*. The indexing value is used when (re)setting a given instance or to indicate which timer instance has expired. When timer primitives **set** and **reset** are used, a duration value should be specified. If specifying a value is undesirable, such primitives cannot be used. As an alternative, three external signals, say *SetTimer*, *ResetTimer* and *TimerExpiry*, could be used between the process *Transmitter* and the environment. Unfortunately, this solution would introduce an unacceptable level of detail into the overall system block interaction diagram and therefore has not been adopted. However, it should be noted that the ESTELLE and LOTOS descriptions of the sliding window protocol model timers without any delay value. Timer management is a convenient feature of SDL.

The dynamic part of the SDL description is, to some extent, implementation-oriented because it suggests algorithms to manipulate concrete data structures such as arrays and queues. However, the real purpose of any such algorithm is to show what the protocol does and not how it does it.

The formal description of the sliding window protocol is hopefully self-explanatory; very few comments were felt to be necessary.

The diagrams of Figure 7.4 refer to the macro *DataTypeDef* given below. This macro defines data types and instances that are applicable at system level. The formal description makes extensive use of complex data structures. A queue is used to store messages for which an acknowledgement is awaited. Two arrays with as many components as the receiver window size are used to support the receiver window mechanism. By using external synonyms, the description is parameterised with respect to the transmit and receive window sizes, the timeout period, and the checksum field lengths. Although the informal description does not mention the use of a CRC *(Cyclic Redundancy Check)* to protect protocol data units against corruption, it has been specified for realism. The format of the CRC depends on the kind of message (data or acknowledgement).

```
macrodefinition DataTypeDef;

synonym tws Integer = external;            /* Transmitter window */
synonym rws Integer = external;            /* Receiver window */
synonym delta Duration = external;         /* Timeout period */
synonym LenDataCrc Integer = external;     /* Data CRC length */
synonym LenAckCrc Integer = external;      /* Ack CRC length */

generator Queue (type Item)
  literals qnew;
  operators
    qadd :      Item, Queue      -> Queue;
    qfirst :    Queue            -> Item;
    qrest :     Queue            -> Queue;
    qconcat:    Queue, Queue     -> Queue;
    qdelete :   Integer, Queue   -> Queue;
    qempty :    Queue   -> Boolean;
  axioms
    qfirst (qnew) == error!;
    qfirst (qadd (x, qnew)) == x;
    qfirst (qadd (x1, qadd (x2, q))) == qfirst (qadd (x2, q));
    qrest (qnew) == qnew;
    qrest (qadd (x, qnew)) == qnew;
```

```
    qrest (qadd (x1, qadd (x2, q))) == qadd (x1, qrest (qadd (x2, q)));
    qconcat (qnew, q) == q;
    qconcat (qadd (x1, q1), q2) == qadd (x1, qconcat (q1, q2));
    qdelete (0, q) == q;
    qdelete (i, q) == qdelete (i – 1, qrest (q));
    qempty (qnew);
    not (qempty (qadd (x, q)));
endgenerator Queue;

syntype DataCrcIndex = Integer
  constants 1 : LenDataCrc
endsyntype DataCrcIndex;

syntype AckCrcIndex = Integer
  constants 1 : LenAckCrc
endsyntype AckCrcIndex;

syntype Tsn = Integer                 /* Integer in range 0 .. tws – 1 */
  constants 0 : tws – 1
endsyntype Tsn;

syntype Rsn = Integer                 /* Integer in range 0 .. rws – 1 */
  constants 0 : rws – 1
endsyntype Rsn;

syntype SeqnoType = Natural
endsyntype SeqnoType;

newtype DataCrc array (DataCrcIndex, Bit)
  /* For a given sequence number and user data field, calculate the
  CRC for an MDT protocol data unit */
  operators dcheck : SeqnoType, BitString –> DataCrc;
endnewtype DataCrc;

newtype AckCrc array (AckCrcIndex, Bit)
  /* For a given sequence number, calculate the CRC for an MAK
  protocol data unit */
  operators acheck : SeqnoType –> AckCrc;
endnewtype AckCrc;

newtype MsgBuf array (Rsn, BitString);
endnewtype MsgBuf;
```

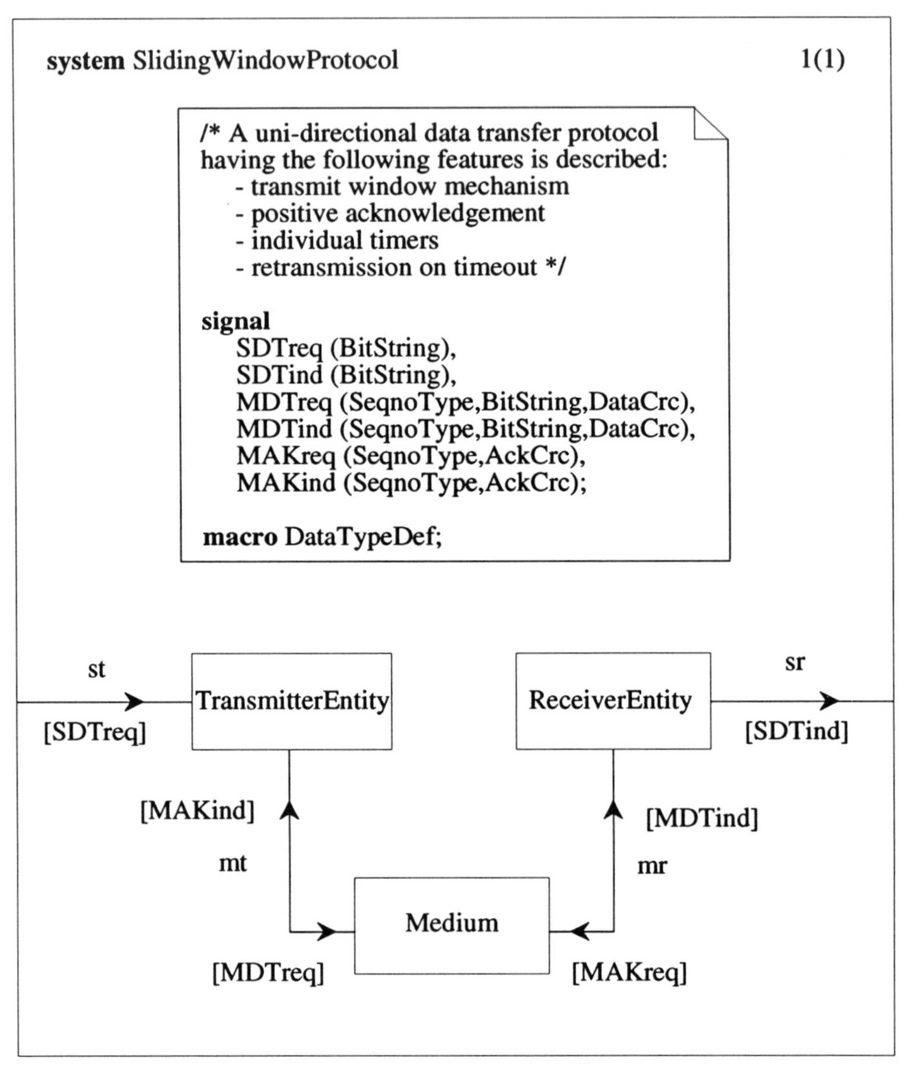

Figure 7.4: Sliding Window Protocol in SDL – Graphical Description

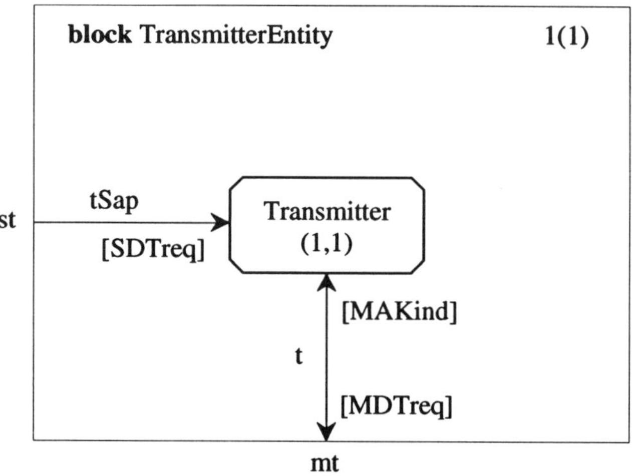

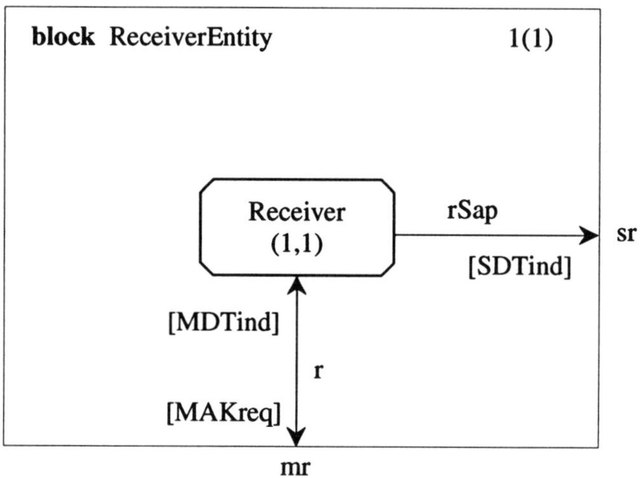

Figure 7.4 *(continued)*

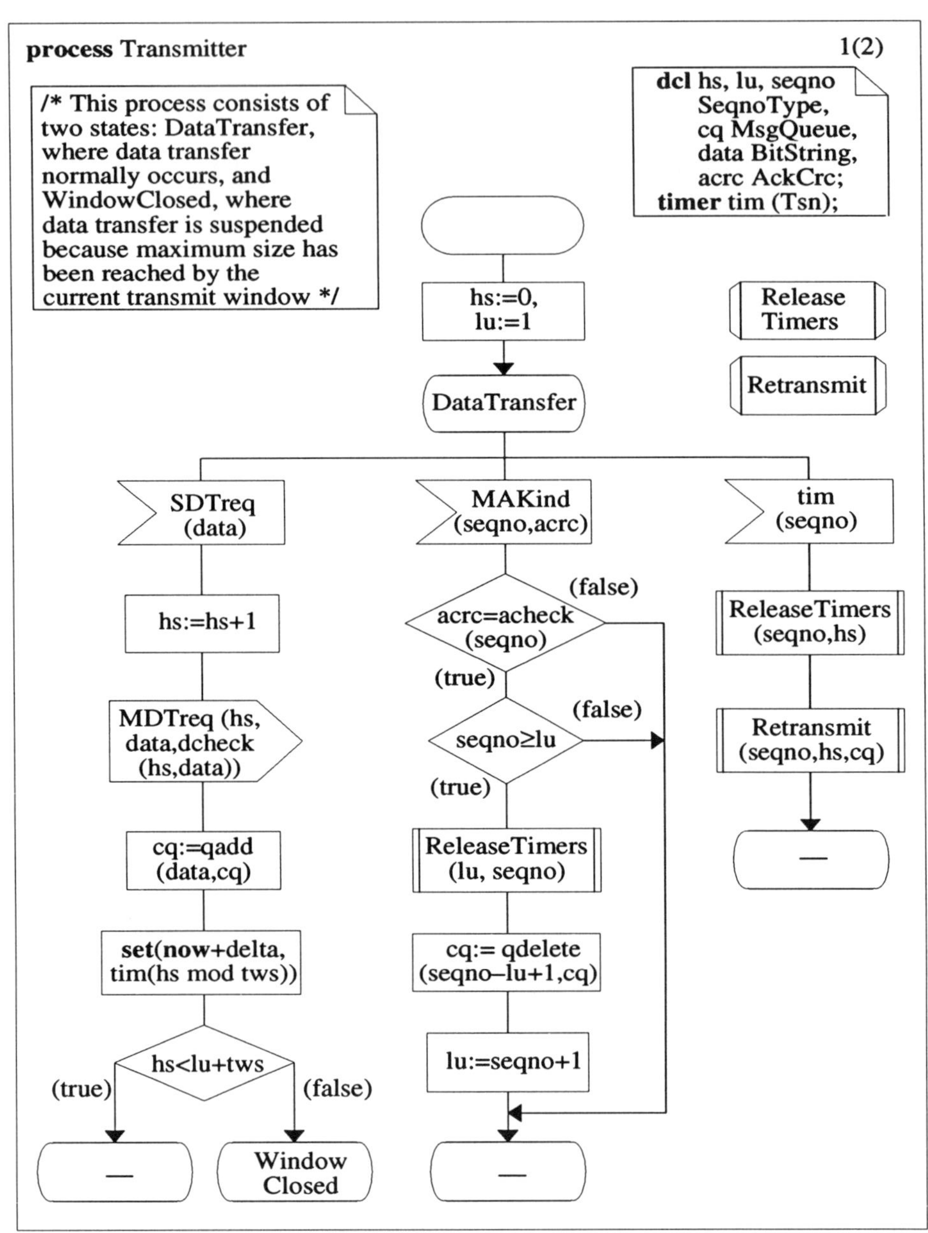

Figure 7.4 *(continued)*

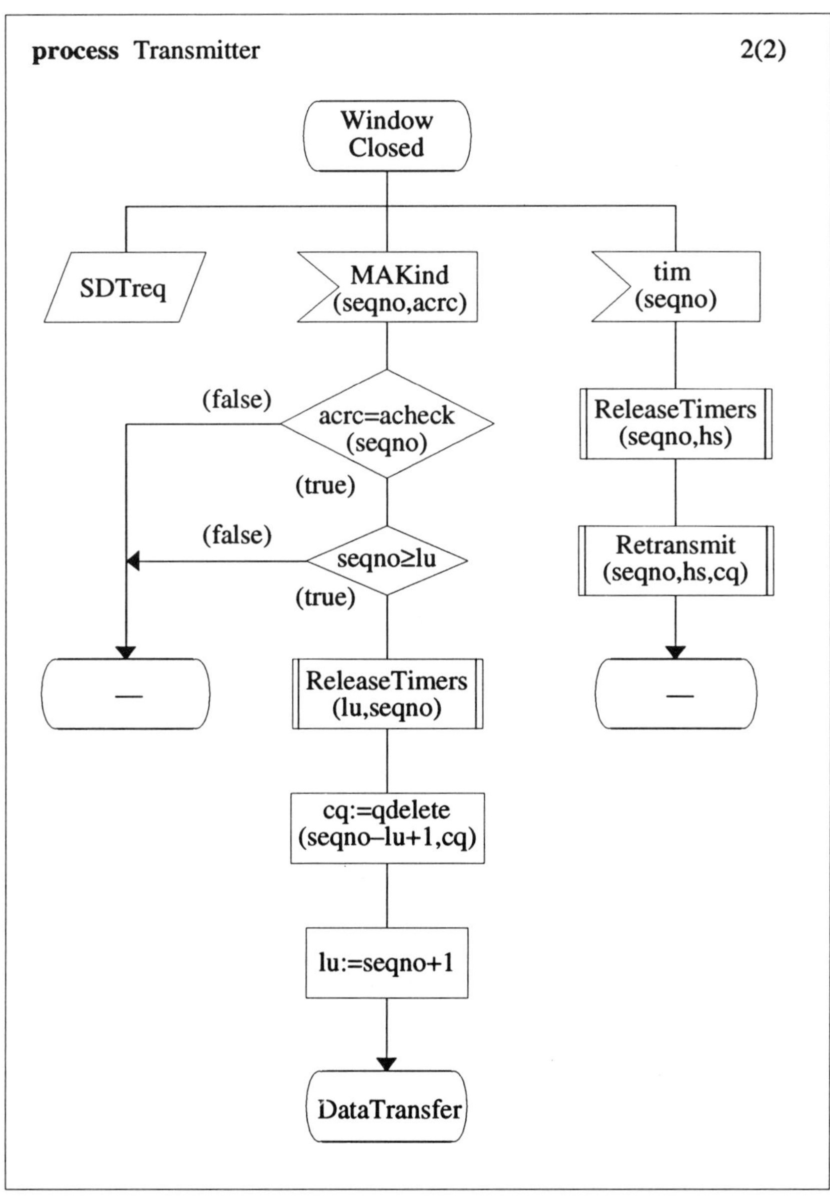

Figure 7.4 *(continued)*

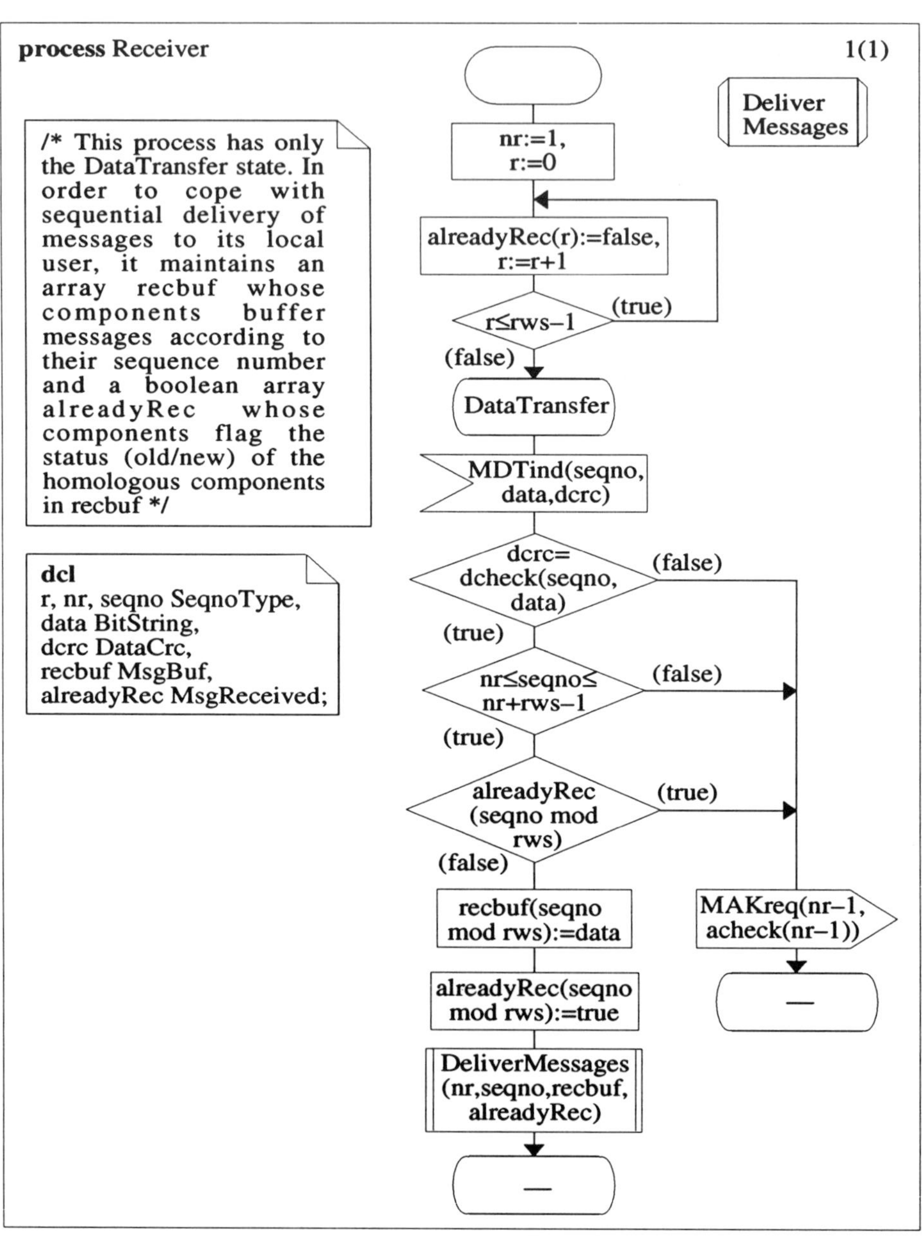
process Receiver
1(1)
Deliver Messages
/* This process has only the DataTransfer state. In order to cope with sequential delivery of messages to its local user, it maintains an array recbuf whose components buffer messages according to their sequence number and a boolean array alreadyRec whose components flag the status (old/new) of the homologous components in recbuf */
dcl
r, nr, seqno SeqnoType,
data BitString,
dcrc DataCrc,
recbuf MsgBuf,
alreadyRec MsgReceived;
nr:=1,
r:=0
alreadyRec(r):=false,
r:=r+1
r≤rws–1
(true)
(false)
DataTransfer
MDTind(seqno, data,dcrc)
dcrc= dcheck(seqno, data)
(false)
(true)
nr≤seqno≤ nr+rws–1
(false)
(true)
alreadyRec (seqno mod rws)
(true)
(false)
recbuf(seqno mod rws):=data
alreadyRec(seqno mod rws):=true
DeliverMessages (nr,seqno,recbuf, alreadyRec)
—
MAKreq(nr–1, acheck(nr–1))
—

Figure 7.4 *(continued)*

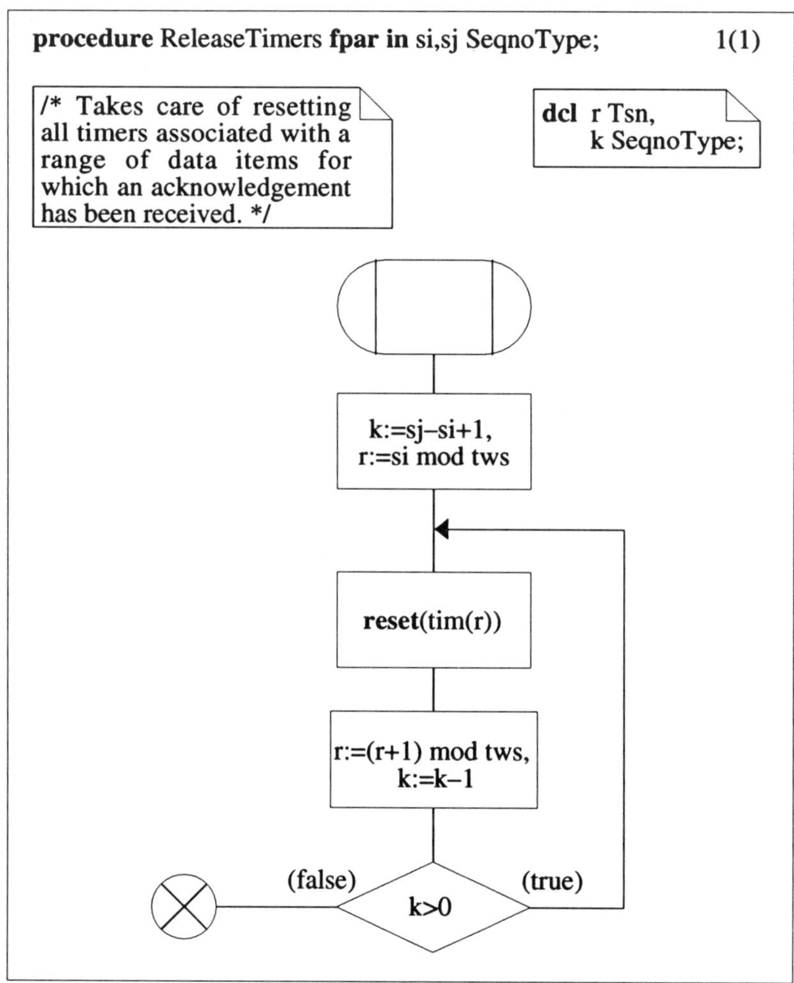
procedure ReleaseTimers **fpar in** si,sj SeqnoType;
1(1)
/* Takes care of resetting all timers associated with a range of data items for which an acknowledgement has been received. */
dcl r Tsn,
k SeqnoType;
k:=sj–si+1,
r:=si mod tws
reset(tim(r))
r:=(r+1) mod tws,
k:=k–1
(false)
k>0
(true)

Figure 7.4 *(continued)*

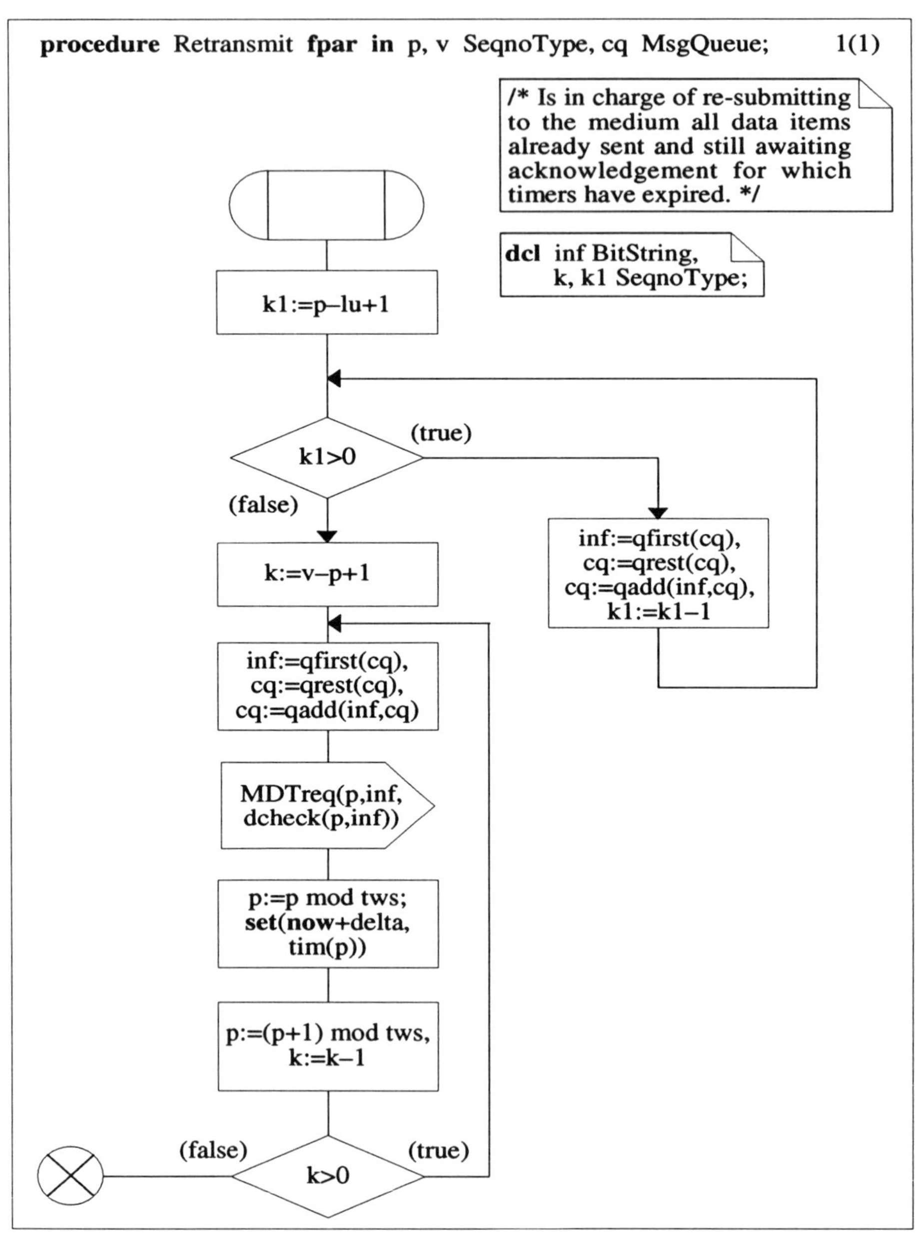

Figure 7.4 *(continued)*

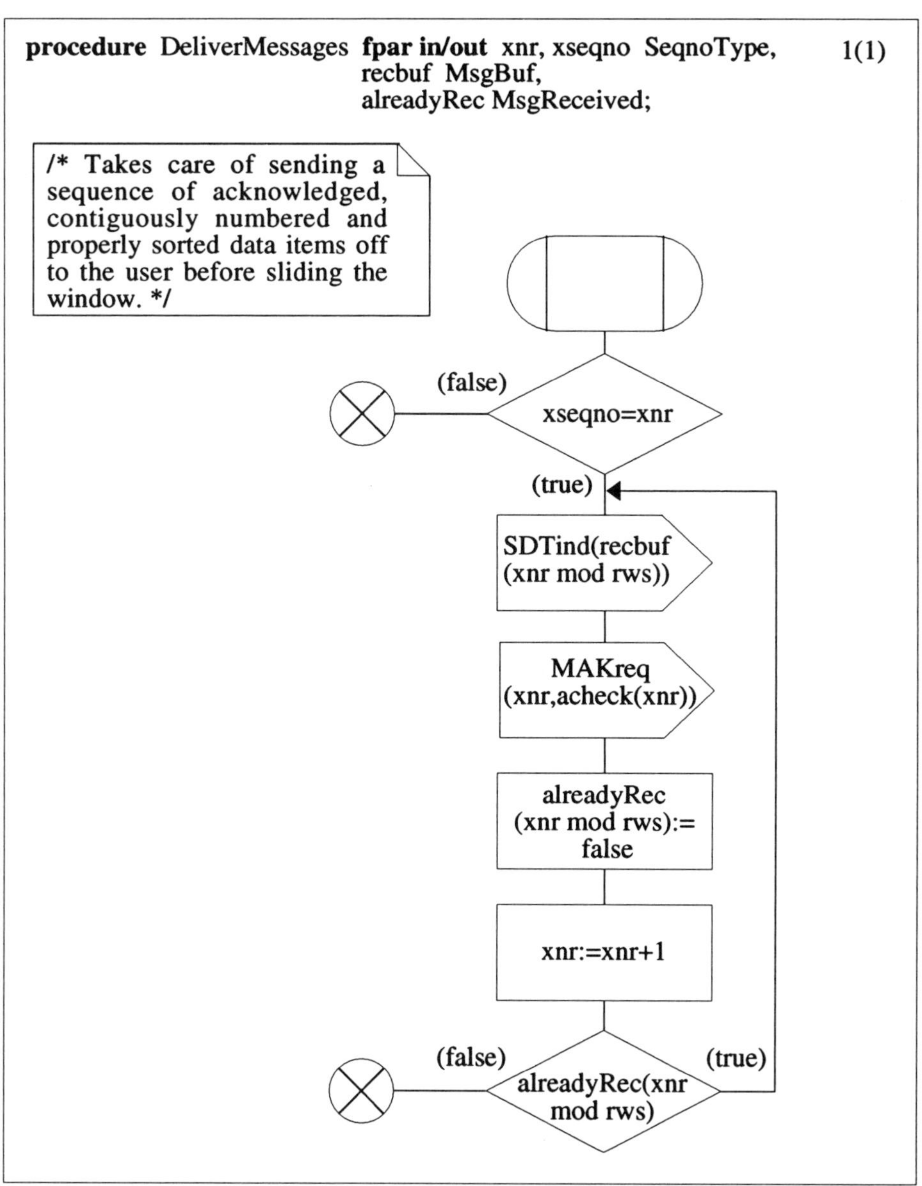
procedure DeliverMessages fpar in/out xnr, xseqno SeqnoType,
recbuf MsgBuf,
alreadyRec MsgReceived;
1(1)
/* Takes care of sending a sequence of acknowledged, contiguously numbered and properly sorted data items off to the user before sliding the window. */
(false)
xseqno=xnr
(true)
SDTind(recbuf (xnr mod rws))
MAKreq (xnr,acheck(xnr))
alreadyRec (xnr mod rws):= false
xnr:=xnr+1
(false)
(true)
alreadyRec(xnr mod rws)

Figure 7.4 *(continued)*

```
newtype MsgReceived array (Rsn, Boolean);
endnewtype MsgReceived;

newtype MsgQueue Queue (BitString);
endnewtype MsgQueue;

newtype BitString string (Bit,'');
endnewtype BitString;

newtype Bit
  literals 0, 1;
endnewtype Bit;

endmacro DataTypeDef;
```

7.6 Conclusion[10]

This example is fairly typical of the style of protocol descriptions. The deficiencies found in the informal description included the usual straight errors or lack of information. However, some interesting and general types of errors were found:

- It is easy to forget to state whether the extreme values of a range are included or excluded.
- The word 'and' can be ambiguous in natural language. For example, it is commonplace in restaurant menus to see that a meal is followed by 'coffee and tea'!
- A natural language description can easily lapse into 'elegant variation'[11]. For example, the same thing may be called a 'unit', a 'component', a 'subsystem', and a 'module'. Although this is acceptable in a literary work, such a style leads to imprecision in a specification.
- A deep and lengthy discussion took place between the authors of the formal descriptions as to how to interpret the 'time-out' parameter. The informal description refers to 'a timer' being started. Such use of the word 'a' is ambiguous. In this case it could reflect the fact that each message has an individual timer, that some particular value is used for each message timer, or that any timer value (perhaps different from timer values used on other occasions) is used.

---

[10] Section 7.6 is by K. J. Turner.

[11] This is the phrase used by Fowler (1968).

- The issue of time-outs is also tied up with the distinction between a non-deterministic specification and a partial specification. A non-deterministic specification of a timer could say that the timer value would be chosen (by some means that could not be determined). A partial specification could indicate that a single timer value would be used, but that the precise value would be defined when the specification was made total (i.e. at a later stage in the design).

8 Abracadabra Service

The unreliable medium of Chapter 6 provides a simple connection-less service to support a variety of protocols. This chapter presents the converse situation – a simple connection-oriented service that may be realised by a variety of protocols. The major new complexity introduced by this example is the concept of the phase of a service, with the need to progress between phases and the possibility of both ends becoming out of step. This places demands on the structuring features of FDTs. The Abracadabra example was devised by K. J. Turner as a vehicle for evaluating formal specification languages. The reason for the name will become evident in Chapter 9.

8.1 Informal Description[1]

The **Abracadabra Service** operates between a pair of users, addressed as *UserA* and *UserB*. Each user is presumed to have some local interface to the underlying protocol entity. The service *'A'* is connection-oriented and transfers data reliably. The service primitives supported by the service provider are as follows:

Phase	Kind	Name	Parameters
Connection	Request	ConReq	-
	Indication	ConInd	-
	Response	ConResp	-
	Confirmation	ConConf	-
Data	Request	DatReq	Service Data Unit
	Indication	DatInd	Service Data Unit
Disconnection	Request	DisReq	-
	Indication	DisInd	-

Only the data primitives carry a parameter – an SDU *(Service Data Unit)* that contains user data. The basic relationship between service primitives is shown in Figure 8.1. More complex situations are described below.

[1]Section 8.1 is by K. J. Turner.

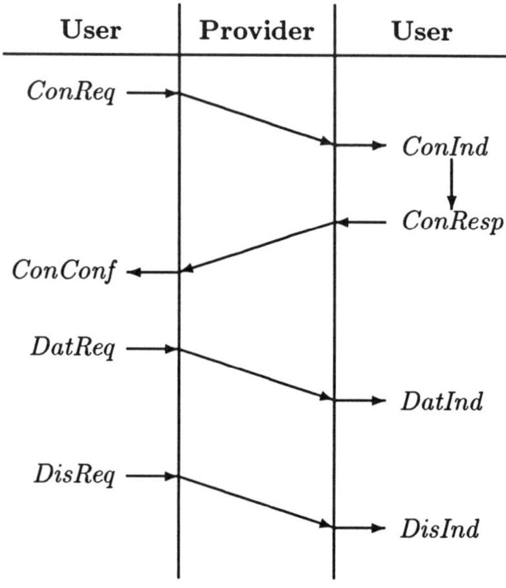

Figure 8.1: Abracadabra Service – Relationship between Primitives

A connection may be established through the service by either user. The normal sequence of primitives is *ConReq*, *ConInd*, *ConResp*, *ConConf*. However, if both users simultaneously initiate a connection then each end sees only *ConReq*, *ConConf*. A connection establishment attempt may be abandoned by the initiator sending *DisReq* before receiving *ConConf*. A connection establishment attempt may also be abandoned by the responder sending a *DisReq* following *ConInd*.

Once a connection is established, either user may send a *DatReq* which will be delivered as *DatInd*. Data messages are preserved in sequence and content, except when a disconnection occurs. In this case, an undefined number of data messages already in the service provider may be lost. Data transfer is subject to flow control by back-pressure.

Either user may terminate an established connection by issuing a *DisReq*. This normally leads to a *DisInd* being delivered to the other user, but if the other user issues a *DisReq* in the meantime then the connection is terminated immediately.

The service provider itself may abandon a connection attempt or may terminate the connection. Normally each user that knows of a connection (attempt) is informed of provider termination by *DisInd*. However, if the user issues *DisReq* in the meantime then the *DisInd* is not delivered.

Once a connection has been terminated, either user may initiate a new connection with *ConReq*.

8.2 Errors in the Informal Description[2]

8.2.1 *Flow Control*

Is it reasonable that the informal description should require flow control by back-pressure since this depends on implementation features?

Flow control by back-pressure is an implicit feature of many service definitions in OSI *(Open Systems Interconnection)*, although it is not normally referred to by this explicit name. The mechanisms for realising flow control by back-pressure lie partly in the service provider (i.e. the protocol) and partly in the interface between the service users and the service provider. The latter is dependent on the actual implementation. Although the precise mechanisms for achieving flow control by back-pressure would not normally be included in a service definition, it is permissible to refer to the end-to-end effect of these.

---

[2]Section 8.2 is by K. J. Turner, based on problems found by the authors of the formal descriptions.

8.2.2 *Repeated Connection Request*

Should *ConReq* be accepted while a connection is being attempted or is current? More generally, should the behaviour of the service under incorrect use by the service user be described?

The intention was that a *ConReq* should be issued only once to establish a connection. In general, the actual FDT being used affects how service user misbehaviour should be described most naturally.

8.2.3 *Simultaneity*

What does 'simultaneously' mean in the context of both users initiating a connection, or 'in the meantime' if both users try to disconnect?

The intended meaning was the period of time between one user initiating an action and its effect at the other user.

8.3 Formal Description in Estelle[3]

The modules and interaction points for the Abracadabra Service description are shown in Figure 8.2. The service provider is modelled by two identical processes, one for each SAP. Of course, there are other solutions possible that use only one process. The reason for choosing two processes is that there may be a delay between the acceptance of a service primitive by the service provider and the delivery of the corresponding service primitive to the respective service user. This delay is modelled by the communication via channel *Internal* between the two *SAPManager* modules. If a service description were produced using only one process for the service provider, time constraints would have to be introduced for the delivery of service primitives corresponding to submitted ones. The two-process solution has been used for the sake of simplicity.

When one *SAPManager* receives a service primitive at a service access point, it will send an internal message to the *SAPManager* for the other service access point. This will the result in a service primitive being delivered to the user at this service access point. For example, a *ConReq* from user *A* will generate the internal message *IConReqInd*, resulting in a *ConInd* to user *B*. The names for the internal messages are hopefully obvious.

The processes of the service provider do not have to communicate through an unreliable medium that supports the underlying protocol. Instead, the inability of the service provider to establish or maintain a connection due to an internal error is modelled in the service description by the use of non-determinism.

The transitions in the following are numbered only for convenient reference.

[3]Section 8.3 is by D. Hogrefe.

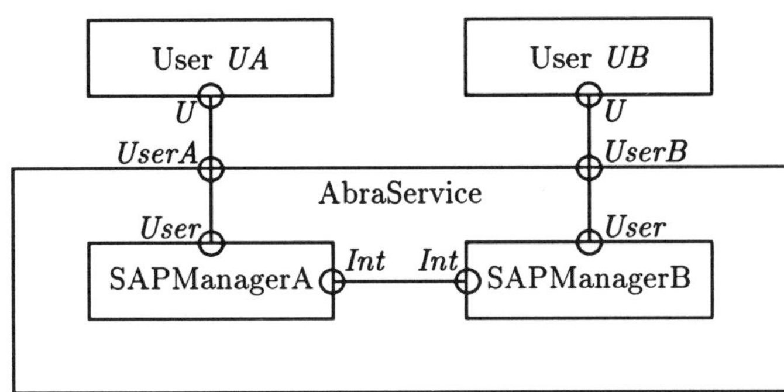

Figure 8.2: Abracadabra Service in ESTELLE – Architecture

```
specification AbracadabraService;

default individual queue;

type
  UserDataType = ...;            { Some suitable type, e.g. a string }

channel SSAP(User, Provider);
  by User:
    ConReq;
    ConResp;
    DatReq(UserData: UserDataType);
    DisReq;
  by Provider:
    ConInd;
    ConConf;
    DatInd(UserData: UserDataType);
    DisInd;

channel Internal(A, B);
  by A, B:
    IConReqInd;
    IConRespConf;
    IDatReqInd(UserData: UserDataType);
    IDisReqInd;
```

```
module User systemprocess;
  ip U: SSAP(User);
end;

body UserBody for User;
external;

module AbraService;
  ip
    UserA: SSAP(Provider);
    UserB: SSAP(Provider);
end;

body AbraServiceBody for AbraService;

  module SAPManagerA systemprocess;
    ip
      User: SSAP(Provider);
      Int: Internal(A);
  end;

  body SAPManagerBodyA for SAPManagerA;

    state DISCONNECTED, CALLED, CALLING, CONNECTED;

    stateset DISallowed = [CALLED, CALLING, CONNECTED];

    initialize to DISCONNECTED
      { There are no variables }
      begin
      end;

    trans

    { *** Connection *** }

    from DISCONNECTED to same
      when User.ConReq
        { Provider refuses connection attempt }
        begin { 1 }
          output User.DisInd;
        end;
```

```
from DISCONNECTED to same
  when Int.IDatReqInd(UserData)
    begin { 2 }
      output Int.IDisReqInd;
    end;
from DISCONNECTED to CALLING
  when User.ConReq
    begin { 3 }
      output Int.IConReqInd;
    end;
from DISCONNECTED to CALLED
  when Int.IConReqInd
      begin { 4 }
        output User.ConInd;
      end;
from CALLED to CONNECTED
  when User.ConResp
    begin { 5 }
      output Int.IConRespConf;
    end;
from CALLED to CONNECTED
  { Collision situation }
  when User.ConReq
    begin { 6 }
      output User.ConConf;
      output Int.IConRespConf;
    end;
from CALLING to CONNECTED
  when Int.IConRespConf
    begin { 7 }
      output User.ConConf;
    end;
from CALLING to CONNECTED
  { Collision situation }
  when Int.IConReqInd
    begin { 8 }
      output User.ConConf;
      output Int.IConRespConf;
    end;

{ *** Data transfer *** }
```

```
from CONNECTED to same
  when User.DatReq(UserData)
    begin { 9 }
      output Int.IDatReqInd(UserData);
    end;
from CONNECTED to same
  when Int.IDatReqInd(UserData)
    begin { 10 }
      output User.DatInd(UserData);
    end;

{ *** Disconnection *** }

from CONNECTED to DISCONNECTED
  when User.DatReq(UserData)
    begin { 11 }
      output User.DisInd;
      output Int.IDisReqInd;
    end;
from CONNECTED to CALLED
  when Int.IConReqInd
    begin { 12 }
      output User.ConInd;
    end;
from DISallowed to DISCONNECTED
  { Spontaneous disconnection by the provider }
  begin { 13 }
    output User.DisInd;
    output Int.IDisReqInd;
  end;
from DISallowed to DISCONNECTED
  when User.DisReq
    begin { 14 }
      output Int.IDisReqInd;
    end;
from DISallowed to DISCONNECTED
  when Int.IDisReqInd
    begin { 15 }
      output User.DisInd;
    end;

end; { SAPManagerBodyA }
```

```
module SAPManagerB systemprocess;
  ip
    User : SSAP(Provider);
    Int: Internal(B);
end;

body SAPManagerBodyB for SAPManagerB;

  state DISCONNECTED, CALLED, CALLING, CONNECTED;

  stateset DISallowed = [CALLED, CALLING, CONNECTED];

  initialize to DISCONNECTED
    { There are no variables }
    begin
    end;

  trans

  { *** Connection *** }

  from DISCONNECTED to same
    when User.ConReq
      { Provider refuses connection attempt }
      begin { 1 }
        output User.DisInd;
      end;
  from DISCONNECTED to same
    when Int.IDatReqInd(UserData)
      begin { 2 }
        output Int.IDisReqInd;
      end;
  from DISCONNECTED to CALLING
    when User.ConReq
      begin { 3 }
        output Int.IConReqInd;
      end;
  from DISCONNECTED to CALLED
    when Int.IConReqInd
        begin { 4 }
          output User.ConInd;
        end;
```

```
from CALLED to CONNECTED
  when User.ConResp
    begin { 5 }
      output Int.IConRespConf;
    end;
from CALLED to CONNECTED
  { Collision situation }
  when User.ConReq
    begin { 6 }
      output User.ConConf;
      output Int.IConRespConf;
    end;
from CALLING to CONNECTED
  when Int.IConRespConf
    begin { 7 }
      output User.ConConf;
    end;
from CALLING to CONNECTED
  { Collision situation }
  when Int.IConReqInd
    begin { 8 }
      output User.ConConf;
      output Int.IConRespConf;
    end;

{ *** Data transfer *** }

from CONNECTED to same
  when User.DatReq(UserData)
    begin { 9 }
      output Int.IDatReqInd(UserData);
    end;
from CONNECTED to same
  when Int.IDatReqInd(UserData)
    begin { 10 }
      output User.DatInd(UserData);
    end;

{ *** Disconnection *** }

from CONNECTED to DISCONNECTED
  when User.DatReq(UserData)
```

```
        begin { 11 }
          output User.DisInd;
          output Int.IDisReqInd;
        end;
    from CONNECTED to CALLED
      when Int.IConReqInd
        begin { 12 }
          output User.ConInd;
        end;
    from DISallowed to DISCONNECTED
      { Spontaneous disconnection by the provider }
      begin { 13 }
        output User.DisInd;
        output Int.IDisReqInd;
      end;
    from DISallowed to DISCONNECTED
      when User.DisReq
        begin { 14 }
          output Int.IDisReqInd;
        end;
    from DISallowed to DISCONNECTED
      when Int.IDisReqInd
        begin { 15 }
          output User.DisInd;
        end;

  end;  { SAPManagerBodyB }

  { Main body for AbraServiceBody }

  modvar
    A: SAPManagerA;
    B: SAPManagerB;

  initialize
    begin
      init A with SAPManagerBodyA;
      init B with SAPManagerBodyB;
      attach UserA to A.User;
      attach UserB to B.User;
      connect A.Int to B.Int;
    end;
```

```
end; { AbraServiceBody }

{ Main body for specification AbracadabraService }

modvar
  UA, UB: User;
  AS : AbraService;

initialize
  begin
    init UA with UserBody;
    init UB with UserBody;
    init AS with AbraServiceBody;
    connect UA.U to AS.UserA;
    connect UB.U to AS.UserB;
  end;

end. { AbracadabraService }
```

8.4 Formal Description in LOTOS[4]

8.4.1 *Architecture of the Formal Description*

The specification follows the constraint-oriented approach. This style emphasises the orthogonality of certain restrictions, or constraints, on behaviour. It permits the specifier to avoid repeating the same restrictions in different parts of the specification (though it cannot, of course, prevent a specifier from doing so!).

The constraints are combined using the parallel operator '||'. A behaviour expression of the form *b1* || *b2* permits a behaviour if and only if both *b1* and *b2* permit it. This allows each of *b1* and *b2* separately to permit a wider range of behaviour than is permitted by their combination, provided that the other behaviour expression precludes the extraneous behaviours. The constraint-oriented style thus composes individual constraints which each permit more than their combination.

The individual constraint may be composed from other constraints or may be constructed from individual interactions placed in some temporal ordering by operators for sequencing (';'), choice ('[]'), etc. This style of description is similar to the state-machine approach often used to model services and protocols.

[4]Section 8.4 is by A. J. Tocher and F. M. Fournón y González-Barcia.

The specification describes the behaviour of a single connection between two service access points. The description has been written in a more general way than is strictly necessary in order to illustrate how to specify more general services. For example, it could easily be extended to deal with a number of service access points and to deal with new kinds of service primitives. The reason for choosing a more abstract approach was to show how more complex services could be described.

Each interaction has three parts: the service boundary at which the interactions occur, the address within the service boundary, and the service primitive that occurs. The service boundary is represented throughout the specification by a single gate, *a*. The address at which interactions occur is denoted by a value of sort *ASAP*. The service primitive is denoted by a value of sort *ASP*. The structure of a typical interaction is therefore represented by

```
a ! address ! sp
```

Where more than one possibility is permitted, the more general form is used:

```
a ? User : ASAP ? sp : ASP [Predicate]
```

This introduces two bound variables, *User* and *sp*, and permits any interaction such that the predicate holds over those variables.

The overall structure of the specification in terms of the nesting of definitions is:

```
specification AbracadabraService

  library

  type ASAP
  type ASDU
  type SetOfASAP
  type ASP
  type Object

  behaviour

  process Connection
    process CEPs
      process CEP
        process PrimitiveOrdering
          process DataTransfer
          process Disconnect
        process Addressing
```

```
        process Association
          type BasicMedium
          type DisconnectedMedium
          type Medium
          process Assoc
            process TransferIn
            process TransferOut
      process BackPressure
```

8.4.2 *Top-Level Specification*

The description is parameterised by the gate that represents the service boundary at which all interactions will occur.

```
specification AbracadabraService [a] : noexit
```

8.4.3 *Basic Types*

Library Types

The standard library types used in this specification are the Booleans, natural numbers, octet strings, decimal digits and sets.

```
library
    Boolean, NaturalNumber, OctetString, DecDigit, Set
endlib
```

Service Access Points

It is sufficient to introduce two distinct addresses, *UserA* and *UserB*, at which the service may be used. Boolean equality and inequality are defined for addresses.

```
type ASAP is Boolean
  sorts ASAP
  opns
    UserA, UserB :                      -> ASAP
    _eq_, _ne_ :        ASAP, ASAP      -> Bool
  eqns
    forall a1, a2 : ASAP
      ofsort Bool
        UserA eq UserA          = true;
        UserA eq UserB          = false;
```

```
        UserB eq UserA          = false;
        UserB eq UserB          = true;
        a1 ne a2                = not (a1 eq a2)
endtype (* ASAP *)
```

Service Data Units

The service data units have the same structure and operations as the standard type *OctetString*, but the values are of sort *ASDU* rather than *OctetString*.

```
type ASDU is OctetString renamedby
  sortnames ASDU for OctetString
endtype (* ASDU *)
```

Sets of Service Access Points

Sets of service access points are represented by the type *SetOfASAP* that is an instantiation of the standard library type *Set* with element sort *ASAP*.

```
type SetOfASAP is Set actualizedby ASAP, Boolean using
  sortnames
    ASAP            for Element
    Bool            for FBool
    SetOfASAP       for Set
endtype (* SetOfASAP *)
```

Service Primitives

The service primitives are represented by values of sort *ASP*. There are eight constructors corresponding to the eight kinds of primitive. Of these constructors, only those constructing data requests and data indications take a parameter – a service data unit.

For each constructor (e.g. *ConReq*) there is a recogniser (e.g. *IsConReq*) that indicates whether its argument is of the corresponding kind. There are also recognisers for whether a given primitive is a request or indication.

The function *SDUOf* extracts the user data from its argument: if there is no data then the result is the null user data value, '<>'.

The auxiliary function *map* is used to simplify the definition of the recognisers (each of which would otherwise have to be defined over the eight distinct forms of primitive!). The important property of *map* is that it is injective: any other such function would suffice.

Lastly, Boolean equality is defined over service primitives, based on equality of the kind of primitive and the user data carried.

```
type ASP is Boolean, ASDU, DecDigit
  sorts ASP
  opns
    ConReq, ConInd, ConResp, ConConf :              -> ASP
    DatReq, DatInd :            ASDU                -> ASP
    DisReq, DisInd :                                -> ASP
    SDUOf :                     ASP                 -> ASDU
    map      :                  ASP                 -> DecDigit
    IsConReq, IsConInd, IsConResp, IsConConf,
      IsDatReq, IsDatInd,
        IsDisReq, IsDisInd :    ASP                 -> Bool
    IsReq, IsInd :              ASP                 -> Bool
    _eq_ :                      ASP, ASP            -> Bool
  eqns
    forall d : ASDU, sp, sp1, sp2 : ASP
      ofsort ASDU
        SDUOf (ConReq)          = <>;
        SDUOf (ConInd)          = <>;
        SDUOf (ConResp)         = <>;
        SDUOf (ConConf)         = <>;
        SDUOf (DatReq (d))      = d;
        SDUOf (DatInd (d))      = d;
        SDUOf (DisReq)          = <>;
        SDUOf (DisInd)          = <>
      ofsort DecDigit
        map (ConReq)            = 0;
        map (ConInd)            = 1;
        map (ConResp)           = 2;
        map (ConConf)           = 3;
        map (DatReq (d))        = 4;
        map (DatInd (d))        = 5;
        map (DisReq)            = 6;
        map (DisInd)            = 7
      ofsort Bool
        IsConReq (sp)           = map (sp) eq 0;
        IsConInd (sp)           = map (sp) eq 1;
        IsConResp (sp)          = map (sp) eq 2;
        IsConConf (sp)          = map (sp) eq 3;
        IsDatReq (sp)           = map (sp) eq 4;
        IsDatInd (sp)           = map (sp) eq 5;
        IsDisReq (sp)           = map (sp) eq 6;
        IsDisInd (sp)           = map (sp) eq 7;
```

```
        IsReq (sp)              =
          IsConReq (sp) or IsConResp (sp) or IsDatReq (sp) or
            IsDisReq (sp);
        IsInd (sp)              = not (IsReq (sp));
        sp1 eq sp2              =
          (map (sp1) eq map (sp2)) and (SDUOf (sp1) eq SDUOf (sp2))
endtype (* ASP *)
```

Service Objects

While in transit, the information encoded in a request/response or indication/confirmation is represented as a service object. The concept of service object is introduced since request/response and indication/confirmation reflect the two directions of information flow *between* the service and a user of the service. However *within* the service itself, that particular notion of direction has no meaning and is not relevant for information in transit within the service[5].

There is a distinct kind of object for each request–indication or response–confirmation pair. The naming of objects is straightforward, apart from *Con* (for connection request/indication) and *Cak* (connection acknowledgement, for connection response/confirmation). The operation *object* transforms primitives to objects. The operations *indication* and *altindication* ('alternative indication') transform objects to indications or confirmations respectively. Boolean equality is defined over sort *Object*.

```
type Object is ASP
  sorts Object
  opns
    object :            ASP               -> Object
    indication,
      altindication :   Object            -> ASP
    IsCon, IsCak,
      IsDat, IsDis :    Object            -> Bool
    _eq_ :              Object, Object    -> Bool
  eqns forall sp : ASP, obj, obj1, obj2 : Object, data : ASDU
    ofsort Bool
      IsCon (object (sp))       = IsConReq (sp) or IsConInd (sp);
      IsCak (object (sp))       = IsConResp (sp) or IsConConf (sp);
      IsDat (object (sp))       = IsDatReq (sp) or IsDatInd (sp);
      IsDis (object (sp))       = IsDisReq (sp) or IsDisInd (sp);
      obj1 eq obj2              =
        (indication (obj1) eq indication (obj2)) and
          (altindication (obj1) eq altindication (obj2))
```

[5]Put another way, this avoids the problem of when a request become an indication.

```
    ofsort ASP
      indication (object (ConReq))              = ConInd;
      indication (object (ConInd))              = ConInd;
      indication (object (ConResp))             = ConConf;
      indication (object (ConConf))             = ConConf;
      indication (object (DatReq (data)))       = DatInd (data);
      indication (object (DatInd (data)))       = DatInd (data);
      indication (object (DisReq))              = DisInd;
      indication (object (DisInd))              = DisInd;
      altindication (object (ConReq))           = ConConf;
      altindication (object (ConInd))           = ConConf;
      altindication (object (ConResp))          = ConInd;
      altindication (object (ConConf))          = ConInd;
      altindication (object (DatReq (data)))    = DatInd (data);
      altindication (object (DatInd (data)))    = DatInd (data);
      altindication (object (DisReq))           = DisInd;
      altindication (object (DisInd))           = DisInd
endtype (* Object *)
```

8.4.4 *Top-Level Behaviour*

The constraints on the behaviour of the service are decomposed into two principal areas of concern:

- the single bidirectional connection between addresses *UserA* and *UserB* without regard to back-pressure (process *Connection*)
- back-pressure in the system as a whole (process *BackPressure*).

```
behaviour
  Connection [a] (UserA, UserB)
||
  BackPressure [a]

where
```

8.4.5 *A Single Connection*

The constraint on a single bidirectional connection between two given addresses is decomposed into constraints concerning:

- the relative order of service primitives within each endpoint separately without reference to the relative order between endpoints (process *CEPs*)
- the relative order of service primitives at opposite endpoints without reference to the relative order within each endpoint (process *Association*).

```
process Connection [a] (UserA, UserB: ASAP) : noexit :=
   CEPs [a] (UserA, UserB)
||
   Association [a] (UserA, UserB)

   where
```

Both Connection Endpoints

The constraints on the relative order of primitives at each end of the connection are independent of each other. The constraint on a single endpoint is described by process *CEP* at a given endpoint address. Their independence is represented by the use of the interleaving operator '|||' in composing the constraints.

```
process CEPs [a] (UserA, UserB : ASAP) : noexit :=
   CEP [a] (UserA)
|||
   CEP [a] (UserB)

   where
```

A Single Connection Endpoint

The constraint at a single endpoint is decomposed into two constraints concerning:

- the order of primitives (process *PrimitiveOrdering*)
- the address at which the interactions occur (process *Addressing*).

```
process CEP [a] (UserX : ASAP) : noexit :=
   PrimitiveOrdering [a]
||
   Addressing [a] (UserX)

   where
```

Primitive Ordering

The order of primitives is constrained to begin with a *ConReq* or *ConInd*, after which the disconnection phase (process *Disconnect*) may be entered at any stage. Until the disconnection phase is entered, any next interaction must be either a *ConConf* or *ConResp* according to the kind of the first interaction and after this the data transfer phase (process *DataTransfer*) may be entered.

```
process PrimitiveOrdering [a] : noexit :=
  a ? User : ASAP ? sp1 : ASP
    [IsConReq (sp1) or IsConInd (sp1)];
  (
    a ? User : ASAP ? sp2 : ASP
      [(IsConReq (sp1) implies IsConConf (sp2)) and
        (IsConInd (sp1) implies IsConResp (sp2))];
    DataTransfer [a]
  [>
    Disconnect [a]
  )

  where
```

Data Transfer Phase

The data transfer phase constraint permits only *DatReq* and *DatInd* service primitives.

```
process DataTransfer [a] : noexit :=
  a ? User : ASAP ? sp : ASP
    [IsDatReq (sp) or IsDatInd (sp)];
  DataTransfer [a]
endproc (* DataTransfer *)
```

Disconnection Phase

The disconnection phase constraint permits an initial *DisReq* or *DisInd*. After the initial interaction the constraint reverts to the primitive ordering on a connection.

```
process Disconnect [a] : noexit :=
  a ? User : ASAP ? sp : ASP
    [IsDisReq (sp) or IsDisInd (sp)];
  PrimitiveOrdering [a]
endproc (* Disconnect *)

endproc (* PrimitiveOrdering *)
```

Constraining the Address

The constraint on addressing permits any interactions provided they occur at the given address, *UserX*.

```
process Addressing [a] (UserX : ASAP) : noexit :=
  a ! UserX ? sp : ASP;
  Addressing [a] (UserX)
endproc (* Addressing *)

endproc (* CEP *)

endproc (* CEPs *)
```

8.4.6 *Bidirectional Transfer of Service Primitives*

The end-to-end constraint on the bidirectional transfer of service primitives is that transfer in each direction separately satisfies the constraint on unidirectional transfer of service primitives (process *Assoc*). The transfers in opposite directions are mutually independent, modelled here by the interleaving operator '|||'. The instantiations of *Assoc* are parameterised by the addresses of each endpoint and an initial empty medium.

```
process Association [a] (UserA, UserB : ASAP) : noexit :=
  Assoc [a] (UserA, UserB, empty)
|||
  Assoc [a] (UserB, UserA, empty)

  where
```

8.4.7 *The Medium*

The service behaves as a medium with specific reordering properties. This is more complex than the Unreliable Medium of Chapter 6, so an alternative and more general approach has been taken. The data type representing the medium is defined in three stages:

- a basic medium is defined as a simple FIFO *(First-In First-Out)* queue, formalised in type *BasicMedium*
- this is augmented in type *DisconnectedMedium* with the transformations associated with the occurrence of provider disconnects
- this in turn is augmented in type *Medium* with the transformations associated with possible reorderings of objects in the medium.

The Basic Medium

A medium may have the value *empty*. If it is non-empty, it is equivalent to some other medium, *asm*, with an additional object, *aso*, appended. In this case the resulting medium is denoted by *aso +-- asm*.

A non-empty medium may alternatively be viewed as having a head object, *aso*, and a remainder, *asm*. This view is denoted by *asm --+ aso* and is useful when removing the first element of a medium. The relationship between the two views is expressed in the first two equations.

The reason for not defining 'head' and 'tail' operations is to avoid error values in the definitions (i.e. head or tail of an empty medium). In the behavioural part of the specification, a medium is used declaratively ('choose head and tail values which combine to form the current medium') rather than imperatively ('decompose the current medium into its head and tail').

As usual, Boolean equality is also defined.

```
type BasicMedium is Object, Boolean
  sorts Medium
  opns
    empty :                          -> Medium
    _+--_ :     Object, Medium       -> Medium
    _--+_ :     Medium, Object       -> Medium
    _eq_ :      Medium, Medium       -> Bool
  eqns
    forall sm, sm1, sm2 : Medium, obj, obj1, obj2 : Object
      ofsort Medium
        obj +-- empty                = empty --+ obj;
        (obj2 +-- (sm --+ obj1)) =
          ((obj2 +-- sm) --+ obj1)
      ofsort Bool
        sm eq sm                     = true;
        (obj2 +-- sm2) eq empty      = false;
        empty eq (obj1 +-- sm1)      = false;
        (obj2 +-- sm2) eq (obj1 +-- sm1) =
          ((obj2 eq obj1) and (sm2 eq sm1))
endtype (* BasicMedium *)
```

Provider Disconnection of the Medium

The ability of the service provider to cause one or more disconnects at any time is now added in the definition of type *DisconnectedMedium*. For medium *s* and medium *t*, the expression *s disconnects t* is true if and only if *s* can be derived by adding zero or more (provider) disconnects to the end of *t*.

```
type DisconnectedMedium is BasicMedium
  opns
    _disconnects_ : Medium, Medium -> Bool
  eqns
    forall obj, obj1 : Object, sm, sm1 : Medium
      ofsort Bool
        empty disconnects empty              = true;
        empty disconnects (obj +-- sm)       = false;
        (obj1 +-- sm1) disconnects sm        =
          (((obj1 +-- sm1) eq sm) or
            (IsDis (obj1) and (sm1 disconnects empty)))
endtype (* DisconnectedMedium *)
```

Reorderings of the Medium

The ability of the provider to reorder and destroy objects in the medium at any time is modelled much as for provider disconnection, namely by defining how two media are related.

Two auxiliary relations are introduced. The ability of a disconnect to cancel a preceding connect is expressed in the relation *negate*. The ability of a disconnect to overtake and delete any preceding object other than a connect is expressed in the relation *destroy*.

One medium , *m1*, is a valid reordering of another medium, *m2*, if and only if *m1* can be derived from *m2* by the application of one or more negations or destructions. The first three equations relating to *reorders* state that an empty medium can be a reordering only of an empty medium or a medium initially containing a disconnect immediately following a connect.

The next three equations address the case where the reordered medium is non-empty. The first of these states that a non-empty medium cannot arise from an empty one. The second states that a non-empty medium can arise from one containing precisely one object only if the two media are the same. The third, and most complex, equation states that a non-empty medium can arise from an original medium containing at least two objects only if one of the following conditions holds:

- their respective last objects are the same and the front of the resulting medium is a valid reordering of the front of the original
- the first two objects of the original medium negate each other and the remainder can be transformed to give the resulting medium
- the last object of the original medium can destroy the penultimate object, and the remaining medium can be validly transformed to the resulting medium.

```
type Medium is DisconnectedMedium
  opns
    _negates_,
      _destroys_ :          Object, Object    -> Bool
    _reorders_ :            Medium, Medium -> Bool
  eqns
    forall m, m0, m1, m2 : Medium,
      obj, obj0, obj1, obj0a, obj1a : Object
    ofsort Bool
      obj1 destroys obj0                                   =
        IsDis (obj1) and (not (IsCon (obj0)));
      obj1 negates obj0                                    =
        IsDis (obj1) and IsCon (obj0);
      empty reorders empty                                 = true;
      empty reorders (obj0 +-- empty)                      = false;
      empty reorders (obj1 +-- (obj0 +-- m))               =
        (obj1 negates obj0) and (empty reorders m);
      (obj +-- m) reorders empty                           = false;
      (obj +-- m) reorders (obj0 +-- empty)                =
        (obj eq obj0) and (m reorders empty);
      (obj +-- m) reorders (obj1 +-- (obj0 +-- m0)) =
        ((obj eq obj1) and
              (m reorders (obj0 +-- m0))) or
                ((obj1 negates obj0) and
                  ((obj +-- m) reorders m0)) or
                    ((obj1 destroys obj0) and
                      ((obj +-- m) reorders (obj1 +-- m0)))
endtype (* Medium *)
```

8.4.8 *Using the Medium*

Process *Assoc* uses the medium in defining the behaviour of unidirectional transfer between two addresses (*UserA* and *UserB*, in either order). It repeatedly offers to transfer a primitive into or out of the medium (processes *TransferIn* and *TransferOut*).

Process *Assoc* accepts requests and responses at address *UserX* and delivers indications at address *UserY*. For a given state of medium, *sm*, acceptance or delivery of a primitive leads to a new state of the medium, *sm1*. After this, and before the next external interaction, the state of the resulting medium may be transformed by any valid combination of provider disconnections and then reordering. This is done in the following stages.

All media, *sm3*, are identified which could be derived as a reordering of another medium, *sm2*, which in turn could be derived as a disconnection of the given medium, *sm1*. In the most general case, the future behaviour will offer a range of choices one based on each possible derived medium, *sm3*.

However, if it is possible for *sm3* to be non-empty (i.e. it can be decomposed into a head, *obj*, and a tail, *sm4*) and it is possible for a disconnect object to have reached the head of the queue, then the provider may unilaterally choose to offer future behaviour based only on that specific transformation of the medium. (This is indicated by the internal event **i**.) Similarly, if it is possible for the transformed medium to be empty, then the provider may unilaterally choose to offer future behaviour based solely on that transformation of the medium. (Again, the internal event **i** is used to indicate this.)

```
process Assoc [a] (UserX, UserY : ASAP, sm : Medium) :
 noexit :=
  (
    TransferIn [a] (UserX, sm)
  []
    TransferOut [a] (UserY, sm)
  )
>>
  accept sm1 : Medium in
    (
      choice sm2, sm3 : Medium []
        [(sm2 disconnects sm1) and
         (sm3 reorders sm2)] ->
          (
            choice sm4 : Medium, obj : Object []
              [sm3 = (sm4 --+ obj)] ->
                (
                  Assoc [a] (UserX, UserY, sm3)
                []
                  [IsDis (obj)] ->
                    i;
                    Assoc [a] (UserX, UserY, sm3)
                )
            []
              [sm3 = empty] ->
                i;
                Assoc [a] (UserX, UserY, sm3)
          )
    )
```

```
where
```

8.4.9 *Medium Input and Output*

Process *TransferIn* accepts any request or confirmation at a given address and appends it to the given medium. Conversely, process *TransferOut* offers delivery of the indication or confirmation corresponding to the object, if any, at the head of the given medium. (This is possible when the given medium can be decomposed into a head and tail.) If the given medium is empty, then process *TransferOut* is unable to offer any delivery.

```
process TransferIn [a] (User : ASAP, sm : Medium) :
 exit (Medium) :=
   a ! User ? sp : ASP [IsReq (sp)];
   exit (object (sp) +-- sm)
endproc (* TransferIn *)

process TransferOut [a] (User : ASAP, sm : Medium) :
 exit (Medium) :=
   choice sm1 : Medium, obj : Object []
     [sm = (sm1 --+ obj)] ->
       a ! User ? sp : ASP
         [(sp eq indication (obj)) or
           (sp eq altindication (obj))];
       exit (sm1)
endproc (* TransferOut *)

endproc (* Assoc *)

endproc (* Association *)

endproc (* Connection *)
```

8.4.10 *Back-pressure Flow Control*

The constraint associated with back-pressure flow control is that data requests may be prohibited at any address at any time. The decision as to where and when to prohibit data requests rests solely with the service provider, and appears to a service user as uncontrollable non-determinism.

```
process BackPressure [a] : noexit :=
  choice RefuseDatReq : SetOfASAP []
    i;
    a ? User : ASAP ? sp : ASP
      [(IsDatReq (sp) implies (User NotIn RefuseDatReq))];
    BackPressure [a]
endproc (* BackPressure *)

endspec (* AbracadabraService *)
```

8.5 Formal Description in SDL[6]

The SDL description of the Abracadabra Service appears in Figure 8.3. The service is modelled as a system *AbraService* consisting of a single block *Serv* communicating with the environment via two channels, *UserA* and *UserB*, representing the service access points. The service users are located in the environment. The service primitives are represented by means of signals; only *DatReq* and *DatInd* have a *UserDataType* parameter.

The service provider behaves non-deterministically in that it may refuse connection attempts and may disrupt established connections on its own initiative for some internal reasons. The channels *AServOnOff* and *BServOnOff* from the environment to block *Serv* have therefore been introduced. They carry signals *ServiceOn* and *ServiceOff* asynchronously and unpredictably, causing service availability to change.

Block *Serv* comprises processes *SAPManagerA* and *SAPManagerB* that mirror each other. The processes are active from system start-up, and model the behaviour of the service at each service access point. Channels to/from the environment are mapped one-to-one onto corresponding signalroutes within the block. Peer processes *SAPManagerA* and *SAPManagerB* communicate via signalroute *Internal* to transfer four possible 'objects' in each direction: connection request/indication, connection response/confirmation, data and disconnection.

The formal description deals with two key aspects of behaviour:

- local behaviour, i.e. correct sequencing of service primitives transferred at one access point
- end-to-end behaviour, i.e. correct relationship between service primitives transferred at different access points.

Local behaviour is described independently by processes *SAPManagerA* and *SAPManagerB*. End-to-end behaviour is described by the mapping that each

[6]Section 8.5 is by S. Trigila.

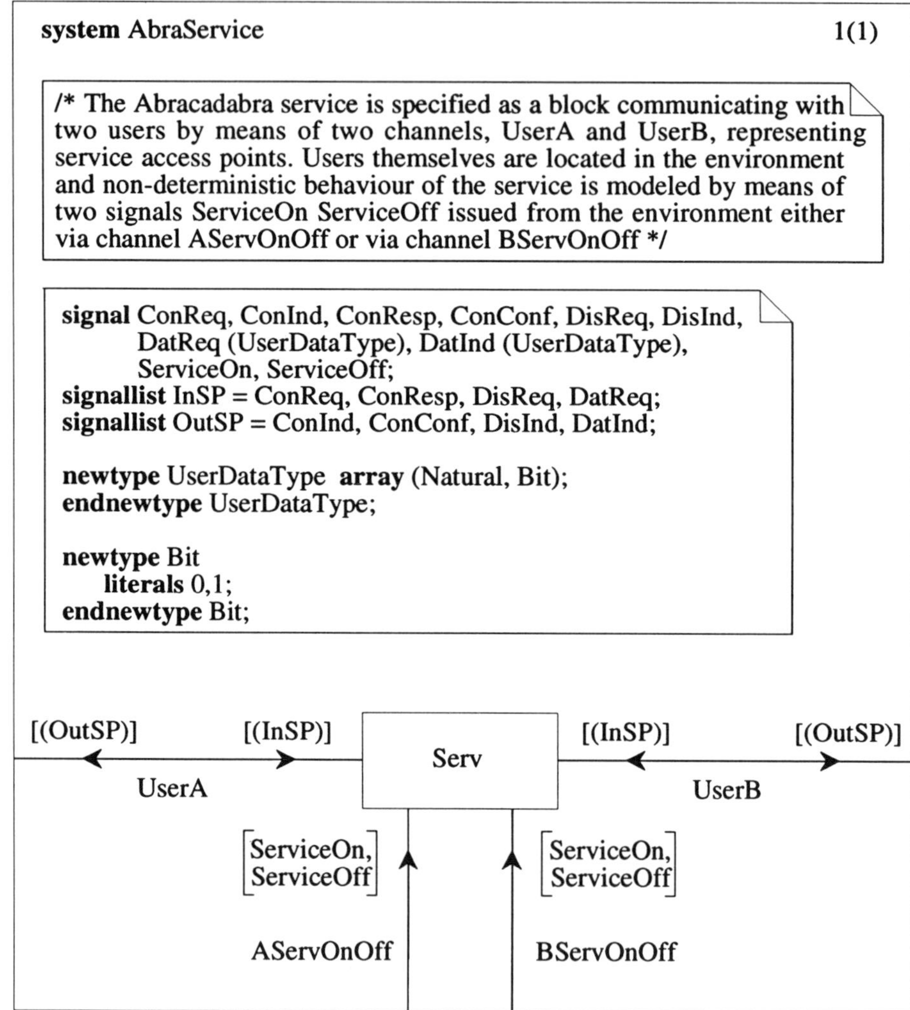

system AbraService
1(1)
/* The Abracadabra service is specified as a block communicating with two users by means of two channels, UserA and UserB, representing service access points. Users themselves are located in the environment and non-deterministic behaviour of the service is modeled by means of two signals ServiceOn ServiceOff issued from the environment either via channel AServOnOff or via channel BServOnOff */
signal ConReq, ConInd, ConResp, ConConf, DisReq, DisInd, DatReq (UserDataType), DatInd (UserDataType), ServiceOn, ServiceOff;
signallist InSP = ConReq, ConResp, DisReq, DatReq;
signallist OutSP = ConInd, ConConf, DisInd, DatInd;
newtype UserDataType array (Natural, Bit);
endnewtype UserDataType;
newtype Bit
literals 0,1;
endnewtype Bit;
[(OutSP)]
[(InSP)]
Serv
[(InSP)]
[(OutSP)]
UserA
UserB
ServiceOn, ServiceOff
ServiceOn, ServiceOff
AServOnOff
BServOnOff

Figure 8.3: Abracadabra Service in SDL – Graphical Description

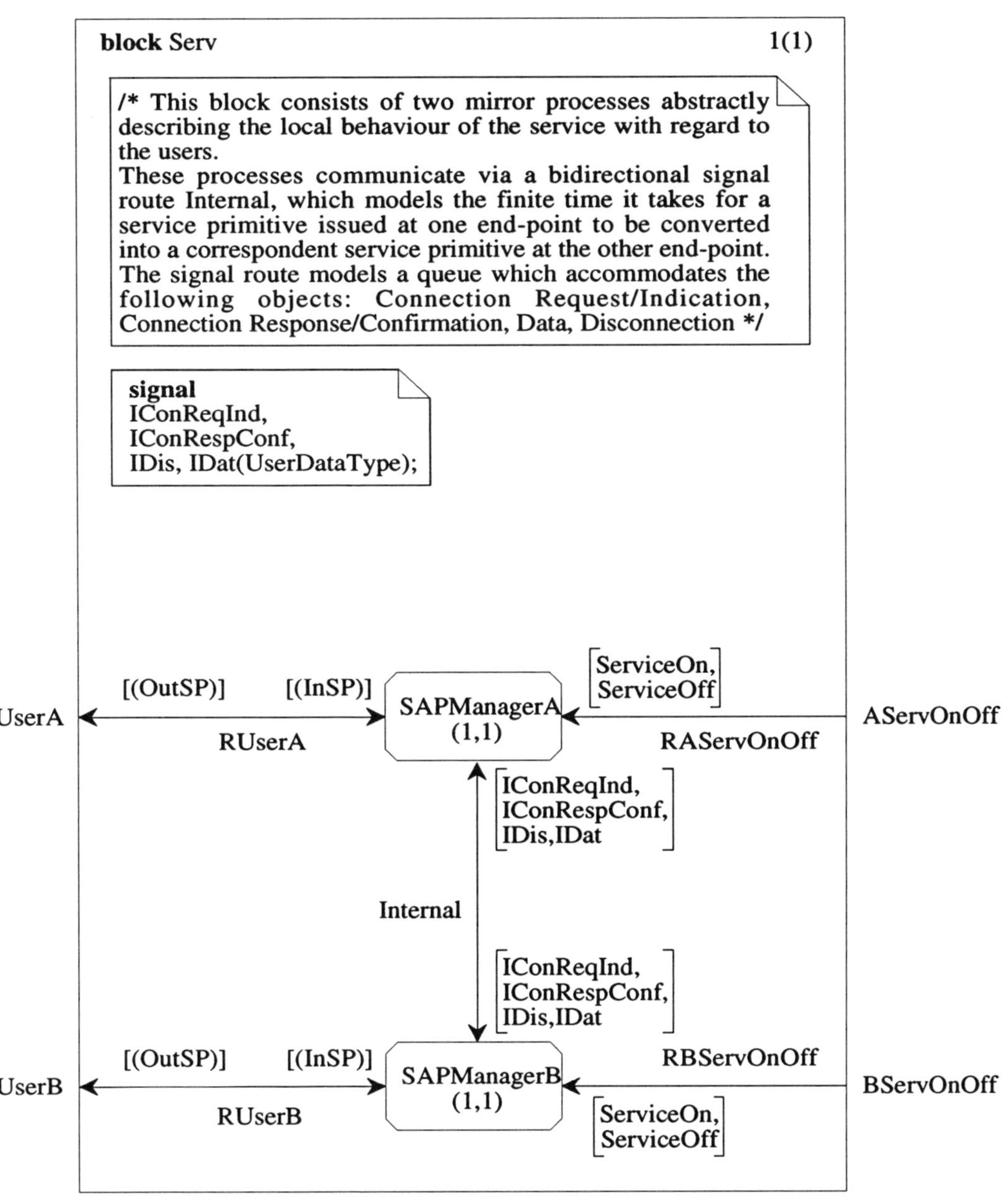

Figure 8.3 *(continued)*

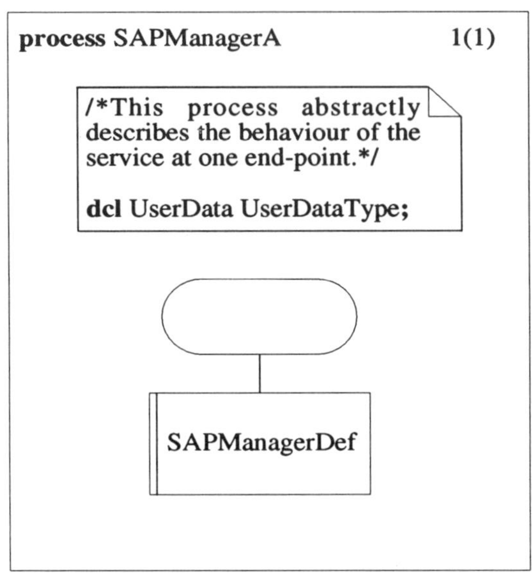

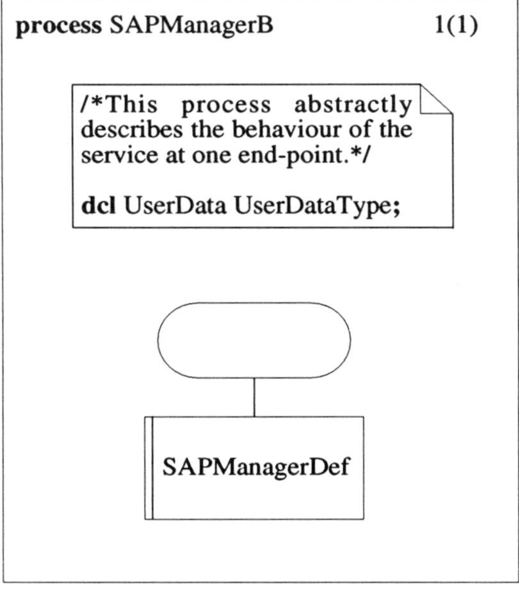

Figure 8.3 *(continued)*

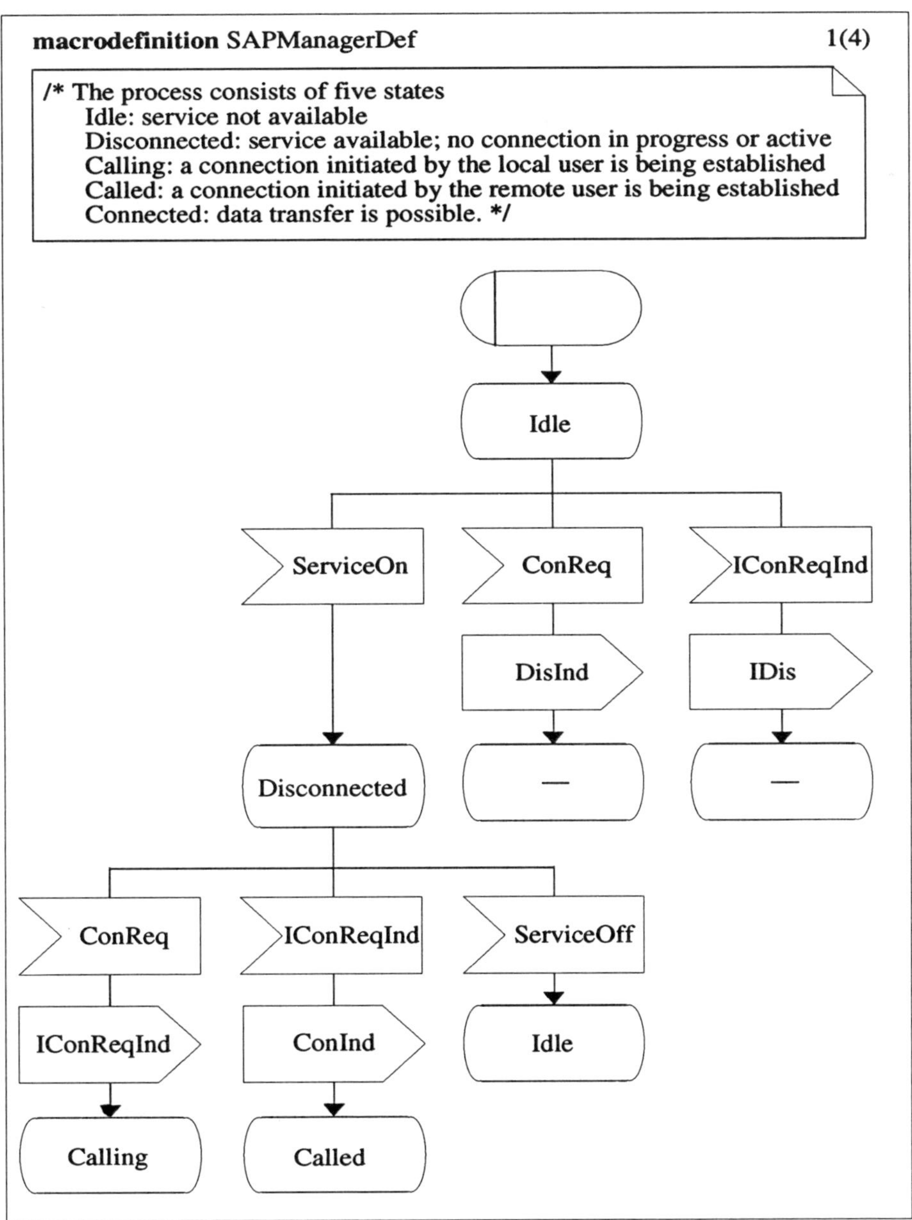

Figure 8.3 *(continued)*

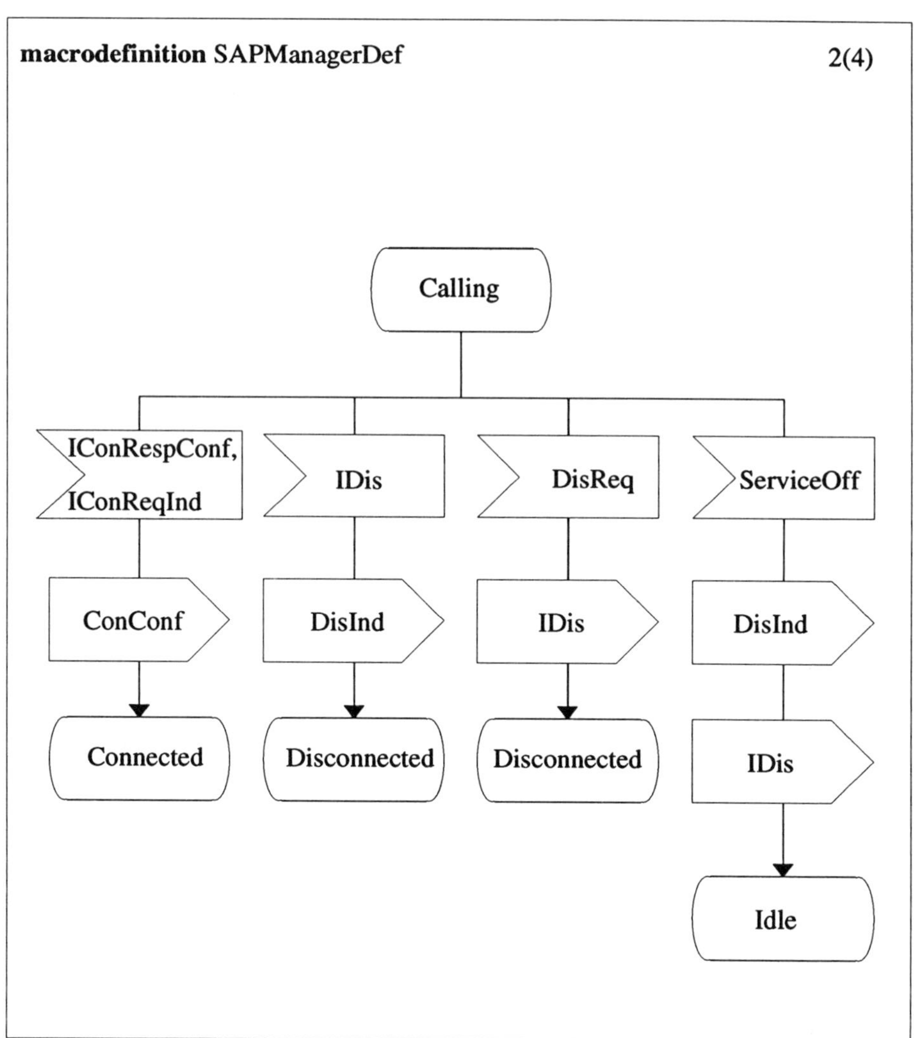

Figure 8.3 *(continued)*

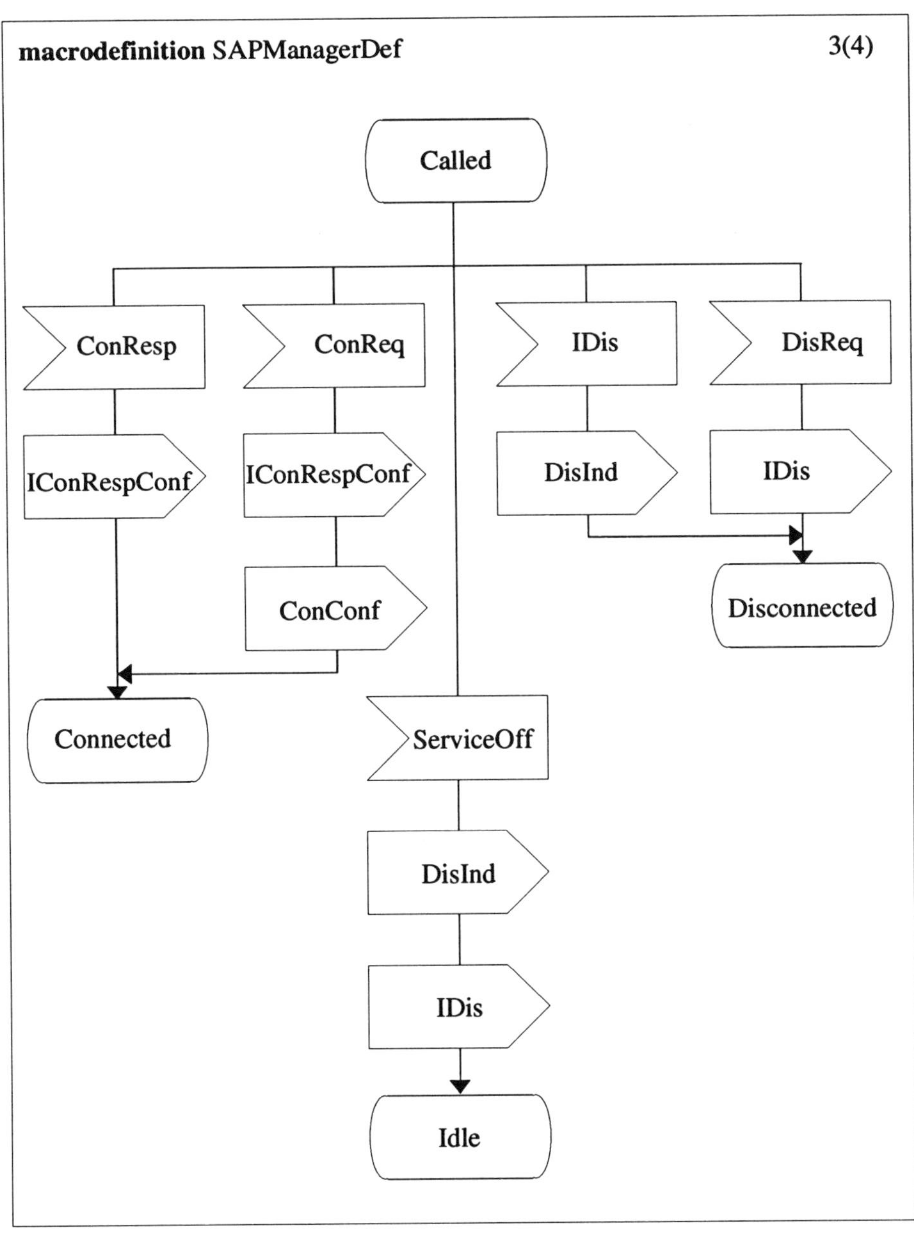

Figure 8.3 *(continued)*

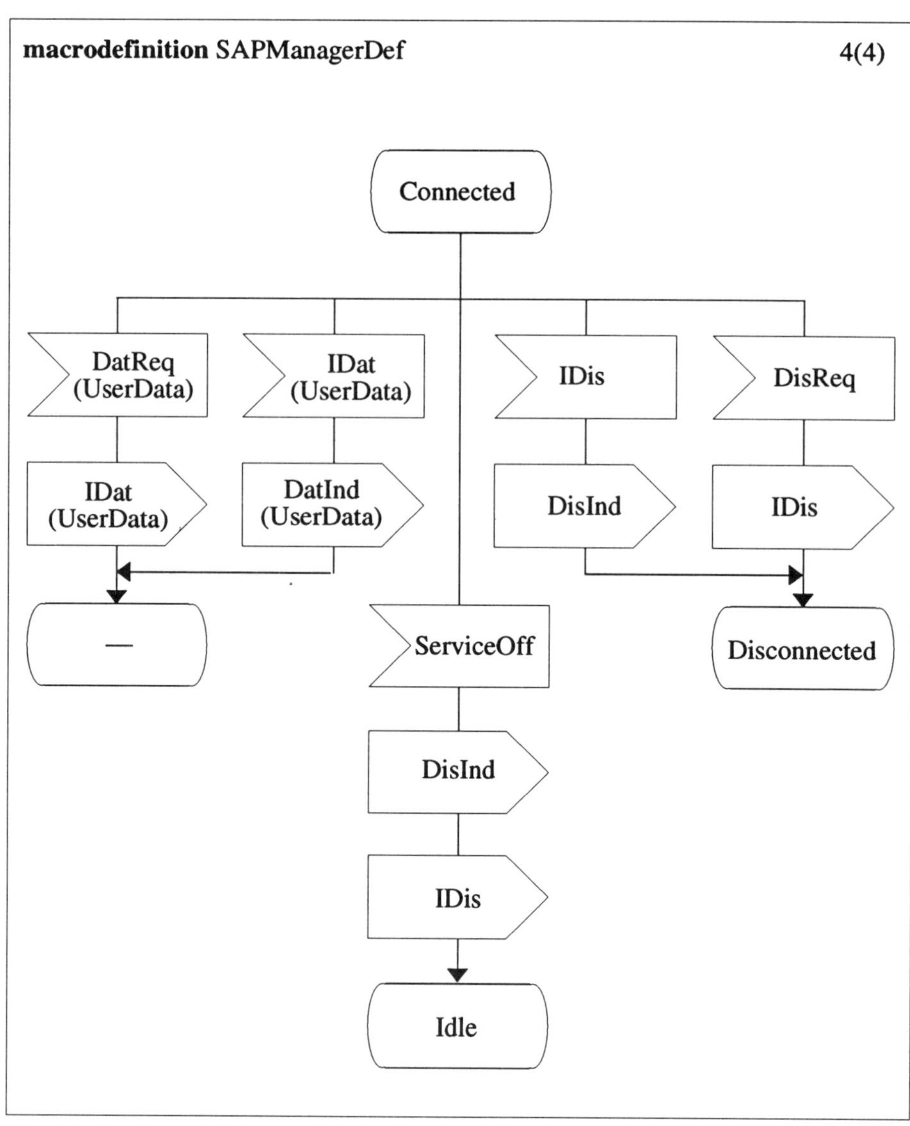

Figure 8.3 *(continued)*

process performs between service primitives on the user signalroute and objects on the internal signalroute. The implicit underlying queue mechanism models the delay from a service primitive being accepted at one SAP to the delivery of the corresponding service primitive at the remote SAP. Signals *ServiceOn* and *ServiceOff* may be independently received by either of the *SAPManager* processes. This explains why two distinct but equivalent channels have been defined.

Since *SAPManagerA* and *SAPManagerB* have identical behaviour, they have been described by means of macro *SAPManagerDef* which acts as a kind of process template. There are five states in it: *Idle*, *Disconnected*, *Calling*, *Called* and *Connected*. Their informal meaning is given through comments embedded in the formal description. Note the difference between *Idle* and *Disconnected*. In the *Idle* state, no connection can be set up because some unspecified internal condition makes the service provider unavailable. In the *Disconnected* state, a connection attempt is allowed when a connection request primitive or a connection object arrives.

The Abracadabra Service example shows that SDL can satisfactorily describe connection-oriented services. Informal service definitions in standards sometimes use state machines to represent the service; however, what they actually represent is a local view of the service at one end-point. This information is not enough to describe all possible sequences of service primitives, so further specification of allowed service interactions has to be provided – a time-sequence diagram. The SDL description in this section uses a state-oriented approach, but deals adequately with an end-to-end view of the service. The description captures the distributed nature of the service provider, with its characteristic behaviour of relating information exchanges occurring at different service access points.

An abstract style of specification is demonstrated in this example. Nondeterministic behaviour is modelled by using signals from the environment and corresponding channels to convey them. The only channels used for concrete information are *UserA* and *UserB*; the others exist in the abstract model only.

8.6 Conclusion[7]

Writing formal descriptions of the Abracadabra Service revealed similar kinds of deficiencies in the informal description as were found with the Unreliable Medium of Chapter 6. However, the connection-oriented nature of the Abracadabra Service exposed new kinds of problem:

[7]Section 8.6 is by K. J. Turner.

- Realistic systems may have 'phase change' problems, when the boundary between different phases of operation is not clearly delineated. It is important to describe these cases fully.

- The distributed nature of a service has a marked effect on how it is formally described. If the basic nature of interactions in an FDT is asynchronous, care must be taken to deal with change-over situations (e.g. a disconnection has been signalled but data is still waiting in the channel to be received). If the basic nature of interactions is synchronous, buffering must be introduced in the description to reflect the distributed operation of the service.

- It is difficult to decide how best to describe user misbehaviour. If user errors are explicitly addressed as part of the informal description then they will be reflected in a formal description. However, a service is often an abstraction of an interface and is not necessarily implemented in exactly the same way. Service descriptions therefore tend to avoid dealing with interface errors. However, a formal description has to ascribe some meaning to invalid behaviour. A formal description could omit an explicit description of invalid user behaviour and so be a partial specification. However, the formal description would still have some implicit meaning in these cases.

  Interestingly, the philosophy of each FDT is different when it comes to dealing with such error conditions. In ESTELLE, invalid user behaviour would result in deadlock. ESTELLE experts therefore prefer to describe invalid user interactions as being accepted but ignored. In LOTOS, invalid user behaviour would also result in deadlock. However, because LOTOS experts prefer to take an abstract view, no explicit description would normally be included for user misbehaviour. In SDL, invalid behaviour cannot arise from the point of view of the system since invalid signals are discarded.

9 Abracadabra Protocol

The Abracadabra Service of Chapter 8 needs to be supported by a connection-oriented protocol. Because of the extra complexity required to handle connection and disconnection, the protocol has been simplified to have limited flow control and error recovery.

The essence of the Sliding Window Protocol in Chapter 7 is its flow control mechanism. The Abracadabra Protocol described in this chapter is effectively a Sliding Window Protocol with a window size of 1. This degenerate case has been widely studied as the Alternating Bit Protocol, so-called because its sequence numbers alternate between 0 and 1. Although the Sliding Window Protocol allows its sequence numbers to increase indefinitely, most protocols recycle sequence numbers when they reach some limiting value. Sequence numbers in this protocol are modulo 2.

The Alternating Bit Protocol supports a unidirectional flow of information with a positive handshake on each transfer. The Abracadabra Service is symmetrical, however, so the Alternating Bit Protocol is used for each direction of transfer. This extra structure is the final touch needed to complete the series of graded examples illustrating the use of FDTs. The bibliography in Appendix A lists sources of more complex or more realistic formal descriptions.

9.1 Informal Description[1]

9.1.1 *Overall Structure*

The **Abracadabra Protocol** is so named because it has:

- Alternating Bit sequence numbers, Retransmission on timeout, and Acknowledgements in one direction

- Connection And Disconnection

[1]Section 9.1 is by K. J. Turner.

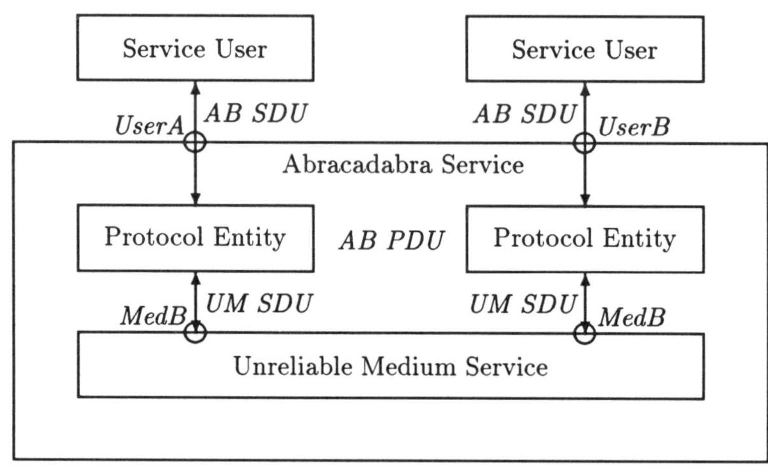

Figure 9.1: Abracadabra Protocol in Context

- Alternating Bit sequence numbers, Retransmission on timeout, and Acknowledgements in the other direction.

The protocol operates over a full-duplex, unreliable communications medium between two stations. The two stations communicate by transfer of PDUs *(Protocol Data Units)*. The protocol is two-way simultaneous, symmetrical and reliable. The protocol may be in one of several phases: connection, data transfer, disconnection or error.

Figure 9.1 shows the Abracadabra Protocol in the context of the underlying medium and the Abracadabra Service.

9.1.2 *Protocol Data Units and Parameters*

The protocol data units of the protocol are tabulated below; only DT and AK carry parameters. Each service data unit is carried in one DT protocol data unit, and each protocol data unit is carried in one service data unit of the underlying medium. In communications terms this means that the protocol does not support blocking, segmentation or concatenation.

The protocol is parameterised by two constants N and P. N (a positive integer) is the maximum number of attempts to transmit a PDU without receiving an acknowledgement. P (which exceeds the round-trip transit delay) is the time period that should elapse before attempting retransmission.

Purpose	Name	Parameters	Corresponding Service Primitives
Connection Request	CR	-	ConReq, ConInd
Connection Confirmation	CC	-	ConResp, ConConf
Data Transfer	DT	Service Data Unit	DatReq, DatInd
		Sequence Number	
Acknowledgement	AK	Sequence Number	-
Disconnection Request	DR	-	DisReq, DisInd
Disconnection Indication	DC	-	-

9.1.3 *Connection Phase*

A connection attempt is made following *ConReq* by sending a *CR*. If a *CC* is received, a *ConConf* is issued and the data transfer phase is entered; the same is true if *CR* is received instead. If *DR* is received or *DisReq* occurs, the disconnection phase is entered. If any PDU other than *CC*, *CR* or *DR* is received it is ignored. If no response to *CR* is received within period P, the *CR* is retransmitted. A maximum of N connection attempts (i.e. N periods of value P) is permitted. After this, the error phase is entered.

When no connection is set up, receipt of a *CR* causes a *ConInd*; any other PDU is ignored. If a *ConResp* follows, then *CC* is sent and the data transfer phase is entered. If, however, the connection attempt is abandoned with *DisReq* then the disconnection phase is entered.

9.1.4 *Data Transfer Phase*

A *DatReq* leads to a *DT* being sent. On receipt of the corresponding *AK*, a further *DatReq* may be accepted. If the corresponding *AK* is not received within period P, the *DT* is retransmitted. A maximum of N transmission attempts (i.e. N periods of value P) is permitted. After this, the error phase is entered.

DT and *AK* PDUs carry a one-bit sequence number that is independent for each direction of transmission. The sequence number starts at 0 after connection. A correct acknowledgement to a *DT* bears the next (i.e. other) sequence number[2]. If an *AK* with the wrong sequence number is received then the error phase is entered.

When a *DT* is received, it is acknowledged by an *AK* with the next sequence number after the one in the *DT*. However, if a further *DT* is received before the *AK* is sent then the error phase is entered. If a *DT* bears the sequence

[2]Note that the receiver in the Sliding Window Protocol sends the sequence number of the message being acknowledged. The Abracadabra Protocol follows the more common rule of sending the sequence number of the *next* message expected.

number expected then a *DatInd* is issued, otherwise the *DT* is not delivered to the user.

A *CC* is sent in response to a *CR* that is received initially in the data transfer phase, before any *DT* or *AK* PDUs. If a *DR* is received by either station the disconnection phase is entered. If any PDU apart from *DT*, *AK*, *CR* (initial transmission only) or *DR* is received then the error phase is entered.

9.1.5 *Disconnection Phase*

A *DisReq* leads to a *DR* being sent. On receipt of *DC* the connection is terminated and a new connection may be attempted; the same is true if *DR* is received instead. If a further *DR* is received, *DC* is sent. Any other kind of PDU is ignored. If no response to *DR* is received within period P, the *DR* is retransmitted. A maximum of N disconnection attempts (i.e. N periods of value P) is permitted. After this, the connection is considered to have been terminated and a new connection may be attempted.

When a *DR* is received, it is acknowledged with *DC*. If a connection is established, a *DisInd* is issued. After this, a new connection may be attempted. Any PDU other than *DR* or *CR* that arrives subsequently is ignored.

9.1.6 *Error Phase*

A protocol error leads to the error phase being entered and *DR* being sent. This is identical to the disconnection phase except that the station detecting the error also issues *DisInd* before sending the *DR*.

9.1.7 *Underlying Medium Service*

The unreliable medium service of Chapter 6 could, in principle, be used to support the Abracadabra Protocol. However, to simplify the mapping of data units it was assumed in Chapter 6 that the medium supported separate data and acknowledgement service primitives. This approach is not general, however, since a service should not need to know about the protocol data units used by a protocol. The medium of Chapter 6 is unidirectional, whereas a bidirectional medium is needed for the Abracadabra Protocol. The medium is also allowed to corrupt, duplicate or re-order messages as well as lose them; the Abracadabra Protocol is designed to deal with message loss only.

A simpler unreliable medium is therefore appropriate for this example. The medium supports a pair of service access points, addressed as *MedA* or *MedB*. The service is accessed by service primitives *Mreq* and *Mind (Medium Request/Indication)* that carry service data units corresponding to protocol data units. The medium service is connection-less, bidirectional and transparent.

Messages may be lost, but may not be corrupted, duplicated, re-ordered or created. Either station may issue an *Mreq*, which will be delivered as an *Mind* with the same data or will be lost.

9.2 Errors in the Informal Description[3]

9.2.1 *Premature Transmission of DT*

Is it reasonable that Section 9.1.4 should consider it an error if a further *DT* is received before an *AK* can be transmitted?

The intention was to trap misuse of the protocol by the transmitter, or to detect that the timeout period was too short. However, this was perhaps an unnecessary complication.

9.2.2 *Stopping Retransmissions*

Should Sections 9.1.3 and 9.1.4 explicitly say that retransmission of a *CR* or *DT* is stopped if the error phase is entered?

Retransmission a timed out PDU was intended to cease on entry to the error phase.

9.2.3 *Retransmission Limit and Period*

What should be the behaviour of the protocol if parameters N and P of Section 9.1.2 are not positive?

The intention was that the protocol should refuse to accept or transmit any messages.

9.2.4 *DR when Disconnected*

Section 9.1.3 says that receipt of any PDU other than *CR* is ignored when no connection is set up. However, Section 9.1.5 says that if a further *DR* is received in the disconnection phase it should result in *DC*. Which is correct?

The description of the disconnection phase is correct. Receipt of *DR* when not connected was intended to result in *DC*.

[3]Section 9.2 is by K. J. Turner, based on problems found by the authors of the formal descriptions. As reported by de Saqui-Sannes and Courtiat (1990), Blumer and Parker (1990), and Tenney (1992) the protocol can fail to operate incorrectly under extreme conditions, e.g. when P is too small or repeated transmissions fail to get through.

9.2.5 *Connection Refusal*

If *DR* is received in response to *CR*, should a *DisInd* be given to the User? Section 9.1.3 says only that the disconnection phase is entered.

The intention was to inform the initiating user by *DisInd* if the connection is refused.

9.2.6 *Connection Refusal*

Should the disconnection phase be entered if the connection is refused by the other party, i.e. is it correct to follow the sequence *CR*, *DR*, *DC*? This is implied by Sections 9.1.3 and 9.1.5.

Although the informal description is valid, it is more usual to find that protocols refuse a connection by the sequence *CR*, *DR*. The informal description should therefore refer to *DR* being sent and a 'not connected' state being entered, rather than the disconnection phase being entered.

9.2.7 *Ignoring Out-of-Sequence Data*

Section 9.1.4 says that a DT with an incorrect sequence number is not delivered to the user. Should this say that the corresponding *DatInd* is not delivered?

The informal description is worded rather loosely and should have referred to *DatInd*.

9.3 Formal Description in ESTELLE[4]

The description modules are **systemprocesses**, and so run asynchronously. As the modules are not refined into submodules, the global behaviour of the description would not change if they were designated **systemactivities**. The crucial point is that they are distinct systems.

The modules and interaction points for the Abracadabra Protocol description are shown in Figure 9.2. The structure illustrates one way to solve the common case of peer-to-peer communication. Peer protocol entities logically communicate with each other, but they actually communicate via an underlying service. When describing a protocol it is thus not possible for an entity to 'send a protocol data unit'. Instead, it must package a protocol data unit up into a service data unit and send it via a request to the underlying service. The peer entity must unwrap the protocol data unit from the service data unit that appears in the corresponding indication from the underlying service.

[4]Section 9.3 is by T. P. Blumer and R. L. Tenney.

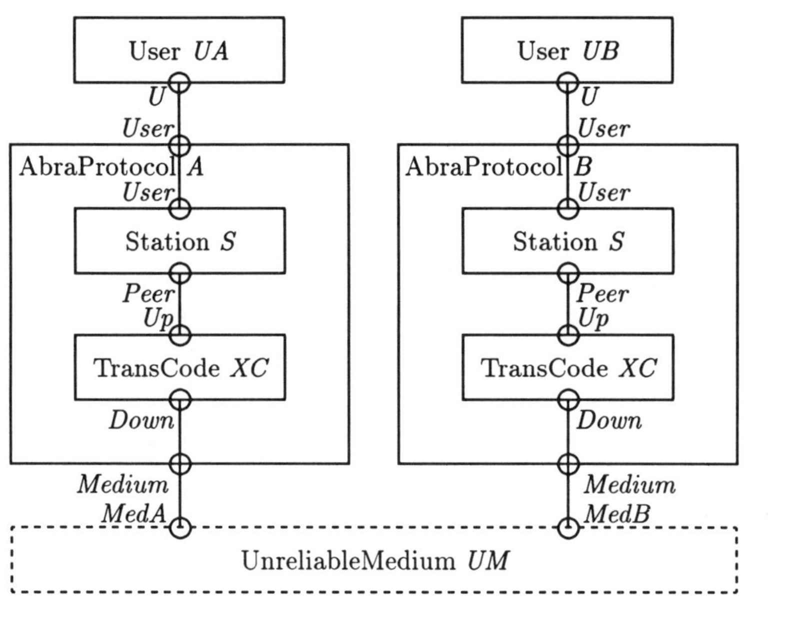

Figure 9.2: Abracadabra Protocol in ESTELLE – Architecture

The description is broken up into several modules. The protocol itself is described in the *Station* module, the main one of interest. The *Station* modules have been written as though they were communicating directly, so they have the illusion of sending or receiving a protocol data unit directly. To permit this, a *TransCode* module has been interposed between each *Station* module and the underlying medium service. The *TransCode* module encodes the protocol data unit from the *Station* module in an *Mreq* primitive of the medium. Conversely, the *TransCode* module decodes an *Mind* primitive from the medium.

The structuring into modules uses ESTELLE features that make the substructures 'invisible' to the rest of the system. The *AbraProtocol* module simply serves to form the substructures and connect them together; it does not have any transitions of its own. Note that the *TransCode* module has only one (unnamed) state, so **from** and **to** clauses are unnecessary for its transitions.

The Abracadabra Protocol description in ESTELLE is fairly straightforward since the order of the transitions of the *StationBody* closely follows the order in the original description. Indeed, this portion of the formal description was written almost as a translation of the informal description.

The main differences between the Abracadabra Service and Protocol descriptions arise from the service being an abstraction of the protocol. The interface to the user is, of course, identical in both cases. In the service description there are no retransmissions and no alternating bit since these are invisible to the user. Furthermore, the processes of the service provider at the service access points do not have to communicate through an underlying service. Instead, the inability of the service provider to establish or maintain a connection (where the protocol's retransmissions have failed) is modelled in the service description by the use of non-determinism.

Although back-pressure flow control has a global end-to-end effect, its exact realisation depends on local implementation of the interfaces. The protocol description therefore does not deal with it, but could be modified to do so as explained at the end of this section.

Since the Abracadabra Protocol is significantly more complex than the other examples, Figure 9.3 has been provided to show which transition numbers are applicable for which inputs in which states.

```
specification AbracadabraProtocol;

default individual queue;

timescale seconds;

const
  N = any integer;                { Number of transmission tries }
  P = any integer;                { Delay amount for timers }
```

Input	State				
	CLOSED	*CRSENT*	*CRRECV*	*ESTAB*	*DRSENT*
ConReq	2	35	35	35	35
ConResp	36	36	10	36	36
DatReq	37	37	37	13	37
DisReq	38	6	11	23	38
CR	9	4	30	17, 18	30
CC	31	3	31	19	31
DT	32	32	32	16	32
AK	33	33	33	14, 15	33
DR	27	5	12	26	25
DC	34	34	34	20	24

Figure 9.3: Abracadabra Protocol in ESTELLE – Transitions

```
type
  SeqType = 0..1;                    { Sequence number type }
  UserDataType = ...;                { Some suitable type, e.g. a string }
  PDUType = (CR, CC, DT, AK, DR, DC);
  SDUType =
    record
      PDU : PDUType;
      SeqNo : SeqType;
      UData : UserDataType
    end;

channel SSAP(User, Provider);
  by User:
    ConReq;
    ConResp;
    DatReq(UserData : UserDataType);
    DisReq;
  by Provider:
    ConInd;
    ConConf;
    DatInd(UserData : UserDataType);
    DisInd;
```

```
channel PeerCode(Peer, Coder);
  by Peer, Coder:
    CR;
    CC;
    DT(Seq : SeqType; UserData : UserDataType);
    AK(Seq : SeqType);
    DR;
    DC;

channel MSAP(User, Provider);
  by User:
    Mreq(SDU: SDUType);
  by Provider:
    Mind(SDU: SDUType);

module User systemprocess;
  ip U : SSAP(User);
end;

body UserBody for User;
external;

module UnreliableMedium systemprocess;
  ip MedA, MedB : MSAP(Provider);
end;

body UnreliableMediumBody for UnreliableMedium;
external;

module AbraProtocol systemprocess;
  ip
    User : SSAP(Provider);
    Medium : MSAP(User);
end;

body AbraProtocolBody for AbraProtocol;

  module Station process;
    ip
      User : SSAP(Provider);
      Peer : PeerCode(Peer);
  end;
```

```
body StationBody for Station;

  state
    CLOSED, CRSENT, CRRECV, ESTAB, DRSENT;

  stateset
    CRignore = [CRRECV, DRSENT];
    CCignore = [CLOSED, CRRECV, DRSENT];
    DTignore = [CLOSED, CRSENT, CRRECV, DRSENT];
    AKignore = [CLOSED, CRSENT, CRRECV, DRSENT];
    DCignore = [CLOSED, CRSENT, CRRECV];

    ConReqIgnore = [CRSENT, CRRECV, ESTAB, DRSENT];
    ConRespIgnore = [CLOSED, CRSENT, ESTAB, DRSENT];
    DatReqIgnore = [CLOSED, CRSENT, CRRECV, DRSENT];
    DisReqIgnore = [CLOSED, DRSENT];

  var
    Sending : boolean;
    SendSeq, RecvSeq : SeqType;
    OldSendSeq : SeqType;
    CRRetranRemaining : integer;
    DTRetranRemaining : integer;
    DRRetranRemaining : integer;
    OldData : UserDataType;
    DTorAK : boolean;

  procedure InitVar;

    begin
      Sending := false;
      SendSeq := 0;
      RecvSeq := 0;
      { Setting the following counters to -1 guarantees that
      the predicates that check them will fail }
      CRRetranRemaining := -1;
      DTRetranRemaining := -1;
      DRRetranRemaining := -1;
      DTorAK := false;
    end;

  initialize
```

```
  to CLOSED
    begin { 1 }
      { Variables are initialised on leaving CLOSED since the
      protocol module may cycle through CLOSED repeatedly }
    end;

trans

{ *** Connection phase *** }

  { User requests connection }
  from CLOSED to CRSENT
    when User.ConReq
      begin { 2 }
        { Initialise module variables on leaving CLOSED }
        InitVar;
        output Peer.CR;
        CRRetranRemaining := N − 1;
      end;

  { Other user accepted connection }
  from CRSENT to ESTAB
    when Peer.CC
      begin { 3 }
        output User.ConConf;
        CRRetranRemaining := −1;
      end;

  { Colliding CRs }
  from CRSENT to ESTAB
    when Peer.CR
      begin { 4 }
        output User.ConConf;
        CRRetranRemaining := −1;
      end;

  { Other user rejected connection }
  from CRSENT to CLOSED
    when Peer.DR
      begin { 5 }
        output User.DisInd;
        CRRetranRemaining := −1;
      end;
```

```
{ Sender requests disconnection }
from CRSENT to DRSENT
  when User.DisReq
    begin { 6 }
      output Peer.DR;
      CRRetranRemaining := −1;
      DRRetranRemaining := N − 1;
    end;

{ Retransmission timer for CR fires }
from CRSENT to same
  provided CRRetranRemaining > 0
    delay (P)
      begin { 7 }
        CRRetranRemaining := CRRetranRemaining − 1;
        output Peer.CR;
      end;

{ Terminate retransmission of CR }
from CRSENT to DRSENT
  provided CRRetranRemaining = 0
    delay (P)                    { Allow time for last CR }
      begin { 8 }
        { Enter error phase }
        output User.DisInd;
        output Peer.DR;
        CRRetranRemaining := −1;
        DRRetranRemaining := N − 1;
      end;

{ Receive connect request from peer entity }
from CLOSED to CRRECV
  when Peer.CR
    begin { 9 }
      { Initialise module variables on CLOSED }
      InitVar;
      output User.ConInd;
    end;

{ User accepts connection }
from CRRECV to ESTAB
  when User.ConResp
```

```
        begin { 10 }
          output Peer.CC;
        end;

    { User rejects connection }
    from CRRECV to CLOSED
      when User.DisReq
        begin { 11 }
          output Peer.DR        { Just once }
        end;

    { Other user disconnected }
    from CRRECV to CLOSED
      when Peer.DR
        begin { 12 }
          output User.DisInd;
          output Peer.DC;
        end;

  { *** Data transfer phase *** }

    { Send data in DT PDU }
    from ESTAB to same
      when User.DatReq
        provided not Sending
          begin { 13 }
            OldData := UserData;
            output Peer.DT(SendSeq, OldData);
            OldSendSeq := SendSeq;
            SendSeq := (SendSeq + 1) mod 2;
            Sending := true;
            { Turn on retransmission timer }
            DTRetranRemaining := N − 1;
          end;

    { Receive acknowledgement with correct sequence number in
    AK PDU }
    from ESTAB to same
      when Peer.AK
        provided Seq = SendSeq
          begin { 14 }
            Sending := false;
```

```
            { Turn off retransmission timer }
            DTRetranRemaining := −1;
            DTorAK := true;
          end;

  { Receive acknowledgement with incorrect sequence number in
  AK PDU }
  from ESTAB to DRSENT
    when Peer.AK
      provided Seq <> SendSeq
        begin { 15 }
          { Enter error phase }
          output User.DisInd;
          output Peer.DR;
          DTorAK := true;
          DTRetranRemaining := −1;
          DRRetranRemaining := N − 1;
        end;

  { Receive data in DT PDU }
  from ESTAB to same
    when Peer.DT
      begin { 16 }
        if Seq = RecvSeq then
          begin
            output User.DatInd(UserData);
            RecvSeq := (RecvSeq + 1) mod 2;
          end;
        { Send AK with next expected sequence number }
        output Peer.AK(RecvSeq);
        DTorAK := true;
      end;

  from ESTAB to same
    when Peer.CR
      provided not DTorAK
        begin { 17 }
          output Peer.CC;
        end;

  from ESTAB to DRSENT
    when Peer.CR
```

```
    provided DTorAK
      begin { 18 }
        { Enter error phase }
        output User.DisInd;
        output Peer.DR;
        DTRetranRemaining := -1;
        DRRetranRemaining := N - 1;
      end;

from ESTAB to DRSENT
  when Peer.CC
    begin { 19 }
      { Enter error phase }
      output User.DisInd;
      output Peer.DR;
      DTRetranRemaining := -1;
      DRRetranRemaining := N - 1;
    end;
  when Peer.DC
    begin { 20 }
      { Enter error phase }
      output User.DisInd;
      output Peer.DR;
      DTRetranRemaining := -1;
      DRRetranRemaining := N - 1;
    end;

{ Retransmission timer for DT fires }
from ESTAB to same
  provided DTRetranRemaining > 0
    delay (P)
      begin { 21 }
        DTRetranRemaining := DTRetranRemaining - 1;
        output Peer.DT(OldSendSeq, OldData);
      end;

{ Terminate retransmission of DT }
from ESTAB to DRSENT
  provided DTRetranRemaining = 0
    delay (P)
      begin { 22 }
        { Enter error phase }
```

```
            output User.DisInd;
            output Peer.DR;
            DTRetranRemaining := -1;
            DRRetranRemaining := N - 1;
          end;

    { *** Disconnection phase *** }

      { Receive disconnect request from user }
      from ESTAB to DRSENT
        when User.DisReq
          begin { 23 }
            output Peer.DR;
            DTRetranRemaining := -1;
            DRRetranRemaining := N - 1;
          end;

      { Receive DC }
      from DRSENT to CLOSED
        when Peer.DC
          begin { 24 }
            DRRetranRemaining := -1;
          end;

      { Receive DR }
      from DRSENT to CLOSED
        when Peer.DR
          begin { 25 }
            DRRetranRemaining := -1;
          end;

      { Receive DR }
      from ESTAB to CLOSED
        when Peer.DR
          begin { 26 }
            output User.DisInd;
            output Peer.DC;
            DTRetranRemaining := -1;
          end;

      { Reply to retransmitted DR }
      from CLOSED to same
        when Peer.DR
```

```
    begin { 27 }
      output Peer.DC;
    end;

{ Retransmission timer for DR fires }
from DRSENT to same
  provided DRRetranRemaining > 0
    delay (P)
      begin { 28 }
        DRRetranRemaining := DRRetranRemaining − 1;
        output Peer.DR;
      end;

{ Terminate retransmission of DR }
from DRSENT to CLOSED
  provided DRRetranRemaining = 0
    delay (P)
      begin { 29 }
        { The connection is regarded as closed }
        DRRetranRemaining := −1;
      end;

{ Ignore other PDUs }
from CRignore to same
  when Peer.CR
    begin { 30 }
    end;

from CCignore to same
  when Peer.CC
    begin { 31 }
    end;

from DTignore to same
  when Peer.DT
    begin { 32 }
    end;

from AKignore to same
  when Peer.AK
    begin { 33 }
    end;

from DCignore to same
```

```
        when Peer.DC
          begin { 34 }
          end;

      from ConReqIgnore to same
        when User.ConReq
          begin { 35 }
          end;

      from ConRespIgnore to same
        when User.ConResp
          begin { 36 }
          end;

      from DatReqIgnore to same
        when User.DatReq
          begin { 37 }
          end;

      from DisReqIgnore to same
        when User.DisReq
          begin { 38 }
          end;
end; { StationBody }

{ *** TransCode *** }

module TransCode process;
  ip
   Up : PeerCode(Coder);
   Down : MSAP(User);
end;

body TransCodeBody for TransCode;

  var SDU: SDUType;

  procedure BuildCR(var SDU: SDUType);
    begin
      SDU.PDU := CR
    end;
```

```
procedure BuildCC(var SDU: SDUType);
  begin
    SDU.PDU := CC
  end;

procedure BuildDT(Seq: SeqType; Data: UserDataType;
 var SDU: SDUType);
  begin
    SDU.PDU := DT;
    SDU.SeqNo := Seq;
    SDU.UData := Data
  end;

procedure BuildAK(Seq: SeqType; var SDU: SDUType);
  begin
    SDU.PDU := AK;
    SDU.SeqNo := Seq
  end;

procedure BuildDR(var SDU: SDUType);
  begin
    SDU.PDU := DR
  end;

procedure BuildDC(var SDU: SDUType);
  begin
    SDU.PDU := DC
  end;

trans

  when Up.CC
    begin { 1 }
      BuildCC(SDU);
      output Down.Mreq(SDU)
    end;

  when Up.CR
    begin { 2 }
      BuildCR(SDU);
      output Down.Mreq(SDU)
    end;
```

```
when Up.DT
  begin { 3 }
    BuildDT(Seq, UserData, SDU);
    output Down.Mreq(SDU)
  end;

when Up.AK
  begin { 4 }
    BuildAK(Seq, SDU);
    output Down.Mreq(SDU)
  end;

when Up.DR
  begin { 5 }
    BuildDR(SDU);
    output Down.Mreq(SDU)
  end;

when Up.DC
  begin { 6 }
    BuildDC(SDU);
    output Down.Mreq(SDU)
  end;

when Down.Mind
  provided (SDU.PDU = CR)
    begin { 7 }
      output Up.CR
    end;

when Down.Mind
  provided (SDU.PDU = CC)
    begin { 8 }
      output Up.CC
    end;

when Down.Mind
  provided (SDU.PDU = DT)
    begin { 9 }
      output Up.DT(SDU.SeqNo, SDU.UData)
    end;
```

```
    when Down.Mind
      provided (SDU.PDU = AK)
        begin { 10 }
          output Up.AK(SDU.SeqNo)
        end;

    when Down.Mind
      provided (SDU.PDU = DR)
        begin { 11 }
          output Up.DR
        end;

    when Down.Mind
      provided (SDU.PDU = DC)
        begin { 12 }
          output Up.DC
        end;

  end; { TransCodeBody }

  { Main body for AbraProtocolBody }

  modvar
    S : Station;
    XC : TransCode;

  initialize
    begin
      { Instantiate modules and make connections }
      init S with StationBody;
      init XC with TransCodeBody;
      attach User to S.User;
      connect S.Peer to XC.Up;
      attach Medium to XC.Down;
    end;
end; { AbraProtocolBody }

{ Main body for AbracadabraProtocol }

  modvar
    A, B : AbraProtocol;
    UA, UB : User;
    UM : UnreliableMedium;
```

```
initialize
  provided (N > 0) and (P > 0)
    begin { 1 }
      init UA with UserBody;
      init UB with UserBody;
      init A with AbraProtocolBody;
      init B with AbraProtocolBody;
      init UM with UnreliableMediumBody;
      connect UA.U to A.User;
      connect UB.U to B.User;
      connect A.Medium to UM.MedA;
      connect B.Medium to UM.MedB;
    end;

end. { AbracadabraProtocol }
```

To deal with back-pressure flow control it would be possible to introduce primitive functions *ReceiverBlocked* and *MediumBlocked.* These functions would yield 'true' when the recipient of an interaction wished to assert back-pressure flow-control. Being primitive, the functions would clearly show that back-pressure flow control is indeed a local implementation issue that depends on the availability of local channel resources. The firing of transitions with output on a channel would depend on the value of these primitive functions.

The functions for back-pressure flow control would necessarily be primitive; it is unlikely that they could be written in ESTELLE. From the point of view of the formal semantics of ESTELLE, a description is technically incomplete until all primitive functions and procedures have been formally described in terms of the semantic model. However, for an implementation it is enough to have a description of the desired behaviour which is sufficiently detailed for an implementation to be made. The intended meaning of a function like *ReceiverBlocked* could be formalised in terms of the ESTELLE semantic model; it would be defined in terms of the status of the user module queues.

The following changes describe the transmitting and receiving stations as subject to back-pressure flow control. Since the *TransCode* module is a simple translator, its actions are not subject to flow control. Instead the *Station* module is the focus of this activity. The effect of back-pressure on the sending user or underlying medium has not been shown since these modules are external and so unspecified. The following functions should be declared in the body of *Station*:

```
function MediumBlocked: boolean;
primitive;

function ReceiverBlocked: boolean;
primitive;
```

The effect of these functions can be described in terms of the queues of the unreliable medium module *UM* and the user modules *UA* and *UB*. The **provided** clauses for transitions 13 and 16 in the body of *Station.* should become:

```
{ Send data in DT PDU }
from ESTAB to same
  when User.DatReq
    provided not Sending and not MediumBlocked
      begin { 13 }
        { As previously }
      end;

{ Receive data in DT PDU }
from ESTAB to same
  when Peer.DT
    provided not ReceiverBlocked
      begin { 16 }
        { As previously }
      end;
```

9.4 Formal Description in LOTOS[5]

9.4.1 *Top-Level Specification*

The overall structure of the specification in terms of the nesting of definitions is:

```
specification AbracadabraProtocol

  library

  type ASAP
  type ASDU
  type ASP
  type SeqNo
  type PDUs
  type MSAPs
  type MSPs

  behaviour
```

[5]Section 9.4 is by J. A. Mañas and F. M. Fournón y González-Barcia.

```
type TimerEvent

process Timer
  process Count
process Protocol
  process OneConnection
    process UpperAssociation
      process Stick
    process LowerAssociation
      process Stick
    process Coordination
      process Noticer
      process Connection
      process Transfer
        type FIFO
        process Sender
        process Receiver
      process Disconnection
      process TryDisconnect
      process Error
      process DiscConditions
        process AnyMSP
```

Externally, the protocol exchanges data with its environment through two gates: an upper gate *a* at the Abracadabra Service, and a lower gate *m* at the Unreliable Medium Service. A protocol entity must be able to establish a new connection after ending a previous one. The association between service access points is therefore established dynamically when a connection is set up.

There are two parameters that characterise protocol behaviour. Several kinds of PDU may be retransmitted under control of a timer that allows up to N transmissions at intervals of P time units. Natural numbers are used for these parameters.

```
specification AbracadabraProtocol [a, m] (N, P : Nat) : noexit
```

9.4.2 *Basic Types*

The protocol operates between protocol entities that support an upper service (the Abracadabra Service) using a lower service (the Unreliable Medium Service). There are thus three main kinds of data: protocol data units (between Abracadabra Protocol entities), upper service data units (for Abracadabra Service users), and lower service data units (for the Unreliable Medium Service).

Library Types

First of all, the standard library types for booleans, natural numbers, octet strings and decimal digits are needed. As explained later, decimal digits are needed to provide an identification for service primitives in order to simplify their specification.

```
library
  Boolean, NaturalNumber, OctetString, DecDigit
endlib
```

Abracadabra Service Data Types

The Abracadabra Service supports SAPs *(Service Access Points)* at which SPs *(Service Primitives)* are exchanged. Service Primitives may carry SDUs *(Service Data Units)*. The specification of SAPs simply requires a sort with distinguished values (*UserA* and *UserB*).

```
type ASAP is Boolean
  sorts ASAP
  opns UserA, UserB : -> ASAP
endtype (* ASAP *)
```

SDUs are based on the standard type *OctetString*.

```
type ASDU is OctetString renamedby
  sortnames ASDU for OctetString
endtype (* ASDU *)
```

Service primitives are a bit harder to specify. There are three groups of operations. The first group comprises the **constructor** operations that are strictly required to state the primitives that may be exchanged with the Abracadabra Service user. The second group is the auxiliary **selector** operation *SDUOf* that extracts the SDU in a service primitive. The third group provides a number of **recogniser** operations. These are boolean functions that check which kind of SDU (and therefore PDU) is under consideration.

Typically, it is convenient to isolate the exchange of a service primitive from its breakdown into fields. It is therefore usual to find the following kind of thing in a formal description:

```
Gate ... ? sp : ASP [IsDat (sp)];
... SDUOf (sp) ...
```

which shows a *DatReq* or *DatInd* service primitive being accepted and its contents being used somewhere else. Certainly, these auxiliary operations may be avoided with the following approach:

```
choice d : ASDU []
  Gate ... ! DatReq (d) ...;
  ... d ...
[]
  Gate ... ! DatInd (d) ...;
  ... d ...
```

but the resulting specification is more contrived. Of course, it is a matter of taste to choose one or the other style in such a case. The more constructive approach with *SDUOf* has been used for the Abracadabra Protocol.

There is a naive way of specifying the recognisers by means of exhaustive enumeration of all the cases:

```
ofsort Bool
  IsConReq (ConReq)    = true;
  IsConReq (ConInd)    = false;
  IsConReq (ConResp)   = false;
  IsConReq (ConConf)   = false;
  IsConReq (DatReq)    = false;
  IsConReq (DatInd)    = false;
  IsConReq (DisReq)    = false;
  IsConReq (DisInd)    = false;
  IsConInd (ConReq)    = false;
  ...
```

This results in a tedious 8×8 equations. The neatest solution is to identify every kind of SDU with some unique identifier; consecutive decimal digits are used here. Although this is something of a specification 'trick', the simplification it brings is worthwhile. If there are N service primitives to be recognised, direct enumeration requires N^2 equations. Mapping each kind of SDU to some identifier and checking these requires only $2N$ equations.

```
type ASP is Boolean, ASDU, DecDigit
  sorts ASP
  opns
    ConReq, ConInd, ConResp, ConConf :            -> ASP
    DatReq, DatInd :              ASDU            -> ASP
    DisReq, DisInd :                              -> ASP
    SDUOf :                       ASP             -> ASDU
    map        :                  ASP             -> DecDigit
    IsConReq, IsConInd, IsConResp, IsConConf,
      IsDatReq, IsDatInd,
        IsDisReq, IsDisInd :      ASP             -> Bool
    IsCon, IsDat, IsDis :         ASP             -> Bool
```

```
eqns
  forall d : ASDU, sp, sp1, sp2 : ASP
    ofsort ASDU
      SDUOf (ConReq)          = <>;
      SDUOf (ConInd)          = <>;
      SDUOf (ConResp)         = <>;
      SDUOf (ConConf)         = <>;
      SDUOf (DatReq (d))      = d;
      SDUOf (DatInd (d))      = d;
      SDUOf (DisReq)          = <>;
      SDUOf (DisInd)          = <>
    ofsort DecDigit
      map (ConReq)            = 0;
      map (ConInd)            = 1;
      map (ConResp)           = 2;
      map (ConConf)           = 3;
      map (DatReq (d))        = 4;
      map (DatInd (d))        = 5;
      map (DisReq)            = 6;
      map (DisInd)            = 7
    ofsort Bool
      IsConReq (sp)           = map (sp) eq 0;
      IsConInd (sp)           = map (sp) eq 1;
      IsConResp (sp)          = map (sp) eq 2;
      IsConConf (sp)          = map (sp) eq 3;
      IsDatReq (sp)           = map (sp) eq 4;
      IsDatInd (sp)           = map (sp) eq 5;
      IsDisReq (sp)           = map (sp) eq 6;
      IsDisInd (sp)           = map (sp) eq 7;
      IsCon (sp)              =
        IsConReq (sp) or IsConInd (sp) or IsConResp (sp) or
          IsConConf (sp);
      IsDat (sp)              = IsDatReq (sp) or IsDatInd (sp);
      IsDis (sp)              = IsDisReq (sp) or IsDisInd (sp);
endtype (* ASP *)
```

Protocol Data Units

To deal with errors in the delivery of PDUs *(Protocol Data Units)*, a one-bit sequence number is included in some PDUs. Two alternating bit values are specified, *SN0* and *SN1*, and an operation *next* to relate them. The library type *Bit* might have been used here, but it does not have the equivalent of a *next* operation.

```
type SeqNo is
  sorts SeqNo
  opns
    SN0, SN1 :                   -> SeqNo
    next :      SeqNo            -> SeqNo
  eqns
    ofsort SeqNo
      next (SN0) = SN1;
      next (SN1) = SN0;
endtype (* SeqNo *)
```

The core of the data specification is of the PDUs, pieces of information exchanged between peer protocol entities to perform the protocol. Their specification is straightforward from the informal description.

```
type PDUs is SeqNo, ASDU
  sorts PDU
  opns
    CR, CC :                     -> PDU
    DT :        SeqNo, ASDU      -> PDU
    AK :        SeqNo            -> PDU
    DR, DC :                     -> PDU
endtype (* PDUs *)
```

Unreliable Medium Service Data Types

The data types of the Unreliable Medium Service are rather similar to those of the Abracadabra Service.

```
type MSAPs is
  sorts MSAP
  opns MedA, MedB : -> MSAP
endtype (* MSAPs *)

type MSPs is PDUs, Boolean, DecDigit
  sorts MSP
  opns
    Mreq, Mind :                 PDU     -> MSP
    SDUOf :                      MSP     -> ASDU
    SeqNoOf :                    MSP     -> SeqNo
    IsMreq, IsMind :             MSP     -> Bool
    IsCR, IsCC, IsDT,
      IsAK, IsDR, IsDC :         MSP     -> Bool
    map :                        MSP     -> DecDigit
```

```
eqns
  forall b : SeqNo, d : ASDU, pdu : PDU, sp : MSP
    ofsort ASDU
      SDUOf (Mreq (DT (b, d)))      = d;
      SDUOf (Mind (DT (b, d)))      = d;
    ofsort SeqNo
      SeqNoOf (Mreq (DT (b, d)))    = b;
      SeqNoOf (Mind (DT (b, d)))    = b;
      SeqNoOf (Mreq (AK (b)))       = b;
      SeqNoOf (Mind (AK (b)))       = b;
    ofsort DecDigit
      map (Mreq (CR))               = 0;
      map (Mind (CR))               = 0;
      map (Mreq (CC))               = 1;
      map (Mind (CC))               = 1;
      map (Mreq (DT (b, d)))        = 2;
      map (Mind (DT (b, d)))        = 2;
      map (Mreq (AK (b)))           = 3;
      map (Mind (AK (b)))           = 3;
      map (Mreq (DR))               = 4;
      map (Mind (DR))               = 4;
      map (Mreq (DC))               = 5;
      map (Mind (DC))               = 5;
    ofsort Bool
      IsMreq (Mreq (pdu))           = true;
      IsMreq (Mind (pdu))           = false;
      IsMind (Mreq (pdu))           = false;
      IsMind (Mind (pdu))           = true;
      IsCR (sp)                     = map (sp) eq 0;
      IsCC (sp)                     = map (sp) eq 1;
      IsDT (sp)                     = map (sp) eq 2;
      IsAK (sp)                     = map (sp) eq 3;
      IsDR (sp)                     = map (sp) eq 4;
      IsDC (sp)                     = map (sp) eq 5;
endtype (* MSPs *)
```

9.4.3 *Top-Level Behaviour*

The description of the protocol needs a protocol entity and a timeout mechanism. These are modelled at the outermost level by two processes that interact at the internal (hidden) timer gate *timer*. The actual action performed by the protocol on each timer event depends on its state, as specified later.

```
behaviour
  hide timer in
    Timer [timer] (N, P)
  |[timer]|
     Protocol [a, m, timer]

where
```

9.4.4 *Timer*

There are three kinds of event at timer gate *timer*: *Start* (to initiate a transmission attempt), *Retry* (to cause a retransmission) and *Kill* (to abort a transmission attempt).

```
type TimerEvent is
  sorts TimerEvent
  opns Start, Retry, Kill : -> TimerEvent
endtype (* TimerEvent *)
```

On a *Start* event, a count is started. The count is interrupted whenever a new cycle starts. Note that in LOTOS events are just *offered.* There is no way to require an event to occur; only if all partners involved in an event agree will it take place. This meaning is completely different from that in other languages where timeouts may be modelled as preemptive interrupts. This concept must be clearly understood to grasp the modelling of the *Timer* process. It offers the following sequences of events for the protocol to choose:

Start: initiate a transmission attempt

Start, Retry: cause a retransmission

Start, Kill: abort a transmission attempt.

```
process Timer [timer] (N, P : Nat) : noexit :=
  timer ! Start;
  (
    Count [timer] (Succ (0), N, P)
  [>
    Timer [timer] (N, P)
  )

  where
```

As each period P elapses, retransmissions are allowed up to N transmissions in total. When the count reaches N, the retransmission procedure must abort (i.e. engage in *Kill*). LOTOS lacks the concept of a clock, so P cannot be used to influence the LOTOS description at all. All that can be specified is that some internal action occurs to step time on and allows a *Retry* action.

```
process Count [timer] (count, max, P : Nat) : noexit :=
  [count lt max ] ->
    (* Time period P *)
    timer ! Retry;
    Count [timer] (Succ (count), max, P)
[]
  [count eq max] ->
    (* Time period P *)
    timer ! Kill;
    stop
endproc (* Count *)

endproc (* Timer *)
```

This completes the description of the *Timer* process within the expressiveness limitations imposed by LOTOS. The protocol entity synchronises on timer events to take decisions about when to retry or abort a transmission attempt.

9.4.5 *Protocol Entity*

The protocol entity must be able to deal with an indefinite number of sequential connections; when a connection is terminated a new one may be established.

```
process Protocol [a, m, timer] : noexit :=
  OneConnection [a, m, timer]
>>
  Protocol [a, m, timer]

  where
```

One Connection

Each connection requires the coordination of service primitives at the upper (Abracadabra) and lower (Medium) service access points.

```
process OneConnection [a, m, timer] : exit :=
  (UpperAssociation [a] ||| LowerAssociation [m])
|[a, m]|
  Coordination [a, m, timer]
```

where

Service Access Point Association

Service access points are associated when a connection is established, and later disassociated for the next connection. The informal description leaves open how these associations are made, so the LOTOS description is quite abstract. On the first service primitive exchanged, the SAP address is provided by the environment (by whatever means). In the second and later interactions, the gate 'sticks' to the same address until the association is broken.

```
process UpperAssociation [a] : exit :=
  a ? sap : ASAP ? sp : ASP;
  Stick [a] (sap)
[>
  exit

  where

  process Stick [a] (sap : ASAP) : noexit :=
    a ! sap ? sp : ASP;
    Stick [a] (sap)
  endproc (* Stick *)

endproc (* UpperAssociation *)
```

The same remarks apply to the lower gate as well.

```
process LowerAssociation [m] : exit :=
  m ? msap : MSAP ? sp : MSP;
  Stick [m] (msap)
[>
  exit

  where

  process Stick [m] (msap : MSAP) : noexit :=
    m ! msap ? sp : MSP;
    Stick [m] (msap)
  endproc (* Stick *)

endproc (* LowerAssociation *)
```

Coordination Procedures

So far, the architecture of the protocol has been straightforward. The coordination procedures are the architectural core of the description. This refinement step requires a large number of considerations to be taken into account, and the decisions taken here have a major influence on the rest of the description. A wrong architectural decision can easily preclude the proper description of the inner details of the protocol. The activities to be coordinated are:

- the connection phase
- the data transfer phase
- user or medium-initiated disconnection
- an exception mechanism to cope with errors.

To start coordinating all these pieces, first notice that the connection and data transfer phases are neatly independent and strictly sequenced. Data transfer starts only after a connection is established:

```
    Connection [a, m, timer, error]
>>
    Transfer [a, m, timer, error]
```

This models 'normal behaviour' – setting up a connection and transferring data forever. This normal behaviour may be interrupted by disconnection. Either the user may request a disconnection, a disconnection PDU may arrive, or an internal error may cause a disconnection. Any of these requires clearing up the current state of normal behaviour. To achieve this, the disable operator '[>' is used:

```
    (
      Connection [a, m, timer, error]
    >>
      Transfer [a, m, timer, error]
    )
[>
    (
      Disconnection [a, m, timer]
    []
      Error [a, m, timer, exception]
    )
```

where *Error* takes care of internal exceptions, and *Disconnection* of other causes. The rationale for the gates *error* and *exception* is given later.

This model is not yet completely right, however, since disconnection is not allowed before a connection has been established. More precisely, the protocol will allow the user to disconnect only after a connection attempt has been initiated. Furthermore, the reaction of the protocol to an incoming disconnection PDU is completely different depending on whether there is an active connection or not.

It is therefore necessary to filter out some events that are permitted in the description above. This requires a constraint to relate connection establishment state to disconnection procedures:

```
    (
      (
        Connection [a, m, timer, error]
      >>
        Transfer [a, m, timer, error]
      )
    [>
      (
        Disconnection [a, m, timer]
      []
        Error [a, m, timer, exception]
      )
    )
  |[a, m]|
    DiscConditions [a, m] (false)
```

where the *false* parameter of *DiscConditions* says that no connection is initially established.

There is still one more matter to describe, namely errors. Many programming languages have features to deal with exceptions. Upon occurrence of some exception, control is passed to an external piece of code that has access to the state of the system and may take appropriate recovery action. In LOTOS there are no global variables, so it is necessary to rely on 'strong' operators like '[>' to clear up after an error. But disabled behaviour cannot synchronise with disabling behaviour. (In *P* [> *Q*, *P* cannot signal to *Q*.) The behaviour raising the exception therefore has to synchronise with an outer behaviour that in turn synchronises with the exception handler.

There is thus one more element of superstructure that is needed to communicate with both: an 'exception noticer'. When an error is reported by the normal behaviour it is passed onto the exception handler.

Now the architecture is complete, and processes *Coordination* and *Noticer* can be defined in full.

```
process Coordination [a, m, timer] : exit :=
  hide error, exception in
    Noticer [error, exception]
  |[error, exception]|
    (
      (
        (
          Connection [a, m, timer, error]
        >>
          Transfer [a, m, timer, error]
        )
      [>
        (
          Disconnection [a, m, timer]
        []
          Error [a, m, timer, exception]
        )
      )
    |[a, m]|
      DiscConditions [a, m] (false)
    )

  where
```

Process *Noticer* accepts an *error* signal and passes it on as *exception* to the exception handler. An **exit** must always be offered in order to allow the whole behaviour to exit and proceed to a new instantiation of process *OneConnection*. LOTOS requires *all* the parallel behaviours to exit simultaneously.

```
process Noticer [error, exception] : exit :=
  error;
  exception;
  stop
[>
  exit
endproc (* Noticer *)
```

Connection Phase

The *Connection* process deals with setting up a connection, requested by a user or via the medium. *Connection* may exit, when it will enable the data transfer phase. It may also raise an *error* condition that will clear up the steps so far. The choices offered are as follows:

- The user requests a connection. The *Timer* process is started, and the protocol entity tries to establish a connection. If this process exits, the connection is confirmed and the data transfer phase is enabled. Alternatively, the *error* condition may be raised.
- A request to connect comes via a *CR* PDU. This is notified to the local user. If the local user confirms that the connection should be established, the data transfer phase is enabled.
- Any other PDU is ignored.

```
process Connection [a, m, timer, error] : exit :=
  (
    a ? sap : ASAP ! ConReq;
    timer ! Start;
    m ? msap : MSAP ! Mreq (CR);
    TryConnect [a, m, timer, error]
  >>
    a ? sap : ASAP ! ConConf;
    exit
  )
[]
  (
    m ? msap : MSAP ! Mind (CR);
    a ? sap : ASAP ! ConInd;
    a ? sap : ASAP ! ConResp;
    m ? msap : MSAP ! Mreq (CC);
    exit
  )
[]
  (
    m ? msap : MSAP ? sp : MSP
      [IsMind (sp) and not (IsCR (sp) or IsDR (sp))];
    Connection [a, m, timer, error]
  )

  where
```

Process *TryConnect* offers the following choices:

- The connection attempt may be accepted, enabling the data transfer phase.
- Other *Mind* events are ignored.

- If the *Timer* process allows it, retry the connection attempt.
- If the *Timer* allows it, abort the connection attempt and raise the *error* condition.

```
process TryConnect [a, m, timer, error] : exit :=
  m ? msap : MSAP ? sp : MSP
    [IsMind (sp) and (IsCR (sp) or IsCC (sp))];
  exit
[]
  m ? msap : MSAP ? sp : MSP
    [IsMind (sp) and (IsDT (sp) or IsAK (sp) or
      IsDC (sp))];
  TryConnect [a, m, timer, error]
[]
  timer ! Retry;
  m ? msap : MSAP ! Mreq (CR);
  TryConnect [a, m, timer, error]
[]
  timer ! Kill;
  error;
  stop
endproc (* TryConnect *)

endproc (* Connection *)
```

Data Transfer Phase

Process *Transfer* deals with exchange data, coming from the user or received via the medium. It continues forever, until disconnection disables it or an *error* condition occurs. The incoming and outgoing data are basically two independent flows of information that may be directly modelled by means of interleaving.

Both the *Sender* and *Receiver* processes start with a sequence number of *SN0*. The *Receiver* also starts with an empty queue of pending data, and a *beginning* flag set to indicate that no data has yet arrived. This flag is considered later when the details of *Receiver* are presented.

```
process Transfer [a, m, timer, error] : noexit :=
  Sender [a, m, timer, error] (SN0)
|||
  Receiver [a, m, error] (SN0, empty, true)

  where
```

The need for a queue requires justification. According to the informal description, an *AK* is required before a new *DT* may be sent. The *Sender* process thus has to consider only one *DT* at most. But there may be several SDUs 'in transit', and these must be queued up in the *Receiver* process.

The '+' operation appends SDUs to the queue. The *head* operation extract the first one in the queue, while *tail* returns all but the first element in the queue. Lastly, the *HasEntries* predicate checks whether the queue is empty or holds at least one SDU. Note that LOTOS associates infix operators to the left, so that $q + d + dd$ is read as $(q\ +\ d) +\ dd$.

```
type FIFO is Boolean, ASDU
  sorts Queue
  opns
    empty :                              -> Queue
    _ + _ :       Queue, ASDU            -> Queue
    head :        Queue                  -> SDU
    tail :        Queue                  -> Queue
    HasEntries :          Queue          -> Bool
  eqns
    forall d, dd : ASDU, q : Queue
      ofsort ASDU
        head (empty + d) = d;
        head (q + d + dd) = head (q + d);
      ofsort Queue
        tail (empty + d) = empty;
        tail (q + d + dd) = tail (q + d) + dd;
      ofsort Bool
        HasEntries (empty) = false;
        HasEntries (q + d) = true;
endtype (* FIFO *)
```

Process *Sender* takes care of one SDU at a time. If the SDU is successfully acknowledged from the peer entity, a new one may be accepted. Alternatively, an *error* may be notified to clear everything up. On receipt of a *DatReq*, the *Timer* process is started and the *Sender* process tries to send the SDU.

```
process Sender
 [a, m, timer, error] (b : SeqNo) : noexit :=
  a ? sap : ASAP ? sp : ASP [IsDatReq (sp)];
  timer ! Start;
  m ? msap : MSAP ! Mreq (DT (b, SDUOf (sp)));
  TrySend [a, m, timer, error] (b, SDUOf (sp))
>>
  Sender [a, m, timer, error] (next (b))
```

where

The formal description of the *TrySend* process is directly derived from the informal description:

- A correct *AK* lets *Sender* deal with another SDU.
- If *Timer* allows it, a retransmission may be attempted.
- If *Timer* allows it, retransmission may be aborted and the *error* condition raised.
- An incorrect *AK* raises the *error* condition.

```
process TrySend [a, m, timer, error]
 (b : SeqNo, D : ASDU) : exit :=
  m ? msap : MSAP ! Mind (AK (next (b)));
  exit
[]
  timer ! Retry;
  m ? msap : MSAP ! Mreq (DT (b, D));
  TrySend [a, m, timer, error] (b, D)
[]
  timer ! Kill;
  error;
  stop
[]
  m ? msap : MSAP ! Mind (AK (b));
  error;
  stop
endproc (* TrySend *)

endproc (* Sender *)
```

The *Receiver* process is a difficult piece of behaviour to specify. It has to deal with a sequence number and with a queue of SDUs already received but not yet delivered. It needs to react specially to *CR* PDUs before any SDU has been received. These considerations lead to three parameters for the process. The choices offered are as follows:

- Before a *DT* or *AK* is received, a *CR* may be accepted and a *CC* sent in response.
- After a *DT* or *AK* has been received, a *CR* will give rise to an *error* condition.

- If a *CC* or *DC* is received, an *error* condition is raised.
- If a *DT* arrives and then another one before an acknowledgement is sent, an *error* condition is raised[6]. Unless this situation arises, an *AK* will be sent after the DT. If the *DT* has the correct sequence number it is queued for delivery to the user, otherwise it is ignored.
- If there are SDUs queued, the first one may be delivered to the Abracadabra Service User.

Back-pressure flow control might be dealt with in *Receiver*. The Abracadabra Service may refuse to accept further *DatReq* primitives when there are 'too many' SDUs in transit. What constitutes 'too many' depends on the implementation, and usually models the situation where the service provider temporarily runs out of resources. The informal description might be expected to state more precisely how back-pressure flow control arises from the exchange of PDUs, but surprisingly it does not!

There are a number of places to cover this concept in the description, all of them related to the situation of too many SDUs queued in the receiver. What can the receiver do to inform its peer not to accept further *DatReq* primitives? The sender could be forced to retransmit in one of the following ways:

- Delay sending an *AK*. This may force the sender to retry, but it may happen that a new *DT* is received too fast and an *error* condition is raised. This approach is rather dubious.
- Do not send an *AK* at all. This contradicts the informal description, and is subject to the retransmission limit. This behaviour is not ideal either.
- Send an *AK* with the wrong sequence number. The same considerations apply as with not sending an *AK*. This might be the easiest way of 'fixing' the protocol design, but has not been adopted because it is inconsistent with the informal description. The description of *Receiver* would be modified as follows if the protocol were redesigned this way:

```
      ...
  []
    [HasEntries (q)] ->
      i;
      m ? msap : MSAP ! Mreq (AK (b));
      Receiver [a, m, error] (b, q, false)
```

The *Receiver* process is specified as:

[6]This part of the behaviour faithfully reflects the informal description. However, a sensible implementation of the protocol should not cause this error to arise.

```
    process Receiver [a, m, error]
      (b : SeqNo, q : Queue, beginning : Bool) : noexit :=
      [beginning] ->
        m ? msap : MSAP ! Mind (CR);
        m ? msap : MSAP ! Mreq (CC);
        Receiver [a, m, error] (b, q, beginning)
    []
      [not (beginning)] ->
        m ? msap : MSAP ! Mind (CR);
        error;
        stop
    []
      m ? msap : MSAP ? sp : MSP
        [IsMind (sp) and (IsCC (sp) or IsDC (sp))];
      error;
      stop
    []
      m ? msap : MSAP ? sp : MSP
        [IsMind (sp) and IsDT (sp)];
      (
        m ? msap : MSAP ? sp : MSP
          [IsMind (sp) and IsDT (sp)];
        error;
        stop
      []
        m ? msap : MSAP ! Mreq (AK (next (SeqNoOf (sp))));
        (
          [SeqNoOf (sp) = b] ->
            Receiver [a, m, error]
              (next (b), q + SDUOf (sp), false)
        []
          [SeqNoOf (sp) = next (b)] ->
            Receiver [a, m, error] (b, q, false)
        )
      )
    []
      [HasEntries (q)] ->
        a ? sap : ASAP ! DatInd (head (q));
        Receiver [a, m, error] (b, tail (q), beginning)
    endproc (* Receiver *)

endproc (* Transfer *)
```

Disconnection Phase

A disconnection may be started by the user or by an incoming request from the peer protocol entity. When a *DR* is received, a *DC* is sent. If the user is aware of the connection then a disconnection primitive must occur, otherwise the user does not need to be informed and the protocol entity just tidies up itself. The user may issue a *DisReq* or accept a *DisInd*.

```
process Disconnection [a, m, timer] : exit :=
  a ? sap : ASAP ! DisReq;
  timer ! Start;
  m ? msap : MSAP ! Mreq (DR);
  TryDisconnect [a, m, timer]
[]
  m ? msap : MSAP ! Mind (DR);
  m ? msap : MSAP ! Mreq (DC);
  (
    a ? sap : ASAP ? sp : ASP [IsDis (sp)];
    exit
  []
    exit
  )
endproc (* Disconnection *)
```

Process *TryDisconnect* is similar to the *TryConnect* and *TrySend* processes. There is only one new aspect: if an abort is allowed, no *error* condition is raised. Instead the protocol entity just resets itself, becoming ready for a new connection.

```
process TryDisconnect [a, m, timer] : exit :=
  m ? msap : MSAP ? sp : MSP
    [IsMind (sp) and (IsDR (sp) or IsDC (sp))];
  exit
[]
  m ? msap : MSAP ? sp : MSP
    [IsMind (sp) and (IsCR (sp) or IsCC (sp) or
      IsDT (sp) or IsAK (sp))];
  TryDisconnect [a, m, timer]
[]
  timer ! Retry;
  m ? msap : MSAP ! Mreq (DR);
  TryDisconnect [a, m, timer]
[]
```

```
    timer ! Kill;
    exit
endproc (* TryDisconnect *)
```

Error Phase

An *error* condition may be raised from several states during the connection or data transfer phases. It is captured by process *Noticer* that gives control to the *Error* process by means of the *exception* event. *Error* disables normal behaviour, getting control of the protocol entity at the same level as a disconnection request. An exception forces disconnection on the users, and tries to disconnect in a similar way to disconnection initiated by the user or protocol entity.

```
process Error [a, m, timer, exception] : exit :=
    exception;
    a ? sap : ASAP ? sp : ASP [IsDis (sp)];
    timer ! Start;
    m ? msap : MSAP ! Mreq (DR);
    TryDisconnect [a, m, timer]
endproc (* Error *)
```

Imposing Constraints on Disconnection

The formal description so far has a deficiency: it allows disconnection before connecting! The easiest way to handle this is to add constraints on when a connection can be released.

A protocol entity starts in a state where it may *not* disconnect, so the boolean *MayDisconnect* is initially false. The choices offered are as follows:

- The reception of any connection or data primitive on the user side implies that the user is aware of the connection. In this case the user must disconnect (*DisReq*) or be informed of disconnection (*DisInd*). This choice does not impose any constraint on the behaviour of the entity; it just notes that disconnection may now occur.

- If the user is aware of the connection, a *DisReq* may be issued. The guard prevents the user from issuing a *DisReq* before a connection has been started. After the user disconnects, the protocol entity may need to exchange PDUs with its peer in order to disconnect. The precise PDUs and their sequencing are covered in the description of the disconnection phase and are not repeated here. Process *AnyMSP* just absorbs these PDUs.

- An *Mind* must be accepted at any time. Any PDU apart from *DR* requires no further action, so the constraints imposed by the connection and data transfer phases apply. Only *DR* requires special consideration. If it is received when the user is aware of a connection, the user must be informed by *DisInd* unless the user has already invoked *DisReq*. This refines the description of process *Disconnection*. If a *DR* is received when the user is unaware of a connection then *DiscConditions* just exits, forcing *OneConnection* to exit without issuing a *DC*.

- An *Mreq* is always allowed, without influencing the rest of the behaviour. This choice is required because *DiscConditions* synchronises on gate m, and so must synchronise on everything that happens on that gate even if it has no interest in it.

```
process DiscConditions [a, m] (MayDisconnect : Bool) :
  exit :=
  a ? sap : ASAP ? sp : ASP [IsCon (sp) or IsDat (sp)];
  DiscConditions [a, m] (true)
[]
  [MayDisconnect] ->
    a ? sap : ASAP ? sp : ASP [IsDis (sp)];
    AnyMSP [m]
[]
  m ? msap : MSAP ? sp : MSP [IsMind (sp)];
  (
    [IsDR (sp)] ->
      m ? msap : MSAP ! Mreq (DC);
      (
        [MayDisconnect] ->
          a ? sap : ASAP ? sp : ASP [IsDis (sp)];
          exit
      []
        [not (MayDisconnect)] ->
          exit
      )
  []
    [not (IsDR (sp))] ->
      DiscConditions [a, m] (MayDisconnect)
  )
[]
  m ? msap : MSAP ? sp : MSP [IsMreq (sp)];
  DiscConditions [a, m] (MayDisconnect)
```

```
            where

            process AnyMSP [m] : exit :=
              m ? msap : MSAP ? sp : MSP;
              AnyMSP [m]
            []
              exit
            endproc (* AnyMSP *)

          endproc (* DiscConditions *)

        endproc (* Coordination *)

      endproc (* OneConnection *)

    endproc (* Protocol *)

  endspec (* AbracadabraProtocol *)
```

9.4.6 *Development of the Formal Description*

The end result of writing the formal description is satisfying. The formal description has been extensively evaluated against the informal description. The text of this section was used literally for checking by LOTOS tools. Of course, checking can never be complete so there may be remaining flaws.

What is harder to check is whether the informal description has been interpreted correctly. There may almost certainly be other interpretations of the informal description that would imply different formal descriptions. But this is the whole point of having formal descriptions – the meaning cannot be debated.

The process of writing the formal description was not too hard. In LOTOS terms, the stages of development were:

```
    getting to know the informal description
  >>
    writing a service specification (in LOTOS)
  >>
    (
      (
        drafting the protocol specification
      >>
        checking basic capabilities with a simulator
      >>
        extensively checking test cases with a compiler
```

```
    >>
      systematically inspecting states with a simulator
    )
  |[text]|
    documenting the specification
  )
```

Reading and understanding the informal descriptions of the Abracadabra Service and Protocol took one day, including taking plenty of notes, making diagrams and integrating details from various places.

Then a 'throw-away' specification of the Abracadabra Service was written to develop a clearer understanding of the functionality of the Abracadabra Protocol[7]. After writing the throw-away service description, it became clear that only the data types could be used in the protocol description. This was very surprising at first, but in retrospect it was inevitable due to the very different kinds of structure.

Any description starts by specifying the basic data types. The data types used in the service were extended with the types particular to the protocol: PDUs, medium service primitives and medium service access points. When the formal description was first drafted, only constructive operations were specified for the data types. As the behaviour description was developed, the convenience of boolean predicates showed up and the types were extended accordingly. Even later, when equations had to be provided, the convenience of the *map* operations arose and these were introduced.

Behaviour description started at the outermost level and went smoothly down to the level of process *Coordination*. Initially the description did not have a *Timer* process; it was introduced later as explained below. When it became necessary to specify *Coordination*, devising the architecture explained in the text was a significant step. It was not too difficult due to previous experience with similar LOTOS specifications. The need for the different elements was clear from the beginning; the need for a normal behaviour that may be disabled is quite a common situation. Avoiding unwanted behaviours by adding constraints was also a well-known technique. The treatment of the exceptions with a notifier and an error handler is fairly usual too. The basic architectural concepts were therefore available, so it was mainly a matter of combining them with the appropriate LOTOS operators.

The *Timer* process underwent some evolution. In an early version of the description there were only local timers. Every process passed on the N and P parameters, and every *Try...* process had to maintain a count of retries. This worked but was clumsy. Eventually, it was realised that the protocol engages

[7]In fact, the formal description of the Abracadabra Service in Section 8.4 was written in parallel by other authors. The protocol description was harmonised with this service description.

in only one retransmission at a time. It was therefore useful to move the retransmission mechanism to the outermost level and let the different phases of behaviour reuse it. The design of a resettable timer was very easy, and its removal from various places in the description led to a major simplification. This is an important architectural feature that could be useful with other protocols. Even if there were several timers running concurrently, simply adding an identification parameter to *Start*, *Retry* and *Kill* events would suffice to distinguish them, allowing several timers to run in parallel. Concurrent timers were not needed for the Abracadabra Protocol so a simplification could be made.

As the different aspects of process *Coordination* were specified, it was discovered that a few parameters were needed to denote some initial state of a subsidiary behaviour. This required modifying the process instantiations. The same process of iterative refinement arose with respect to the gates passed between processes.

The approach to specifying the *Try...* processes was revised several times in the interests of brevity, clarity and homogeneity. The *Try...* processes conform to same schema; the same approach may work with other protocols too. Apart from the removal of retransmission handling to *Timer*, the other changes were cosmetic.

The most problematic part of the formal description was process *DiscConditions*. Up to this point, every piece of LOTOS was written to formalise a part of the informal description. But *DiscConditions* had to coordinate all those pieces. Informal languages tend to be poor at giving such over-arching constraints. They are usually spread over the whole description, and must be carefully collected from here and there when writing a formal description. They are also usually very specific to the problem under study.

Within one day of beginning work on the formal description a draft was ready for checking. A symbolic simulation was tried; it deadlocked! This was not really a surprise since there a number of processes that must synchronise at every event on gate *m*. A specifier tends to concentrate on 'positive' constraints on events, and may easily forget to explicitly allow behaviour when no constraint is being imposed. This kind of error mostly affected the specification of process *DiscConditions*.

The checking now uncovered a number of editorial errors where *Mreq* and *Mind* had been interchanged. This kind of error could not have been detected by checking static semantics. Another group of errors was found, relating to the acceptance of *Mind*. Although an *Mreq* is issued by the protocol entity without any constraint from the medium, the opposite situation applies to *Mind*. Any *Mind* must be accepted at any moment; it may be discarded by the protocol entity, but must be accepted from the medium. These errors were detected during exhaustive testing, and forced the introduction of more 'null' constraints.

A symbolic simulator was used to exercise the specification, and it discovered the most fundamental flaws. Then a compiler was used to run a large number of test cases, highlighting most of the remaining errors. Lastly, and with great patience, the symbolic simulator was used again for exhaustive inspection. This revealed the final, and really tricky, errors. Note that running tests will check that expected behaviours are there and may occur. But it is hard to check that undesired behaviours may not happen. There are rejection tests, of course, but it is faster to inspect the menus offered during simulation and to check that there are no unexpected offers.

The description was checked, revised and rechecked during a period of three days. This phase of development coincided with writing the explanatory text. A tool was used to combine a narrative description with the LOTOS text. As the description was developed, this allowed changes to be checked immediately by tools and reflected in the up-to-date documentation. In fact, the final checking was undertaken on the literal text of this section.

9.4.7 *Conclusion*

It has proven to be rapid and practicable to specify, check and document the Abracadabra Protocol in LOTOS. Strenuous attempts have been made to produce a specification that is not only correct, but is also readily comprehensible and of general architectural value. The development of the description has been summarised for others to benefit from the experience.

LOTOS is not a simple language to use, and the process of writing formal descriptions in general is still poorly understood. The experience of this section will hopefully be of benefit to the community of specifiers.

9.5 Formal Description in SDL[8]

The SDL description of the Abracadabra Protocol appears in Figure 9.4. The protocol is modelled as a system *Abracadabra*, consisting of only one block *Station* that represents a protocol entity. Accordingly, the boundary of the system is represented by the user service access point (channel *User*) and the medium service access point (channel *Med*).

Block *Station* is refined into two processes, *SenderReceiver* and *Transcode*. *SenderReceiver* describes the protocol entity as an extended finite state machine that relates input service primitives and/or protocol data units to output service primitives and/or protocol data units. *Transcode* describes the lowest level of functionality of the protocol, i.e. PDU encoding and decoding. The *PduType* and *UserDataType* components of a protocol data unit are encoded in an *Mreq* primitive or are decoded from an *Mind* primitive.

Process *SenderReceiver* has five states:

[8]Section 9.5 is by F. Bertolotti, L. Cerchio and S. Trigila.

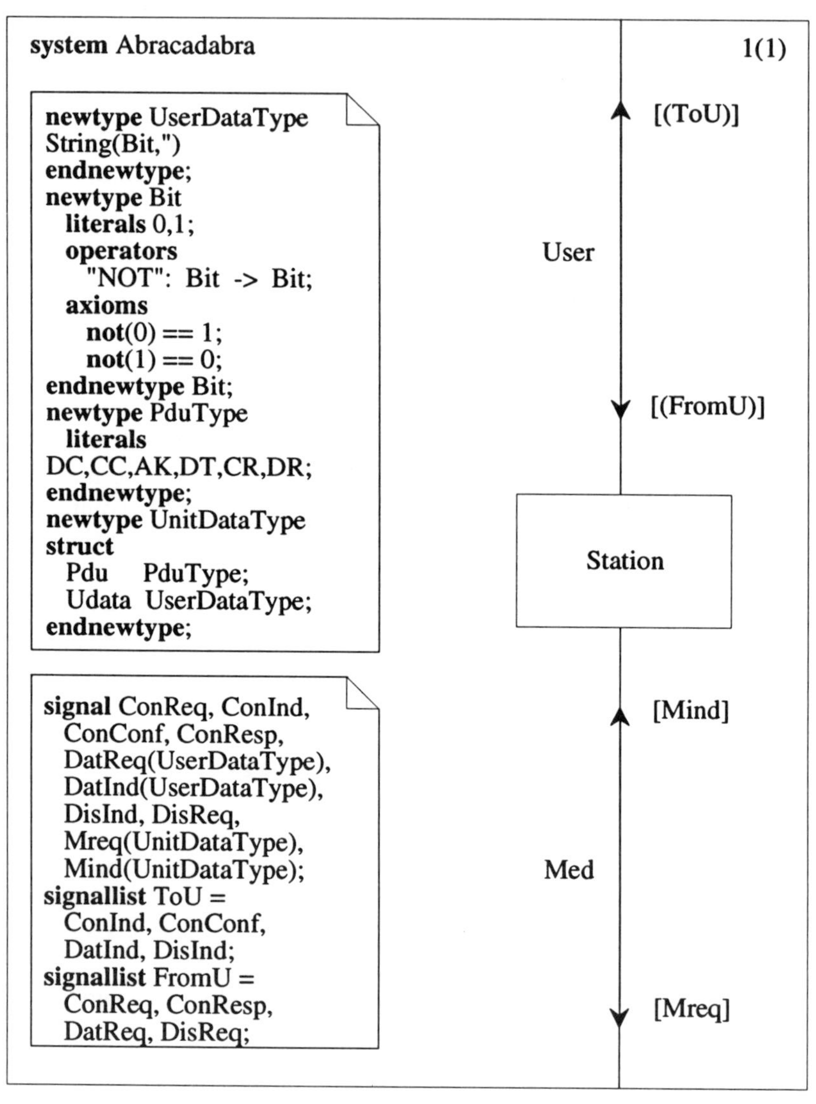

Figure 9.4: Abracadabra Protocol in SDL – Graphical Description

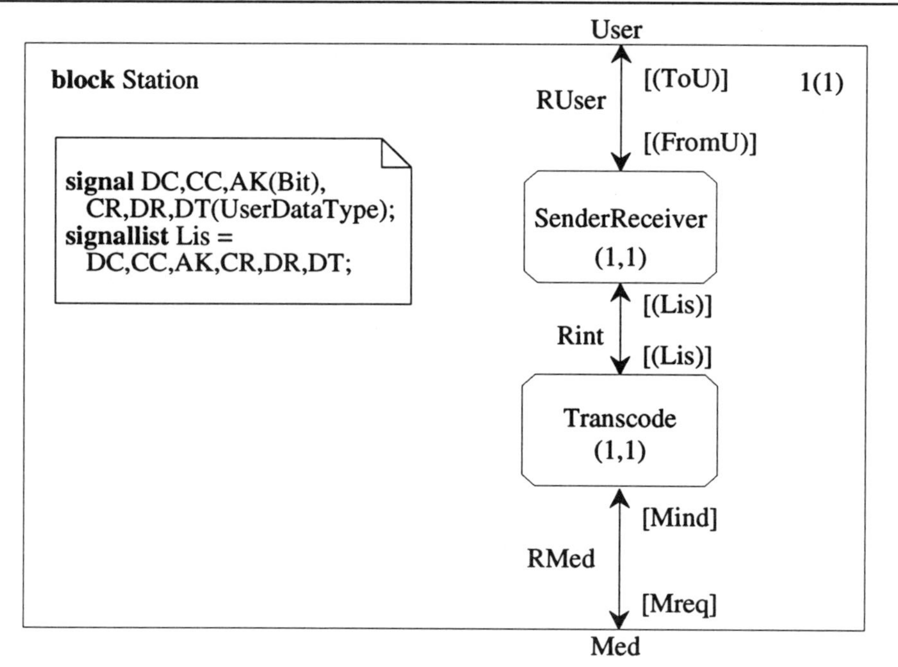

Figure 9.4 *(continued)*

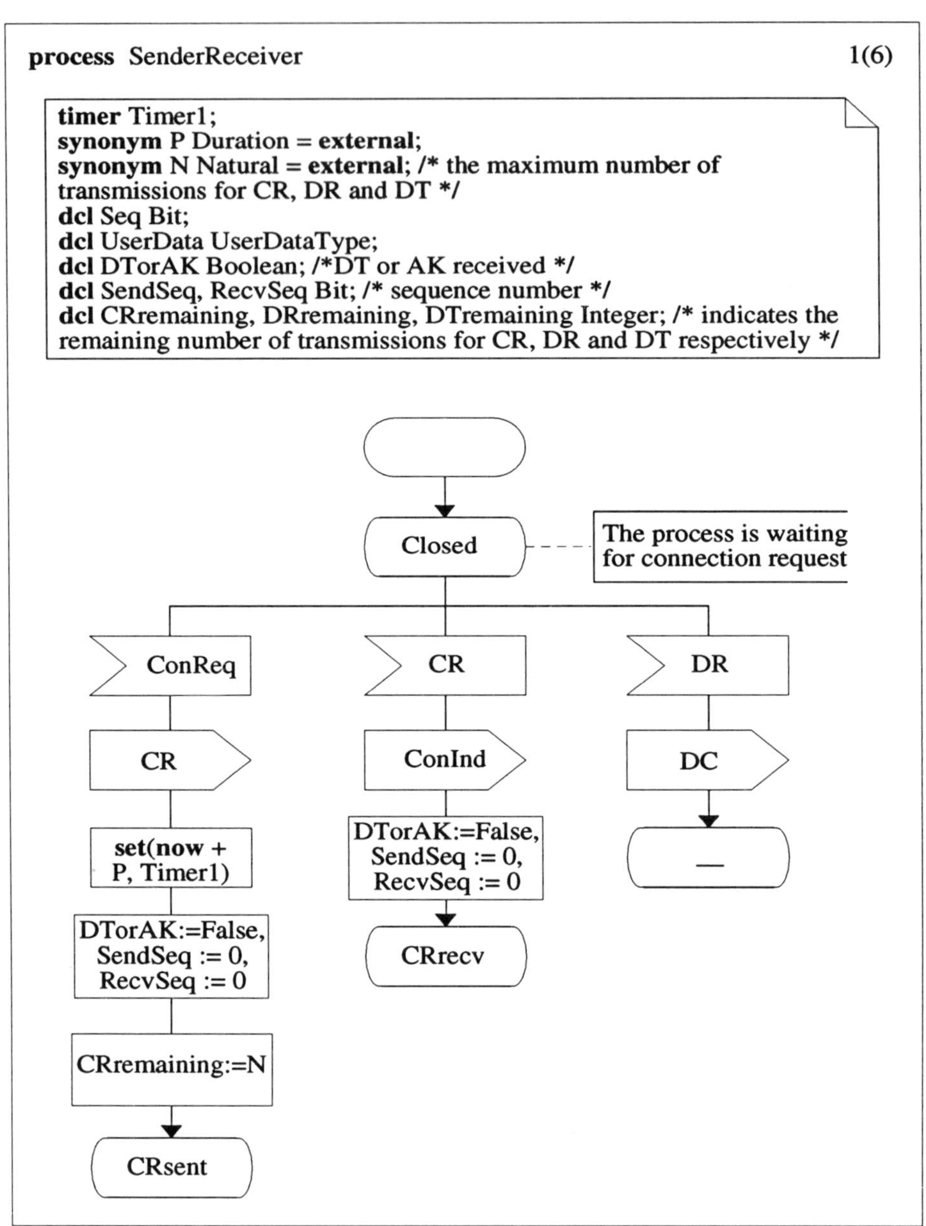

Figure 9.4 *(continued)*

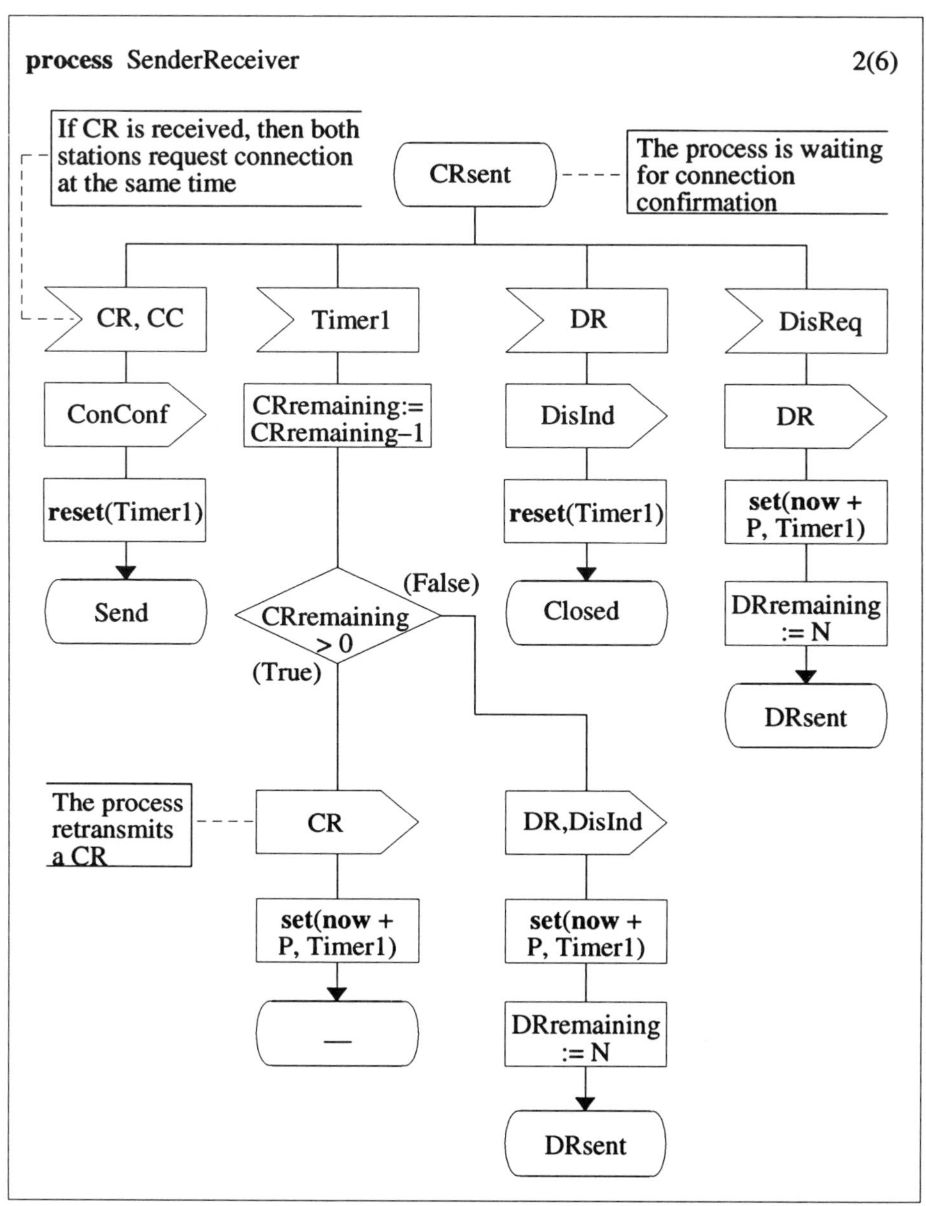

Figure 9.4 *(continued)*

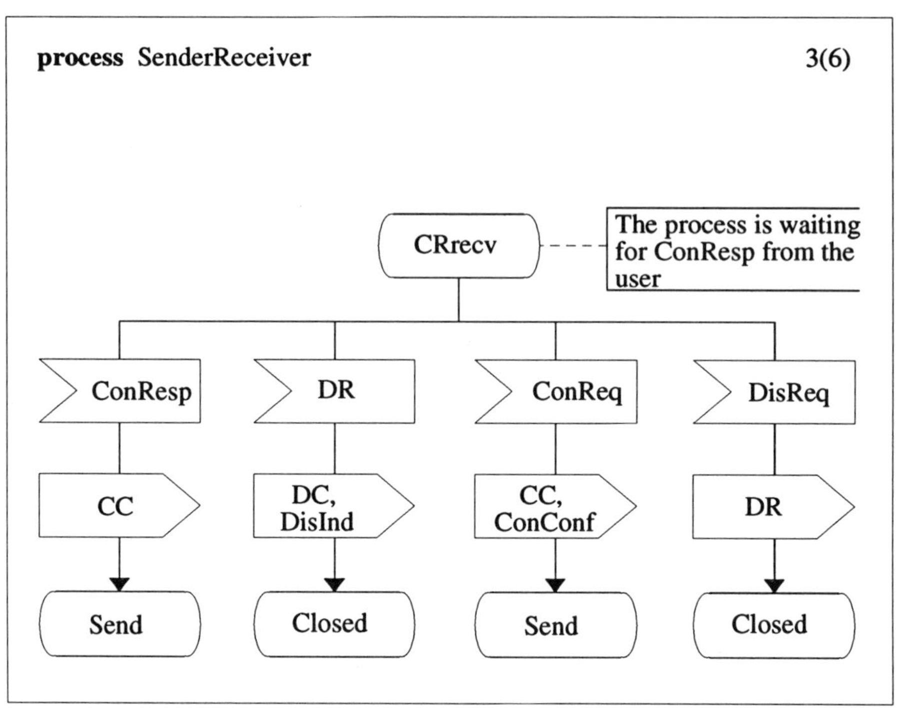

Figure 9.4 *(continued)*

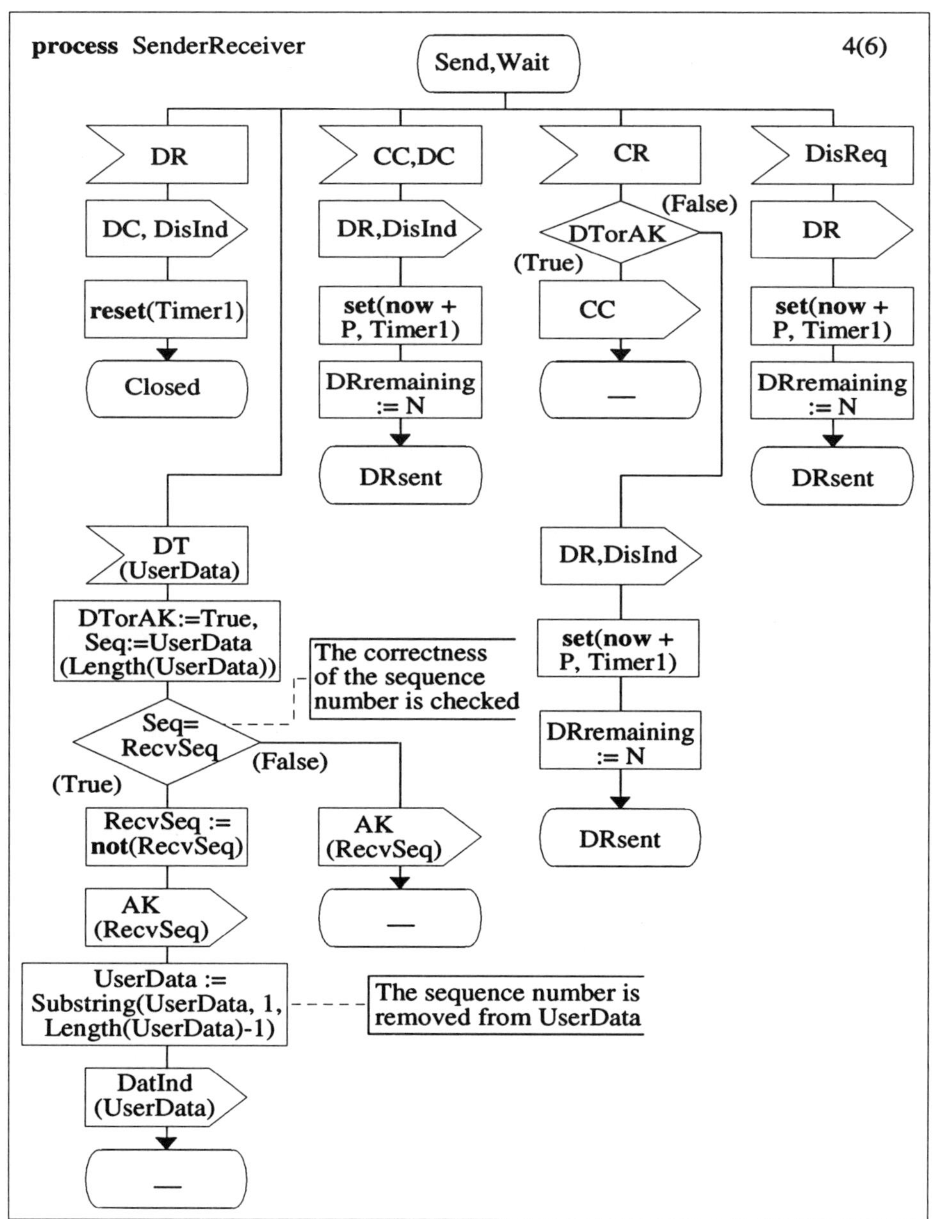

Figure 9.4 *(continued)*

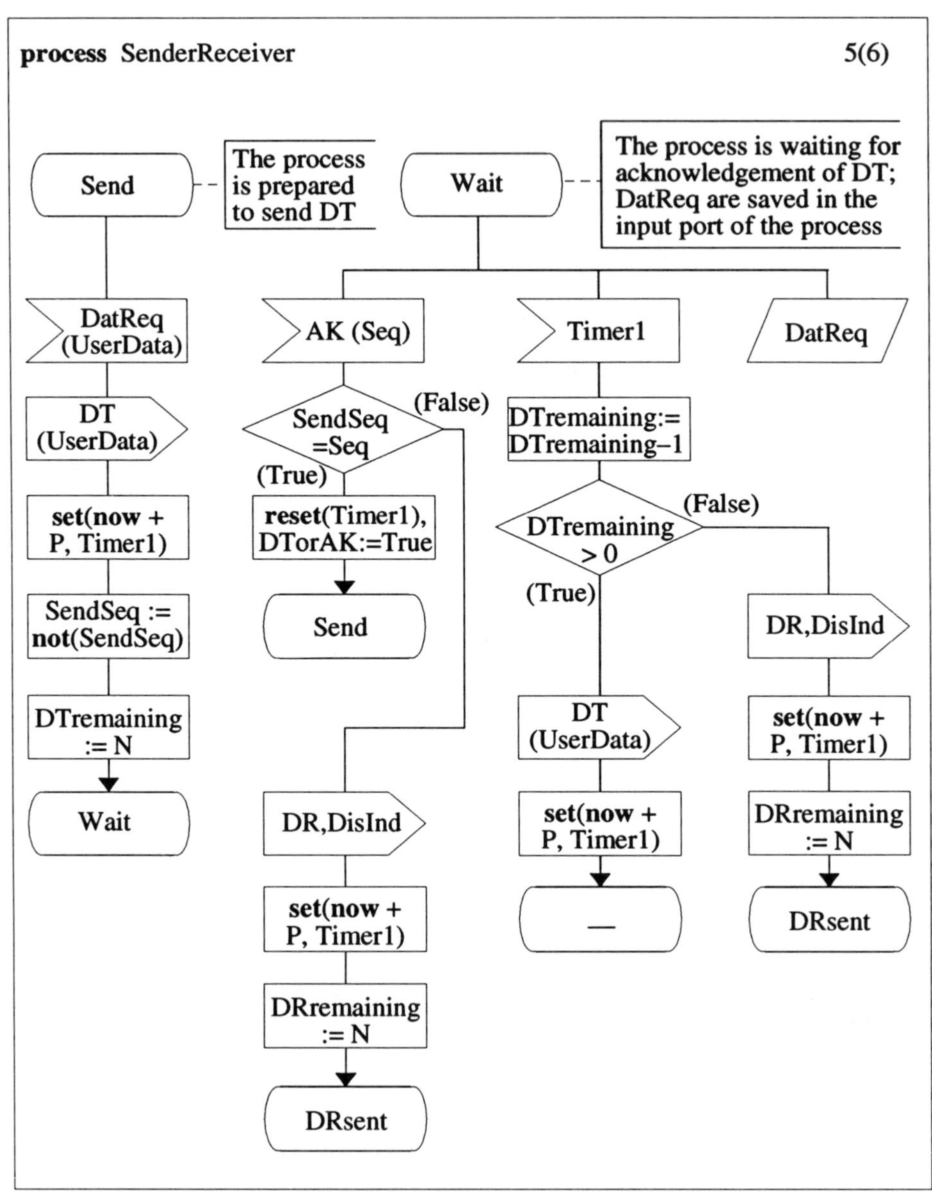

Figure 9.4 *(continued)*

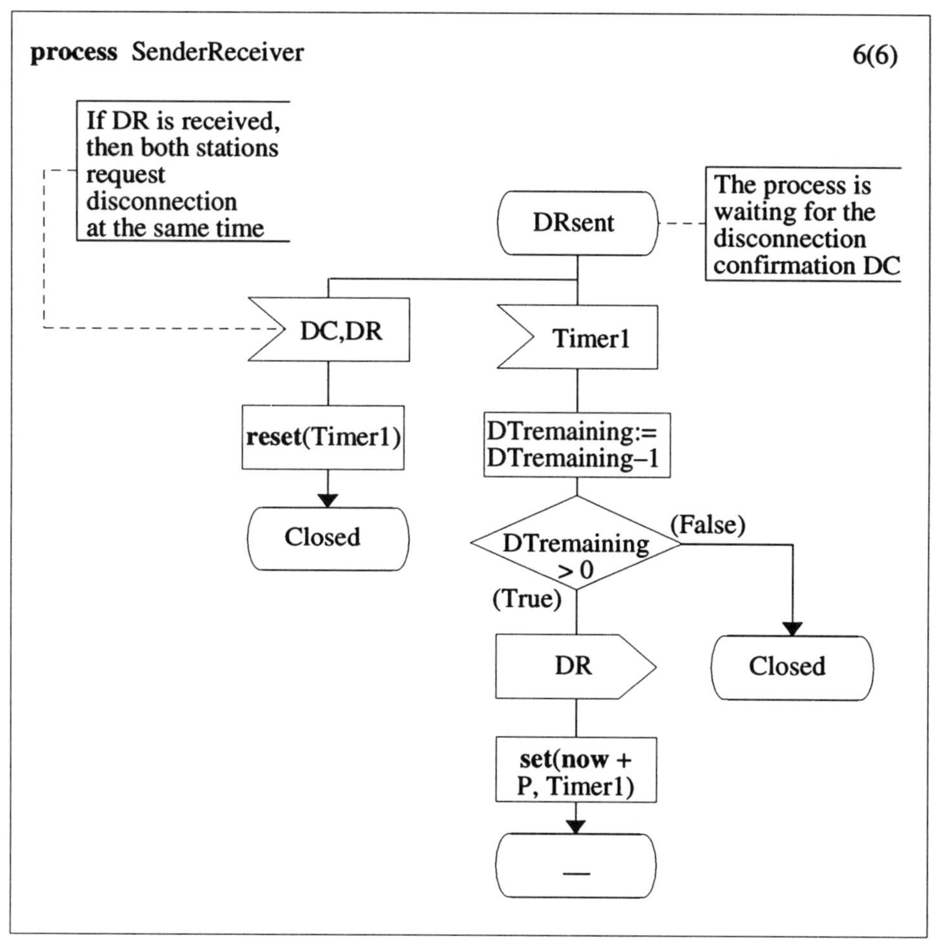

Figure 9.4 *(continued)*

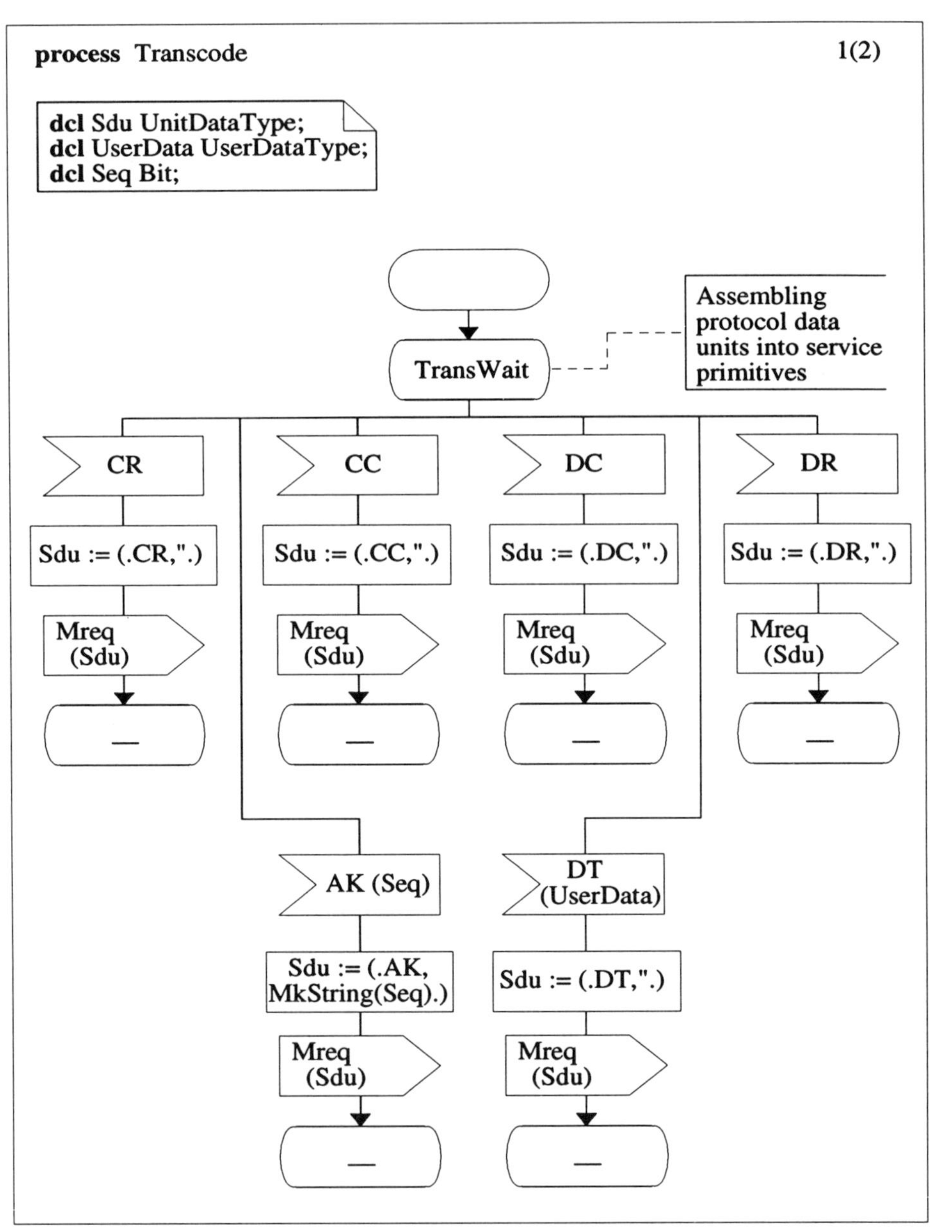

Figure 9.4 *(continued)*

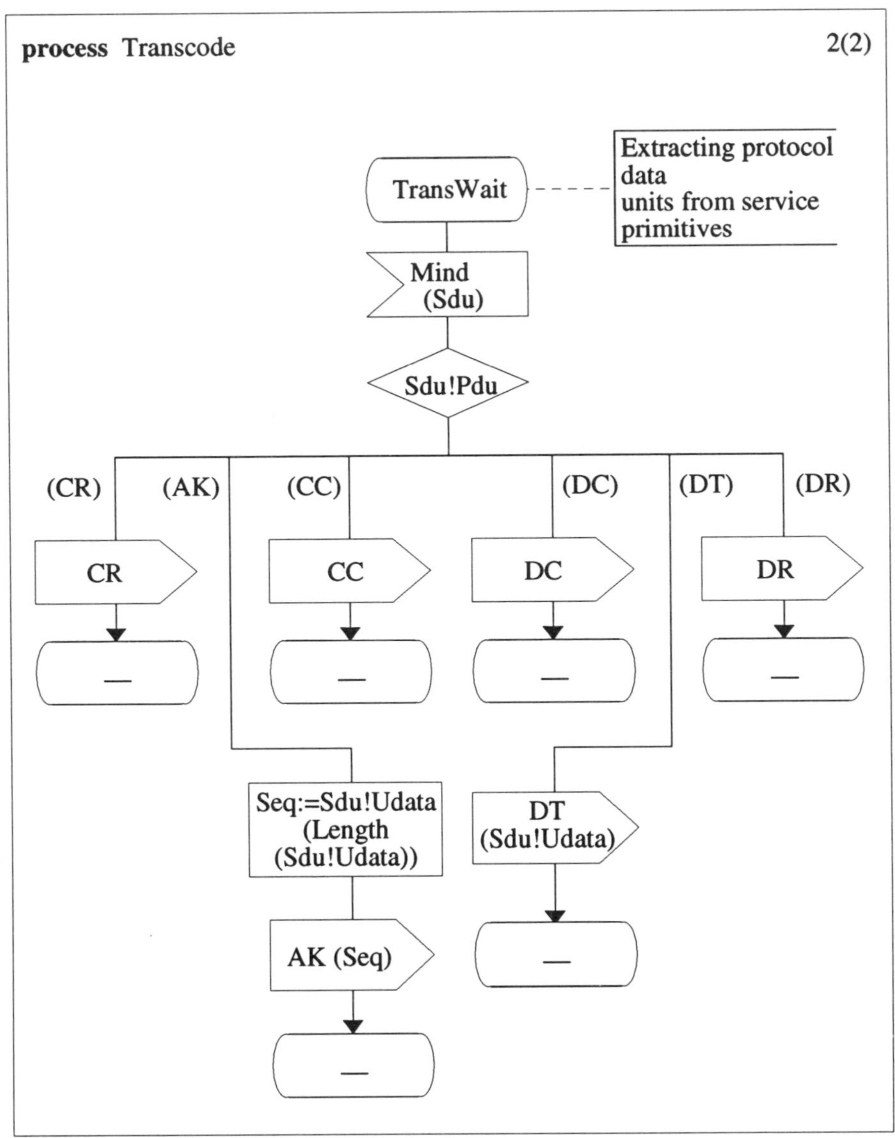

Figure 9.4 *(continued)*

Closed: the protocol entity is ready to accept a Connection Request

CRsent: the protocol entity is waiting for a Connection Confirmation from the peer protocol entity

CRrecv: the protocol entity is waiting for a Connection Response from its user

Send: data transfer is permitted

Wait: data transfer is delayed until previous data is acknowledged; in the meantime, data transfer requests from the user are buffered.

A timer is needed in order to count down the maximum delay for Connection Confirmation and for Data acknowledgement. The SDL built-in constructs for timer management are used, with an instance called *Timer1.*

Process *Transcode* consists of just one state, *Transwait.* In fact, encoding or decoding is always enabled and the mapping function does not require any memory of past conditions.

The approach taken consists of formally describing the protocol by expressing the behaviour of just one party. This is sufficient due to the symmetry of the Abracadabra Protocol. It would not be the case for unsymmetrical protocols, where it would be necessary to describe the individual behaviour of each party.

Interactions with the medium use only the signals *Mreq* and *Mind*, meaning protocol data unit transmission and reception respectively. The medium is implicitly assumed to be ready for transmission or reception at all times.

Isolating low-level features of the protocol such as encoding and decoding greatly improves readability of the formal description. The partitioning of block *Station* into processes *SenderReceiver* and *Transcode* serves this purpose without necessarily imposing this structure on an actual implementation.

The SDL description of the Abracadabra example shows how SDL can satisfactorily express both services and protocols. Nevertheless, it is interesting to note how the approaches taken in describing a service and a protocol may differ substantially. For the service description an end-to-end view was considered appropriate, whereas with the protocol description a local view was chosen. Adopting a local description for the service would have resulted in incomplete specification. This would have failed to capture the distributed nature of the service provider, with its property of delaying information exchange between users. As a consequence, some valid sequences of service primitives would not have been modelled. Conversely, an end-to-end description for the protocol that described both protocol entities would have caused duplication in the description due to their equivalent behaviour.

The approach chosen for the description of the service had to rely on a higher degree of abstraction than was appropriate for the protocol. For example, the solution of using signals from the environment in order to express non-determinism is the only one possible in SDL. Unfortunately it leads to a system interaction diagram where the intuitive mapping between channels and physical pathways for information is no longer valid. However, the approach chosen for the description of the protocol turned out to be quite natural; all the SDL features that have been used are easily justified and intuitively appropriate.

9.6 Conclusion[9]

Considering the comparative complexity of this example, the variety of errors found was quite small. The following types of errors are additional to those discovered while formalising the Abracadabra Service:

- More 'phase change' problems were found in formally describing the protocol than were found with the service. It is frequent in protocols like Abracadabra to find that in error cases one protocol entity has a different view of the state of connection from the other protocol entity (e.g. the so-called 'half-open connection'). It is important to describe change-over or cross-over situations fully.

- It is also important to relate the behaviour of a service to its underlying protocol properly. By theoretical verification, it is possible to show using FDTs that a service is indeed satisfied by its protocol. A degree of confidence may also be established by comparing the results of simulating (symbolically executing) the service and protocol formal descriptions.

- It is easy in an informal description to make loose statements such as 'a protocol data unit is not delivered' where it is actually the user data that is meant. Writing a formal description soon uncovers such vagueness and can be used to improve the informal description.

- Valid limits for system parameters should be clearly stated so that the behaviour of the system under extreme conditions is known.

---

[9]Section 9.6 is by K. J. Turner.

Part III

Development with the FDTs

This part of the book deals with development methods and tools for each of the FDTs. The reader should have a working knowledge of the FDTs from Part I of the book before tackling Part III. Individual chapters in this part are as follows:

Chapter 10 deals with development using ESTELLE.

Chapter 11 deals with development using LOTOS.

Chapter 12 deals with development using SDL.

10 Development with ESTELLE[1]

10.1 Introduction

This chapter illustrates various stages in development using ESTELLE with reference to an integrated set of software tools called the EWS (*ESTELLE Work Station*, Ayache *et al.* (1989)). The ESTELLE Work Station consists of a syntax-driven graphical editor, an ESTELLE-to-C compiler, a simulator and an implementation kernel. The ESTELLE Work Station is the outcome of the project SED *(SEDOS ESTELLE Demonstrator)*, undertaken under the second ESPRIT programme in Europe. The tools were used as industrial prototypes for validating real-sized ESTELLE descriptions in four important areas: computer networks, industrial systems, telecommunications and space communications.

Prior to this work, the ESPRIT project SEDOS *(Software Environment for the Design of Open distributed Systems)* participated in the definition of ESTELLE within ISO. SEDOS developed the research prototype tools described by Diaz *et al.* (1989). These were subsequently enhanced to form industrial prototype tools under the name of the ESTELLE Development Toolset, described by Budkowski (1992). The ESTELLE Development Toolset has also been used to validate real-sized protocol descriptions in ESTELLE.

It will be explained how an ESTELLE description is built, modified, checked, executed, debugged and tested with the aid of a proven methodology. The methodology was developed by the SEDOS project and is the basis for the ESTELLE Work Station and the ESTELLE Development Toolset. Both of these embody further enhancements, resulting in some different tools. All the tools are described in Section 10.3. The methodology helps a user to build a description using the editor, to check the syntax and static semantics[2] with the translator, and to build an internal representation called the **intermediate form**. This representation is used to generate code in a language such as C that can be executed on the ESTELLE Work Station. The C output is the basis for both simulation and implementation environments. The fact that the

[1]Chapter 10 is by V. Chari.

[2]Errors in static semantics include type incompatibilities and scope rule violations.

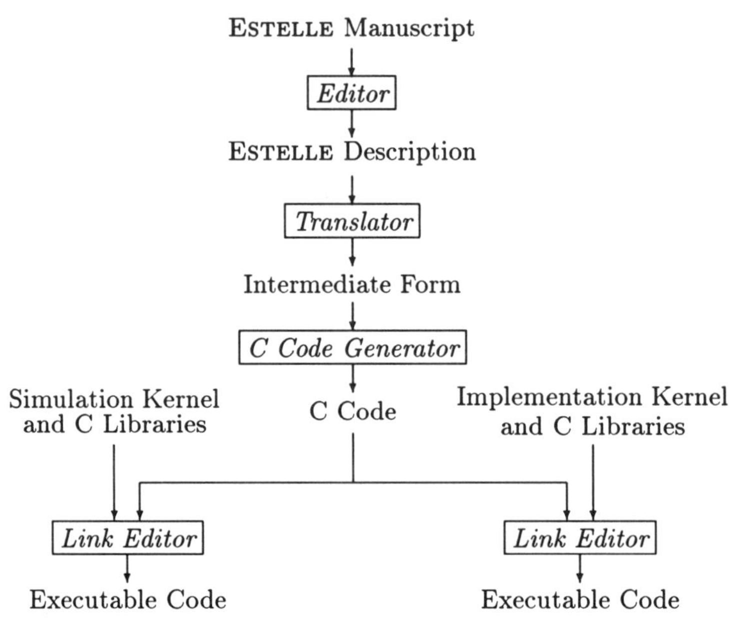

Figure 10.1: Outline Operation of the ESTELLE Work Station

same C code is run through the simulator and then used for implementation is an important advantage of this approach. It ensures a steady progression of confidence in the description as the various tools are used.

Figure 10.1 shows how the different tools are integrated. The result of each processing step is as follows:

- The output of the syntax-driven editor is a list of parsing errors to be corrected, or a correctly parsed and nicely indented ESTELLE description.

- The output of the translator is a list of errors detected during parsing and static semantics checking, or the internal representation of the description in intermediate form. This comprises data structures and access functions that may be handled by programs. It contains the ESTELLE description and, optionally, extra attributes that say how to process the intermediate form (such as obtaining certain variants in code generation for simulation or implementation). The supplementary information does not alter the representation of the ESTELLE description in any way.

- The C code generator maps the ESTELLE description onto C data structures (representing the ESTELLE and PASCAL data structures) and C functions (standing for ESTELLE transitions). It also contains the C translation of the attributes added for further processing.
- The executable code produced for simulation by the link editor comes from the C code generated by the ESTELLE description, the simulator monitor, and the C libraries corresponding to C functions that simulate specific ESTELLE and PASCAL operations.
- Similarly, the executable code produced for implementation by the link editor comes from the same C code for the ESTELLE description, the implementation monitor, and additional libraries to perform specific operations under UNIX.

10.2 Development of the Daemon Game

The Daemon Game example of Chapter 5 will be used to illustrate development with the ESTELLE Work Station. The following refers to the description in Section 5.3.1 with an explicit daemon. The main features of the tools are explained for the following processing steps:

- transformation and refinement using the editor and the compiler
- verification and validation using the compiler and the simulator
- implementation using the implementation kernel
- conformance testing using the simulator on particular scenarios.

10.2.1 *Transformation and Refinement*

Two practical aids offered by the editor are **holophrasting** and **pretty printing**. The holophrasting mechanism is powerful and useful; it gives a view of the description at various levels of detail, ranging from the bare architectural structure of the description to its complete text. Pretty printing is a valuable help in all stages of development.

ESTELLE allows undefined aspects in an abstract description so that implementation detail can be dealt with at a later stage when the implementation context is clear. This gradual refinement of the description is carried out by completing undefined elements in four categories:

- **any** values of constants

- '...' undefined types
- **primitive** procedure or function bodies that depend on the implementation
- **external** module bodies.

In the Daemon Game, the constant value of the number of games is irrelevant at the abstract description level and so is defined as **any** *integer*. At the concrete description level, it has a precise value such as 2 for two players.

The translator may be invoked to check just the syntax and the static semantics while the description is being developed. Only when the specification is complete and correct (for the syntax and static semantics), is the translator in a position to build the intermediate form.

The user may gradually refine the C code to be obtained, both the code generated automatically from the ESTELLE description and also other code programmed directly in C. The latter might include implementation-dependent **primitive** functions, and extra procedures used during simulation for displaying ESTELLE variables. The user refers to the symbolic names in the ESTELLE description; the correspondence with C variables is established by the tools. The association between the different portions of C code can be controlled by the user with the help of special comments. For example, a special comment in the ESTELLE description may instruct the C code generator to insert text in C, or may give the correspondence between a C data structure and an undefined type. The use of special comments is illustrated in Section 10.2.3.

The **external** keyword in ESTELLE allows a module body to be given in a separate compilation unit. This feature is supported by the ESTELLE Work Station.

All the C code is put through a C compiler and link editor in order to produce the executable code. Figure 10.2 shows typical figures drawn from the experiments of the EWS project, giving an insight into the ratio of the various forms of codes. One of the ESTELLE descriptions dealt with aspects of FTAM *(File Transfer And Manipulation)*. This experiment involved the integration of ASN.1 and ESTELLE. The C code automatically generated from ASN.1 and the C code automatically generated from ESTELLE were designed to match.

10.2.2 *Verification and Validation*

The objective of this step is to aid in debugging the C code obtained from the description. The abstract description of the Daemon Game in Section 5.3.1 defines *DaemonBody* and *PlayerBody* as having **external** module bodies. The concrete description must fill these in. The Daemon Game description was executed on the ESTELLE Work Station as three ESTELLE systems with the

Type of Code	Size (bytes)
Estelle description	78561
C automatically generated from ESTELLE	278105
Primitive procedures/functions written directly in C	65500
Object code obtained from C derived from ESTELLE	107479
Object code obtained from directly programmed C	31000
Executable C	155648

Figure 10.2: ESTELLE Code Generation Statistics

attributes of **systemactivity**. The undefined module bodies were therefore elaborated as shown later.

Essentially, the *DaemonBody* is based on a counter called *BumpNumber* which is incremented until it reaches *BumpLimit* (a constant). *DaemonBody* outputs *Bump* interactions. In the *DaemonBody* module, the calls to the **primitive** function *display* print the value of *BumpNumber* on the screen. *DaemonBody* contains three transitions:

- The **initialize** transition sets the initial value of the automaton state to *Active* and sets *BumpNumber* to 0.

- The first transition from state *Active*, introduced by the **delay** clause, has a **provided** clause with a condition that *BumpNumber* must be less than *BumpLimit*. This is called a spontaneous transition because it is eligible to fire when the enabling conditions are true. The **delay** clause has two time bounds (1, 12) which define a time range. If the other clauses of the enabling conditions are continuously true for at least 1 time unit, the transition is eligible for firing and remains eligible for 12 units of time. In between these two time bounds the transition may or may not fire. After 12 time units the transitions must fire. This reflects non-deterministic behaviour. When the description is simulated, the choice depends on the transition selection policy of the simulator. After this transition, the state remains *Active* and *Bump* is output; *BumpNumber* is also increased by one.

- The second transition from state *Active*, introduced by the **delay** clause, has a **provided** clause with a condition that *BumpNumber* must be equal to *BumpLimit*. After the transition is fired, the state changes to *Inactive* and *BumpNumber* is set to 0. Note that there is no other transition from this *Inactive* state so the Daemon Game stops.

The *PlayerBody* module describes the behaviour of two Daemon Game players, introduced by the **initialize** transition. The other transitions deal with the outgoing and incoming interactions from the *Machine* module. Players may take a turn (output *Probe*) or may request a score (output *Result*). They receive transitions introduced by the interactions *Win*, *Lose* and *Score*.

The **initialize** transition sets initial values (identity and previous score) in the simulator data structures for the two players. This illustrates the fact that different PASCAL data structures are handled by the simulator. The state of the automaton is set to *ReadyToPlay*.

The first, and only, transition in the **trans** section is from *ReadyToPlay* to *Playing*. Note that this transition has an empty body. In an alternative description this would be where a player could initiate a new game by outputting the *Newgame* interaction declared in the *GameServer* channel definition. Note also that there is no transition in this description that allows a player to output an *Endgame* interaction. The simulator therefore controls the introduction of the players and stops the game. As mentioned earlier, this occurs in the *DaemonBody* when *BumpLimit* is reached.

There are two **delay** transitions that regulate the output of *Probe* and *Result* interactions by the player. The time bounds have simulator-dependent values.

The last three transitions of the description simulate the player's action on receiving the interactions *Score*, *Win* and *Lose*. All of them have empty bodies here.

```
module Daemon systemactivity;
 ip D : DaemonServer (Provider) individual queue;
end; { Daemon }

body DaemonBody for Daemon;

  const BumpLimit = 10;

  var BumpNumber : integer;

  state Active, Inactive;

  initialize
    to Active
      begin
        BumpNumber := 0;
      end; { initialize }
```

```
  trans
   delay (1, 12)
    from Active
      provided BumpNumber < BumpLimit
        to Active
          name Bump:
            begin
              output D.Bump;
              display (BumpNumber);
              BumpNumber := BumpNumber + 1;
              display (BumpNumber);
            end;

        provided BumpNumber = BumpLimit
          to Inactive
            begin
              BumpNumber := 0;
              display (BumpNumber);
            end;
end; { DaemonBody }

module Player systemactivity;
  ip G : GameServer (Player) individual queue;
end; { Player }

body PlayerBody for Player;

  const
    Min = 1;
    Max = 2;

  type
    ResultRange = Min .. Max;
    PlayerClass = (Advanced, Medium, Novice);
    Result = integer;
    Identity =
      record
        IdentNumber : integer;
        Value : PlayerClass;
      end;
```

```
var
  PlayerId : Identity;
  LastResults : array [ResultRange] of Result;

state ReadyToPlay, Playing;

initialize
  to ReadyToPlay
      begin
        case Id of
          1:
            begin
              PlayerId.IdentNumber := 433;
              PlayerId.value := Medium;
              LastResults[1] := 35;
              LastResults[2] := 28
            end;
          2:
            begin
              with PlayerId do
                begin
                  IdentNumber := 112;
                  Value := Novice;
                end;
              LastResults[1] := -18;
              LastResults[2] := 2
            end
        end; { case }
      end; { initialize }

trans
  from ReadyToPlay
    to Playing
      begin
      end;

trans
  delay (0, 400)
    from Playing
      name Play:
```

```
          begin
            { Player takes a turn }
            output G.Probe
          end;

    delay (3, 5)
      from Playing
        Name MyScore :
          begin
            { Player requests score }
            output G.Result
          end;

  trans
    when G.Score (Nwon)
      from Playing
        to Playing
          begin
          end;

  trans
    when G.Win
      from Playing
        to Playing
          begin
          end;

  trans
    when G.Lose
      from Playing
        to Playing
          begin
          end;

end; { PlayerBody }
```

10.2.3 *Implementation*

The implementation kernel is common to the ESTELLE Work Station and the ESTELLE Development Toolset. The ESTELLE **system** is a task of the host operating system. The communication between systems within one ESTELLE description is handled by the intertask communication facilities of the host operating system. The interface with the operating system is described as operations on mailboxes. A mailbox is viewed as a FIFO *(First-In First-Out)* queue related to the operating system task, i.e. to the ESTELLE system. A special set of **primitive** functions to handle this can be used in an ESTELLE description. These C functions offer buffer management operations on a *BufferType* which appears as an undefined type in the ESTELLE description. This data type and the corresponding functions are completely described in C code.

For handling strings of characters, C is generally preferred to PASCAL but this is an implementation-dependent choice. An abstract ESTELLE description will say that *StringType* is undefined and the string handling functions are **primitive**. For example:

```
type StringType = ...;

function StringLength (s : StringType) : integer;
primitive;

function GetFirstChar (s : StringType) : char;
primitive;

function Concatenate (s1 , s2 : StringType) : StringType;
primitive;
```

Later in development, at the concrete description level, the correspondence between the ESTELLE *StringType* and the C type will be given in an included file. This is achieved by a special ESTELLE comment to be interpreted by the C code generator. For example, the concrete description might say:

```
type
   {$ generate "lstring" "lstring.h"}
   StringType = ...;
```

The C code generated for this would be:

```
#include "lstring.h"

extern int StringLength ();

extern char GetFirstChar ();

extern lstring Concatenate ();
```

10.2.4 *Testing*

An acceptance test for the Daemon Game may be defined in the form of the following tests of valid player behaviour:

- check the ability of the game to accept initialization by *Newgame*
- check the ability of the game to respond with *Win* to *Probe* from the player when the state is *ODD*
- check the ability of the game to respond with *Lose* to *Probe* from the player when the state is *EVEN*
- check the ability of the game to accept *Endgame* from the player.

A test for invalid player behaviour might be:

- check the ability of the game to detect as invalid a *Newgame* interaction from the player during the course of a game.

The executable test cases for these tests are straightforward in the sense that they each represent a transition in *PlayerBody* with appropriate ***display*** functions corresponding to the related variables, e.g. the major state and the *BumpNumber*.

10.3 Tools

This section gives some insight into the various tools that have been developed during the SEDOS and EWS projects. These tools are representative of those developed generally for ESTELLE. A brief list of other ESTELLE tools is also given.

10.3.1 *Book-Keeping Tools*

The ESTELLE Work Station has a syntax-driven screen editor with graphical support. It was produced by Huybrecht (1986) using the MIRA tool. A user who is not completely familiar with ESTELLE syntax may receive more guidance by having keywords and punctuation inserted automatically. A well-acquainted user may create and modify the formal text directly. The usual functions of an editor such as inserting, deleting, substituting and moving text are available. The selection of syntactic units under mouse control is a useful feature. As the text is built up, the editor displays syntactic units after parsing and pretty-printing. The text may be displayed at different levels of abstraction by setting a holophrasting parameter.

The SEDOS ESTELLE editor is also a syntax-driven and interactive. It was based on the MENTOR meta-tool of Donzeau-Gouge *et al.* (1984), enhanced with graphical support. The editor was intended for creating, modifying and beautifying ESTELLE descriptions. It takes input from the terminal or from a file, parses it and formats the text, including holophrasting and pretty printing. The basic MENTOR commands offer the usual editor facilities, with powerful features based on its knowledge of ESTELLE syntax. The command set was extended with macro-commands specially tailored for ESTELLE.

10.3.2 *Front-End and Back-End Tools*

The ESTELLE **compiler** comprises a **translator** and a **code generator**. The translator was generated with the aid of the SYNTAX translator generation tool, Boullier and Deschamp (1985). The translator parses the ESTELLE description and checks the static semantics. It lists any errors, or builds the intermediate form using data structures (e.g. the symbol table and the transition table). The intermediate form is the basis for other tools that continue the processing of descriptions. The translator also outputs a cross-reference listing of all symbols.

The code generator takes the intermediate form as input and produces programming language code for execution in the simulation and implementation environments. Three code generators were produced by the EWS and SEDOS projects; they generate code in PASCAL, ML (*MetaLanguage*, Huet (1985)) and C. The code generator in the ESTELLE Work Station views ESTELLE module instances as tasks that run under the control of the simulation and implementation kernels. Each task has a context consisting of C data structures and C functions. The data environment is made up from the internal and external variables, the interaction points and the control variables. The C functions correspond to transition guards and transition bodies. A library of C functions deals with the execution of ESTELLE-specific operations such as **output** and **init**. PASCAL declaration and statement parts are translated into C data structures and C functions that obey PASCAL semantics. For simulation purposes, *display* functions and other special functions for handling breakpoints are extra features.

The **implementation kernel** is common to the ESTELLE Work Station and the ESTELLE Development Toolset. The kernel offers an environment for the execution of the C code generated from the description. The ESTELLE **system** is executed as a single task within the target operating system. The implementation kernel controls the scheduling of the module instances. Specific data types and memory management functions are supported, as well as an interface to the host operating system; the implementation kernel supports a UNIX system interface.

10.3.3 *Verification Tools*

There has been much research on **simulators** for ESTELLE. In fact, three simulators were developed during the EWS and SEDOS projects: the ESTELLE Work Station simulator, ESTIM and the ESTELLE Debugger.

The ESTELLE Work Station simulator acts as an interactive symbolic debugger. The user has essentially two modes of choice in the selection of transitions to be fired: automatic selection on a random basis, or user choice based on interactively examining the list of firable transitions at a given point in the execution. The simulator offers a wide range of display facilities such as display of major states, module variables and interaction point queues. The hierarchical structure of modules and their instances may be displayed graphically, as well as their dynamic evolution. The display mechanism uses the names of symbols in the ESTELLE description. Specialised functions ensure the correspondence with the symbolic names in C.

The ESTELLE Work Station simulator supports a number of useful additional facilities. The user may combine automatic and interactive modes by letting the simulator execute a given number of transitions automatically before stopping to pass the control to the user. Execution may also be stopped at specific points, including inside a PASCAL procedure or function. The simulator supports backtracking, undoing a given number of transitions. Also, the sequences of given transitions that were executed once may be stored on file and run again during other sessions. A general help facility is available for all operations. The screen is divided into two main sections: one shows the simulation traces; the other shows the text of the transition which was executed last, along with the associated breakpoints that were selected.

ESTIM, de Saqui-Sannes and Courtiat (1988), is an interpreter written ML for ESTELLE; it uses an extended, coloured and timed Petri Net model. ESTIM supports interactive access to various elements of the state, and also allows some of them to be modified.

EDB *(ESTELLE Debugger)* is an interactive symbolic simulator developed by the SEDOS project, subsequently enhanced by Budkowski (1992). The debugger is based on the semantic model described in the ESTELLE standard, reflecting the atomicity of transitions in ESTELLE. This implies that observation and control can be carried out only at the end of the execution of transitions; there is therefore no point of observation or control within a transition. EDB lets the user choose the transitions to be executed interactively or choose the automatic random policy implemented in the simulator. There is an 'observer' facility that allows certain conditions to be prescribed for stopping the simulation. When these conditions are true they execute a set of commands, e.g. to display some state variables. The debugger has other features such as detection of run-time errors associated with Pascal run-time errors appearing in ESTELLE transitions.

These simulators are complemented by the PIPN verifier (see Azema *et al.* (1984), Azema and Papapanagiotakis (1985)). This is a prototype Petri Net-based verifier developed in PROLOG by the SEDOS project. It uses as its underlying model a Predicate Petri Net. The properties of a system may be expressed using temporal logic formulae which are checked against the reachability graph of the Predicate Net model.

More recently, Algayres *et al.* (1991) have developed another tool called VESAR as an aid in design and formal verification of protocols. VESAR has extended ESTELLE by introducing rendezvous synchronisation for communication between modules. Separately programmed modules observe the behaviour of ESTELLE modules.

10.3.4 *Other Tools*

A few of the other projects and institutions involved in developing ESTELLE tools are as follows. In Canada, the Universities of Montreal and British Columbia have developed a compiler, simulators and testing systems for ESTELLE. In the USA, the National Institute of Standards and Technology has produced a compiler, an interpreter (using SMALLTALK) and a large testing system for ESTELLE. Phoenix Technologies have also developed a compiler and an implementation system. Several Universities such as Massachussetts, Delaware and Santa Barbara have used ESTELLE for teaching and have produced various tools in their research projects. In Japan, KDD has developed a prototype compiler for ESTELLE.

In the area of testing, Tenney (1992) recommends some initial tests that should be applied to protocol descriptions. The work is based on experiments conducted by Blumer (1986) using ESTELLE descriptions with an automatic implementation system. The tests expose some weaknesses of the Abracadabra Protocol description discussed in Chapter 9. Favreau and Linn (1987) as well as Vuong and Chan (1988) report other experiences of using ESTELLE for testing.

11 Development with LOTOS[1]

This chapter describes development with LOTOS based on top-down stepwise refinement. It is an instance of the general concept of stepwise refinement particularised to the case in which LOTOS and LOTOS tools are used to help preserve correctness along the design trajectory.

11.1 The Design Process

The design process consists of a set of **design phases**, each of one which can be further subdivided into a set of **design steps**. Design starts with the most abstract description of the system and ends with the actual system constructed.

The important milestones of the design process define its different phases. Four phases can be identified:

- the **requirements capture phase** that produces a requirements document
- the **architectural phase** that defines and formally describes the architecture of the system or subsystem considered
- the **implementation phase** that produces a formal description of the implementation
- the **realisation phase** that produces the actual system.

A design step transforms a description of the system to a more refined description by making new **design decisions**. A design decision selects one design out of the set of possible designs that satisfy the requirements considered relevant to the current design step.

LOTOS provides formal support when designing by stepwise refinement. Different examples of its use have been reported by BEST (1988), Fernandez *et*

[1]Chapter 11 is by J. Quemada, A. Azcorra and S. Pavón.

al. (1988), Turner (1990), LOTOSPHERE (1990), and van Eijk, Vissers and Diaz (1989).

An example of the approach is the design of a network[2], in which the design steps consist of specifying the service provided by a layer, to be implemented by a protocol plus its underlying service (Vissers and Logrippo (1985)). This process is undertaken iteratively until all the layers have been designed.

11.1.1 *Structure of the Design Step*

A precise description of a design step is needed before giving guidance on how to carry out the development process. The model of a design step given now has been conceived with enough generality to allow its use with different design approaches or methods. It is compatible with different models of software life-cycles including the waterfall model, rapid prototyping and the spiral model (Boehm (1988), Davis *et al.* (1988), Zave (1984), ESA (1987)).

A design step is decomposed into concrete tasks, and may have up to three different tasks:

Task 1: formal design

Task 2: assessment

Task 3: implementation or prototyping.

Task 1, formal design, takes as input the previous design and the requirements document. The requirements considered relevant for the step must be identified and the proper design decisions satisfying the requirements must be taken. The design must be then performed and formalised (see Section 11.2).

Task 2, assessment, is performed to achieve confidence in the correctness of the design and/or to detect errors. The task must assess the current design for consistency with the relevant requirements and also with the previous designs. Two types of assessment task can be identified. The first one validates the design by assessing the consistency of the design with respect to the requirements considered relevant at the current step. The second one assesses the consistency of the current design with respect to the previous design steps.

Task 3, implementation or prototyping, consists of transforming a LOTOS description of the design to a non-LOTOS, technology-specific description. A prototype is a minimal implementation that allows the operational validation of the interpretation of the requirements made by the system designers. All the technology-specific descriptions produced at intermediate levels of of the design

[2] In practice, network design has many technological, technical and even political constraints that make a pure top-down approach infeasible.

trajectory can be considered as prototypes. Only the implementation produced from the last refinement can be considered as the implementation of the system. It will be the only one to implement the full functionality of the system.

It is important to notice that the decomposition of the design step distinguishes clearly between *design* tasks and *assessment* tasks, following good software engineering practice. This separation permits the assignment of tasks to different teams such that each team is obliged to make a different interpretation of the requirements.

There may be design steps in which not all of the tasks are performed. Prototyping is typically done only after several consecutive design steps at relevant milestones in the development. The same can be said for the assessment task, although it is usually more frequently performed than prototyping. On the other hand, there may be design steps in which some tasks are performed twice. For example, the assessment task can be undertaken by designers as well as by managers for project control, product acceptance or certification.

The model of a design step can be adapted to a particular approach. For example, it can be adapted to the waterfall model by having the requirements fixed and by eliminating Task 3 (prototyping). It can also be adapted to prototyping approaches by allowing the modification of requirements at some point in the design process, following the early feedback received from prototypes.

11.1.2 *Support provided by LOTOS*

LOTOS allows the formalisation of functional aspects of design at every level of refinement. Design thus has two aspects: a conceptual one and a formal one. Conceptual definition and formalisation should be carried out in Task 1 either together or in close interaction. The reason for dividing the design into two aspects is to have a self-contained conceptual definition that can be analysed by non-technical persons, as well as a formal one for the more technical aspects of the design.

A design step can thus be seen as a transformation of the specification produced in the last step to a new, more refined one. As LOTOS does not allow the representation of non-functional characteristics, these must be treated non-formally in parallel with formalised design. Non-formal aspects are not dealt with in this chapter.

The overhead of producing a formal specification is justified by a number of advantages:

Task 1: Experience has shown that the sole fact of formalising an informal design triggers the detection of a number of contradictions and loopholes. In addition, formal specifications are unambiguous, reducing the risks of different design teams misinterpreting requirements.

Task 2:

Subtask 2.1: The consistency of the formal design with the previous formal designs is achieved by maintaining some algebraic relation between them. Such relations formalise important system design concepts. For example, the black box concept is formalised by the testing equivalence of de Nicola and Hennessy (1984), interface enrichment is formalised by the extension relation of Brinksma and Scollo (1986), and option selection is formalised by the reduction relation of Brinksma and Scollo (1986).

Subtask 2.2: Since LOTOS may be symbolically executed, the consistency of the current design with respect to the relevant requirements for the step may be validated by testing procedures.

Task 3: Prototypes may be obtained from LOTOS specifications in a semi-automatic manner. *Automatic* production of prototypes is not possible due to the abstract nature of LOTOS and its expressive limitations. It is at least necessary that the designer provide the mapping between LOTOS events and real events together with system characteristics that cannot be expressed in LOTOS (e.g. real-time behaviour). As prototyping is actually a realisation problem, Section 11.6 gives a deeper explanation of this subject.

In Subtask 2.1, the verification of algebraic relations requires very large amounts of computation, and is infeasible except for simple cases. However, as the relations are defined in terms of the response of systems to a given set of common tests, validation (partial verification) is possible by selecting a subset of the complete test set (see Section 11.4).

Finally, the content and design goals of each task determine the particular approach taken. For example, if Task 1 is performed by using correctness-preserving transformations, Subtask 2.1 is no longer needed since the approach is transformational.

11.2 Task 1: Producing the Formal Design

The main goal of Task 1 is production of the next design in a conceptual and a formal manner. Both parts are intimately related and should be carried out by the same team, but are intended for persons with different expertise; the conceptual design is for those who do not know LOTOS (e.g. managers), while the formal design is for LOTOS experts. Both outputs should complement each other, and together constitute the formalised design and its documentation.

11.2.1 *Conceptual Definition of the Design*

The conceptual definition of the next design must describe its structure. It embodies the requirements considered relevant in the step. The design decisions taken in this step will also be stated in the conceptual definition. Finally, the conceptual definition will include those aspects that cannot be described in LOTOS.

The most common transformations of specifications performed during this step are:

Functionality Decomposition: A black box description of the system or a part of it is transformed to a white box description, where the internal structure is made visible. Such decomposition may be carried out to obtain a *functional* decomposition or a *physical* decomposition. The relation to be preserved is testing equivalence (see Section 11.4).

Functionality Rearrangement: A white box description of the system or a part of it is transformed to a different white box description, where the internal structure is adapted to the new requirements or goals of the current design step. The relation to be preserved should be testing equivalence when both white box descriptions have their internal interfaces hidden (see Section 11.4).

Functionality Extension: A given system or subsystem (i.e. resource) is enriched. The purpose of this transformation is to include new patterns of behaviour that do not conflict with the old ones, e.g. for error recovery. The relation to be preserved is the extension relation (see Section 11.4).

Functionality Reduction: A given system or subsystem (resource) which has been specified with optional behaviours is reduced in order to fix the desired options. The purpose of this transformation is to remove non-determinism, representing design decisions left unresolved in previous refinements. The relation to be preserved is the reduction relation (see Section 11.4).

A system or subsystem description is transformed to a given LOTOS implementation model. The particular implementation model is dependent on the implementation infrastructure used. For example, for software implementations, a mixture of monolithic and state-oriented styles is the most suitable approach (see Section 11.3); this style has been called extended automata-oriented. The parameterised expansion of Quemada, Pavón and Fernandez (1989) can be used for transforming specifications written in any style to a LOTOS model of an extended automaton.

The design can also be expressed using subsets of LOTOS that can be efficiently implemented. For example, binary rendezvous with one-way data exchange only might be enforced, or selection predicates might be forbidden.

Styles play an important role while performing design steps. Section 11.3 describes some styles and illustrates their use.

The following items should be made explicit in the conceptual definition and description of the succeeding design:

- requirements relevant to the current design step
- functional decomposition
- physical decomposition
- visibility aspects (modification of interfaces existing in design N, creation of new interfaces in design $N + 1$)
- other behavioural implications of the requirements
- design decisions made
- quality criteria
- style and language structuring issues
- relations to be preserved by a transformation
- non-functional design aspects, whether of direct or indirect relevance.

11.2.2 *Formal Description of the Design*

The output of this activity is a formal representation of the system as defined conceptually. Two different approaches can be taken in the production of the formal design:

- hand-coded design
- transformational design.

The first approach, hand-coding of specifications, is always possible but requires a major man-power investment. In this approach, the designer starts from the specification of the previous step and produces a specification that formalises the conceptual design.

The second approach, using correctness-preserving transformations, is more productive in terms of man-power, but its applicability is limited by the current state of the art. The general use of automatic transformations is not likely to be feasible in the near future. There exist, however, useful transformations for a limited set of design steps, e.g. the parameterised expansion of LOLA that derives efficient implementations (Quemada, Pavón and Fernandez (1989)). Transformations in the direction of protocol synthesis would be of particular interest since they would provide the basis for automating transformation of a black box to a white box. Work in this area has been reported by Langerak (1990), Parrow (1989), and Khendek, von Bochmann and Kant (1989).

11.2.3 *Tool Support*

Task 1 needs to be supported by appropriate tool functionalities. Recall that design should be undertaken along with assessment, so that the tools described in this section must be complemented by assessment tools.

Editor: An editor is used to edit specifications, tests and the like. Conventional editors, LOTOS-specific syntax-oriented editors or graphical LOTOS editors may be used.

Debugger: A debugger is used to analyse the cause of errors in specifications. Debuggers are standard tools used with programming languages; LOTOS specifications are pieces of code that have to be debugged too. Existing LOTOS tools most similar to debuggers are simulators (van Eijk (1989), Guillemot, Haj-Hussein and Logrippo (1988)). The functionality of such simulators is less than that of conventional program debuggers.

Transformational Environment: Design should be supported by an environment that automatically produces correctness-preserving transformations. New design decisions should be introduced as parameters of the transformation, or could even by chosen by the tool itself. The behaviour part of LOTOS has a very rich set of possible transformations based on the equational characterisation of relations. The parameterised expansion (Quemada, Pavón and Fernandez (1989)) may be used to derive efficient implementations.

11.3 Specification Styles

It may be hard to understand why a LOTOS specification should be transformed to a different one that describes the same system (viewed as a black box). The reasons for doing so may be illustrated by describing the concept of specification style in LOTOS. According to Vissers, Scollo and van Sinderen (1988), a specification style is effectively a way to use a language to describe a system. Styles play an important role within the design process, and many transformations can be presented as style transformations. From the design point of view, the three most relevant styles are the constraint-oriented style, the resource-oriented style and the extended automata-oriented style (a mixture of monolithic and state-oriented styles).

11.3.1 *Constraint-Oriented Style*

Constraints may be seen as behavioural properties of the system to be specified. The complete system is formed by combining all these properties. The constraint-oriented approach usually allows a straightforward formalisation of requirements.

Constraints are composed by means of the parallel operators. Unsynchronised composition (interleaving) provides an 'or'-like composition, whereas synchronised composition (synchronisation) means an 'and'-like composition. An 'or'-like composition produces the union of the behavioural properties composed. An 'and'-like composition produces the intersection of the behavioural properties composed.

An example of a constraint-oriented specification of the two-key system is given in Section 3.3.6.

11.3.2 *Extended Automata Style*

Extended automata representations are used very frequently for protocol implementations. A combination of monolithic and state-oriented styles in LOTOS provides a model for a class of extended automata.

The monolithic style makes use of mainly the action prefix operator, the choice operator, and processes. The ordering of different events in time is given in a direct fashion, mainly by prefix and choice. Processes are used as a way of abstracting or creating loops.

The state-oriented style is data-oriented. The state space of the system is defined using LOTOS data typing facilities. A state-oriented specification has a unique process whose parameter(s) define the state of the system.

The rules for determining the trade-off between variables (state-oriented) and behaviour (monolithic) are similar to those used for standard extended automata. Variables are used for coding states that have a natural interpretation, such as sequence numbers or other type of numerical or symbolic quantities. These represent a huge number of states in a compressed fashion. Behaviour is used for coding states that depend on interactions with the environment. This means that such states are related to the traces of interactions occurring at the interfaces.

The semantic model of LOTOS allows only automata having one interaction with the environment per transition. Every transition is able to accept an input

Extended Automata	LOTOS
initial state	process containing it
final state	process called after it
transition predicate	guard and/or selection predicate
input or output	event denotation
transition action	process parameter actualisation

Figure 11.1: Automata States and LOTOS Constructs

or to generate an output, but cannot do both in the same transition.

The mapping between extended automata and the corresponding LOTOS model is that the behaviour part represents explicit states, where each state is mapped onto a process. Each process contains the transitions starting at its state. The context variables of an extended automaton are mapped onto process parameters. Every state (process) must have as parameters the context variables at least. This is summarised in Figure 11.1.

An example of an extended automata-oriented specification of the two key system is given in Section 3.6.3.

11.3.3 *Resource-Oriented Style*

In the resource-oriented style, a system is represented as a set of abstract system resources that are interconnected through internal gates (hidden gates). Such gates are models of internal interfaces that are visible only within this refinement. This is considered a white box representation because the internal structure of the specification is made explicit by making the internal resources and interfaces visible.

A specification of the two-key system using the resource-oriented style is given in Section 11.7. This specification also serves the purpose of showing where the resource-oriented style is typically used in the design trajectory.

11.3.4 *Guidelines for the Use of Styles*

In most cases, specifications are written using a mixture of styles. When one of them is predominant, the specification is considered to be written in it. The crucial issue lies in finding the trade-off between styles that leads to a well-structured specification.

A good specification of a complex system depends on the overall decomposition of both the behaviour and the data space in terms of subsystems, as well as the structuring of each of these subsystems. This means that a complex system has to be partitioned into independent subsystems, and each subsystem has to be adequately structured. From this point of view, constraints and resources are relevant elements of a semantically 'modular' design, whereas the proper balance between behaviour and structured state variables is the way to achieve a good structure inside the subsystems. Constraints and resources are considered as parts or subsystems because there is an operator in the language (the parallel operator) that allows them to be combined to form the system.

Constraint-Oriented Style

Constraints represent a different way of structuring a system. Specifying a system as a composition of constraints is a way of decomposing it, and offers a natural way of formalising requirements or other kinds of abstract specifications. On the other hand, while a direct implementation is possible, its execution speed is usually low due to the big run-time overhead introduced by the extensive use of multi-way rendezvous.

The constraint-oriented style should be used for representing systems as black boxes without considering their internal structure. Constraints can be considered as behavioural properties or interface invariants to some extent. This style may lead to a declarative type of representation for the functionality of a system. It is recommended for specifying at a high level of abstraction. For example, it might be used to specify a service, or the preliminary designs in a stepwise refinement process.

Extended Automata Style

This style has a fast, efficient and direct implementation when translated into sequential languages such as C, Pascal and Ada. Consequently, extended automata specifications should be used as implementation models for deriving efficient (in particular, fast) implementations.

Resource-Oriented Style

This style is very well suited for architectural definitions where parts and interfaces are identified. Its primary characteristic is that hidden gates exist for communication between the parts of the system. Such gates are naturally introduced for modelling internal interfaces of a system in an architectural design at different levels of abstraction.

A white box description makes internal structure explicit in terms of the internal subsystems and the interfaces connecting them. Many refinement steps of the methodology presented here consist of taking a constraint-oriented specification representing some service, and transforming it to a resource-oriented one where the resources are the elements used to construct the system at the new level of abstraction.

Sometimes, a clear and short specification can be obtained when introducing hidden events for structuring purposes only. This practice is usually not recommended, unless there are strong reasons for it.

Other Structuring Approaches

There exist other structuring approaches apart from the ones presented up to this point. As a matter of fact, the styles described so far are bound to the usage of the parallel operator and to the balance between behaviour and data typing. The usage of other operators may lead to an alternative structuring of specifications. For example, the sequential composition operator (enabling) combined with synchronised termination (exit) is the basis for structuring the phases of a behaviour. The use of disabling is a way of introducing disrupting (interrupting) behaviours.

11.3.5 *Guidelines for Data Type Specification*

This subsection gives some guidance on specifying data types. The specification of sorts and operations is reasonably obvious, but it is less clear what equations are needed.

Constructors

The first step is to identify operations that are constants. Constants are usually not rewritten to anything else, but there are some cases where this happens (e.g. *2* = *Succ (Succ (0))*). Identify those constants that will not be rewritten. Select operations that will be used in addition to these constants to construct canonical terms. These are referred to as the **constructors** of the sort.

The other operations, those that are not constructors, must be reducible to constructors, so enough equations must be written to allow this. There several ways of identifying the equations needed, including considering every possible combination of constructors as arguments to non-constructors.

In the case of library type *NaturalNumber*, the constructors were chosen to be constant *0* and operation *Succ*. Any natural number is either *0* or the result of repeated applications of *Succ* to *0*. In the case of library type *Boolean*, the constructors were chosen to be constants *true* and *false*. Expressions using *not*, for example, can be reduced to either *true* or *false* by the equations.

The specifier may choose the constructors. Suppose a list of values is to be specified with constructor operations *nil* (empty list) and '~' (prefix). A typical list would be:

```
(e1 ~ (e2 ~ (e3 ~ nil)))
```

The following specification uses these constructors to define derived operations *unit* (to make a one-element list) and '+' (list concatenation):

```
type List is
  sorts Element, List
  opns
    nil :                                  -> List
    unit :        Element                  -> List
    _ ~ _ :       Element, List            -> List
    _ + _ :       List, List               -> List
  eqns
    forall e : Element, l1, l2 : List
      ofsort List
        unit (e) = e ~ nil;
        (e ~ l1) + l2 = e ~ (l1 + l2);
        nil + l2 = l2;
endtype (* List *)
```

If the constructors were chosen to be *nil*, *unit* and '+', so that '~' became a derived operation, the new equations would be:

```
nil + l2 = l2;
unit (e) + nil = unit (e);
(unit (e) + l1) + l2 = unit (e) + (l1 + l2);
e ~ l2 = unit (e) + l2;
```

A typical list would now be constructed as:

```
unit (e1) + (unit (e2) + unit (e3))
```

Both sets of constructors are satisfactory. Other considerations such as personal taste will decide which set is chosen.

Completeness and Consistency of Equations

Specifiers have a second problem to tackle: how many equations are needed? Writing too many equations should not be a problem unless they are inconsistent. Equations should reflect the problem closely. Avoid contrived and clever equations that will be hard to understand later.

There are subtle faults that may sneak into the equations and cause problems. Use of a simulator or compiler is very advisable to ensure confidence, but testing cannot in general say that there are no more errors. There are tools that help in proving completeness and consistency of the equational theory behind the equations. These tools may be useful for most practical cases, but definite answers are not guaranteed in every case since some properties are undecidable.

Auxiliary Operations

Most operations can be put into general categories such as **constants**, **constructors**, **aggregators** (that build composite values), **extractors** (that select elements from composite values), and **recognisers** (that check for some property of values). Other unclassifiable operations may also be required.

Consider the specification of the first five letters of the alphabet, with a binary operation to check for equality:

```
type Letter is Boolean
  sorts Letter
  opns
    a, b, c, d, e :                    -> Letter
    _ eq _ :          Letter, Letter   -> Bool
  eqns
    forall ltr : Letter
      ofsort Bool
        ltr eq ltr = true;
        a eq b = false; a eq c = false; a eq d = false; a eq e = false;
        b eq a = false; b eq c = false; ...
endtype (* Letter *)
```

The example shows a typical situation where a collection of objects and an equality relation among them are required. The first equations says that any letter is equal to itself. It is tedious to say that every letter is different from every other letter, requiring $(n-1)^2$ equations. This would be impracticable for a whole alphabet, or even impossible if the sets of values were infinite.

There is a space-saving solution that requires an **auxiliary operation**. This is a function that is unimportant for the type but helps in stating its properties. Introducing a *map* function that maps letters to natural numbers greatly shortens the definition of equality since it uses the equality already defined for naturals:

```
opns
  ...
  map :          Vowel    -> Nat
eqns
  forall ltr1, ltr2 : Letter
    ofsort Nat
      map (a) = 0;
      map (b) = Succ (map (a));
      map (c) = Succ (map (b));
      map (d) = Succ (map (c));
      map (e) = Succ (map (d));
```

```
ofsort Bool
  ltr1 eq ltr2 = map (ltr1) eq map (ltr2);
```

11.4 Relations

Before describing Task 2 in detail, it is important to introduce the relations among LOTOS specifications that formalise important design ideas. As this chapter is design-oriented, the definition of the relations is given in terms of design ideas and not mathematical ones, although both are possible.

Two relations will be dealt with — testing equivalence and the implementation relation. Both relations are defined using the concepts of test and test response. This makes both relations especially well suited for engineering purposes, because testing is a central component of every design method. Verification is more powerful, but the present state of the art is not advanced enough to make large-scale use feasible.

11.4.1 *Testing Equivalence*

Testing equivalence formalises an important system design concept — the black box. Two systems are testing equivalent (equivalent black boxes) if they cannot be distinguished by testing. This relation abstracts from the internal structure of a system and focusses only on its responses at the visible interfaces (gates in LOTOS).

Testing is therefore a central feature of this kind of equivalence. A test is a LOTOS process that has a special termination event to signal when the successful termination of a test is reached. The test termination event must never appear in the specification being tested. This event is reserved only for test construction. In the examples of this section, the event is called *Success*.

The application of a test to a specification can be represented in LOTOS as the parallel composition of a test process with the specification, synchronising on the union of the gate sets of both except for *Success* events. This will be referred to as the **test composition**. The following example represents such a composition:

```
   SystemUnderTest [Events]
|[Events]|
   Test [Events, Success]
```

When including the δ (successful termination) event associated with **exit** in a test, a small variation of this scheme must be used due to the syntactic restrictions of LOTOS.

Successful termination of a test execution means reaching a state where a transition labelled with *Success* is offered. A test does not terminate in a given execution if it reaches deadlock.

Since LOTOS allows the representation of non-deterministic systems, the response of a system to a test may change in different executions. Two types of test responses must therefore be considered: a **may response** and **must response**. Given a specification S and a test T, T has a *may* response when applied to S if it terminates successfully for at least one execution of the test composition. Given a specification S and a test T, T has a *must* response when applied to S if it terminates successfully for every execution of the test composition. For deterministic systems there is no difference between *may* and *must* tests.

The response of specifications to tests allows the definition of testing equivalence to be made in a simple and straightforward manner. A *may* (*must*) test of S has a *may* (*must*) response when applied to S. The terms '*must* response' or '*must* test' will be used interchangeably if the specification S is implicit.

Two specifications S_1 and S_2 are defined to be testing equivalent if every *may* (*must*) test of S_1 is also a *may* (*must*) test of S_2 and vice versa.

Verifying the equivalence of two specifications can in principle be carried out with existing algorithms, but the complexity of such algorithms is very high. This makes verification infeasible even for quite simple specifications because of state explosion.

The particular interest of testing equivalence stems from the fact that verification is equivalent to demonstrating a similar response of related systems to every test. Consequently, by selecting a set of tests with sufficient coverage and comparing the response of both systems to this set, there is partial or incomplete verification (i.e. validation). Tools exist for automating this process (see Section 11.5).

Acceptance and Rejection Testing

The framework for testing used in the definition of testing equivalence can be used for the derivation of tests. The manual derivation of tests from interpretation of a requirements document makes use of two types of test: **acceptance tests** and **rejection tests**. An acceptance test determines if the system accepts a given set of interactions with the environment. A rejection test determines if the system rejects a set of events in a given state (i.e. after a given trace).

The following describes the *may sequential test* and the *refusal set test*. The *may sequential tests* provide an alternative LOTOS representation of the traces of a specification. They are the basic way to construct acceptance tests. The *refusal set tests* provide an alternative LOTOS representation of the refusals of the specification and are used for constructing rejection tests.

May Sequential Test

A **sequential test** is any test that has only one trace of events ending in *Success*:

```
process Sequential_Test [Events, Success] : noexit :=
   Event_1;
   ...                          (* events of the trace *)
   Event_n;
   Success;
   stop
endproc (* Sequential_Test *)
```

A **may sequential test** of a specification S is a sequential test that has a *may* response when applied to S. The value of a *may* sequential test of S is that it is the LOTOS representation of a trace of S. Traces are possible executions of a specification. The set of all *may* sequential tests of S is therefore the **trace set** of S.

A Refusal Set Test

A **refusal set test** checks if a set of events is rejected in the state where it is applied, as defined by Brinksma and Scollo (1986):

```
process Refusal_Set_Test [Events, Success1, Success2] : noexit :=
   Rejected_Event_1;
   stop
[]
   ...
[]
   Rejected_Event_m;
   stop
[]
   i;
   Success;
   stop
endproc (* Refusal_Set_Test *)
```

A 'trick' is used in this type of test. There is a choice of single events followed by **stop** (deadlock) for the actions to be rejected. If any of the actions to be rejected were accepted, the response would not be *must*. A **refusal set test** is therefore a *must* test with the given structure.

11.4.2 *Implementation Relation*

The **implementation relation** of Brinksma and Scollo (1986) is the composition of two relations: the reduction relation and the extension relation. These formalise two system design concepts.

The **reduction relation** formalises the notion of option selection. The intuition of a reduction is related to the internal choices of a specification. Options are specified as non-deterministic choices. If an option is selected in advance when the specification is written then the internal choice is fixed. A reduction is therefore obtained by removing behaviour that is excluded by pre-selected options.

The **extension relation** formalises the notion of visible enrichment of the behaviour of a specification, while still preserving the original functionality of the system. The intuition of this relation is that any sequence of events that is accepted by the original specification (i.e. does not lead to deadlock) must also be accepted by the extended specification. The original functionality is therefore completely preserved and accessible through the extended behaviour of the specification. An observer of the extended specification is thus able to use the original functionality or the new one. Examples of the use of the extension relation in refinement are the inclusion of error recovery and the addition of compatible new features.

The definition of both relations is given in terms of the responses to tests. The importance of giving the definition in terms of test responses is that the test application can be defined in LOTOS. Tools can be used to analyse the responses to tests, allowing the partial verification of the relation by real testing as in Section 11.4.1.

A specific type of test will now be defined before the notions of extension and reduction are given.

Existential Refusal Set Test

The implementation relation is defined mathematically on the basis of refusal sets after a given observable transition. A new type of test is now defined that tests for existence of a refusal set after a given observable transition. Such a test will be called an **existential refusal set test**, or ERS test for short.

An ERS test must test two facts: the acceptance of a given sequence of observable transitions, and the refusal or rejection of a set of events after this. An ERS test can be constructed from a **may sequential test** and a **refusal set test**. This kind of test needs two success events, *Success1* and *Success2*:

```
process ERS_Test [Events, Success1, Success2] : noexit :=
  Accepted_Event_1;
  ...                         (* events of observable transitions *)
```

```
        Accepted_Event_n;
        i;
        Success1;
        (
          Rejected_Event_1;
          stop
        ...
        []
          Rejected_Event_m;
          stop
        []
          i;
          Success2;
          stop
        )
      endproc (* ERS_Test *)
```

The successful termination of an ERS test applied to S means that the **may sequential test** leads the test composition to a (*may*) success state where the application of the refusal set test has a *must* termination.

Reduction and Extension Relations

A specification S_1 **conforms** to S_2 if any ERS test formed with any *may* sequential test of S_2, followed by any refusal set of actions of S_1 and S_2 which is an ERS test of S_1, is also an ERS test of S_2.

A specification S_1 **extends** S_2, if:

- S_1 conforms to S_2
- the trace set of S_1 contains the trace set of S_2.

A specification S_1 **reduces** S_2 if:

- S_1 conforms to S_2
- the trace set of S_1 is contained in the trace set of S_2.

11.5 Task 2: Assessment

As mentioned in Section 11.1.2, there are two clearly separated assessment subtasks: the assessment of the relation to be preserved in the step, which is an indirect assessment of the requirements fulfilled by all the previous steps; and the assessment of the new requirements to be fulfilled in the step. The following two subsections describe the different nature of these assessment activities.

11.5.1 *Subtask 2.1: Assessing the Relation Maintained*

Verification of the relation to be maintained between two consecutive designs is the goal of this subtask. The algorithms for performing the complete verification of relations are very complex and suffer from state explosion even for very simple specifications. They are not practicable in most realistic cases. The alternative consists of substituting testing for verification.

The work is divided into two consecutive parts. The first part defines the assessment procedure, i.e. the concrete validation strategy plus the set of relation assessment tests. The second part consists of actually performing the assessment with the procedure established in the previous part.

One aspect to be considered in the assessment task is the satisfaction of the requirements for the complete design process. The satisfaction by every new refinement of all the design decisions and requirements introduced in the previous design steps must be achieved by the proper choice of the formal relation between two consecutive refinements. The relation (or mixture of relations) linking consecutive designs must preserve the satisfaction of the relevant requirements throughout the whole design process, such that step N can be proven to be related to any previous step.

The algebraic relations that represent relevant system design concepts are defined through testing and are assessed in this way. Testing is also the most realistic way of assessing requirements. The responses to tests characterise the properties that must be preserved along the sequence of designs. The relations should therefore be linked in such a way that this can be achieved on a global basis.

11.5.2 *Subtask 2.2: Assessing Relevant Requirements*

In most cases, the satisfaction of relevant requirements by new design decisions has to be assessed using informal text as the reference. An interpretation of the informal requirements is therefore necessary in this task. To check the interpretations requires at least two different assessments, preferably by different teams, and checking them for consistency.

An interpretation of requirements is formalised and compared to the design. Two approaches to this can be considered. The first one, which is part of current software engineering practice, is based on testing. The second one is verification-oriented and consists of using a modal logic formula derived from the requirements to assess the design.

In the testing approach, the new design decisions of a step are assessed with tests derived directly from the interpretation of the requirements. The acceptance and ERS tests derived according to testing equivalence (*must*, *may*) are well suited to this kind of assessment (see Section 11.4).

In the approach based on logic, assessment is carried out by expressing properties derived from the relevant requirements as modal formulae defined in terms of a modal calculus for LOTOS. An example of this approach is the H-M calculus (de Nicola and Hennessy (1984), Cleaveland, Parrow and Steffen (1989)). Model checking is used to verify the satisfaction of the properties. However, the theoretical framework is not completely defined for LOTOS, especially for the data typing part. The approach is not mature enough at present to be applied in real design. Only the testing approach has been therefore considered here. As with Subtask 2.1, the work consists of defining the assessment procedure and then applying it.

11.5.3 *Tool Support*

The assessment task needs to be supported by appropriate tools such as:

Test Generator: This tool is for generating test suites from the reference specification. The generator should be able to generate tests to assess testing equivalence, and *must/may* types of tests and to assess the implementation relation. The tests generated should provide sufficient coverage. No tool is available today for full LOTOS, although Brinksma (1988) reports developments that are under way for subsets of the language.

Test-Bed: A test-bed allows extensive analysis of the behaviour of a specification through testing. Automatic analysis of test responses can be undertaken with the expansions of LOLA (Quemada, Pavón and Fernandez (1989)). This tool has a specialised expansion to analyse test responses. A manual approach using existing simulators is also possible.

Verifier: This tool is used to verify relations between specifications. As has already been mentioned, verification for full LOTOS is infeasible for practical reasons at present. A practical verification tool would of course be extremely valuable.

Modal Verifier: This tool is used to verify whether modal formulae are satisfied by a specification. There are no current tools that support full LOTOS in this task. Should they become available, model-checking could be used as a substitute for testing in some cases.

11.6 Task 3: Implementation or Prototyping

The implementation or prototyping task takes as input a low-level LOTOS specification and produces a description of the design using some implementation language(s). The low-level specification is the last LOTOS description of the system being designed and might be considered a LOTOS implementation.

A wide range of implementation languages exist for software designs, such as C, ADA, MODULA 2 and OCCAM. For hardware designs the implementation languages include HHDL, ISP, TI-HDL, VHDL and PAL. Hardware and software designs can be considered to be the main families of implementation technologies. Others are conceivable, or may appear in the future. Mixtures of technologies can also be used for implementations.

The basic idea underlying the implementation procedure is to perform only a change of representation, such that the semantics (the labelled transition system) is preserved in the new representation. This allows tests derived from the LOTOS specification to be used with the implementation description.

Ideally, no design decisions which modify the semantics should be introduced in the new design. However, there is no way to avoid design decisions related to non-functional aspects of the system since these cannot be represented in LOTOS (e.g. timing or priority). These post-LOTOS design decisions modify the behaviour of the implementation with respect to the low-level specification in such a way that testing equivalence is not completely maintained. Only some test responses are preserved.

This task can be seen as a design step that transforms a LOTOS specification to a technology-specific design. An assessment task is therefore needed, but it must be adapted to the new situation. The first subtask assesses that the technology-specific design produced is consistent with the previous design. The second subtask assesses that the design is consistent with new design decisions; these will be mainly related to non-functional aspects.

11.6.1 *Technology-Specific Design*

The implementation or prototype must be constructed using the implementation language. A conceptual and a technology-specific description of the design must also be produced. Both will be intimately related as in the LOTOS-to-LOTOS steps. The reasons for separating both activities in spite of their close relationship are the same as for the LOTOS-to-LOTOS case. Both outputs complement each other and together constitute the technology-specific design and its documentation.

The conceptual definition must contain the mapping of requirements into the current design, such that the *relevant* requirements are made explicit. The design decisions taken in this task will also be stated in it.

As this task must perform a change in representation, the last LOTOS design should be as close as possible to its realisation. Only properties of the design which cannot be expressed in LOTOS should be added at this stage.

The following are the most important individual items to be considered in the conceptual definition:

- requirements relevant for the task
- visibility aspects:
  - mapping of abstract LOTOS events into concrete realisation events
  - mapping of LOTOS abstract data types into concrete realisation types
- mapping of LOTOS statements or constructs onto the implementation language
- quantitative timing
- event priorities
- fairness or probabilistic aspects of events
- performance
- quality criteria
- other non-functional design aspects.

The generation of an implementation description is mainly a change of representation from the low-level LOTOS specification. The change of representation should follow very regular rules, so that compilation should be feasible for most implementation languages. The compilable subset of LOTOS will depend largely on the target implementation language. For example, software implementations will be able to use a larger subset of LOTOS than hardware implementations. The low-level specification must use only the subset of LOTOS which can be translated into the target technology with the required performance.

11.6.2 *Assessment*

Implementations or prototypes must be assessed. Testing equivalence must hold between an implementation and the low-level specification. Testing is feasible in nearly all technology-specific environments and is usually the basis for quality assurance. The assessment must be based on a translation of the LOTOS tests into the technology-specific framework. Once a translation from LOTOS into the implementation language has been made, the testing procedure can also be translated into the implementation language. The relation can then be tested by direct execution in the implementation language.

The new design decisions related to non-functional aspects must also be assessed. No guidelines are given here because it depends on the implementation environment.

The expressive limitations of LOTOS do not allow the LOTOS to non-LOTOS step to consist of only a change of representation that retains exactly the same behaviour. The new representation of the system will now be 'real'. This means that properties of the system that cannot be represented in LOTOS are introduced as additions in the technology-specific design. Timing and priorities are two such aspects. The introduction of precise timing or priority modifies the behaviour of the system, and therefore modifies the response of the implementation to tests. There may be other properties with similar effects.

The addition of timing to the events of an implementation modifies the semantics only when parallel behaviours exist in the low-level specification. Timed models, such as that of Quemada, Azcorra and Frutos (1990), show that timed parallel behaviours do not preserve all the evolutions of a system in the non-timed case.

The addition of priority to the events of the implementation obviously modifies the response to a test when there is a choice of two events at different priority. Both can be accepted in the low-level specification, but in the implementation only the one with higher priority can be accepted. The behavioural modifications caused by the introduction of priority are not completely clear.

The low-level specification is the reference for generating tests. All the *must* and *may* tests should be preserved except the ones whose response in the realisation is modified by timing or priority. The implementation must preserve its responses to the selected tests. Coverage measures and proper test families are necessary here also.

As before, the work consists of defining the assessment procedure and then applying it.

11.6.3 *Tool Support*

Most of the tools needed in this task will be technology-specific. They might include:

Compiler: This should automate the translation into the implementation language. For example, for software implementations in C the TOPO LOTOS-to-C compiler can be used (Mañas and de Miguel (1988)). The compiler supports annotation that introduce non-functional design decisions.

Implementation Environment: This will be highly technology-dependent, and will include tools for compilation and transformation.

Test Generator: This will have similar functionality to the LOTOS test generator. It should ideally consider non-functional aspects, although this is still a research topic.

Implementation Test-Bed: The implementation test-bed should have similar functionality to the LOTOS test-bed, but for the specific implementation technology.

11.7 Example: The Two-Key System

The stepwise refinement design approach will be illustrated by a variation of the **two-key system** example already used in Chapter 3. The new definition of the two-key system reflects a simplified requirements definition:

(1) The two-key system provides controlled access to some resource, e.g. a safety deposit box. It is controlled by two separate magnetic keys.

(2) The two-key system must have both keys inserted before it allows one access.

(3) The extraction of keys is allowed only after access has occurred.

(4) After an access, both keys must be extracted before any key can be re-introduced.

(5) The system is to be implemented using lock and access control devices already chosen, but coordinated by a new controller to be designed.

(6) The lock device peripheral is to be implemented by an existing component with the following features. Each lock interacts with the controller by means of two signals:

   (a) a *Do* command that allows a given operation on the lock when received (key introduction or key extraction)

   (b) an *End* response that tells the controller when the allowed operation has been done.

   Initially, key introduction is blocked. After key introduction, key extraction is automatically blocked until explicitly allowed. After key extraction, re-introduction of keys is disallowed until explicitly permitted.

(7) The access control device peripheral will be implemented with an existing component with the following features. The access control device interacts with the environment via two signals:

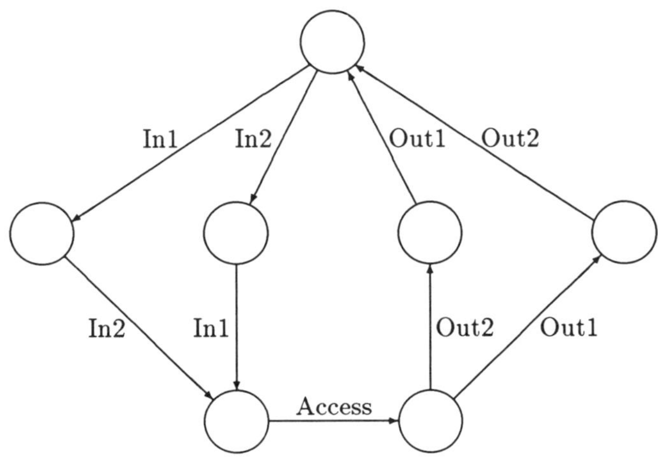

Figure 11.2: The Two-Key System

(a) a *Do* command that allows an access to be made

(b) an *End* response that tells the controller when the access has occurred. Initially, access is disallowed. After access has occurred, new accesses are disallowed until explicitly permitted.

These requirements specify what the system will do, but they also put constraints on how the system must be implemented. The following LOTOS specifications represent the system at different levels of abstraction, corresponding to the refinements of the system shown in this chapter.

The first refinement concerns the system as a black box, where only the interactions with the outside world are shown. The first four requirements are related to it. This description can be considered as a service.

The model of the system at the service level differentiates five events. *In1* and *In2* represent the action of introducing each magnetic card into the lock. *Out1* and *Out2* represent the action of extracting each magnetic card from the lock. *Access* represents access to the protected resource. The automaton of such a system is represented graphically in Figure 11.2.

The second refinement is a white box description that shows how the system is constructed. The last three requirements are related to it. The resource-oriented style described in Section 11.3.3 is suited to providing such white box descriptions; the detailed LOTOS model for the internal structure of the system is given in this refinement.

The third refinement represents a possible implementation of the system using the TOPO LOTOS-to-C compiler (Mañas and de Miguel (1988)) in order to annotate and translate the controller design.

Step 1, Task 1

The first refinement represents the description of the two-key system as a black box (at a high level of abstraction). It has a cyclic behaviour consisting of three phases. In the first phase, the keys can be introduced in either order. The second phase is when access actually occurs. In the third phase, the keys can be extracted in either order. The relevant requirements in this step are (1), (2), (3) and (4).

```
process Two_Key_System_1 [In1, In2, Access, Out1, Out2] : noexit :=
  (
    In1; exit
  |||
    In2; exit
  )
>>
  Access; exit
>>
  (
    Out1; exit
  |||
    Out2; exit
  )
>>
  Two_Key_System_1 [In1, In2, Access, Out1, Out2]
endproc (* Two_Key_System_1 *)
```

This specification does not have a clear style according to the taxonomy in Section 11.3. Its structuring makes use of phases, interleaving and synchronised termination. However, the structure is a natural model of this system.

Step 1, Subtask 2.2

The procedure chosen to assess requirements is testing with the *test expansion* function of LOLA (Quemada, Pavón and Fernandez (1989)). The test suite must include acceptance and rejection tests. Only an example of an acceptance and a rejection test is given. A real test suite should, of course, have a much larger coverage.

The first test is an example of a *must* test used as an acceptance test. It tests an instance of an access cycle:

```
process Test1 [In1, In2, Access, Out1, Out2, Success] : noexit :=
  In1; In2; Access; Out2; Out1; Success; stop
endproc (* Test1 *)
```

The second test is an example of a rejection test. It is a *refusal set* test that assesses whether, after accepting *In1* and *In2*, the two-key system does indeed reject events *Out1* and *Out2* if access has not occurred:

```
process Test2 [In1, In2, Access, Out1, Out2, Success1, Success2]
 : noexit :=
  In1; In2;
  (
    Out2; stop
  []
    Out1; stop
  []
    i; Success
  )
endproc (* Test2 *)
```

Step 2, Task 1

The transformation performed in this design step is functionality decomposition (black box into white box), which produces an abstract implementation of the system above. It is composed of a controller and three peripherals — two locks and an access device. The models of the peripherals have to be derived from the requirements.

This step designs the controller in a particular way. The controller first enables the input of both keys, waiting for them to be inserted. It then enables the access, waiting for its completion. Finally it enables the extraction of both keys, waiting for them to be removed. The relevant requirements in this step are (5), (6) and (7).

A formal model of a lock device according to requirement (6) is:

```
process Lock [Do, Input, Output, End] : noexit :=
  Do; Input; End; Do; Output; End;
  Lock [Do, Input, Output, End]
endproc (* Lock *)
```

A formal model of the access control device according to requirement (7) is:

```
process AccessDev [Do, Access, End] : noexit :=
  Do; Access; End;
  AccessDev [Do, Access, End]
endproc (* AccessDev *)
```

The structure of the specification using these processes is:

```
process Two_Key_System_2 [In1, In2, Access, Out1, Out2] : noexit :=
  hide DoIn1, DoIn2, EndOut1, EndOut2, DoAccess, EndAccess in
    (
      Lock [DoIn1, In1, Out1, EndOut1]
    |||
      Lock [DoIn2, In2, Out2, EndOut2]
    |||
      AccessDev [DoAccess, Access, EndAccess]
    )
  |[DoIn1, DoIn2, EndOut1, EndOut2, DoAccess, EndAccess]|
    Controller
      [DoIn1, DoIn2, EndOut1, EndOut2, DoAccess, EndAccess]
endproc (* Two_Key_System_2 *)
```

where process *Controller* is defined as:

```
process Controller
 [DoIn1, DoIn2, EndOut1, EndOut2, DoAccess, EndAccess] : noexit :=
  DoIn2; DoIn1; EndOut1; EndOut2;
  DoAccess; EndAccess;
  DoIn1; DoIn2; EndOut2; EndOut1;
  Controller [DoIn1, DoIn2, EndOut1, EndOut2, DoAccess, EndAccess]
endproc (* Controller *)
```

Step 2, Subtask 2.1

The transformation changed a black box into a white box. The relation to be assessed in this case is therefore testing equivalence between *Two_Key_System_1* and *Two_Key_System_2*. Here, all the tests from the previous step must provide the same result when applied to the design in this step. Although verification is possible here because of the simplicity of the example, testing must be used in realistic cases.

Subtask 2.1 should also be carried out. The models of the peripherals and of the controller should be assessed against the requirements.

Step 3, Task 1 (LOTOS to non-LOTOS)

Suppose that the controller will be built with microprocessor-controlled hardware for which a C compiler exists. The TOPO LOTOS-to-C compiler could be used to generate the software of the controller by compiling the annotated *Controller* process shown below. The lock and access devices are physical devices that are connected to the controller hardware.

The complete descriptions of the peripherals and hardware would be the input for this step. They would be used to define the C routines of the annotations.

```
process Controller
 [DoIn1, DoIn2, EndOut1, EndOut2, DoAccess, EndAccess] : noexit:=
  DoIn2 (*| C DoLock(2) |*);
  DoIn1 (*| C DoLock(1) |*);
  (*| wait EndLock(1) |*) EndOut1;
  (*| wait EndLock(2) |*) EndOut2;
  DoAccess (*| C DoAccess |*);
  (*| wait EndAccess |*) EndAccess;
  DoIn1 (*| C DoLock(1) |*);
  DoIn2 (*| C DoLock(2) |*);
  (*| wait EndLock(2) |*) EndOut2;
  (*| wait EndLock(1) |*) EndOut1;
  Controller [DoIn1, DoIn2, EndOut1, EndOut2, DoAccess, EndAccess]
endproc (* Controller *)
```

Annotations are executable comments written in C which are inserted in the LOTOS specification. Each annotation has an associated C function (*DoLock(x)*, *EndLock(x)*, *DoAccess*, and *EndAccess*) that links an abstract event with a real event. Two types of annotations are used in this example:

(*| C *C-Code* **|*)** annotations are used to implement output actions. The *C-Code* associated with it activates the corresponding *do* command of each peripheral.

(*| wait *C-Function* **|*)** annotations are used to implement input actions. As input actions have to wait for the signal to come from the outside world, the annotation delays the occurrence of the associated event until the *C-Function* returns a non-zero value. The *C-Function* will do something like reading a hardware port that signals the end by setting some status flag. The function will return a non-zero value when the end is detected, or a zero value otherwise.

12 Development with SDL[1]

12.1 Introduction

The effective usage of SDL for the development of systems is helped by giving some general methodological guidelines. The guidelines need not form a single, coherent and complete methodology since they will be adapted and incorporated by SDL users into their overall methodologies, and tailored for target applications and specific needs. The guidelines should cover the following topics:

- modelling of target application architectures
- refinement of target applications
- production of an SDL specification
- derivation of implementations from an SDL specification
- data modelling
- relation to complementary non-SDL information
- formal approaches to verification and testing
- auxiliary diagrams
- documentation aspects
- tool aspects.

A complete set of guidelines for the above topics would require a separate book. This chapter therefore focusses on the production of an SDL specification. However, there is also some discussion of implementation, validation, conformance testing and tools.

[1]Chapter 12 is by F. Belina.

12.1.1 *Overview of the Method*

SDL specifications can be produced with respect to **structure**, **behaviour** and **data**. A specification is not, of course, complete until all three aspects have been completely covered. However, it can be formally valid before that stage.

In the following, all three aspects will be considered in parallel. The principles followed for the definition of the steps are that each step:

- should be a natural halting point in the production process.
- should produce a self-contained result that appears meaningful and can be checked, preferably by tools.
- should not (or to a small extent) be dependent on succeeding steps.

Each step is discussed under three headings:

Description: This is the conceptual process for the step. It is formulated using general concepts and the corresponding SDL concepts (in italics). Wherever possible, heuristic guidance is given.

Result: This is the result of performing the step.

Example: This illustrates the step applied to the specification of a simple lift (elevator) system. The complete specification is given in Section 12.1.4. The example part has been omitted for some steps in order to save space.

12.1.2 *Enrichment Relations*

Three classes of (partial) process specifications are considered in the steps that follow: P_{skel} (skeleton), P_{inf} (informal) and P_{for} (formal). In order to correlate these, three relations are identified between process specifications.

B' is an **external enrichment** of B if and only if:

- each *state* of B is a *state* of B'
- for an empty *state transition* in B leading back to the same *state* (e.g. a valid input *signal* not mentioned in a *state*), a non-empty *state transition* may be added to B'
- for each *state transition* in B, a corresponding *state transition* exists in B' that can be composed by inserting *outputs* and *creates* into the *state transition* in B.

B' is an **internal enrichment** of B if and only if:

- each *state* of B is a *state* of B'
- for each *state transition* in B, a corresponding *state transition* exists in B' that can be composed by inserting internal actions (i.e. *tasks*, *decisions*) in the *state transition* of B; one *branch* of each *decision* introduced must lead towards the termination of the original *state transition*.

B' is a **formalisation** of B if and only if:

- for each *informal text* in B, the same *informal text* exists in B' or it has been formalised in B'
- B' is an internal enrichment of B or B' is an external enrichment of B.

External enrichment implies that new subtraces may be inserted. The expansion of *states* implies insertion of *inputs* in new *states*. The expansion of *state transitions* implies possible insertion of *outputs* in the *state transitions*. Internal enrichment implies that a new alternative subtrace may be inserted in a *state transition* through branching. It is believed to be relatively easy to let a tool check whether a certain enrichment is fulfilled. The enrichment relations have to some extent been pragmatically chosen.

12.1.3 *The Steps*

Step 1: System Boundary

Description:

- Delimit the *system* from its environment. Find a suitable name for the *system*. Identify the agents in the environment of the *system* (i.e. the different entities which the *system* will interact with). Describe the purpose and characteristics of the *system* informally in a *comment*.
- Specify one *channel* for each identified agent in the environment, and give a suitable name corresponding to the name of the agent.
- Introduce one dummy *block* within the *system*. This *block* will later be replaced by the actual system structure.
- Identify the information flow through the *system* boundary in terms of discrete events. These events constitute the system alphabet, and are modelled by *signals*. The *signals* for external communication are specified at the *system* level. State the purpose of each *signal* in a comment for each *signal specification*. Identify the information to be conveyed by *signals*, and indicate the *sort* of *signal parameters*. Use predefined *sorts* as far as possible. Associate *signals* with *channels*, either directly or by using *signal lists*.

- Provide a skeleton specification (without signatures) for each new *sort* introduced.

Keep in mind that the number of *signals* can be reduced by qualifying *signals* with *signal parameters.* This step is a great simplification of the considerable effort needed in the early phases of requirements capture, analysis, etc. It may be profitable to use techniques other than SDL as a prelude to this step.

Result: The specification of the boundary of a *system*, having its internal structure undefined.

Example:

```
system lift;

/************************************************************

A lift consists of a car with 'goto(floor)' buttons and floor controls
at each floor where users can ask for upwards or downwards service.
The specification does not model the mechanical part of the lift.

The order of serving floors is that if there are more floors to be
served in the current direction, the lift continues to the next of
these floors. If there are only floors to be served in the opposite
direction, the lift moves the other way. If there are no floors waiting
to be served, the lift stays at the current floor.

A user can control the lift by:

  • pressing a button at any floor for service in the desired direction
  • pressing a button in the lift car for a certain floor.

In addition, the specification also covers some unusual cases,
such as starting and stopping the operation of the lift.

************************************************************/

block dummy;
/* Minimal block syntax */

  process dummy;
    start;
```

```
    stop;
  endprocess;

endblock;

channel car
  from env to dummy with (cin);
endchannel;

channel floors
  from dummy to env with (fout);
  from env to dummy with (fin);
endchannel;

channel maintenance
  from dummy to env with alarm;
  from env to dummy with maint_start, maint_stop;
endchannel;

signal
  goto(floor),                      /* Request for floor */
  floor_req(direction, floor),      /* Request for lift */
  open_door(floor),                 /* Open door at floor */
  ...

signallist cin = goto, ...
signallist fin = floor_req, ...
signallist fout = open_door, ...

syntype floor ...

newtype direction ...

endsystem;
```

Step 2: System Structure

Description:

- Identify the main conceptual components of the system and name them. These are the *blocks* of the *system*. Find a suitable name for each *block*, and describe the *block* and its relation to its environment (the enclosing structure) informally in a *comment* within the *block specification.*

- Connect the *blocks* to the *system* boundary with the *channels* introduced in Step 1.
- Identify the information flow (*channels* and associated *signals*) between *blocks.* Specify new *signals* introduced at the system level, as in Step 1.
- Provide a skeleton specification of each new *sort* introduced at the system level, as in Step 1.

It is advisable not to have many *blocks* in the same enclosure. If the number of *blocks* is too large and hinders an overview, nesting should be used (see Step 3). A *block* must have strong internal cohesion and must be easily understandable on its own. A block must correspond to a self-contained concept, e.g. a lift drive mechanism or a lift controller.

The properties to be taken into account when identifying *blocks* are as follows. A *block* delimits visibility, so local *signals* and *sorts* can be specified within a *block.* Communication between *blocks* (i.e. *channels*) involves possible delay. A *block* is considered as a *system* in its own right; it defines an external alphabet for the subsystem inside the *block,* and acts as a boundary to its environment.

A *block* can be specified directly as a *block instance.* However, object-oriented SDL makes a clear distinction between *type* and *instance*; see, for example, CCITT (1991). If the *block* or another *block* similar to it, is going to be used somewhere else in the *system,* it is necessary to identify first the more basic features of the similar *blocks* in a *block type.* The actual *blocks* can then be instantiated from the general type or specialisations of the general type. This observation is a simplification of object-oriented methods which advocate the definition of concepts in *type hierarchies.*

A *channel* may be associated with a transmission delay, so special modelling effects can be achieved by having several *channels* between two *blocks.* Normally, two *blocks* within the *system* need only be interconnected via one *channel*, but using more *channels* can be useful in special cases.

The use of an MSCs *(Message Sequence Charts)* can be considered at this step to get a useful overview of typical communication scenarios between system components. The use of MSCs is elaborated in Step 5.

Result: Identification of *blocks* at *system* level.

Example:

```
block control;
/* In this example only one block is needed, and it is specified
   directly. It controls the complete lift system. Minimal process
   syntax is used here. */

  process dummy;
    start;
    stop;
  endprocess;

endblock;
```

Step 3: Block Partitioning

Description:

- Partition each complex *block* into *subblocks*, just as in Step 2 for the *system*. Repeat this until there are no complex *blocks* left.

If the system is large, some *blocks* can be considered as *systems* in their own right; they can be further partitioned according to the rules given for a *system*. This results in nesting of *blocks*. In the resulting structure, each *unpartitioned block* is a placeholder for specification of behaviour. The behaviour is described in successive steps by a number of *processes* within each *block*.

Result: A *block* tree having the *system* as the root and *unpartitioned blocks* as the leaves.

Example: None, since the lift controller is so small that substructuring is not needed.

Step 4: Block Components

Description:

- Identify the activities within each *unpartitioned block*. These are the *process sets* of the *block*. Find a suitable name for each *process set*, and describe it and its relation to its environment (the enclosing *block*) informally in a *comment* within the *process specification*.
- Connect the *process sets* to *channels* at the *block* boundary with *signal routes*.
- Identify the information flow (*signal routes* and associated *signals*) between *process sets*. Specify the new *signals* introduced, as in Step 1.

- Provide a skeleton specification of each new *sort* introduced, as in Step 1.

Specify for each *process set* the *number of instances*, i.e. the *initial* and *maximum number* of instances. For each *block*, at least one *process set* must have an *initial number* greater than zero. It can be useful to state the *maximum number* if each *process instance* corresponds to a limited resource (e.g. some hardware device). The considerations of *type* identification mentioned in Step 2 apply here to *process types.*

Guidelines for the identification of *process sets* are that each *process set* represents a pattern of activity, and that this pattern can exist in a number of concurrent instances. Most of the heuristics from Step 2 apply to this step as well.

The input alphabet of a *process set* can be specified by *signal routes* or by a *signal set.* A *signal route* is a communication path between *process sets* within a *block*, or between *process sets* and the surroundings of a *block.* Compare this with a *channel*, which is a communication path between *blocks* and their surroundings.

Result: Identification of *process sets* within the unpartitioned *blocks.*

Example:

```
block control;

  process control (0, 1);
  /* Controls the operation of the lift */
    start;                          /* Minimal process syntax */
    stop;
  endprocess;

  process maint (1, 1);
  /* Initialises the operation of the lift */
    start;                          /* Minimal process syntax */
    stop;
  endprocess;

  signal route r_car
    from env to control with (cin);

  signal route r_floors
    from control to env with (fout);
    from env to control with (fin);
```

```
signal route r_start
  from env to maint with maint_start;

signal route r_alarm
  from env to control with maint_stop;
  from control to env with alarm;

connect car and r_car;
connect floors and r_floors;
connect maintenance and r_alarm, r_start;

endblock;
```

Step 5: Skeleton Process Specifications

Description:

- Identify the typical use cases, and describe these using MSCs for example.
- Make necessary additional decisions concerning how to model the behaviour. This may require the introduction of new *signals* and *sorts*, as specified in Step 1.
- Write a skeleton *process specification* covering the typical use cases, but do not consider the combination of these yet.
- Consider using *procedures* to hide details and *timers* for time supervision. Introduce *external synonyms* for unspecified values.

The order of events on the vertical axis of an MSC defines one ordering of events in a *process specification*, as illustrated in Figure 12.1. This ordering constitutes (part of) a skeleton *process specification*. Dynamic *process* creation can also be deduced from an MSC. An MSC can even be used in earlier steps to define the communication within the *system*. In this case, a vertical line in the MSC may denote a whole *block*.

Beginning at the *start* symbol of each *process specification*, build a tree of *states* by considering the 'normal' behaviour of the *process*. Introduce dynamic *creation* of *process instances* if needed, but do not include *parameters* for *process* creation yet. Indicate *parameters* in *inputs* and *outputs*.

Also deal with time supervision; this can be shown on an MSC if required. Time supervision is used to model elapsed time within the model, to supervise the release of a resource, and to supervise replies from unreliable

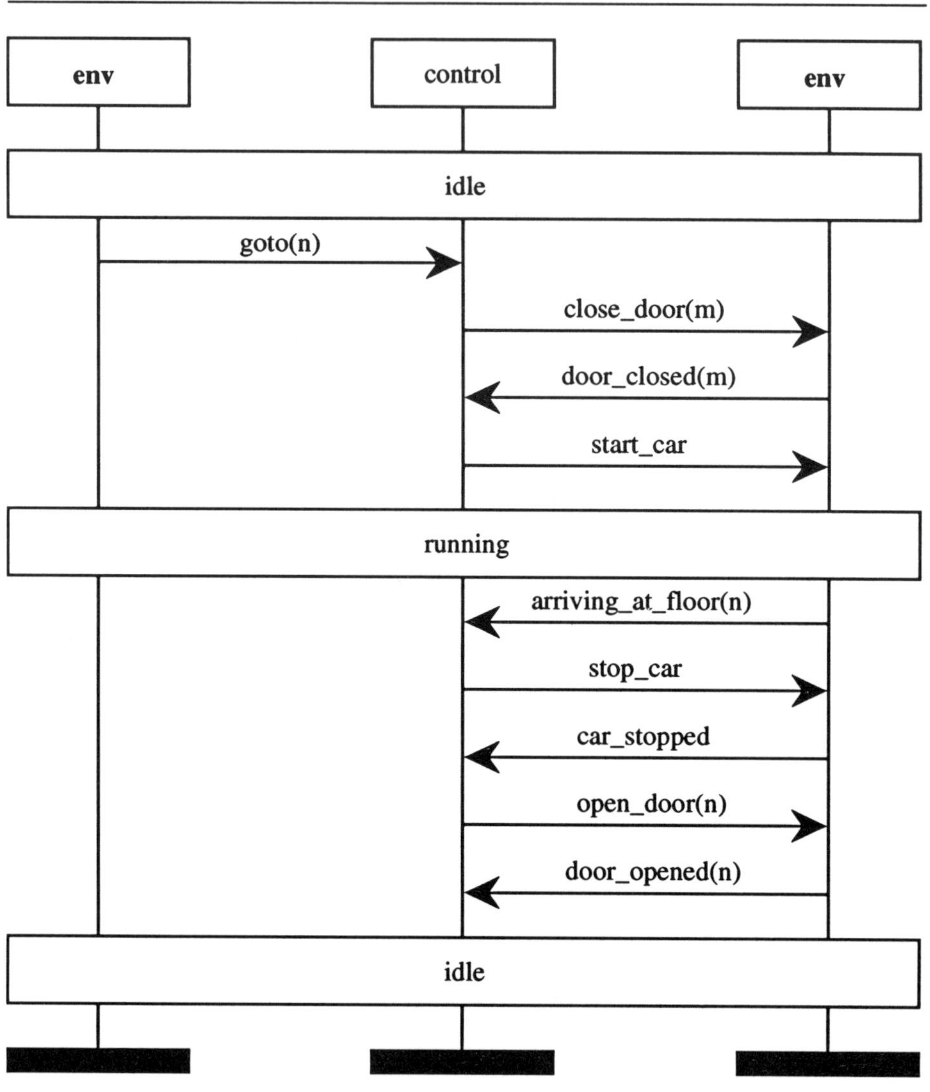

Figure 12.1: Sample Message Sequence Chart

sources. Time supervision is achieved by the introduction of *timers* and by *set* and *reset* actions.

If some values are naturally left unspecified (e.g. the top floor in the lift example), this can be expressed by using *external synonyms.* Considering which parts of a specification should be generic is important for increasing the usefulness of a specification.

Result: MSCs and a skeleton *process specification*, P_{skel}.

Example: Some decisions about modelling lift behaviour must be made, e.g. how to indicate the arrival of the lift car at a floor. This is done here by the reception of a signal *arriving_at_floor* from the environment.

The skeleton *process specification* below was produced partly from the MSC in Figure 12.1 which describes the following simple situation. A user standing at the *m*th floor enters the lift car (which happens to be at the floor). The user presses the button *goto(n)* and is transported to the *n*th floor, where the door opens on arrival. Note that only the vertical control axis is within the SDL system.

The skeleton *process specification* also covers the situation when the lift car happens to be waiting at another floor, so the user must first call for the lift. This could be also expressed by an MSC very similar to the one in Figure 12.1.

The skeleton *process specification* covers the single-user case. Some detailed signalling is hidden by procedures *open_door* and *close_door.*

```
process control_skel;
  procedure open_door referenced;
  procedure close_door referenced;
  start;
    nextstate idle;
  state idle;
    input goto(/* n */);
      call close_door(/ *m */);
      nextstate running;
    input floor_req(/* n */);
      call close_door(/* m */);
      nextstate running;
  state running;
    input arriving_at_floor;
      call open_door(/* n */);
    nextstate idle;
endprocess;
```

Step 6: Informal Process Specifications

Description:

- Consider the combination of typical use cases, and describe these with an MSC if appropriate.
- Identify the information that needs to be stored in the *processes*. Introduce *tasks* and *decisions* using only *informal text* at this stage. Introduce any new *states* required.
- Write a skeleton specification of each *procedure*, and indicate the *sort* of *procedure parameters.*
- Indicate the *sort* of *process formal parameters.* Specify each new *sort* introduced, as in Step 1.

A choice of *inputs* is made according to *state.* A choice of *outputs* is made using an *informal decision.* A choice of *inputs* and *outputs* uses a combination of *state* and *informal decisions.*

Result: Informal *process specifications*, P_{inf}, that must be an internal enrichment of P_{skel}.

Example: For a lift that supports multiple users, *goto* and *floor_req* can be received while the lift car is running; these requests must be stored in a reservation table. A new state *floor_stop* is introduced for a temporary stop at a floor, the duration being determined by timer *floor_delay.*

```
synonym wait_time duration = external;
                                    /* Time for one floor */

process control_inf;
  procedure open_door referenced;
  procedure close_door referenced;
  timer floor_delay;                /* Timer for one floor */
  start;
    task 'initialise variables';
    call open_door (/* current */);
    nextstate idle;
  state idle;
    input goto(/* goal */), floor_req(/* goal */);
      decision 'goal = current floor';
        'yes': task 'ignore';
        'no': task 'update reservations';
      enddecision;
```

```
        call close_door (/* current */);
        nextstate running;
  state running;
    input arriving_at_floor;
      decision 'floor to be served';
        'yes':
          task 'remove floor from reservations';
          call open_door (/* current */);
          set(now+wait_time, floor_delay);
          nextstate floor_stop;
        'no':
          task 'continue';
          nextstate -;
      enddecision
  state floor_stop;
    input floor_delay;
      decision 'more floors to be served';
        'yes':
          call close_door (/* current */);
          nextstate running;
        'no': nextstate idle;
      enddecision
  state running, floor_stop;
    input goto(/* goal */), floor_req(/* goal */);
      decision 'goal = current floor';
        'yes': task 'ignore';
        'no': task 'update reservations';
      enddecision;
      nextstate -;
endprocess;
```

Step 7: Complete Process Specifications

Description:

- Now consider unusual cases such as error situations. Complete the *procedure specifications* accordingly. Check that all *signal-state* combinations are covered.

This step terminates when no new *nextstate* is introduced in a *state transition*. A new *nextstate* corresponds to a *state* that has not been considered yet.

Result: Complete but informal *process specifications*, P_{inf}, that must be an external enrichment of the *process specifications* obtained in the preceding step.

Step 8: Formal Process Specifications

Description:

- Identify *sorts* for stored information. Specify the *signature* of each *sort* introduced so far, and use *informal text* for *equations*.
- Specify *variables* for stored information and *input parameters*. Specify *process formal parameters*.
- Change *informal text* in *tasks*, *decisions* and *answers* to *assignments* and *expressions*.
- Add parameters to *inputs*, *outputs*, *creates* and *procedure calls*.

The *signature* of a *sort* deals with *literals* and *operator* argument/result sorts. Use predefined *sorts* as far as possible. Identify (in *comments*) the basic set of *operators* and *literals* to construct all possible *values*. These are the constructors of the *sort*. Specify *equations* for the constructors first. Then specify *equations* for the remaining *operators* and *literals*.

Result: Semi-formal *sort specifications* and formal *process specifications*, P_{for}. P_{for} must be a formalisation of P_{inf}.

Example:

```
newtype direction
  literals up, down;
  operators
    change_dir: direction -> direction;
  axioms
    'if direction is up then down, else up'
endnewtype;

process control_for;
dcl
  here floor,                 /* Floor the lift is at */
  moving direction,           /* Actual direction */
  table reservations,         /* Floor requests */
  goal floor,                 /* Goal of floor request */
  towards direction;          /* Direction from user */
endprocess
```

The task:

task 'initialise variables';

becomes:

task here := bot_floor;
task moving := up;
task table := empty_serv;

Similarly, the decision:

decision 'goal = current floor';

becomes:

decision goal = here;

Step 9: Formal Sort Specifications

Description:

- Formalise the *equations* by replacing informal *equations* with formal ones. Complete the *sort specifications* with *equations.*

The specifications are complete when all expressions with non-constructor *operators* and *literals* can be rewritten as expressions containing only constructor *operators* and *literals.* During this step, *sorts* may also be made more constructive (and therefore suitable for automatic term rewriting).

Result: Complete and formal *sort* specifications.

Example:

```
newtype direction
  literals up, down;
  operators
    change_dir: direction -> direction;
  axioms
    change_dir (up) == down;
    change_dir (down) == up;
endnewtype;
```

12.1.4 *Full Specification of Lift Controller*

```
system lift;

/*************************************************************

A lift consists of a car with 'goto (floor)' buttons and floor controls
at each floor where users can ask for upwards or downwards service.
The specification does not model the mechanical part of the lift.

The order of servicing floors is that if there are more floors to be
served in the current direction, the lift continues to the next of
these floors. If there are only floors to be served in the opposite
direction, the lift moves the other way. If there are no floors waiting
to be served, the lift stays at the current floor.

A user can control the lift by:

  • pressing a button at any floor for service in the desired direction
  • pressing a button in the lift car for a certain floor.

In addition, the specification also covers some unusual cases,
such as starting and stopping the operation of the lift.

*************************************************************/

signal
  goto(floor),                          /* Request for floor */
  floor_req(direction, floor),          /* Request for lift */
  arriving_at_floor,                    /* Arrival at floor */
  open_door(floor),                     /* Open door at floor */
  door_opened(floor),                   /* Door opened at floor */
  close_door(floor),                    /* Close door at floor */
  door_closed(floor),                   /* Door closed at floor */
  stop_car(floor),                      /* Stop car at floor */
  car_stopped(floor),                   /* Car stopped at floor */
  start_car(direction),                 /* Start car in direction */
  emergency_stop,                       /* Stop car immediately */
  restart,                              /* Restart stopped car */
  alarm,                                /* Alarm message */
  maint_start,                          /* Start lift operation */
  maint_stop;                           /* Stop lift operation */
```

```
synonym top_floor natural = external;      /* The top floor */
synonym bot_floor natural = external;      /* The bottom floor */
synonym wait_time duration = external;  /* Time for one floor */

signallist cin = goto, emergency_stop restart;
signallist fin =
  floor_req, arriving_at_floor, door_closed, door_opened, car_stopped;
signallist fout = open_door, close_door, stop_car, start_car;

syntype floor = natural
  constants bot_floor : top_floor
endsyntype;

newtype direction
  literals up, down;
  operators
    change_dir: direction -> direction;
  axioms
    change_dir(up) == down;
    change_dir(down) == up;
endnewtype;

newtype floor_indicator
  struct upwards boolean; downwards boolean;
endnewtype;

newtype reservations array(floor, floor_indicator) adding
  literals empty_serv;
  operators
      goto_req: reservations, floor, floor -> reservations;
        /* Marks request to go from current floor to another */
      floor_req: reservations, floor, direction -> reservations;
        /* Marks request to go from floor in given direction */
      floor_stop: reservations, direction, floor -> boolean;
        /* Checks if floor has requested service in given direction */
      cancel_res: reservations, direction, floor -> reservations;
        /* Removes service request from floor in given direction */
      more_floors: reservations, direction, floor -> boolean;
        /* Checks for more floors to be served from current floor
            to top or bottom, depending on current direction */
      more_floors!: reservations, direction, integer -> boolean;
```

```
        /* Additional operator to iterate over a range */
  axioms
    empty_serv == Make!(Make!(false, false));
    goal /= here ==>
      goto_req(r, here, goal) ==
        Modify!(r, goal,
          if goal > here
            then upwardsModify!(Extract!(r, goal), true)
            else downwardsModify!(Extract!(r, goal), true)
          fi);
    goto_req(r, here, here) == Error!;
    floor_req(r, goal, d) ==
      Modify!(r, goal,
        if d = up
          then upwardsModify!(Extract!(r, goal), true)
          else downwardsModify!(Extract!(r, goal), true)
        fi);
    floor_stop(r, d, f) ==
        if d = up
            then upwardsExtract!(Extract!(r, f))
            else downwardsExtract!(Extract!(r, f))
        fi;
    cancel_res(r, d, f) ==
    Modify!(r, f,
        if d = up
            then upwardsModify!(Extract!(r, f), false)
            else downwardsModify!(Extract!(r, f), false)
        fi);
    more_floors(r, d, f) ==
        if d = up
            then more_floors!(r, d, f+1)
            else more_floors!(r, d, f-1)
        fi;
    more_floors!(r, d, f) ==
        upwardsExtract!(Extract!(r, f)) or
          downwardsExtract!(Extract!(r, f)) or
            if d = up
              then more_floors!(r, d, f+1)
              else more_floors!(r, d, f-1)
            fi;
endnewtype reservations;
```

```
channel car
  from env to control with (cin);
endchannel;

channel floors
  from control to env with (fout);
  from env to control with (fin);
endchannel;

channel maintenance
  from control to env with alarm;
  from env to control with maint_start, maint_stop;
endchannel;

block control referenced;

endsystem;

block control;
/* The block describes the controls of the complete lift system */

  process control (0, 1) referenced;
  process maint (1, 1) referenced;

  signal route r_car
    from env to control with (cin);

  signal route r_floors
    from control to env with (fout);
    from env to control with (fin);

  signal route r_start
    from env to maint with maint_start;

  signal route r_alarm
    from env to control with maint_stop;
    from control to env with alarm;

  connect car and r_car;
  connect floors and r_floors;
  connect maintenance and r_alarm, r_start;

endblock;
```

```
process control;
/* Controls the operation of the lift */
  procedure open_door referenced;
  procedure close_door referenced;
  timer floor_delay;                          /* Timer for one floor */

  dcl
    here floor,                               /* Floor the lift is at */
    moving direction,                         /* Actual direction */
    table reservations,                       /* Floor requests */
    goal floor,                               /* Goal of floor request */
    towards direction;                        /* Direction from user */

  start;
    task here := bot_floor;
    task moving := up;
    task table := empty_serv;
    call open_door(here);
    nextstate idle;

  /* The lift is waiting at the floor designated by 'here' */

  state idle;
    input goto(goal);
      decision goal = here;
          (true): nextstate -;                /* Ignore */
          (false):
            task table := goto_req(table, here, goal);
            task moving :=
              if goal > here then up else down fi;
            task here := if moving = up then here+1 else here-1 fi;
            call close_door(here);
            nextstate running;
      enddecision;
    input floor_req(towards, goal);
      decision goal = here;
        (true): nextstate -;                  /* Ignore */
        (false):
            task table := floor_req(table, goal, towards );
            task moving := if goal > here then up else down fi;
```

```
        task here := if moving = up then here+1 else here-1 fi;
        call close_door(here);
        nextstate running;
      enddecision;

/* The lift is running between two floors */

state running;
  input arriving_at_floor;
    decision floor_stop(table, moving, here);
      (true):
        task table := cancel_res(table, moving, here);
        set(now+wait_time, floor_delay);
        call open_door(here);
        nextstate floor_stop;
      (false):
        decision more_floors(table, moving, here);
          (false):
            set(now+wait_time, floor_delay);
            call open_door(here);
            nextstate floor_stop;
          (true):
            task here := if moving = up then here+1 else here-1 fi;
            nextstate -;
        enddecision;
    enddecision;
  input goto(goal);
    decision goal = here;
      (true):
        task table := floor_req(table, goal, moving);
        nextstate -;
          (false):
            task table := goto_req(table, here, goal);
            nextstate -;
    enddecision;
  input floor_req(towards, goal);
    task table := floor_req(table, goal, towards);
    nextstate -;
  input emergency_stop;
    output alarm;
    nextstate stopped;
```

```
/* The lift makes a temporary stop */

state floor_stop;
  input goto(goal);
    decision goal = here;
      (true):
      (false):
        task table := goto_req(table, here, goal);
    enddecision;
    nextstate -;
  input floor_req(towards, goal);
    decision goal = here;
      (true):
      (false):
        task table := floor_req(table, goal, towards);
    enddecision;
    nextstate -;
  input floor_delay;
    task moving :=
      if more_floors(table, moving, here)
        then moving
        else change_dir(moving)
      fi;
      task table := cancel_res(table, moving, here);
      decision more_floors(table, moving, here);
        (false): nextstate idle;
        (true):
          task here := if moving = up then here+1 else here-1 fi;
          call close_door(here);
          nextstate running;
      enddecision;

state *;
  input maint_stop;
    stop;

stopped *;
  input restart;
    nextstate running;

endprocess control;
```

```
process maint;
  start;
    nextstate idle;
  state idle;
    input maint_start;
    nextstate idle;
    create control;
endprocess maint;

procedure open_door;
  fpar here floor;
  dcl f floor;
  start;
    output stop_car(here);
    nextstate wait1;
  state wait1;
    input car_stopped(f);
      output open_door(f);
      nextstate wait2;
  state wait2;
    input door_opened(f);
      return;
  state *;
    save *;
endprocedure;


procedure close_door;
  fpar
    here floor,
    towards direction;
  dcl f floor;
  start;
    output close_door(here);
    nextstate wait;
  state wait;
    input door_closed(f);
      output start_car(towards);
      return;
  state *;
    save *;
endprocedure;
```

12.2 Implementation

The problem addressed in this section is how to bridge the conceptual gap between abstract systems modelled by SDL and concrete systems made from real-world hardware and software components. Real-world components normally differ from abstract components in structure as well as in behaviour. Adaptations are therefore needed at both the abstract and the concrete level in order to ensure that the SDL specification faithfully models the functionality of the real system. Documentation in addition to pure SDL is needed to describe the concrete system and its relationships to the abstract system.

During the life-time of a system, SDL specifications are used for at least three purposes:

- At an early stage, SDL specifications are used to specify and to validate the functionality (behaviour) required by the user environment. For this purpose the external behaviour should be emphasised, and irrelevant internal design details should be discarded.
- Design-oriented SDL specifications are then used to provide a firm basis for implementation design, i.e. finding the optimum realisation. Premature design decisions should therefore not be embedded in SDL specifications. However, it is legitimate to give additional guidance in the form of design constraints, i.e. properties that the implementation must have in addition to those expressed in the SDL specification.
- After implementation design, implementation-oriented SDL specifications are used to describe (and therefore document) the complete functional properties of the system as implemented. For this purpose, the SDL specifications must normally be adapted to the underlying implementation.

SDL systems are constructed from abstract components well suited to the first purpose above — modelling the observable behaviour of systems in a clear and unambiguous way. But they are also well suited for the second purpose — acting as the basis for implementation design. The abstract mechanisms of SDL have the useful feature of combining implementation independence with implementability (except for non-constructive abstract data types). There are normally no fundamental problems in implementing SDL specifications effectively. There is usually a choice of alternative implementations that are functionally equivalent, but different in non-functional properties such as cost, modularity and speed. This enables the designer to select an optimum implementation with respect to design constraints (the non-functional properties).

In designing an implementation, it is necessary to be aware of the differences between the abstract world of SDL and the real world of hardware and software.

Real-world components may be used to build systems that are functionally equivalent to one expressed in SDL. A designer must know the various ways in which the gap can be bridged. The real world differs from the abstract world in the following respects:

- processing takes time
- errors do occur
- signals must cross physical space
- communication primitives may be different
- concurrency may be different
- synchronisation primitives may be different
- resources are limited.

Implementation design should ideally be orthogonal to the functionality given in the source SDL specification, but this is not always possible. If the implementation is to be distributed in a network, for instance, some of the SDL channels will be implemented using network protocols. These protocols add functionality in a distributed implementation compared to a centralised solution. Since parts of a distributed system can fail while other parts remain operational, error handling is different compared to a centralised system.

Implementation design can be seen as defining the mapping from an abstract SDL system to a concrete system made up of hardware and software components. How should this mapping be defined? Clearly, SDL can be restructured and refined up to a point where it reflects much of the low-level design. But the SDL specification will still be abstract and implementable in different ways. Something is thus needed in addition to pure SDL to document the implementation design. This could be achieved by inserting design information as comments in the SDL specification, but this would tie the SDL specification to a particular implementation design. By documenting the implementation design separately, it will be easier to reuse SDL specifications in systems with different implementations.

An SDL specification will have to accommodate the implementation design decisions. Feedback from implementation design will normally occur, leading to restructuring and refinement of the functional design. There are thus two aspects of implementation design: a feedforward aspect aiming at an implementation, and a feedback aspect that affects the functional design (and sometimes the requirements specification).

But even an implementation-oriented SDL specification will leave some design decisions open. There will still be alternative ways to implement it, but they will differ only in non-functional properties. There is consequently an orthogonal aspect that needs to be documented too — how the functionality is implemented in the physical system. For this purpose, some information must be provided in addition to the formal SDL specification.

12.3 Validation

12.3.1 *Validation Support*

The objective of validation is to determine if a specification fulfils the requirements of users and the environment of the system. In validation, as in other system development activities, one of the major benefits of an FDT is the possibility of using computer-based tools. The availability of tools is, of course, a direct consequence of the formal semantics of the language, since this allows automatic interpretation of the meaning of a specification. Computer-based tools relevant to SDL validation are basically of two types: simulation tools, and analysis/verification tools based on state-space exploration.

Simulation tools allow an SDL specification to be executed, allowing interactive investigation of behaviour. Signals can be sent to the system and system responses can be checked. It is usually possible to force the system into some pre-defined state (e.g. by changing variable values or creating process instances) and continuing the simulation from this state. Simulation tools for SDL are commercially available from different vendors.

State-space exploration analysis/verification tools are intended to check if certain specific properties are true of a given SDL system. These properties can be general ones like absence of deadlock or other general errors, or they can be system-specific properties defined by the designer of the SDL system.

For small SDL systems it is possible to verify the absence of undesirable properties, but in general it is not possible due to problems with state explosion. Nonetheless, this type of automatic analysis has been found to be very useful even for large and complex systems. Such tools perform a more extensive test than is possible with simulation tools. State exploration tools are used to complement simulation tools, mainly to detect design errors involving infrequent system behaviours. Several state exploration tools are in use but are not commercially available yet. This approach must therefore be considered as somewhat research-oriented at the moment.

12.3.2 *Validation Method*

A method that employs simulation and state space exploration tools is outlined below. The major ideas in this validation method are:

- use of a simulation tool to validate the capabilities of the SDL system, i.e. to check that the expected behaviour is indeed included in the specification

- use of state-space exploration tool to find problems caused by unexpected behaviours, such as infrequent combinations of signals and timeouts.

Before the validation process can begin, however, it is necessary to have a complete and formal SDL system. This can be achieved by using a conventional SDL analysis tool to make certain that the specification has valid syntax and static semantics.

Given this statically analysed SDL specification, the first step in the validation process is to use a simulation tool. The purpose of the simulation is mainly to test that the capabilities described in the requirements specification have been correctly included in the SDL specification. This is accomplished by executing the simulation tool on prescribed cases, for example those given in message sequence charts. The simulation will look for major design flaws. As a by-product it will also help to find minor errors that could not be detected by static analysis.

The second step is to use a state-space exploration tool on the specification. This sometimes also includes making modifications or extensions to the SDL system to reduce the state-space that has to be explored. In practice, this might include limiting the number of instances allowed for some process types, limiting the length of channel queues, or making a fairly detailed specification of the system environment. Analysis with a state-space exploration tool can reveal subtle design errors. These could be unexpected signal races or infrequent timeouts — things that are very difficult to find using simulation or manual inspection.

12.4 Conformance Testing

12.4.1 *Need for Formality*

The aim of conformance testing, according to ISO (1991c), is to determine if an implementation conforms to the requirements given in a standard. In this context, the standard is a specification of the externally observable behaviour of an OSI protocol.

Each such standard has a standardised test suite specified in TTCN *(Tree and Tabular Combined Notation)*. The test suite is executed against the implementation. If the implementation passes all the test cases in the test suite, it is considered to conform to the standard. Standards specify requirements on only observable behaviour, so no implementation details are known when performing tests. Tests therefore have to be devised without an inner knowledge of the implementation.

Current standards are usually given in natural language, in some cases accompanied by state tables, so test suites must be developed manually. This gives rise to problems since there is no possibility of formally verifying that a test suite specifies the same set of requirements as the standard does.

It is believed that the use of FDTs in standardised specifications is a way to overcome this problem. When formal specifications are available, computer-supported tools can be used to derive and validate test suites. Much research effort has been spent on test suite derivation during the past few years. Two approaches have been identified for SDL: automatic derivation, and test derivation based on simulation.

12.4.2 *Automatic Test Derivation*

Automatic test derivation uses techniques developed from hardware testing, or techniques similar to the ones used in validation (e.g. state-space exploration). The main characteristic of the approach is that a representation of the externally observable behaviour of the system is computed. From this representation the test suite is then automatically generated. The limitation of the approach in the context of SDL is that the techniques used to compute the observable behaviour impose restrictions on which SDL constructs can be used.

One example of a technique used to compute observable behaviour is based on finite state machines. The processes in the system are transformed into a set of finite state machines which then are composed in order to compute their observable behaviour. Since the semantics of SDL uses *extended* finite state machines, it is not possible in general to perform this transformation. Currently, there are no available tools that can directly and automatically generate test suites from SDL specifications.

12.4.3 *Simulator-Assisted Test Derivation*

The use of a simulator can assist the test derivation process in different ways. The test designer can become familiar with the behaviour of the specification by using a simulator. Once it is known which behaviours are appropriate to test, the simulator can assist the derivation of the test cases by interactively 'walking-through' the specification. Although SDL simulators are commercially available, interactive simulation is hard and time-consuming if the specification is complex.

Test derivation can also be partly automated by the use of a 'special purpose' simulator. In this case, the test designer guides test generation by interactively making decisions as to which behaviour to test, but the actual test generation is performed automatically. There are several research prototypes of this kind of simulator, so the technique will probably be available within a few years.

12.5 Tools

Tool support is highly desirable for effective use of an FDT. The kind of tool support depends on the characteristics of the FDT and on the type of activities for which the FDT is to be used. Tools for SDL can be classified as follows, the order below indicating their time of appearance.

Graphical Editor: This kind of tool emerged first, since SDL was used rather informally in the beginning. The major concern was handling the ever-popular SDL diagrams, whose creation and update requires great effort.

Static Analyser: This checks syntactic and static correctness using the textual representation. Conversion from graphical to textual representation is therefore normally part of the static analyser.

Document Generator: SDL specifications are only a subset of the complete documentation of a system. This kind of tool converts SDL specifications to documents according to the in-house rules of an organisation.

Syntax Converter: Textual representation is used as a standard exchange format between tools from different tool makers. In such cases a syntax converter may be necessary to convert from the textual representation to the graphical representation. This is not an easy task, and most tool makers do not provide this kind of conversion.

Simulator: Simulation tools allow interactive execution/animation of an SDL specification in order to gain a better understanding of dynamic properties.

Dynamic Analyser: This checks if some given dynamic properties are true of an SDL system.

Code Generator: Within industry, the main emphasis is on handling detailed implementation descriptions as a basis for producing system instances. A largely automatic translation from SDL specifications to implementation descriptions is therefore a prerequisite for broad industrial use of SDL. A code generator produces programs in a chosen programming language from an SDL specification.

A good knowledge of SDL tools can be acquired at the biennial SDL Forum. Initially, many papers were presented at this conference on tools, partly to discuss design problems and partly to advertise. Nowadays, such papers are not accepted; instead the tool makers are encouraged to give demonstrations at the Forum and to provide informative material. Figure 12.2 is based on the demonstrations given at the fifth SDL Forum in 1991. Since some tool makers were unable to attend the Forum, the list is not claimed to be a full one. The summary in the figure is also necessarily rather brief.

Name	Owner	Environment	Features	Avail.
CROCOS	CRIN-CNRS, INRIA Lorraine (France)	Sun	Graphical editor, static analyser and dynamic analyser; needs Concerto	No
EDDIE/DOC	CPqD, Telebras (Brazil)	IBM PC, Sun	Graphical editor, document generator	Yes
ESCORT	KDD Laboratories (Japan)	Sun	Graphical editor, static analyser, document generator, simulator, dynamic analyser, MSCs semantically linked to specifications	No
GEODE	Verilog (France)	HP 9000, IBM RS 6000, Sun, VaxStation, X-Terminal	Graphical editor, static analyser, document generator, syntax converter, simulator, dynamic analyser, C/ADA code generator, MSCs semantically linked to specifications	Yes
GTS	BT Laboratories (UK)	Sun	Test specifications and code generator for validated protocol specifications	No
MELBA	RMIT (Australia)	IBM PC, Sun	Graphical editor, static analyser, dynamic analyser, C code generator	Yes
RIGA-SDL	University of Latvia (Latvia)	IBM PC	Graphical editor, static analyser, dynamic analyser, PASCAL code generator, MSC editor	Yes
SDL Environment	Private Individual (UK)	HP 9000, IBM RS 6000, Sun, VaxStation	Graphical editor, static analyser, syntax converter; needs Concerto	Yes
SDL-Tool	Jutland Telephone (Denmark)	IBM PC	Graphical editor, static analyser, MSC editor	Yes
SDT	Telelogic (Sweden)	HP 9000, IBM PC, IBM RS 6000, Sun, VAX	Graphical editor, static analyser, document generator, syntax converter, simulator, dynamic analyser, C code generator	Yes
SIGRAPH-SET	Siemens Nixdorf Inf. (Germany)	Apollo, HP 9000, SNI Workstation	Graphical editor, static analyser, simulator, C code generator, MSC editor	Yes

Figure 12.2: Sample SDL Tools

Part IV

Appendixes

This part of the book contains reference material for the rest of the book. Individual appendixes in this part are as follows:

Appendix A lists references and gives other sources of information on FDTs.

Appendix B is an index to the main components of each example specification.

Appendix C is the main index.

A References and Other Sources

A.1 References

Algayres, B. *et al.* (1991). 'VESAR: un outil pour la specification et la verification formelle des protocoles', Proc. of *Colloque Francophone sur Ingenierie des Protocoles 91*, Hermes Publishing.

Ansart, J. P. *et al.* (1982). 'Protocol Description and Implementation Language (PDIL)', Proc. of *Protocol Specification, Testing and Verification II*, North-Holland, Amsterdam.

Ayache, J. M. *et al.* (1989). 'Presentation of the SEDOS ESTELLE Demonstrator project', Proc. of *Esprit Technical Week 1989*, North-Holland, Amsterdam.

Azema, P. *et al.* (1984). 'Specification and verification of distributed systems using PROLOG-interpreted Petri Nets', Proc. of *7th Int. Conf. on Software Engineering*, IEEE Computer Press.

Azema, P. and Papapanagiotakis, G. (1985). 'Analysis by using Predicate Nets', Proc. of *Protocol Specification, Testing and Verification V*, North-Holland, Amsterdam.

BEST (1988). 'BEST — Broadband European Software Technology', Proc. of *RACE 88 — The RACE Program in 1988*, Vol. OTR 112 - R 1023, Commission of the European Communities, Brussels.

Blumer, T. P. (1986). *ESTELLE Development System — User Manual*, Phoenix Technologies Ltd., Cambridge, Massachusetts, USA.

Blumer, T. P. and Parker, J. (1990). 'Testing of ESTELLE protocols via automatic implementation', Technical Report BCCS-90-05, Boston College, USA.

Blumer, T. P. and Tenney, R. L. (1982). 'An automated formal specification technique for protocols', *Computer Networks and ISDN Systems*, *6*, pp. 201–217, North-Holland, Amsterdam.

von Bochmann, G. (1978). 'Finite state description of communication protocols', *Computer Networks and ISDN Systems*, *2*, pp. 361–378, North-Holland, Amsterdam.

von Bochmann, G. and Sunshine, C. (1980). 'Formal methods in communication protocol design', *IEEE Transactions on Communications*, *COM-28*, pp. 624–631.

Boehm, B. W. (1988). 'A spiral model of software development and enhancement', *IEEE Computer*, pp. 61–72.

Boullier, P. and Deschamp, P. (1985). *Manuel d'Utilisation et Mise en Oeuvre du Système SYNTAX*, INRIA, Rocquencourt, France.

Brinksma, E. and Scollo, G. (1986). 'Formal notions of implementation and conformance in LOTOS', Technical report, Universiteit Twente, Enschede, The Netherlands.

Brinksma, E. (1988). 'A theory for the derivation of tests', Proc. of *Protocol Specification, Testing and Verification VIII*, North-Holland, Amsterdam.

Budkowski, S. (1992). 'ESTELLE Development Toolset (EDT)', *Computer Networks and ISDN Systems*, *23* (5), North-Holland, Amsterdam.

Budkowski, S. and Dembinski, P. (1987). 'An introduction to ESTELLE: a specification language for distributed systems', *Computer Networks and ISDN Systems*, *14* (1), pp. 3–23, North-Holland, Amsterdam.

Bull (1989). *ESTELLE Simulator/Debugger — User Reference Manual*, Bull S.A., Les Clayes s/s Bois, France.

Bull and Marben (1989). ESTELLE-*to-C Compiler User Reference Manual*, Bull S.A., Les Clayes s/s Bois, France.

CCITT (1988). *Specification and Description Language*, CCITT Z.100, International Consultative Committee on Telegraphy and Telephony, Geneva.

CCITT (1991). 'Tutorial on Object-Oriented SDL', CCITT SG X/D.74, International Consultative Committee on Telegraphy and Telephony, Geneva.

CCITT (1992g). *Guidelines for the Application of ESTELLE, LOTOS, and SDL*, CCITT Manual, International Consultative Committee on Telegraphy and Telephony, Geneva.

CCITT (1992s). *Specification and Description Language*, CCITT Z.100, International Consultative Committee on Telegraphy and Telephony, Geneva.

Cleaveland, R., Parrow, J. and Steffen, B. (1989). 'The concurrency workbench', *Automatic Verification Methods for Finite State Systems*, pp. 24–37, Grenoble, France.

Danthine, A. S (1980). 'Protocol representation with finite-state models', *IEEE Trans. on Communications, COM-28*, pp. 632–643.

Davis, A. M. *et al.* (1988). 'A strategy for comparing alternative software development cycle models', *IEEE Trans. on Software Engineering*, 14 (10), pp. 1453–1461.

Dembinski, P. and Budkowski, S. (1989). 'The specification language ESTELLE', *in* Diaz *et al.* (1989), pp. 35–75.

Diaz, M. *et al.* (1989). *The Formal Description Technique ESTELLE*, North-Holland, Amsterdam.

Donzeau-Gouge, V. *et al.* (1984). 'Programming environments based on structure editors: the MENTOR experience', *in* Barstow, D., Sandewall, E. and Shrobe, H. *(eds.)*: *Interactive Programming Environments*, pp. 128–140, McGraw-Hill.

Ehrig, H. and Mahr, B. (1985). *Fundamentals of Algebraic Specification 1*, *EATCS Monographs on Theoretical Computer Science*, *6*, Springer-Verlag, Berlin.

van Eijk, P. H. J. (1989). 'LOTOS simulator', *in* van Eijk, Vissers and Diaz (1989), pp. 391–396.

van Eijk, P. H. J., Vissers, C. A. and Diaz, M. (1989). *The Formal Description Technique LOTOS*, North-Holland, Amsterdam.

ESA (1987). 'Software engineering standards', Technical Report, European Space Agency, Noordwijk, Netherlands.

Favreau, J.-P. and Linn, R. (1987). 'Automatic generation of test scenario skeletons from specifications written in ESTELLE', Proc. of *Protocol Specification, Testing and Verification VI*, North-Holland, Amsterdam.

Fernandez, A. *et al.* (1988). 'PRODAT — the derivation of an implementation from its LOTOS formal description', Proc. of *Protocol Specification, Testing and Verification VIII*, North-Holland, Amsterdam.

Fowler, H. (1968). *Modern English Usage*, Oxford University Press, Oxford.

Guillemot, R., Haj-Hussein, M. and Logrippo, L. (1988). 'Executing large LOTOS specifications', Proc. of *Protocol Specification, Testing and Verification VIII*, North-Holland, Amsterdam.

Hoare, C. A. R. (1985). *Communicating Sequential Processes*, Prentice-Hall International, Englewood Cliffs, New Jersey.

Huet, G. (1985). 'The ML handbook', FORMEL Project, INRIA, Rocquencourt, France.

Huybrecht, H. (1986). *MIRA: A Computer-Aided Software Engineering Tool*, User Manual, Expert Software Systems, Ghent, Belgium.

ISO (1982). *Programming Language — PASCAL*, ISO/IEC 7185, International Organization for Standardization, Geneva.

ISO (1988). *Information Processing Systems — Open Systems Interconnection — Connection Oriented Transport Protocol Specification*, ISO/IEC 8072, International Organization for Standardization, Geneva.

ISO (1989e). *Information Processing Systems — Open Systems Interconnection — ESTELLE — A Formal Description technique based on an Extended State Transition Model*, ISO/IEC 9074, International Organization for Standardization, Geneva.

ISO (1989l). *Information Processing Systems — Open Systems Interconnection — LOTOS — A Formal Description Technique based on the Temporal Ordering of Observational Behaviour*, ISO/IEC 8807, International Organization for Standardization, Geneva.

ISO (1991c). *Information Processing Systems — Open Systems Interconnection — Conformance Testing Methodology and Framework*, ISO/IEC 9646, International Organization for Standardization, Geneva.

ISO (1991g). *Information Processing Systems — Open Systems Interconnection — Guidelines for the Application of ESTELLE, LOTOS and SDL*, ISO/IEC TR 10167, International Organization for Standardization, Geneva.

ISO (1991t). *Information Processing Systems — Open Systems Interconnection — ESTELLE — A Formal Description Technique based on an Extended State Transition Model — Proposed Draft Amendment 1: ESTELLE Tutorial*, ISO/IEC SC21/N5710, International Organization for Standardization, Geneva.

Khendek, F., von Bochmann, G. and Kant, C. (1989). 'New results on deriving protocol specifications from service specifications', *SIGCOM '89 Symposium Communications Architectures and Protocols, Computer Communications Review*, 19 (4), pp. 136–145.

Langerak, R. (1990). 'Decomposition of functionality: a correctness-preserving LOTOS transformation', Proc. of *Protocol Specification, Testing and Verification X*, pp. 203–218, North-Holland, Amsterdam.

Linn, R. J. (1987). 'Tutorial on the features and facilities of ESTELLE', ICST Technical Report, National Bureau of Standards, Washington, USA.

LOTOSPHERE (1990). *Task 1.1 Deliverable*, ESPRIT project 2304, Commission of the European Communities, Brussels.

Mañas, J. A. and de Miguel, T. (1988). 'From LOTOS to C', Proc. of *Formal Description Techniques I*, North-Holland, Amsterdam.

Merlin, P. M. (1979). 'Specification and validation of protocols', *IEEE Trans. on Communications*, *COM-27*, pp. 1671–1680.

Milner, A. J. R. G. (1989). *Communication and Concurrency*, Addison-Wesley, Reading, Massachusetts.

de Nicola, R. and Hennessy, M. (1984). 'Testing equivalences for processes', *Theoretical Computer Science*, 34 (1, 2), pp. 83–133.

Parrow, J. (1989). 'Verifying a CSMA/CD protocol with CCS', Technical report, Swedish Institute of Computer Science, Kista, Sweden.

Quemada, J., Pavón, S. and Fernandez, A. (1989). 'State exploration by transformation with LOLA', *Workshop on Automatic Verification Methods for Finite State Systems*, Grenoble, June 1989.

Quemada, J., Azcorra, A. and Frutos, D. (1990). 'A timed calculus for LOTOS', Proc. of *Formal Description Techniques II*, North-Holland, Amsterdam.

de Saqui-Sannes, P. and Courtiat, J.-P. (1988). 'ESTIM, the ESTELLE simulator prototype of the ESPRIT SEDOS project', Proc. of *Formal Description Techniques I*, North-Holland, Amsterdam.

de Saqui-Sannes, P. and Courtiat, J.-P. (1990). 'From the simulation to the verification of ESTELLE* specifications', Proc. of *Formal Description Techniques II*, North-Holland, Amsterdam.

Stenning, V. (1976). 'A sliding window protocol', *Computer Networks and ISDN Systems*, *1*, pp. 99–110, North-Holland, Amsterdam.

Tenney, R. L. (1980). 'Specification technique', *Formal Description Techniques for Network Protocols*, Technical Report ICST/HLNP-80-3, National Bureau of Standards, Washington, USA.

Tenney, R. (1992). 'Tutorial on ESTELLE and early testing', Tutorial for Proc. of *Formal Description Techniques IV*, published by Overseas Telecommunications Corporation, Sydney.

Turner, K. J. (1990). 'A LOTOS-based development method', Proc. of *Formal Description Techniques II*, North-Holland, Amsterdam.

Vissers, C. A., Tenney, R. L. and von Bochmann, G. (1983). 'Formal Description Techniques', *IEEE Trans. on Communications, COM-71*, pp. 1356–1364.

Vissers, C. A. and Logrippo, L. (1985). 'On the importance of the service concept in the design of data communication protocols', Proc. of *Protocol Specification, Testing and Verification V*, North-Holland, Amsterdam.

Vissers, C. A., Scollo, G. and van Sinderen, M. (1988). 'Architecture and specification style in formal descriptions of distributed systems', Proc. of *Protocol Specification, Testing and Verification VIII*, North-Holland, Amsterdam.

Vuong, S. T. and Chan, W. Y. L. (1988). 'Validation of the Ferry Clip local testing system using an ESTELLE-C compiler', Proc. of *Formal Description Techniques I*, pp. 337–351, North-Holland, Amsterdam.

Zave, P. (1984). 'The operational versus the conventional approach to software development', *Comm. of the ACM*, 27 (2), pp. 104–118.

A.2 Other Sources of Information

The following information is correct at time of publication, but may change in future.

Most computer science journals, particularly those dealing with data communications, feature papers on FDTs from time to time. There are two annual conferences that devote a large part of their proceedings to FDTs: PSTV *(Protocol Specification, Testing and Verification)* and FORTE *(Formal Techniques)*. Both are sponsored by IFIP WG6.1, whose chairman circulates a regular electronic newsletter:

Dr. Harry Rudin
IBM Research Division
Zurich Research Laboratory
Saumerstraße 4
CH-8803 Rüschlikon
SWITZERLAND

Electronic Mail:	csaddr.ifip-6-1-request@bbn.com	(newsletter requests)
	hr@zurich.ibm.com	(personal enquiries)

The *SDL Forum* takes place every two years, and acts as an important means of reporting SDL activities. There are also newsletters for FDT users. For more information contact:

Dr. R. L. Tenney
ESTELLE Newsletter Editor
Department of Mathematics and Computer Science
University of Massachusetts
70 Bow Road
Belmont MA 02178
USA

Electronic Mail: rlt@cs.umb.edu

Prof. K. J. Turner
LOTOS Newsletter Editor
Department of Computing Science and Mathematics
University of Stirling
Stirling FK9 4LA
SCOTLAND

Electronic Mail: kjt@compsci.stirling.ac.uk

Mr. F. Belina
SDL Newsletter Editor
Telia Research AB
PO Box 85
Hjälmaregatan 3
S-201 20 Malmö
SWEDEN

Electronic Mail: ferenc.belina@malmo.trab.se

There are many groups world-wide who develop and use FDT tools, so it is difficult to single out any particular groups for mention. However, the individuals below have agreed to help readers of this book by acting as initial contact for information on tools to support a particular FDT.

Dr. R. L. Tenney
ESTELLE Tools Contact
Department of Mathematics and Computer Science
University of Massachusetts
70 Bow Road
Belmont MA 02178
USA

Electronic Mail: rlt@cs.umb.edu

Prof. J. A. Mañas
LOTOS Tools Contact
Departmento Ingenieria Telematica
ETSI Telecomunicacion
Polytechnic University of Madrid
E-28040 Madrid
SPAIN

Electronic Mail: lotos@dit.upm.es (general LOTOS enquiries)
jmanas@dit.upm.es (personal enquiries)

Mr. O. Færgemand
SDL Tools Contact
TFL
Lyngso Alle 2
DK-2970 Horshølm
DENMARK

Electronic Mail: ove@tfl.dk

B Index to Formal Descriptions

The following is an index for the example formal descriptions, referencing each major specification component (e.g. type, channel, procedure, process, block, module).

C Index

Compound nouns are indexed under the main noun, but also under subsidiary words where relevant; for example, 'child module' is indexed under 'module' but also under 'child module'. Acronyms are indexed under the abbreviation but are cross-referenced from the full form; for example, 'Specification and Description Language' is indexed under 'SDL'. Specification identifiers are listed separately, printed in *italics*. Keywords are listed separately, printed in **bold**. Non-alphabetic entries in the index are mainly sorted according to their ASCII code.